ZB
SPELLING
CONNECTIONS

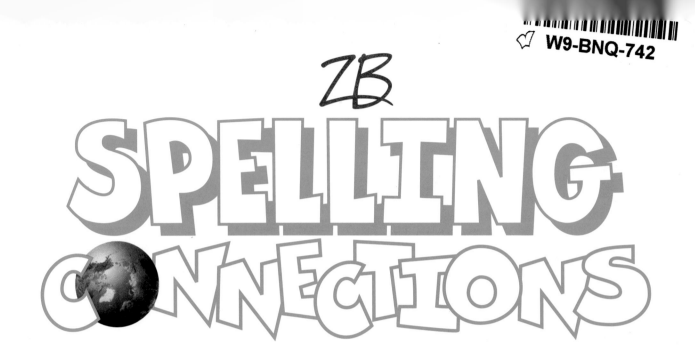

J. Richard Gentry, Ph.D.

5

Series Author
J. Richard Gentry, Ph.D.

Editorial Development: Cottage Communications

Art and Production: PC&F

Photography: George C. Anderson: cover, pages 1, 4, 6, 7, 254, 256, 257; Tony Stone Images ©: p. 266, © Jim Stamates; p. 274, © Royal Philharmonic Orchestra; p. 275, © Douglas Struthers; p. 279, © Stuart Westmoreland; p. 284, © Nick Vedros, Vedros & Associates; p. 287; p. 295, © Christopher Arnesen; p. 303, © Tom Walker; p. 305, © George Kavanaugh; Artville ©: p. 276, p. 277, p. 301, p. 302, p. 310; The Stock Market ©: p. 278, © 95 Al Francekevitch; p. 282, © DRS Productions, Taos Pueblo, NM; p. 290, © 98 Jon Feingersh; p. 299, © 97 Tom Brakefield; p. 306, © DRS Productions, Taos Pueblo, NM; p. 312, © 97 Pete Saloutos; Corbis Bettmann ©: p. 285; p. 292, Robbie Jack

Illustrations: Laurel Aiello: pages 16, 21, 27, 46, 106, 229, 233, 247; Dave Blanchette: pages 9, 10, 22, 33, 34, 51, 58, 82, 88, 105, 119, 131, 161, 167, 173; Nan Brooks: pages 135, 141, 160, 166; Len Ebert: page 63; Tom Elliot: pages 73, 96, 109, 133; Ruth Flanigan: pages 11, 17, 23, 29, 35, 47, 53, 59, 65, 71, 83, 89, 95, 101, 107; Collin Fry: pages 57, 117, 137, 143, 155, 179, 191, 197, 201, 203, 208; Kate Gorman: pages 190, 196, 209; Steve Henry: pages 189, 202, 215; Larry Nolte: pages 39, 40, 75, 76, 78, 110, 112, 114, 146, 147, 148, 183, 184, 186, 218, 219, 220, 221, 222; Bill Ogden: pages 28, 69, 81, 87, 93, 99, 125, 153, 171, 172; Vicki Woodworth: page 177

The following references were used in the development of the **Word Study** activities included on the **Vocabulary Connections** pages in each developmental spelling unit:

Ayto, John. *Arcade Dictionary of Word Origins: The Histories of More Than 8,000 English-Language Words*. New York: Arcade Publishing, Little, Brown, and Company, 1990.

Barnhart, Robert K., ed. *The Barnhart Dictionary of Etymology: The Core Vocabulary of Standard English*. New York: The H.W. Wilson Company, 1988.

Makkai, Adam, ed. *A Dictionary of American Idioms*. New York: Barron's Educational Series, Inc., 1987.

Rheingold, Howard. *They Have a Word for It: A Lighthearted Lexicon of Untranslatable Words and Phrases*. Los Angeles: Jeremy P. Tarcher, Inc., 1988.

Terban, Marvin. *Time to Rhyme: A Rhyming Dictionary*. Honesdale, PA: Wordsong, Boyds Mills Press, 1994.

ISBN: 0-7367-2063-4

Zaner-Bloser, Inc., P.O. Box 16764, Columbus, Ohio 43216-6764 (1-800-421-3018)
www.zaner-bloser.com
Printed in the United States of America   12 13 14 15 16 (330) 13 12 11 10 9

Contents

Spelling Study Strategy

Look  **Say** **Cover** **See** **Write** **Check**

1 **Look** at the word.

2 **Say** the letters in the word. Think about how each sound is spelled.

3 **Cover** the word with your hand or close your eyes.

4 **See** the word in your mind. Spell the word to yourself.

5 **Write** the word.

6 **Check** your spelling against the spelling in the book.

Spelling and Thinking

READ THE SPELLING WORDS

1.	operate	*operate*	He can **operate** the new motor.
2.	claim	*claim*	I **claim** the black male kitten.
3.	needle	*needle*	A **needle** and thread will fix that tear.
4.	beneath	*beneath*	Wolf Lake glittered **beneath** the moon.
5.	foggy	*foggy*	Carry a flashlight on **foggy** nights.
6.	gasoline	*gasoline*	Pump the **gasoline** into the tank.
7.	eighty	*eighty*	We saw **eighty** birds this week.
8.	freight	*freight*	New cars arrived on a **freight** train.
9.	complete	*complete*	The workers must **complete** the job.
10.	scary	*scary*	Spiders are hairy and **scary**.
11.	neighbor	*neighbor*	Their only **neighbor** was a mile away.
12.	daily	*daily*	Dad runs five miles **daily**.
13.	screen	*screen*	On the porch **screen** sat a huge fly.
14.	police	*police*	The **police** stopped the speeding car.
15.	explain	*explain*	Now, can you **explain** your answer?
16.	feature	*feature*	Her lovely eyes are her best **feature**.
17.	straight	*straight*	Connect the dots with a **straight** line.
18.	memory	*memory*	Ed has a good **memory** for names.
19.	contain	*contain*	The books **contain** facts about dogs.
20.	populate	*populate*	Unusual animals **populate** the island.

SORT THE SPELLING WORDS

1.–2. Write the words that have both a **long a** and a **long e** sound. Circle the letters that spell these vowel sounds.

3.–10. Write the other words that have the **long a** sound.

11.–20. Write the other words that have the **long e** sound.

REMEMBER THE SPELLING STRATEGY

Remember that the **long a** sound is spelled **ai**, **a-consonant-e**, or **ei**.
The **long e** sound is spelled **ee**, **ea**, **e-consonant-e**, **y**, or **i-consonant-e**.

---

long a and long e

1. _____

2. _____

long a

3. _____

4. _____

5. _____

6. _____

7. _____

8. _____

9. _____

10. _____

long e

11. _____

12. _____

13. _____

14. _____

15. _____

16. _____

17. _____

18. _____

19. _____

20. _____

Spelling ^{and} Vocabulary

Word Meanings

Write the spelling word that most closely matches each definition.

1. misty
2. seventy plus ten
3. frightening
4. every day
5. the ability to remember
6. to state strongly; to assert
7. type of grate
8. to work or control
9. to supply with residents
10. without curves

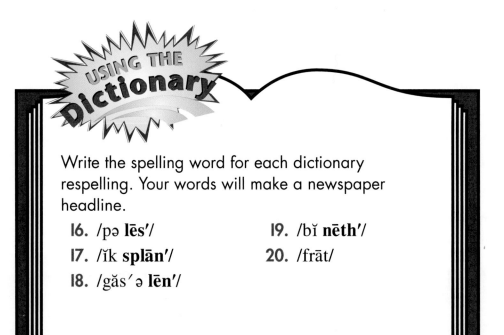

Word Structure

11.–15. Replace the first syllable in each of the following words to make a spelling word: **labor, creature, cradle, deplete,** and **retain.**

USING THE Dictionary

Write the spelling word for each dictionary respelling. Your words will make a newspaper headline.

16. /pə lēs'/
17. /ĭk splān'/
18. /găs'ə lēn'/
19. /bĭ nēth'/
20. /frāt/

Word Meanings
1.
2.
3.
4.
5.
6.
7.
8.
9.
10.
Word Structure
11.
12.
13.
14.
15.
Using the Dictionary
16.
17.
18.
19.
20.

Spelling and Reading

operate	claim	needle	beneath	foggy
gasoline	eighty	freight	complete	scary
neighbor	daily	screen	police	explain
feature	straight	memory	contain	populate

Solve the Analogies Write a spelling word to complete each analogy.

1. **Rope** is to **anchor** as **thread** is to ____.
2. **Over** is to **under** as **above** is to ____.
3. **Wet** is to **steamy** as **rainy** is to ____.
4. **Injure** is to **hurt** as **finish** is to ____.
5. **Throw** is to **hold** as **release** is to ____.

Complete the Sequences Write the spelling word that belongs in each group.

6. ____, weekly, monthly   8. ____, window, shutters
7. study, learn, ____

Replace the Words Write a spelling word that could replace the underlined word or words in these sentences.

9. A long neck is a <u>trait</u> of a giraffe.
10. Please <u>ask for</u> your luggage at the door.
11. Take this package to your <u>person next door</u>.
12. The <u>cargo</u> was sent by truck.
13. Several types of shark <u>inhabit</u> these waters.
14. We stopped for <u>fuel</u> after hours of driving.
15. Her <u>remembrance</u> of the event differed from mine.

Complete the Paragraph Read this paragraph. Write the word from the box that fits the meaning.

A car going __16.__ miles an hour forced Ray to drive into a ditch. After the state __17.__ arrived, we drove Ray __18.__ to the hospital. We had a pretty __19.__ night. Some people should not __20.__ a car.

operate
straight
scary
police
eighty

Solve the Analogies
1. 2. 3. 4. 5.

Complete the Sequences
6. 7. 8.

Replace the Words
9. 10. 11. 12. 13. 14. 15.

Complete the Paragraph
16. 17. 18. 19. 20.

10

Spelling ᴬⁿᵈ Writing

Proofread a News Story

Six words are not spelled correctly in this news story.
Write the words correctly.

DAILY NEWS

SEARCH FOR CLUES GOES ON

The polise needed flashlights to check the scary crime scene this fogy morning. One officer questioned the nabor in the corner house. Just as she started to explane what she had seen, the detective saw a clue beneeth her daley newspaper.

Proofreading Marks

≡ Make a capital.

/ Make a small letter.

∧ Add something.

℮ Take out something.

⊙ Add a period.

New paragraph

ⓢⓟ Spelling error

Write a News Story

Narrative Writing

Choose one of the headlines below, or make up a headline, and write your own short news story.

Giant Footprints Uncovered

Scientists Discover Talking Rabbit

- Answer Who, What, When, Where, and Why.
- Get as much information as you can into the story.

Use as many spelling words as you can.

Proofread Your Writing During →

Proofread your writing for spelling errors as part of the editing stage in the writing process. Be sure to check each word carefully. Use a dictionary to check spelling if you are not sure.

Writing Process

Prewriting

⇩

Drafting

⇩

Revising

⇩

Editing

⇩

Publishing

11

VOCABULARY CONNECTIONS

Strategy Words

Review Words: Long a, Long e

Write a word from the word box to complete each sentence. The word you write will rhyme with the underlined word.

brain	fame	lady	peach	speed

1. We saw that tall _____ under a tree that was <u>shady</u>.
2. I will be delighted to slice you <u>each</u> a juicy, firm, and golden _____.
3. As Sam strolled down the <u>lane</u>, thoughts rolled around his _____.
4. The hare was built for _____, but the tortoise took the <u>lead</u>.
5. If it is all the <u>same</u>, I will choose fortune over _____.

Preview Words: Long a, Long e

Write the word from the box that matches each clue.

complain	daydream	freeze	geology	sleigh

6. When you do this, your mind wanders.
7. Water will do this at 32° Fahrenheit.
8. This is the study of Earth's surface.
9. You can ride over the snow in this.
10. When you are displeased, you do this.

Review Words

1. _____
2. _____
3. _____
4. _____
5. _____

Preview Words

6. _____
7. _____
8. _____
9. _____
10. _____

Content Words

Science: Weather

Write the word from the box that fits each definition.

cyclone	monsoon	fury	blizzard	hurricane

1. small but powerful circular wind
2. severe snowstorm
3. large tropical storm
4. a season of wind and rain
5. frenzy

Language Arts: Genres

Write the word from the box that matches each clue.

adventure	fiction	mystery	drama	biography

6. This writing is not based on facts.
7. It uses dialogue and stage directions.
8. A person's life is described.
9. The story has a puzzle to be solved.
10. The characters risk physical danger.

Apply the Spelling Strategy

Circle the letters that spell the **long a** or the **long e** sound in four of the Content Words you wrote.

Word Study

Word Roots

Many words have their roots in ancient languages. **Graph** comes from an old Greek word that meant "to draw" or "to write." Write the Content Word that has this root.

Science: Weather

1. _____
2. _____
3. _____
4. _____
5. _____

Language Arts: Genres

6. _____
7. _____
8. _____
9. _____
10. _____

Word Roots

1. _____

Spelling and Thinking

READ THE SPELLING WORDS

1.	arrive	*arrive*	When they **arrive,** yell "Surprise!"
2.	slope	*slope*	The gentle, green **slope** led to a brook.
3.	growth	*growth*	Rings show a tree's yearly **growth**.
4.	locate	*locate*	After you **locate** the trail, go to camp.
5.	design	*design*	Carla can **design** the sets for the play.
6.	supply	*supply*	Coach Pirotta will **supply** sliced oranges.
7.	chosen	*chosen*	Three men were **chosen** for guard duty.
8.	type	*type*	Dad can **type** fifty words a minute.
9.	froze	*froze*	We **froze** the lemonade for popsicles.
10.	polite	*polite*	The **polite** child shook my hand.
11.	spoken	*spoken*	I have **spoken** to her before.
12.	tone	*tone*	A mellow **tone** floated across the lake.
13.	describe	*describe*	Use sense words to **describe** the setting.
14.	silent	*silent*	With a **silent** wink, the hero rode away.
15.	thrown	*thrown*	Have you **thrown** away the potato peels?
16.	deny	*deny*	I cannot **deny** my fear of crowds.
17.	excite	*excite*	If you **excite** the wasp, it may sting you.
18.	bowl	*bowl*	Please beat the eggs in the green **bowl**.
19.	style	*style*	Margaret's writing **style** is formal.
20.	decide	*decide*	Please **decide** quickly where to sit.

long i
1.
2.
3.
4.
5.
6.
7.
8.
9.
10.
11.

long o
12.
13.
14.
15.
16.
17.
18.
19.
20.

SORT THE SPELLING WORDS

1.–11. Write the words that have the **long i** sound spelled **y, i-consonant-e,** or **i**. Circle the letters that spell this vowel sound.

12.–20. Write the words that have the **long o** sound spelled **o-consonant-e, ow,** or **o**. Circle the letters that spell this vowel sound.

REMEMBER THE SPELLING STRATEGY

Remember that the **long i** sound can be spelled **y, i-consonant-e,** or **i**. The **long o** sound can be spelled **o-consonant-e, ow,** or **o**.

Spelling and Vocabulary

Word Meanings

Write spelling words to complete the sentences.

1.–2. A written thank-you note is even more _____ than a _____ thank you.

3.–4. The water _____. Except for faint creaking sounds, the lake was _____.

5.–6. I think I can _____ the right fabric if you _____ on the colors you want.

7.–8. We should _____ quietly so we do not _____ the dogs.

9.–10. Because of sudden _____, the gardener has _____ to prune the roses.

11.–12. It is difficult to _____ my emotion as I was _____ from the horse's back.

thrown
describe
froze
growth
chosen
excite
polite
silent
locate
spoken
decide
arrive

Word Clues

Write a spelling word for each clue.

13. It contains the word **sign**.

14. It rhymes with **bone**.

15. It begins like **slap** and ends like **hope**.

16. It contains the word **owl**.

USING THE Dictionary

A dictionary lists the parts of speech of each entry word. Here is an example:

ex•cite /ĭk sīt'/ -v.

Write these spelling words. Then write **n** if the word is a noun or **v** if the word is a verb. Two words can be both.

17. type

18. supply

19. style

20. deny

Word Meanings

1. _____
2. _____
3. _____
4. _____
5. _____
6. _____
7. _____
8. _____
9. _____
10. _____
11. _____
12. _____

Word Clues

13. _____
14. _____
15. _____
16. _____

Using the Dictionary

17. _____
18. _____
19. _____
20. _____

Spelling and Reading

arrive	slope	growth	locate	design
supply	chosen	type	froze	polite
spoken	tone	describe	silent	thrown
deny	excite	bowl	style	decide

Solve the Analogies   Write a spelling word to complete each analogy.

1. **Saucer** is to **plate** as **cup** is to _____.
2. **Dark** is to **light** as **loud** is to _____.
3. **Go** is to **come** as **leave** is to _____.
4. **Mountain** is to **hill** as **cliff** is to _____.
5. **Hard** is to **soft** as **rude** is to _____.
6. **Find** is to **lose** as **accept** is to _____.
7. **Cool** is to **heat** as **soothe** is to _____.

Complete the Rhymes   Write the spelling word that completes each sentence and rhymes with the underlined word.

8. After the dog got a <u>bone</u>, her bark had a gentler _____.
9. As soon as the writer's ideas were <u>ripe</u>, he sat at his desk and began to _____.
10. The figure skaters practiced, and after <u>awhile</u>, each one developed her own _____.
11. After several hours, the popsicles _____, and the hot, tired kids forgot their <u>woes</u>.
12. After the winning pass was _____, the other team let out a <u>groan</u>.

Complete the Sentences   Write spelling words from the list to complete the sentences.

13.–14. Let me _____ to you the dress I have _____.
15.–16. After each candidate had _____, I was ready to _____ who would get my vote.
17.–18. I will _____ the tools if you can _____ the nails.
19.–20. Amahl will _____ the garden so that there is plenty of room for plant _____.

growth
chosen
spoken
locate
supply
describe
design
decide

Solve the Analogies
1. _____
2. _____
3. _____
4. _____
5. _____
6. _____
7. _____

Complete the Rhymes
8. _____
9. _____
10. _____
11. _____
12. _____

Complete the Sentences
13. _____
14. _____
15. _____
16. _____
17. _____
18. _____
19. _____
20. _____

Spelling and Writing

Proofread a Design Plan

Six words are not spelled correctly in this design plan. Write the words correctly.

In the center of my model town of Friendship, there will be a grassy park. I have choasen to put most of the open land downtown. Four major streets will sloep down to the town from the surrounding hills. The town offices and library will be built in an open desine. Each shop owner will descreib to me the style of his or her store. Then I will build the shops. The town will have the shape of a shallow bole. There will be room for grothe because the park takes the place of large yards for each house.

Proofreading Marks

≡ Make a capital.

╱ Make a small letter.

∧ Add something.

℘ Take out something.

⊙ Add a period.

⌗ New paragraph

🆂🅿 Spelling error

Write a Design Plan

Expository Writing

Imagine that it is the year 3000. The mayor has asked you to design the perfect city. Write your plan. Ask yourself questions like these:

- What will the city be called?
- What will it look like?
- What kinds of buildings will I design?
- How will the people in the city live, work, play, and travel?

Use as many spelling words as you can.

Proofread Your Writing During ▶

Proofread your writing for spelling errors as part of the editing stage in the writing process. Be sure to check each word carefully. Use a dictionary to check spelling if you are not sure.

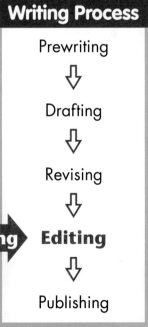

Writing Process

Prewriting

⇩

Drafting

⇩

Revising

⇩

Editing

⇩

Publishing

VOCABULARY CONNECTIONS

Strategy Words

Review Words: Long i, Long o

Write the word from the box that matches each clue.

beside	cycle	lone	role	shown

1. job; area of responsibility
2. pedal a two-wheeled vehicle
3. displayed; pointed out
4. next to
5. solitary; by oneself

Preview Words: Long i, Long o

Write a word from the box that completes each rhyme.

assign	classify	donate	exponent	strike

6. Four times <u>nine</u> is the first problem to ____.
7. One of the things we really <u>like</u> is to see our pitcher throw a ____.
8. In the math contest, my first <u>opponent</u> arrived at an answer with an ____.
9. Every Thanksgiving, we pick and ____ fruits and vegetables by the <u>crate</u>.
10. She can <u>pacify</u> her little brother by giving him stones and shells to ____.

Review Words

1. _____
2. _____
3. _____
4. _____
5. _____

Preview Words

6. _____
7. _____
8. _____
9. _____
10. _____

Content Words

Language Arts: Poetry

Write the word from the box that matches each definition.

prose	limerick	poetry	verse	rhyme

1. a humorous poem of five lines
2. uses rhythm and sound to express ideas or emotions
3. the ordinary form of language
4. words that end with the same sound
5. a stanza; a group of lines that follow a pattern

Social Studies: Pioneers

Write the word from the box that matches each clue.

frontier	coonskin	homestead	settler	moccasins

6. This cap has a tail.
7. You live on it and farm it.
8. This person makes a home in a new place.
9. This area is at the edge of a known land.
10. People can walk quietly in these soft shoes.

Apply the Spelling Strategy

Circle the two Content Words you wrote in which the **long o** sound is spelled **o-consonant-e**. Circle the one Content Word you wrote in which the **long i** sound is spelled **y**.

Word Study

Words From Other Languages

Many words in English came from Native American languages. Write the Content Word that came from Algonquian and Ojibwa words for a kind of footwear.

Language Arts: Poetry
1. _____
2. _____
3. _____
4. _____
5. _____

Social Studies: Pioneers
6. _____
7. _____
8. _____
9. _____
10. _____

Words From Other Languages
1. _____

Spelling and Thinking

READ THE SPELLING WORDS

1.	humid	*humid*	The **humid** jungle air is full of odors.
2.	remove	*remove*	Please **remove** your hat as you enter.
3.	prove	*prove*	Can we **prove** that dinosaurs are extinct?
4.	costume	*costume*	Sara made her own Halloween **costume**.
5.	rescue	*rescue*	Firefighters **rescue** people and animals.
6.	unit	*unit*	The hospital **unit** for infants was warm.
7.	annual	*annual*	Our club holds an **annual** dance.
8.	suit	*suit*	On Sunday, Rita wore a yellow **suit**.
9.	include	*include*	Both of these recipes **include** butter.
10.	continue	*continue*	The swimmers will **continue** for ten laps.
11.	future	*future*	Your **future** may include an electric car.
12.	beauty	*beauty*	The **beauty** of the canyon is awesome.
13.	movies	*movies*	Orson Welles made great **movies**.
14.	value	*value*	The new roof added **value** to her home.
15.	humor	*humor*	W.C. Fields is known for his **humor**.
16.	museum	*museum*	My town has an art **museum**.
17.	avenue	*avenue*	This **avenue** runs east; that street runs south.
18.	produce	*produce*	Bees **produce** honey and carry pollen.
19.	amuse	*amuse*	This birthday card will **amuse** Mom.
20.	youth	*youth*	Grandpa won many races in his **youth**.

SORT THE SPELLING WORDS

1.–8. Write the words that have the /o͞o/ sound. Circle the letters that spell this vowel sound.

9.–20. Write the words that have the /yo͞o/ sound. Circle the letters that spell this vowel sound.

REMEMBER THE SPELLING STRATEGY

Remember that the /o͞o/ vowel sound may be spelled **ui**, **o-consonant-e**, **u-consonant-e**, **o**, and **ue**. The /yo͞o/ vowel sound may be spelled **u**, **you**, **u-consonant-e**, **ue**, and **eau**.

/o͞o/
1.
2.
3.
4.
5.
6.
7.
8.

/yo͞o/
9.
10.
11.
12.
13.
14.
15.
16.
17.
18.
19.
20.

Spelling and Vocabulary

Word Sequences

Write the spelling word that belongs in each group.

1. build, create, ____
2. ____, maturity, age
3. lane, road, ____
4. notice, welcome, ____
5. question, experiment, ____
6. weekly, monthly, ____

Word Meanings

Write the spelling word that fits each clue.

7. Precious art is protected in this place.
8. You wear this matching outfit.
9. When you do this, you keep on without stopping.
10. Both friendship and gold have a lot of this.
11. Actors may wear one in a play.
12. You have to do this to the shells before you eat certain foods.
13. This means "to save someone who is in danger."
14. These are moving pictures shown on a screen.
15. This means "damp" or "moist."

USING THE Dictionary

Match a syllable in Column A with a syllable from Column B to complete the dictionary respelling. Then write the spelling words.

A	B
16. byoo′	mər
17. ə	nĭt
18. hyoo′	chər
19. yoo′	myooz′
20. fyoo′	tē

Word Sequences
1. _____
2. _____
3. _____
4. _____
5. _____
6. _____

Word Meanings
7. _____
8. _____
9. _____
10. _____
11. _____
12. _____
13. _____
14. _____
15. _____

Using the Dictionary
16. _____
17. _____
18. _____
19. _____
20. _____

21

Spelling ᵃⁿᵈ Reading

humid	remove	prove	costume	rescue
unit	annual	suit	include	continue
future	beauty	movies	value	humor
museum	avenue	produce	amuse	youth

Solve the Analogies Write a spelling word to complete each analogy.

1. **Clear** is to **foggy** as **dry** is to _____.
2. **Yesterday** is to **tomorrow** as **past** is to _____.
3. **Give** is to **take** as **add** is to _____.
4. **Begin** is to **end** as **stop** is to _____.
5. **Fish** is to **aquarium** as **art** is to _____.
6. **Tragedy** is to **sadness** as **comedy** is to _____.

Complete the Sentences Write a spelling word to complete each sentence.

7. The _____ of the mountains was captured by her pictures.
8. We will walk along this tree-lined _____.
9. Can you _____ that the answer is correct?
10. The lifeguard will _____ that cat in the pool.
11. Our class has an _____ bake sale in May.
12. Grandma has been a great reader since her _____.
13. The clown will _____ the bored children.

Complete the Paragraph Write the spelling words that complete the paragraph.

In Hollywood, making __14.__ is a big business. Many hard-working people are needed to __15.__ a movie. The tasks __16.__ choosing a good script, finding actors, and planning the sets and __17.__ designs that will __18.__ both the plot and the characters. Each department, or __19.__, in a movie company, no matter how small, has a job of great __20.__ to perform.

Solve the Analogies
1.
2.
3.
4.
5.
6.

Complete the Sentences
7.
8.
9.
10.
11.
12.
13.

Complete the Paragraph
14.
15.
16.
17.
18.
19.
20.

Spelling and Writing

Proofread a Fable

Six words are not spelled correctly in the fable below.
Write the words correctly.

> The lesson is that byooty is only skin deep. The plot is that a costoom makes Princess Hilda fall in love with an evil man named Tim. His appearance blinds Hilda to selfish Tim's faults. Her two friends, Sal and Edith, reskyew her from Tim. They remoov his mask and show Hilda his mean eyes and cruel mouth. In the fyoochur, Hilda will have the man she loves proov his goodness. She must continue to look for that man. As the fable ends, she meets Will, whose beauty and kindness are real.

Write a Fable

Narrative Writing

When you write a fable, decide first on the lesson the fable will teach. Then choose a main character and develop a plot.

- Choose a lesson that the fable will teach.
- Make sure you describe the characters.

Use as many spelling words as you can.

Proofread Your Writing During → Editing

Writing Process

Prewriting
⇩
Drafting
⇩
Revising
⇩
Editing
⇩
Publishing

Proofread your writing for spelling errors as part of the editing stage in the writing process. Be sure to check each word carefully. Use a dictionary to check spelling if you are not sure.

VOCABULARY CONNECTIONS

►Strategy Words◄

Review Words

1. _____
2. _____
3. _____
4. _____
5. _____

Preview Words

6. _____
7. _____
8. _____
9. _____
10. _____

Review Words: Vowel Sounds: /o͞o/, /yo͞o/

Write the word from the box that matches each clue.

cube	fruit	glue	human	lose

1. Apples, peaches, and pears are examples.
2. Ice often comes in this form.
3. The baseball team with the lowest score will do this.
4. It rhymes with **blue**.
5. It's the two-syllable word.

Preview Words: Vowel Sounds: /o͞o/, /yo͞o/

Write the word from the box that completes each sentence.

approve	cruise	introduce	refuse	tissue

6. Mother and Father do not _____ of makeup for children.
7. We can use _____ to fill the gift box.
8. Debby had a cold, so she had to _____ an invitation to swim.
9. May I _____ you to my cousin?
10. The _____ left from Miami, Florida, and sailed all over the world.

Content Words

Science: Experiments

Write the word from the box that could best replace the underlined word or words.

| beaker | mixture | chemical | residue | dilute |

1. Dr. Shepherd put salt in the glass pitcher.
2. We stirred the combination.
3. We poured in water to make it thinner.
4. We removed the material that was left.
5. This experiment included a material-combining process.

Science: Elements

Write the word from the box that matches each clue.

| element | molecule | hydrogen | phosphorus | iodine |

6. This is the smallest unit into which something can be divided and still be a substance.
7. This is a common gas.
8. This might keep a cut from becoming infected.
9. This cannot be separated into simpler parts by ordinary chemical methods.
10. This is a shiny yellow or white substance.

Apply the Spelling Strategy

Circle the letters that spell the /$\overline{oo}$/ sound or the /y$\overline{oo}$/ sound in three of the Content Words you wrote.

Word Study

Homographs

Homographs are words that are spelled alike but have different pronunciations and meanings. Write the one Strategy Word that can be pronounced two different ways to fit these meanings:

- deny or decline
- trash

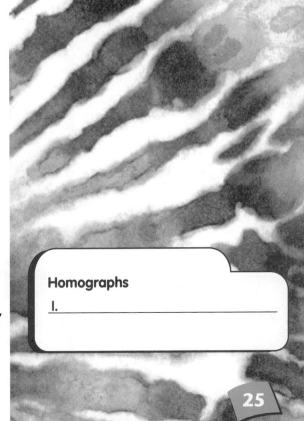

Science: Experiments

1. _____
2. _____
3. _____
4. _____
5. _____

Science: Elements

6. _____
7. _____
8. _____
9. _____
10. _____

Homographs

1. _____

25

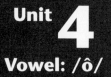

Spelling and Thinking

o, oa

1. _____
2. _____
3. _____
4. _____

au, aw, or a + l

5. _____
6. _____
7. _____
8. _____
9. _____
10. _____
11. _____
12. _____
13. _____
14. _____
15. _____
16. _____
17. _____
18. _____
19. _____
20. _____

READ THE SPELLING WORDS

1. launch	*launch*	NASA will **launch** a satellite to Mars.
2. shawl	*shawl*	Margy wore a **shawl** in the cold room.
3. false	*false*	The **false** information misled us.
4. author	*author*	Not every **author** wants fame.
5. install	*install*	Cleo will **install** the bookcase.
6. loss	*loss*	The Hawks had one **loss** this season.
7. broad	*broad*	Ducks float on the **broad** lake.
8. audience	*audience*	A hush fell over the **audience**.
9. drawing	*drawing*	Lara was **drawing** the boy's portrait.
10. caution	*caution*	Use **caution** when you write in ink.
11. lawyer	*lawyer*	Clay needed a **lawyer** to defend him.
12. recall	*recall*	Does Rita **recall** what time Bill left?
13. astronaut	*astronaut*	Ho is preparing to be an **astronaut**.
14. office	*office*	A doctor's **office** is a busy place.
15. scald	*scald*	We **scald** the tomatoes first.
16. automobile	*automobile*	Nat's first **automobile** had extra lights.
17. drawn	*drawn*	The curtains were **drawn** shut.
18. broth	*broth*	Chicken **broth** soothes the stomach.
19. awful	*awful*	The **awful** weather added to our dismay.
20. flaw	*flaw*	That argument has a **flaw** in it.

SORT THE SPELLING WORDS

1.–4. Write the words that spell the /ô/ sound with **o** or **oa**. Circle the letters that spell this vowel sound.

5.–20. Write the words that spell the /ô/ sound with **au**, **aw**, or **a** followed by **l**. Circle the letters that spell this vowel sound.

REMEMBER THE SPELLING STRATEGY

Remember that the /ô/ vowel sound you hear in **author** can be spelled in different ways: **au** in **author**, **aw** in **flaw**, **a** followed by **l** in **false** and **install**, **o** in **loss**, and **oa** in **broad**.

Spelling and Vocabulary

Related Meanings

Write a spelling word to complete each analogy.

1. **Painting** is to **artist** as **book** is to _____.
2. **Electricity** is to **lamp** as **gasoline** is to _____.
3. **Ball** is to **throw** as **rocket** is to _____.
4. **Leather** is to **shoe** as **wool** is to _____.
5. **Clean** is to **dirty** as **true** is to _____.
6. **Short** is to **tall** as **narrow** is to _____.

Word Sequences

Write the spelling word that belongs in each group.

7. driver, pilot, _____
8. telephone, desk, _____
9. idea, sketch, _____
10. stew, soup, _____
11. warm, heat, _____
12. problem, mistake, _____

Word Meanings

Write the spelling word that completes each sentence.

13. With his loudspeaker, Al has _____ a crowd.
14. After the _____ of his tooth, Jake lisped.

USING THE Dictionary

Write the spelling words for the dictionary respellings. Underline the syllable that is stressed in each word.

15. /kô′ shən/
16. /ĭn stôl′/
17. /rĭ kôl′/
18. /ô′ dē əns/
19. /ô′ fəl/
20. /lô′ yər/

◆ ◆ ◆

Dictionary Check Be sure to check the respellings in your **Spelling Dictionary**.

Related Meanings
I. _____
2. _____
3. _____
4. _____
5. _____
6. _____

Word Sequences
7. _____
8. _____
9. _____
10. _____
11. _____
12. _____

Word Meanings
13. _____
14. _____

Using the Dictionary
15. _____
16. _____
17. _____
18. _____
19. _____
20. _____

27

launch	shawl	false	author	install
loss	broad	audience	drawing	caution
lawyer	recall	astronaut	office	scald
automobile	drawn	broth	awful	flaw

Complete the Sentences

Write a spelling word to complete each sentence.

1. Henry Ford invented the Model T _____.
2. Add some beef _____ to this stew.
3. My mother's _____ is on Main Street.
4. The _____ of the horses was done in charcoal.
5. The play made the _____ laugh and cry.
6. The spacecraft is on the _____ pad.
7. Do not _____ your hand in the boiling water.

Replace the Words

Replace the underlined word or words with a spelling word.

8. The losing of the game does not matter.
9. We crossed a wide river.
10. There is no defect in the movie.
11. We have sketched you a map.
12. The plumber will put in a sink.
13. The attorney argued the case.
14. The terrible storm battered the coast.

Complete the Story

Write a spelling word from the box to fill in each blank in the story.

An __15.__ sat at her desk and wrote. She wore a __16.__ around her shoulders. She was writing about an __17.__. She could __18.__ many stories about the space program in the 1960s. However, she wrote with __19.__. She did not want to include __20.__ information.

astronaut
author
caution
recall
false
shawl

Complete the Sentences
1.
2.
3.
4.
5.
6.
7.

Replace the Words
8.
9.
10.
11.
12.
13.
14.

Complete the Story
15.
16.
17.
18.
19.
20.

Spelling and Writing

Proofread a Biography

Six words are not spelled correctly in the biography below.
Write the words correctly.

On April 4, 1968, our country mourned the lose of Dr. Martin Luther King, Jr. His brod vision and courage gave African American people a sense of their heritage and pride. He helped eliminate fals ideas that many people had about African Americans.

King believed that a major flau in our society was segregation, or the separation of the races. Many Americans helped him lawnch nonviolent protests. Millions today can recawl his work and his message. Dr. King's audience is larger than ever.

Proofreading Marks

≡ Make a capital.

/ Make a small letter.

∧ Add something.

℮ Take out something.

⊙ Add a period.

⌗ New paragraph

(SP) Spelling error

Write a Biography

Expository Writing

Decide first on your subject. Then read about him or her in newspapers, books, and magazines. If possible, find diaries, articles, or letters written by your subject.

- Include quotations from your subject.
- Check your facts in more than one source.

Use as many spelling words as you can.

Writing Process

Prewriting

⇩

Drafting

⇩

Revising

⇩

Editing

⇩

Publishing

Proofread Your Writing During Editing

Proofread your writing for spelling errors as part of the editing stage in the writing process. Be sure to check each word carefully. Use a dictionary to check spelling if you are not sure.

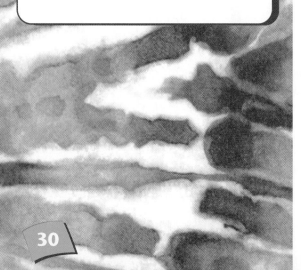

VOCABULARY CONNECTIONS

Strategy Words

Review Words: Vowel /ô/

Write a word from the box to complete each sentence.

because	bought	daughter
taught	thought	

1. Rain falls to the earth ____ of gravity.
2. My mother ____ me how to sing.
3. Sonya's ____ studies marine biology.
4. Martin's brother ____ a used taxicab.
5. Grandpa ____ the sky would be clear.

Preview Words: Vowel /ô/

Write a word from the box that matches each clue.

autumn	autograph	officer
pause	thoughtless	

6. Get one from a person you admire.
7. A person who cuts ahead in line is this.
8. This is a colorful season.
9. Do this before you answer.
10. He or she could be wearing a uniform.

Review Words
1.
2.
3.
4.
5.

Preview Words
6.
7.
8.
9.
10.

Content Words

Language Arts: Writing

Write a word from the box that matches each clue.

clause	preposition	composition	subject	predicate

1. This contains a subject and a verb.
2. This has at least one verb.
3. This writing has a main idea supported by details.
4. This is what a sentence is about.
5. One of these always has an object.

Fine Arts: Dancing

Write a word from the box that fits each blank.

polka	waltz	ballroom	jazz	square dance

6. traditional _____ dancing
7. a lively Polish _____
8. a caller for a _____
9. some New Orleans _____
10. a romantic, graceful _____

Apply the Spelling Strategy

Circle the letters that spell the /ô/ sound in three of the Content Words you wrote.

Word Study

Word Roots

The root **auto** came from a Greek word that meant "self." For example, something that is **automatic** operates by itself. Write the Strategy Word that has this root and means "writing by one's own self."

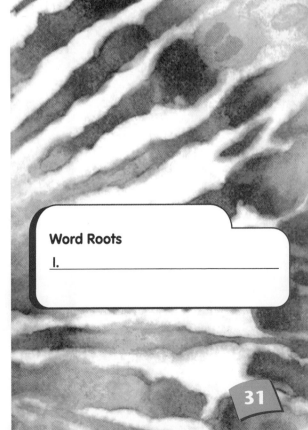

Language Arts: Writing
1. _____
2. _____
3. _____
4. _____
5. _____

Fine Arts: Dancing
6. _____
7. _____
8. _____
9. _____
10. _____

Word Roots
1. _____

Spelling and Thinking

READ THE SPELLING WORDS

a, e

1. _____
2. _____
3. _____
4. _____
5. _____
6. _____
7. _____
8. _____
9. _____

i, o, u

10. _____
11. _____
12. _____
13. _____
14. _____
15. _____
16. _____
17. _____
18. _____
19. _____
20. _____

1. magic	*magic*	Jane has learned to do **magic** tricks.
2. credit	*credit*	He got **credit** for his heroic effort.
3. exist	*exist*	Turtles can **exist** on land or in water.
4. deposit	*deposit*	We can **deposit** the money at the bank.
5. staff	*staff*	Five new nurses joined the **staff**.
6. direct	*direct*	Sam took a **direct** flight to Nigeria.
7. splendid	*splendid*	A **splendid** rainbow framed the falls.
8. business	*business*	Ellen took on the family **business**.
9. sense	*sense*	Jonas could **sense** Dana behind him.
10. discuss	*discuss*	Can we **discuss** the problem calmly?
11. contest	*contest*	Claire won the spelling **contest**.
12. building	*building*	Landscaping surrounded the **building**.
13. swift	*swift*	The deer made a **swift** departure.
14. interest	*interest*	Mark has no **interest** in football.
15. exact	*exact*	At that **exact** moment, the bell rang.
16. promise	*promise*	Robert made a **promise** he could keep.
17. habit	*habit*	Kim makes a **habit** of speaking politely.
18. thus	*thus*	I just ate. **Thus,** I am not hungry.
19. active	*active*	Granddad remained **active** by cycling.
20. solve	*solve*	Sherlock Holmes can **solve** the case.

SORT THE SPELLING WORDS

1.–9. Write the words that contain the **short a** or **short e** sound in the stressed syllable. Circle the letters that spell this vowel sound.

10.–20. Write the words that contain the **short o, short i,** or **short u** sound in the stressed syllable. Circle the letters that spell this vowel sound.

REMEMBER THE SPELLING STRATEGY

Remember that short vowel sounds may be spelled in a variety of ways.

Spelling ᵃⁿᵈ Vocabulary

Word Meanings

Write the spelling word that fits each clue.

1. If you feel this, you pay attention.
2. This place of shelter is made by people.
3. Money is offered for goods or services.
4. This means "rapid, very fast."
5. This is the opposite of **nonsense**.
6. If you do this, the mystery is all cleared up.
7. One meaning of this word is "a walking stick."

Word Structure

Write the spelling word that solves each equation.

8. them – em + us = _____
9. disc + us + s = _____
10. create – ate + dit = _____
11. image – i – e + ic = _____

Related Words

Write the spelling word for each related word.

12. depository
13. splendor
14. indirectly
15. existence

USING THE Thesaurus

A **synonym** is a word that has the same or nearly the same meaning as another word. Write the spelling word that is a synonym for each of the following words.

16. competition
17. lively
18. custom
19. pledge
20. precise

Word Meanings

1. _____
2. _____
3. _____
4. _____
5. _____
6. _____
7. _____

Word Structure

8. _____
9. _____
10. _____
11. _____

Related Words

12. _____
13. _____
14. _____
15. _____

Using the Thesaurus

16. _____
17. _____
18. _____
19. _____
20. _____

Spelling and Reading

magic	credit	exist	deposit	staff
direct	splendid	business	sense	discuss
contest	building	swift	interest	exact
promise	habit	thus	active	solve

Solve the Analogies   Write a spelling word to complete each analogy.

1. **Horse** is to **ride** as **problem** is to _____.
2. **Do** is to **act** as **be** is to _____.
3. **Pen** is to **writing** as **trick** is to _____.
4. **Foggy** is to **clear** as **vague** is to _____.
5. **Remove** is to **add** as **withdraw** is to _____.
6. **Bad** is to **good** as **horrid** is to _____.

Complete the Sentences   Write a spelling word to complete each sentence.

7. Who will judge the skating _____?
8. Please enter on the right side of the _____.
9. I am trying to break my nail-biting _____.
10. We were successful; _____ the audience cheered.
11. Charlie's good _____ saved the sailors.
12. Maggie deserves _____ for that speech.
13. Mr. Boyd is an _____ member of several charities.

Complete the Paragraph   Write a spelling word from the box to fill in each blank in the paragraph.

Here is a chance for you to learn to sell tacos. You must have an __14.__ in Mexican food. You will have __15.__ contact with our cooking __16.__. We promise customers __17.__ delivery. If you can __18.__ to work six hours a week, stop in to __19.__ this great __20.__ opportunity.

promise
business
staff
interest
discuss
direct
swift

Solve the Analogies
1.
2.
3.
4.
5.
6.
Complete the Sentences
7.
8.
9.
10.
11.
12.
13.
Complete the Paragraph
14.
15.
16.
17.
18.
19.
20.

Spelling and Writing

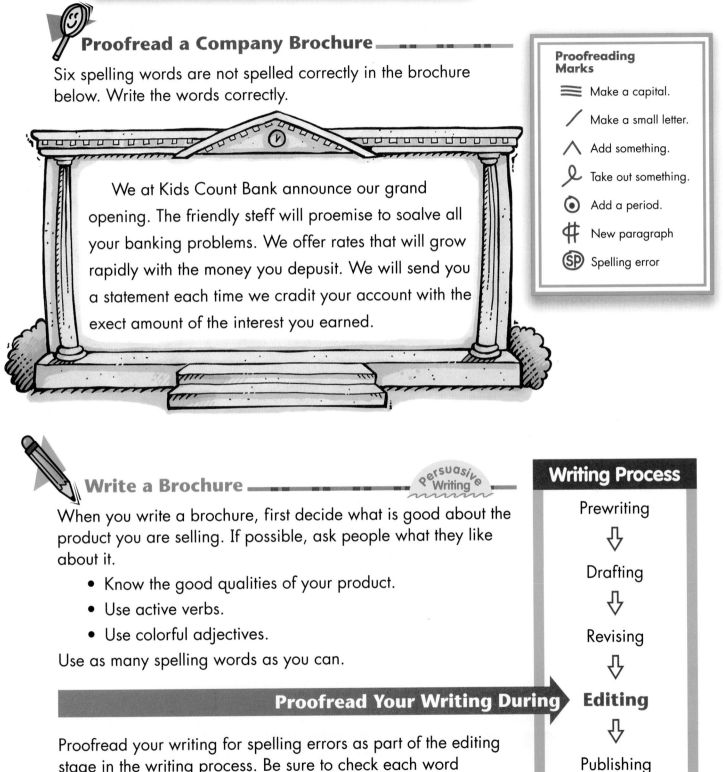

Proofread a Company Brochure

Six spelling words are not spelled correctly in the brochure below. Write the words correctly.

We at Kids Count Bank announce our grand opening. The friendly steff will proemise to soalve all your banking problems. We offer rates that will grow rapidly with the money you depusit. We will send you a statement each time we cradit your account with the exect amount of the interest you earned.

Proofreading Marks

≡ Make a capital.

/ Make a small letter.

∧ Add something.

℮ Take out something.

⊙ Add a period.

New paragraph

SP Spelling error

Write a Brochure

Persuasive Writing

When you write a brochure, first decide what is good about the product you are selling. If possible, ask people what they like about it.

- Know the good qualities of your product.
- Use active verbs.
- Use colorful adjectives.

Use as many spelling words as you can.

Writing Process

Prewriting
⇩
Drafting
⇩
Revising
⇩
Editing
⇩
Publishing

Proofread Your Writing During ➡ Editing

Proofread your writing for spelling errors as part of the editing stage in the writing process. Be sure to check each word carefully. Use a dictionary to check spelling if you are not sure.

VOCABULARY CONNECTIONS

Strategy Words

Review Words: Short Vowel Sounds

Write a word from the box to complete each rhyme. Each rhyming word is underlined.

brick	collar	edge	pass	trust

1. You would not want to <u>kick</u> something as hard as a _____.
2. To bake the bread with the crispiest <u>crust</u>, it is Cal we can always _____.
3. I sat on the <u>grass</u> to watch the bird _____.
4. The dry cleaner charged an extra <u>dollar</u> to sew the rip in my dad's _____.
5. Down below the walk, there is a <u>ledge</u>. Be careful; don't go near the _____.

Preview Words: Short Vowel Sounds

Write a word from the box to complete each analogy.

consider	excellent	invisible	rapid	stubborn

6. **Boring** is to **dull** as **determined** is to _____.
7. **Hear** is to **silent** as **see** is to _____.
8. **Bad** is to **terrible** as **good** is to _____.
9. **Look** is to **watch** as **notice** is to _____.
10. **Slow** is to **sluggish** as **fast** is to _____.

Review Words

1. _____
2. _____
3. _____
4. _____
5. _____

Preview Words

6. _____
7. _____
8. _____
9. _____
10. _____

Content Words

Language Arts: Critiques

Write a word from the box to fill each blank in the paragraph.

essay	viewpoint	critical	revise	comment

   A good writer will ask people to ___1.___ on his or her
writing. These readers may be ___2.___ of the writer's language
or ideas. They might even write an ___3.___ explaining their
thoughts about the piece of writing. The writer can consider
each reader's perspective, or ___4.___. Then the writer can ___5.___
the work sensibly.

Math: Ordinal Numbers

Write a word from the box to complete each sentence.

eighteenth	fifteenth	sixteenth	nineteenth	seventeenth

6. The year 1889 was in the _____ century.
7. The year 1776 was in the _____ century.
8. The year 1402 was in the _____ century.
9. The year 1525 was in the _____ century.
10. The year 1617 was in the _____ century.

Apply the Spelling Strategy

Circle the letters in six of the Content Words you wrote that
spell the short vowel sound in the stressed syllable.

Word Study

Idioms

An **idiom** is a saying that doesn't mean what the words
in it say. If you are **up against a brick wall,** you are
unable to continue something. Write a Strategy Word to
finish this saying, which means "to be nervous, excited, or
impatient": **on ____ .**

Language Arts: Critiques
1. _____
2. _____
3. _____
4. _____
5. _____

Math: Ordinal Numbers
6. _____
7. _____
8. _____
9. _____
10. _____

Idioms
1. _____

Assessment and Review

Assessment — Units 1–5

Each Assessment Word in the box fits one of the spelling strategies you have studied over the past five weeks. Read the spelling strategies. Then write each Assessment Word under the unit number it fits.

Unit 1 _____

1.–4. The **long a** sound may be spelled **ai**, **a-consonant-e**, or **ei**. The **long e** sound may be spelled **ee**, **ea**, **e-consonant-e**, **y**, or **i-consonant-e**.

Unit 2 _____

5.–8. The **long i** sound can be spelled **y**, **i-consonant-e**, or **i**. The **long o** sound can be spelled **o-consonant-e**, **ow**, or **o**.

Unit 3 _____

9.–12. The /$\overline{oo}$/ vowel sound may be spelled **ui**, **o-consonant-e**, **u-consonant-e**, **o**, and **ue**. The /$y\overline{oo}$/ vowel sound may be spelled **u**, **you**, **u-consonant-e**, **ue**, and **eau**.

Unit 4 _____

13.–16. The /ô/ vowel sound you hear in **author** can be spelled in different ways: **au** in **author**, **aw** in **flaw**, **a** followed by **l** in **false** and **install**, **o** in **loss**, and **oa** in **broad**.

Unit 5 _____

17.–20. Short vowel sounds may be spelled in a variety of ways.

marry
throne
rude
walnut
timid
olive
scrawl
funeral
lying
haste
cease
bestow
soup
salty
demand
closet
sausage
pure
desire
failure

Unit 1
1. _____
2. _____
3. _____
4. _____

Unit 2
5. _____
6. _____
7. _____
8. _____

Unit 3
9. _____
10. _____
11. _____
12. _____

Unit 4
13. _____
14. _____
15. _____
16. _____

Unit 5
17. _____
18. _____
19. _____
20. _____

| neighbor | scary | straight | memory | contain |
| complete | police | explain | screen | beneath |

Complete each sentence by writing a spelling word that rhymes with the underlined word.

1. Watch out, <u>Keith</u>! There's a rock ____.
2. Ask <u>Denise</u> to call the ____.
3. We helped our ____ with the <u>labor</u>.
4. Phil will <u>carry</u> the costume that's ____.
5. Does the road <u>rate</u> crooked or ____?
6. We can't be <u>seen</u> behind the ____.
7. Our computer, "Emory," has a huge ____.
8. The doctor couldn't ____ the cause of my <u>pain</u>.
9. The teacher told <u>Pete</u> his task was ____.
10. How much <u>rain</u> does this bucket ____?

Review Unit 2: Long i, Long o

| decide | excite | thrown | describe | bowl |
| arrive | spoken | supply | type | silent |

Write the spelling word by adding the missing letters.

11. descr __ b __
12. b __ __ l
13. a __ __ ive
14. d __ c __ de
15. __ xc __ te
16. thr __ __ n
17. s __ l __ nt
18. t __ pe
19. su __ __ ly
20. sp __ k __ n

Unit 1

1. _____
2. _____
3. _____
4. _____
5. _____
6. _____
7. _____
8. _____
9. _____
10. _____

Unit 2

11. _____
12. _____
13. _____
14. _____
15. _____
16. _____
17. _____
18. _____
19. _____
20. _____

1.	
2.	
3.	
4.	
5.	
6.	
7.	
8.	
9.	
10.	

Unit 4

11.	
12.	
13.	
14.	
15.	
16.	
17.	
18.	
19.	
20.	

Review Unit 3: Vowel Sounds /o͞o/, /yo͞o/

beauty	produce	prove	suit	future
unit	continue	value	movies	youth

Some of the sentences below do not make sense. Replace the underlined word in each sentence with the spelling word that makes sense.

1. We were impressed by the <u>ugliness</u> of the sunset.
2. These valuable cows <u>collect</u> lots of milk every day.
3. Scientists can <u>deny</u> that the earth is round.
4. This spelling <u>book</u> is about words with /o͞o/ and /yo͞o/ sounds.
5. The class will <u>stop</u> this interesting discussion.
6. This is a jewel of great <u>worthlessness</u>.
7. Juan wore a handsome gray <u>shirt</u> to the meeting.
8. Only <u>adults</u> under the age of 10 can participate.
9. There have been three full-length <u>paintings</u> starring this new actress.
10. What do you think will happen to the forests in the <u>past</u>?

Review Unit 4: Vowel /ô/

loss	caution	author	false	office
audience	awful	drawing	shawl	drawn

Write the spelling word that belongs in each group.

11. had painted, had sketched, had _____
12. robe, scarf, _____
13. painting, sketching, _____
14. terrible, horrible, _____
15. ruin, injury, _____
16. care, watchfulness, _____
17. listeners, observers, _____
18. writer, creator, _____
19. lobby, workplace, _____
20. wrong, incorrect, _____

Review

Unit 5: Short Vowel Sounds

building	business	direct	interest	sense
exact	thus	discuss	solve	promise

Write the word that fits each meaning and has the given vowel sound in the stressed syllable.

1. sight and smell (**short e**)
2. correct (**short a**)
3. and so (**short u**)
4. talk about (**short u**)
5. work out (**short o**)
6. pledge (**short o**)
7. structure (**short i**)
8. company (**short i**)
9. straight (**short e**)
10. attraction (**short i**)

Unit 5

1. _____
2. _____
3. _____
4. _____
5. _____
6. _____
7. _____
8. _____
9. _____
10. _____

GAME Spelling Study Strategy

Ask a Question

Swap any spelling lists you want to study with a partner. Take turns reading all the words to be sure you both know every word.

Ask your partner to read the first word on your list. Write the word on a piece of scrap paper. Ask your partner to check your spelling. If you're correct, you get two points.

If you're not correct, ask one question about the spelling of the word. (You could ask for the last letter of the word.) Write the word again. If you're correct this time, you get one point. If you're still not correct, your partner will spell the word for you. You don't get any points.

Now it's your partner's turn. Read the first word on your partner's list. Your partner should write the word.

Keep going until you have practiced all the words.

Unit **6** enrichment

Grammar, Usage, and Mechanics

Complete Subjects and Complete Predicates

Every sentence has a subject and a predicate. The complete subject is made up of a noun or pronoun and words that tell about it. The subject tells whom or what the sentence is about.

The complete predicate is made up of a verb and words that tell what the subject is, has, or does.

One girl in my class | gave an oral report.

↑   ↑

complete subject   complete predicate

Practice Activity

Write **subject** or **predicate** to show which part of the sentence is underlined.

1. Two houses on my street look scary.
2. Many birds build nests beneath this cliff.
3. Early settlers discovered gold.
4. We lost our towels on the foggy beach.
5. Those model trains move quickly.
6. Most students in the audience laughed.
7. Trees drop their leaves in the fall.
8. My neighbor moved to the city.
9. A police officer in uniform directs traffic daily.
10. The screen in my bedroom window is ripped.
11. The hot soup spilled from the bowl.
12. We met the author of several popular books.
13. The office of the manager seems small.
14. A large and noisy audience greeted the president.
15. The citizens demanded a meeting with the mayor.

Practice Activity

1. _____
2. _____
3. _____
4. _____
5. _____
6. _____
7. _____
8. _____
9. _____
10. _____
11. _____
12. _____
13. _____
14. _____
15. _____

WORKSHOP

Box It Up!

Good writers always proofread their work for spelling errors. Here's a strategy that you can use to proofread your papers.

Take a small piece of paper and cut a small hole or box in it. Slide it along your work so that only one or two words appear inside the box. This way, you do not see an entire sentence at one time. Instead of seeing **This author wrote a very funny book**!, you might see **author wrote** or **very funny**.

Reading your paper this way helps you focus on the spelling of words instead of on the meaning of sentences. Try it!

Electronic Spelling

Search Engines

Computers allow you to find information in many places, such as CD-ROMs, online libraries, and the Internet. Usually, a search engine helps you find the information you want.

With a search engine, you type in a word or phrase. Then the search engine looks for material that contains that word or phrase. If you misspelled the word, you may not find the information that you want.

Make sure each word is spelled and capitalized correctly. For example, if you entered **George Washington bridge,** you might learn about George Washington and the game called bridge, not about the George Washington Bridge.

Write these proper names correctly. Write **OK** if a name is correct.

1. Fewture Farmers
2. York police Department
3. First Street
4. Best School Supply
5. Baeuty and the Beast
6. Tipe and Tools

Electronic Spelling

1. _____
2. _____
3. _____
4. _____
5. _____
6. _____

Spelling and Thinking

READ THE SPELLING WORDS

1.	shadow	*shadow*	A **shadow** fell over the table.
2.	cheap	*cheap*	We cannot find **cheap** scuba gear.
3.	social	*social*	Are cats **social** creatures?
4.	motion	*motion*	Wind causes most of a wave's **motion**.
5.	bunch	*bunch*	Will you rinse this **bunch** of celery?
6.	nature	*nature*	Science studies the laws of **nature**.
7.	publish	*publish*	Mary will **publish** her diary.
8.	ancient	*ancient*	The **ancient** tree is still healthy.
9.	picture	*picture*	Susan wore bells in her baby **picture**.
10.	shelter	*shelter*	Alex ran to the barn for **shelter**.
11.	special	*special*	Karl has **special** heated socks.
12.	delicious	*delicious*	Raw corn tastes **delicious** in salads.
13.	chest	*chest*	Is there a hammer in the tool **chest**?
14.	official	*official*	An **official** asked for my passport.
15.	exchange	*exchange*	We can **exchange** phone numbers.
16.	shoulder	*shoulder*	My **shoulder** aches this morning.
17.	patient	*patient*	The **patient** tigress fed three cubs.
18.	kitchen	*kitchen*	There are roses on the **kitchen** table.
19.	furniture	*furniture*	Their **furniture** was made of shells.
20.	pasture	*pasture*	The racehorse retired to the **pasture**.

SORT THE SPELLING WORDS

1.–11. Write the words that contain the **/sh/** sound spelled **sh, ti,** or **ci**. Circle the letters that spell this sound.

12.–20. Write the words that contain the **/ch/** sound spelled **ch, tch,** or **tu**. Circle the letters that spell this sound.

REMEMBER THE SPELLING STRATEGY

Remember that the **/sh/** sound can be spelled in different ways: **sh** in **shelter**, **ti** in **patient**, and **ci** in **ancient**. The **/ch/** sound can be spelled in different ways: **ch** in **cheap**, **tch** in **kitchen**, and **tu** in **nature**.

/sh/

1. _____

2. _____

3. _____

4. _____

5. _____

6. _____

7. _____

8. _____

9. _____

10. _____

11. _____

/ch/

12. _____

13. _____

14. _____

15. _____

16. _____

17. _____

18. _____

19. _____

20. _____

Spelling ^{and} Vocabulary

Related Meanings

Write a spelling word to complete each statement.

1. **Painting** is to **art** as **chair** is to _____.
2. **Pig** is to **pen** as **horse** is to _____.
3. **Bread** is to **food** as **house** is to _____.
4. **Plain** is to **fancy** as **ordinary** is to _____.
5. **Bed** is to **bedroom** as **stove** is to _____.
6. **Leg** is to **hip** as **arm** is to _____.
7. **Promote** is to **promotion** as **move** is to _____.
8. **Port** is to **export** as **change** is to _____.

Word Replacements

Write a spelling word that could replace each word or group of words.

9. inexpensive
10. group
11. large container with drawers
12. friendly
13. the world of living things
14. formal
15. tasty
16. good at waiting

USING THE Dictionary

Many English words come from other languages. For example, the word **pasture** came originally from the Latin word **pascere,** meaning "to feed." Write the spelling words that came from these words:

17. the Latin **ante,** meaning "before"
18. the Old English **sceadu,** meaning "shade"
19. the Latin **publicare,** meaning "to make public"
20. the Latin **pingere,** meaning "to paint"

Related Meanings

1. _____
2. _____
3. _____
4. _____
5. _____
6. _____
7. _____
8. _____

Word Replacements

9. _____
10. _____
11. _____
12. _____
13. _____
14. _____
15. _____
16. _____

Using the Dictionary

17. _____
18. _____
19. _____
20. _____

shadow   cheap   social   motion   bunch
nature   publish   ancient   picture   shelter
special   delicious   chest   official   exchange
shoulder   patient   kitchen   furniture   pasture

Complete the Paragraph Write the spelling words that complete the paragraph.

Behzad looked thoughtfully at the black-and-white __1.__ of his horse. The horse was standing with her left __2.__ facing the camera, nibbling the grass in the __3.__. The sun made the horse cast a __4.__ across the fence and the walkway beyond. Behzad's little sister had tied a __5.__ of flowers in the mare's mane.

Name the Categories The following words are smaller parts of something bigger. Write the spelling word that names that bigger something.

6. lungs, heart: _____
7. plants, animals: _____
8. roof, walls: _____
9. couch, bureau: _____
10. run, jump: _____
11. refrigerator, sink: _____
12. print, distribute: _____
13. give, take: _____

Complete the Sentences Write a spelling word from the box to complete each sentence.

14. The _____ sparrow waits hours for the worm.
15. Sid is our _____ team captain.
16. Rosa's _____ skill is juggling.
17. These _____ teeth belonged to a dinosaur.
18. Many people find toasted marshmallows _____.
19. Your party is on my _____ calendar.
20. We bought a very _____ bike at a yard sale.

patient
cheap
official
social
special
ancient
delicious

Complete the Paragraph
1.
2.
3.
4.
5.

Name the Categories
6.
7.
8.
9.
10.
11.
12.
13.

Complete the Sentences
14.
15.
16.
17.
18.
19.
20.

Spelling and Writing

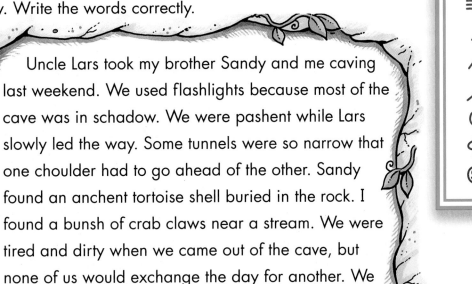

Proofread a Diary Entry

Six spelling words are not spelled correctly in the diary entry below. Write the words correctly.

Uncle Lars took my brother Sandy and me caving last weekend. We used flashlights because most of the cave was in schadow. We were pashent while Lars slowly led the way. Some tunnels were so narrow that one choulder had to go ahead of the other. Sandy found an anchent tortoise shell buried in the rock. I found a bunsh of crab claws near a stream. We were tired and dirty when we came out of the cave, but none of us would exchange the day for another. We felt we had discovered something very spetial.

Proofreading Marks

≡   Make a capital.

/   Make a small letter.

∧   Add something.

℘   Take out something.

⊙   Add a period.

⌗   New paragraph

(SP)   Spelling error

Write a Diary Entry

Narrative Writing

Think of a new experience that you had recently. Maybe you visited a new place or moved to a new school. How did the experience change you? Write a diary entry about it.

- Tell how you felt in the new situation.
- Tell what you learned from the experience.
- Use specific adjectives.
- Use active verbs.

Use as many spelling words as you can.

Proofread Your Writing During

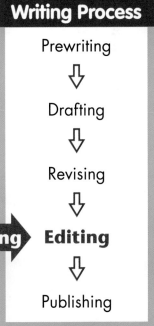

Writing Process

Prewriting

⇩

Drafting

⇩

Revising

⇩

Editing

⇩

Publishing

Proofread your writing for spelling errors as part of the editing stage in the writing process. Be sure to check each word carefully. Use a dictionary to check spelling if you are not sure.

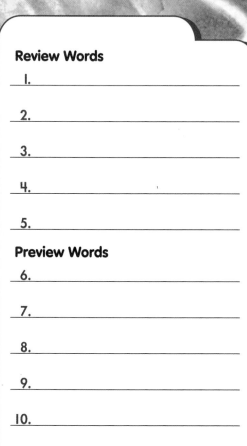

VOCABULARY CONNECTIONS

►Strategy Words◄

Review Words: Consonant Sounds /sh/, /ch/

Write a word from the box to complete each sentence.

chart	nation	reach	shell	shower

1. The conch _____ I found today on the beach looks like a beautiful horn.
2. The captain used a _____ to plot his course through the narrow channel.
3. In ten minutes, we will _____ the snow-covered mountains of Vermont.
4. A hot _____ felt good after sledding.
5. Even though she loves this country, Sara still misses the _____ of her birth.

Preview Words: Consonant Sounds /sh/, /ch/

Write a word from the box to complete each analogy.

appreciate	channel	direction	patience	shield

6. **Dislike** is to **detest** as **like** is to _____.
7. **Rain** is to **umbrella** as **sword** is to _____.
8. **Instruct** is to **instruction** as **direct** is to _____.
9. **Stream** is to **gully** as **river** is to _____.
10. **Unkindness** is to **kindness** as **impatience** is to _____.

Review Words

I. _____
2. _____
3. _____
4. _____
5. _____

Preview Words

6. _____
7. _____
8. _____
9. _____
10. _____

Content Words

Social Studies: Symbols

Write words from the box to complete the paragraph.

statue	torch	emblem	tired	homeless

Miss Liberty is a __1.__ in New York Harbor. She is an __2.__ of America's welcome to immigrants. Written on her base is an invitation to the __3.__ and __4.__ of the world. She holds her __5.__ high to light the way.

Social Studies: Government

Write the word from the box that matches each clue.

constitution	proclaim	faith	represent	history

6. In a democracy, one person can _____ many.
7. The Declaration of Independence was meant to _____ freedom from British rule.
8. Many nations do not have a written _____.
9. Most United States voters have _____ in democracy.
10. We can learn from our past if we study _____.

Apply the Spelling Strategy

Circle the letters that spell the /**ch**/ and /**sh**/ sounds in three of the Content Words you wrote.

Word Study

Homophones

Words that sound alike but have different spellings and meanings are **homophones**. **Eight** and **ate** are homophones. Write the Strategy Word that is a homophone for **patients**.

Social Studies: Symbols
1. _____
2. _____
3. _____
4. _____
5. _____

Social Studies: Government
6. _____
7. _____
8. _____
9. _____
10. _____

Homophones
1. _____

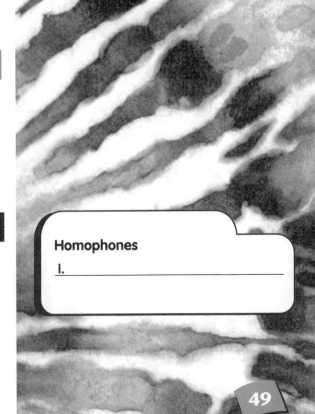

/əl/ spelled al, el, or il

1.
2.
3.
4.
5.
6.
7.
8.
9.
10.
11.
12.
13.
14.
15.
16.

/əl/ spelled le

17.
18.
19.
20.

Spelling and Thinking

READ THE SPELLING WORDS

1. humble — *humble* — A **humble** person does not brag.
2. angel — *angel* — Marcie played an **angel** in the show.
3. council — *council* — The **council** planned a town park.
4. pupil — *pupil* — The new **pupil** likes art class.
5. final — *final* — The **final** batter hit a home run.
6. normal — *normal* — A **normal** school day lasts six hours.
7. angle — *angle* — An **angle** of thirty degrees is acute.
8. syllable — *syllable* — Mark pronounced each **syllable**.
9. festival — *festival* — Mardi Gras is a huge **festival**.
10. panel — *panel* — The **panel** is made of oak.
11. evil — *evil* — An **evil** king took all their land.
12. rural — *rural* — On the **rural** road, we saw sheep.
13. fossil — *fossil* — The **fossil** had the shape of a bone.
14. scramble — *scramble* — Please **scramble** my eggs for me.
15. marvel — *marvel* — A thousand-year-old tree is a **marvel**.
16. loyal — *loyal* — A German shepherd is a **loyal** pet.
17. general — *general* — The **general** idea seemed reasonable.
18. parcel — *parcel* — A lumpy **parcel** sat on the table.
19. civil — *civil* — In a **civil** debate, no one yells.
20. counsel — *counsel* — Ann can **counsel** you about baby-sitting.

SORT THE SPELLING WORDS

1.–16. Write the words that spell the final /əl/ sound with an **l** at the end. Circle the letters that spell the /əl/ sound with **al**, **el**, or **il**.

17.–20. Write the words that spell the final /əl/ sound with an **e** at the end. Circle the letters that spell the /əl/ sound with **le**.

REMEMBER THE SPELLING STRATEGY

Remember that the final **schwa-l** sound can be spelled in different ways: **le** in **angle**, **el** in **panel**, **il** in **civil**, and **al** in **final**.

Spelling and Vocabulary

Word Clues

Write the spelling word that fits each clue.

1. someone who is very kind
2. opposite of **urban**
3. celebration, holiday
4. faithful to a person or idea
5. no more after this
6. opposite of **unusual**
7. You do it if you hurry.
8. If you are polite, you are this.
9. part or all of a word
10. opposite of **good**

Word Replacements

Write the word that could replace each underlined word.

11. The mail carrier delivered a large <u>package</u>.
12. Every teacher was once a <u>student</u>.
13. Let's cover this wall with an oak <u>board</u>.
14. In the stone was a <u>trace</u> of a leaf.
15. The <u>overall</u> idea is to run the bases.
16. There is a sharp <u>turn</u> in the road.
17. Yuka has great talent, but she is <u>modest</u>.
18. This giant pumpkin is a <u>miracle</u>.

USING THE Dictionary

A **homophone** is a word that sounds like another word but has a different spelling and different meaning. Study the definitions for **council** and **counsel**. Write the correct word to complete each sentence.

19. At the _____ meeting, the town leaders decided to build a town pool.
20. I always ask for Mom's _____ for hard choices.

Word Clues
1. _____
2. _____
3. _____
4. _____
5. _____
6. _____
7. _____
8. _____
9. _____
10. _____

Word Replacements
11. _____
12. _____
13. _____
14. _____
15. _____
16. _____
17. _____
18. _____

Using the Dictionary
19. _____
20. _____

Spelling and Reading

humble	angel	council	pupil	final
normal	angle	syllable	festival	panel
evil	rural	fossil	scramble	marvel
loyal	general	parcel	civil	counsel

Solve the Analogies

1.
2.
3.
4.
5.
6.
7.

Complete the Sentences

8.
9.
10.
11.
12.
13.
14.
15.

Complete the Paragraph

16.
17.
18.
19.
20.

Solve the Analogies Write a word to complete each analogy.

1. **Glass** is to **pane** as **wood** is to _____.
2. **Team** is to **athlete** as **class** is to _____.
3. **Talk** is to **speak** as **advise** is to _____.
4. **Car** is to **tire track** as **dinosaur's foot** is to _____.
5. **Paragraph** is to **sentence** as **word** is to _____.
6. **Diner** is to **restaurant** as **party** is to _____.
7. **Part** is to **whole** as **particular** is to _____.

Complete the Sentences Write a spelling word to complete each sentence.

8. Citizens' liberties are protected by _____ rights.
9. For once, the city _____ members all agreed.
10. The story was about an _____ and a human being.
11. His temperature has returned to _____.
12. Two walls meet at a right _____.
13. Chad is _____ about his talents.
14. People say that an _____ monster once ruled these woods.
15. Everyone is trying to _____ to the windows to see the snow.

Complete the Paragraph Write the spelling words from the box to complete the paragraph.

What happens to a letter or __16.__ after you drop it off at the post office? You would __17.__ at the machines and people who keep the mail system moving. Postal workers must be __18.__ and honest employees. Mail is sorted according to its __19.__ destination. Mail carriers then deliver the mail in the cities and __20.__ areas.

> marvel
> final
> parcel
> loyal
> rural

52

Spelling and Writing

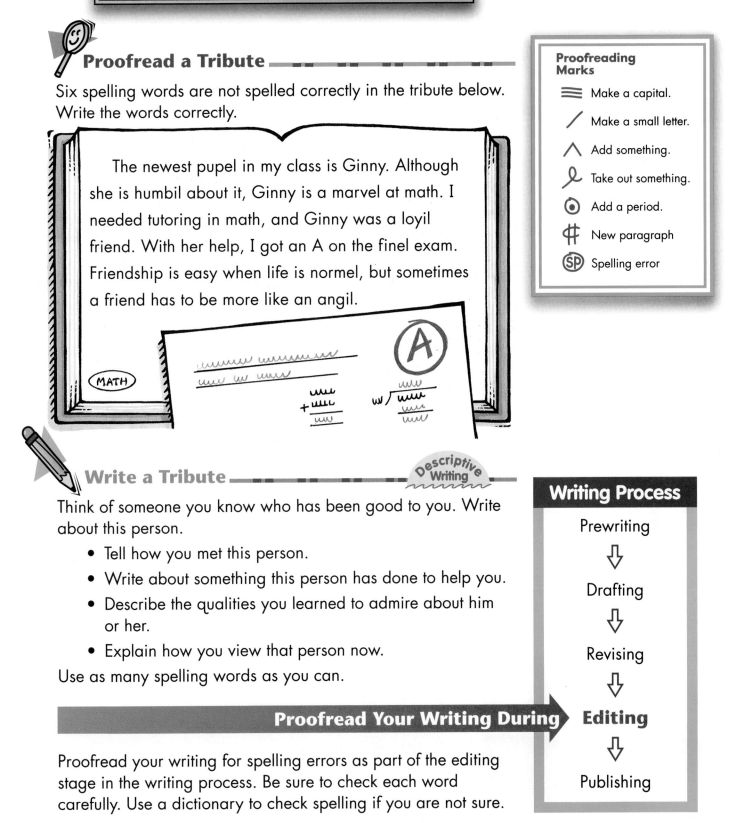

Proofread a Tribute

Six spelling words are not spelled correctly in the tribute below. Write the words correctly.

> The newest pupel in my class is Ginny. Although she is humbil about it, Ginny is a marvel at math. I needed tutoring in math, and Ginny was a loyil friend. With her help, I got an A on the finel exam. Friendship is easy when life is normel, but sometimes a friend has to be more like an angil.

MATH

Proofreading Marks

≡ Make a capital.

/ Make a small letter.

∧ Add something.

℮ Take out something.

⊙ Add a period.

New paragraph

SP Spelling error

Write a Tribute

Descriptive Writing

Think of someone you know who has been good to you. Write about this person.

- Tell how you met this person.
- Write about something this person has done to help you.
- Describe the qualities you learned to admire about him or her.
- Explain how you view that person now.

Use as many spelling words as you can.

Proofread Your Writing During

Proofread your writing for spelling errors as part of the editing stage in the writing process. Be sure to check each word carefully. Use a dictionary to check spelling if you are not sure.

Writing Process

Prewriting

⇩

Drafting

⇩

Revising

⇩

Editing

⇩

Publishing

VOCABULARY CONNECTIONS

►Strategy Words◄

Review Words
1. _____
2. _____
3. _____
4. _____
5. _____

Preview Words
6. _____
7. _____
8. _____
9. _____
10. _____

Review Words: Final /əl/

Write a word from the box to complete each rhyme.

battle	eagle	jungle	royal	vowel

1. A perfect pet would be a <u>beagle</u>, but you should not try to keep an _____.
2. Reading maps we do not <u>bungle</u>, when exploring in the _____.
3. Though hard to rid of dust and <u>soil</u>, velvet is the fabric _____.
4. That newborn baby sure can <u>howl</u>, but she seems to know just one _____.
5. Some kept sheep, and some raised <u>cattle</u>. Over land for each, there was many a _____.

Preview Words: Final /əl/

Write the word from the box that belongs in each group.

cancel	favorable	label	rational	tunnel

6. schedule, reschedule, _____
7. negative, neutral, _____
8. illogical, eccentric, _____
9. identify, name, _____
10. road, underpass, _____

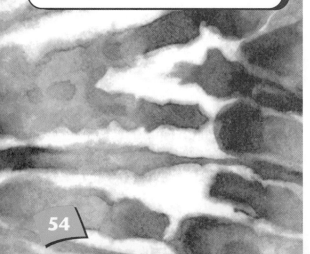

Content Words

Health: Teeth

Write the word from the box that fits each clue.

tartar	enamel	plaque	decay	fluoride

1. This rot is caused by bacteria.
2. Some towns add this to their water supply.
3. This is the hard outer layer of a tooth.
4. This is a thin film that can collect on a tooth's surface.
5. This is a hard deposit on teeth that a dentist removes.

Science: Animals

Write the word from the box that fits each clue.

buffalo	coyote	wolf	weasel	porcupine

6. This animal has large, curved horns.
7. This animal looks like a wolf.
8. This animal has quills.
9. This animal has short legs and a long tail; we sometimes call a sneaky person this.
10. This animal usually travels in packs; it sometimes appears in fairy tales as cruel and dangerous.

Apply the Spelling Strategy

Circle the letters that spell the final /əl/ sound in two of the Content Words you wrote.

Word Study

Word History

This Content Word came from an old Latin term, **porcus spinosis,** which meant "pig of spines." Write the word.

Health: Teeth

1. _____
2. _____
3. _____
4. _____
5. _____

Science: Animals

6. _____
7. _____
8. _____
9. _____
10. _____

Word History

1. _____

55

Spelling and Thinking

READ THE SPELLING WORDS

1.	citizen	*citizen*	Jules is a **citizen** of Belgium.
2.	profession	*profession*	Nursing is a rewarding **profession**.
3.	companion	*companion*	A good **companion** can make you laugh.
4.	governor	*governor*	The **governor** called a statewide meeting.
5.	solution	*solution*	Is there a **solution** to the problem?
6.	mention	*mention*	Did Claire **mention** my party?
7.	common	*common*	The **common** room is shared by all.
8.	senator	*senator*	The term of a **senator** is six years.
9.	mission	*mission*	Our **mission** is to send aid to them.
10.	section	*section*	The first **section** of the book is exciting.
11.	million	*million*	Several **million** stars filled the sky.
12.	oven	*oven*	Preheat the **oven** before baking.
13.	differ	*differ*	My parents **differ** on some issues.
14.	bother	*bother*	These flies **bother** my dog.
15.	mayor	*mayor*	Our town elected the same **mayor** again.
16.	copper	*copper*	Electricity flows through **copper**.
17.	dozen	*dozen*	A **dozen** eggs are needed for the cake.
18.	motor	*motor*	The **motor** in the clock is broken.
19.	onion	*onion*	Raw **onion** brings tears to my eyes.
20.	remember	*remember*	May Ling can **remember** the 1950s.

/ən/
1.
2.
3.
4.
5.
6.
7.
8.
9.
10.
11.
12.

/ər/
13.
14.
15.
16.
17.
18.
19.
20.

SORT THE SPELLING WORDS

1.–12. Write the words that contain the final /ən/ sound spelled **en, on,** or **ion**. Circle the letters that spell the /ən/ sound.

13.–20. Write the words that contain the final /ər/ sound spelled **er** or **or**. Circle the letters that spell the /ər/ sound.

REMEMBER THE SPELLING STRATEGY

Remember that the **schwa-n** sound can be spelled in different ways: **en** in **oven, on** in **common,** and **ion** in **companion.** The **schwa-r** sound can also be spelled in different ways: **er** in **copper** and **or** in **motor.**

Spelling and Vocabulary

Rhymes

Write the spelling word that completes each rhyme. The rhyming words are underlined.

1. Her cake had a top hat on the last <u>layer</u>. She had just been elected _____.

2. If Jane had only one more <u>cousin</u>, she would have had an even _____.

3. I am lucky to have a very good <u>father</u>. To him, I am never, ever a _____.

4. Do you know that a <u>billion</u> is many times more than a _____?

Synonyms

Write the spelling word that is a synonym for each word.

5. engine
6. occupation
7. answer
8. friend
9. portion
10. ordinary

USING THE Dictionary

Write the spelling word for each dictionary respelling. Next to each word write **n** if the word is a noun or **v** if the word is a verb.

11. /rĭ **mĕm′** bər/
12. /**sĭt′** ĭ zən/
13. /**ŭv′** ən/
14. /**ŭn′** yən/
15. /**mĭsh′** ən/
16. /**kŏp′** ər/
17. /**mĕn′** shən/
18. /**dĭf′** ər/
19. /**sĕn′** ə tər/
20. /**gŭv′** ər nər/

Rhymes
1. _____
2. _____
3. _____
4. _____

Synonyms
5. _____
6. _____
7. _____
8. _____
9. _____
10. _____

Using the Dictionary
11. _____
12. _____
13. _____
14. _____
15. _____
16. _____
17. _____
18. _____
19. _____
20. _____

Spelling and Reading

citizen	profession	companion	governor
solution	mention	common	senator
mission	section	million	oven
differ	bother	mayor	copper
dozen	motor	onion	remember

Solve the Analogies Write a spelling word to solve each analogy.

1. **Fruit** is to **apple** as **vegetable** is to _____.
2. **Refrigerator** is to **freezer** as **stove** is to _____.
3. **Hardship** is to **hard** as **companionship** is to _____.
4. **Food** is to **people** as **fuel** is to _____.
5. **Shoes** is to **pair** as **eggs** is to _____.

Complete the Sentences Write a spelling word to complete each sentence.

6. We sat in the first _____ of the audience.
7. Do not _____ the puppy while it is eating.
8. I just thought of a _____ to the problem.
9. Often used for wiring, _____ is an excellent conductor of heat and electricity.
10. Did I hear someone _____ my name?
11. Your smile is worth a _____ dollars.

Complete the Paragraph Write the spelling words that complete the paragraph.

Every __12.__ should __13.__ that the government is composed of national, state, and local branches. All three branches __14.__ in the powers and duties of their elected offices. The local government of a city or town is run by the __15.__. The top officer of a state is the __16.__. At the federal level is the __17.__, two for each state. It is __18.__ for an elected official to gain experience in his or her __19.__ by being elected to a minor office. With a __20.__ to serve in a greater role, a politician may go on to higher office.

Solve the Analogies

1. _____
2. _____
3. _____
4. _____
5. _____

Complete the Sentences

6. _____
7. _____
8. _____
9. _____
10. _____
11. _____

Complete the Paragraph

12. _____
13. _____
14. _____
15. _____
16. _____
17. _____
18. _____
19. _____
20. _____

Spelling and Writing

Proofread a Speech

Six spelling words are not spelled correctly in the speech below. Write the words correctly.

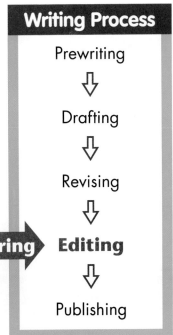

Every citizin here will remember this century. My missien is to have more freedom and peace in the next. There are too many concerns to mention today, but I will be your companian as we face them. We may diffur in our methods, but we have in commen our hope for the future.

Proofreading Marks

≡ Make a capital.

/ Make a small letter.

∧ Add something.

℮ Take out something.

⊙ Add a period.

⌗ New paragraph

(SP) Spelling error

Write a Speech

Persuasive Writing

Imagine that you have been elected president of your school's student government. Write a speech telling how you will make your school a better place.

- Name your new position.
- State your plan for improving the school.
- Use specific adjectives.
- Use active verbs.

Use as many of the spelling words as you can.

Proofread Your Writing During ➤ Editing

Writing Process

Prewriting

⇩

Drafting

⇩

Revising

⇩

Editing

⇩

Publishing

Proofread your writing for spelling errors as part of the editing stage in the writing process. Be sure to check each word carefully. Use a dictionary to check spelling if you are not sure.

VOCABULARY CONNECTIONS

Strategy Words

Review Words

1. _____
2. _____
3. _____
4. _____
5. _____

Preview Words

6. _____
7. _____
8. _____
9. _____
10. _____

Review Words: Final /ən/, Final /ər/

Write the word from the box that matches each clue.

lighten	major	thicken	tractor	water

1. It is the opposite of **minor**.
2. You might have to do this to a stew.
3. This can pull another large vehicle.
4. It is the opposite of **darken**.
5. This is made up of hydrogen and oxygen.

Preview Words: Final /ən/, Final /ər/

Write the word from the box that completes each sentence.

carbon	diameter	emotion	mirror	permission

6. This circle is eighteen inches in _____.
7. Joy is the _____ he feels most often.
8. Everyone needs _____ to go on the field trip.
9. All animal and plant matter contains a certain amount of _____.
10. That _____ is too high for me to see myself.

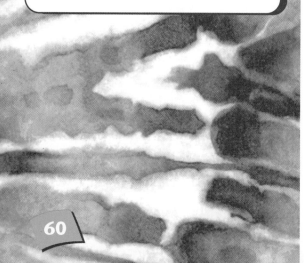

Content Words

Math: Operations

Write the word from the box that matches each clue.

calculate	estimate	calculator	signs	compute

1. If you do this, you might say "about."
2. You could use one to do long division.
3. These tell you to add, subtract, multiply, or divide.
4. This is another word for **calculate**.
5. To do this, you could add and multiply.

Social Studies: Business

Write a word from the box that completes each sentence.

retail	industry	consume	monitor	commerce

6. Experts in sales ____ customer behavior.
7. The computer ____ changes quickly.
8. A ____ shop sells to the general public.
9. Business, trading, buying, and selling are all part of ____.
10. Food is meant for people to ____.

Apply the Spelling Strategy

Circle the letters that spell the final /ər/ sound in two of the Content Words you wrote.

Word Study

Word Roots

The root **dia** comes from an old Greek word that meant "through" or "across." Write the Strategy Word that has this root and means "the length through or across an object."

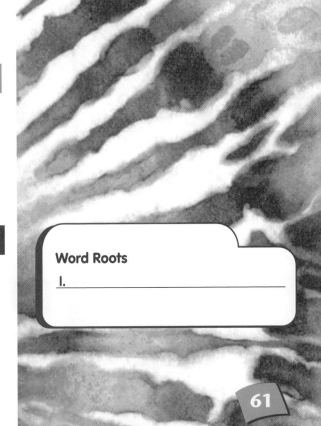

Math: Operations
1. _____
2. _____
3. _____
4. _____
5. _____

Social Studies: Business
6. _____
7. _____
8. _____
9. _____
10. _____

Word Roots
1. _____

61

Spelling and Thinking

READ THE SPELLING WORDS

1.	rehearse	*rehearse*	The band will **rehearse** every Tuesday.
2.	perfume	*perfume*	The smell of **perfume** filled the room.
3.	murmur	*murmur*	In a **murmur,** the shy girl gave her name.
4.	worth	*worth*	Your education is **worth** saving for.
5.	external	*external*	This lotion is for **external** use only.
6.	circulate	*circulate*	Please let air **circulate** in this room.
7.	service	*service*	My parents run a taxi **service**.
8.	disturb	*disturb*	Please do not **disturb** the baby.
9.	world	*world*	Few have seen the **world** from space.
10.	internal	*internal*	We sent the staff an **internal** memo.
11.	alert	*alert*	Please do not **alert** the newspapers.
12.	search	*search*	We can **search** in the attic for your hat.
13.	further	*further*	After **further** thought, Ben agreed.
14.	current	*current*	What is your **current** address?
15.	burnt	*burnt*	Dad likes his toast **burnt**.
16.	worst	*worst*	Our **worst** winter storm was in March.
17.	purpose	*purpose*	My **purpose** is to weed the garden.
18.	deserve	*deserve*	Kai and Becca **deserve** our applause.
19.	squirrel	*squirrel*	Have you ever seen a flying **squirrel**?
20.	conserve	*conserve*	In the desert, people **conserve** water.

/ûr/
1.

/ûr/ spelled er
2. 3. 4. 5. 6. 7. 8.

/ûr/ not spelled er
9. 10. 11. 12. 13. 14. 15. 16. 17. 18. 19. 20.

SORT THE SPELLING WORDS

1. Write the word that spells the /ûr/ sound in two different ways. Circle the letters that spell the /ûr/ sound.
2.–8. Write the other words that spell the /ûr/ sound **er**.
9.–20. Write the other words that do not spell the /ûr/ sound **er**. Circle the letters that spell the /ûr/ sound.

REMEMBER THE SPELLING STRATEGY

Remember that the **r**-controlled vowel sound you hear in **service** (/ûr/) can be spelled in different ways: **er** in **alert**, **ear** in **search**, **ir** in **circulate**, **ur** in **burnt**, and **or** in **world**.

Spelling and Vocabulary

Related Meanings

Write a spelling word to complete each analogy.

1. **Dream** is to **wish** as **goal** is to _____.
2. **Praise** is to **compliment** as **pester** is to _____.
3. **Receive** is to **request** as **find** is to _____.
4. **Lake** is to **fish** as **tree** is to _____.
5. **Better** is to **best** as **worse** is to _____.
6. **Do** is to **plan** as **perform** is to _____.
7. **Strive** is to **try** as **merit** is to _____.

Synonyms

Write the spelling word that is a synonym for each of these words.

8. attentive
9. travel
10. beyond
11. assistance
12. fragrance
13. value
14. inside
15. earth

USING THE Dictionary

Write the spelling word that fits each definition.

16. a past tense and past participle of **burn**
17. to protect from loss
18. the movement of water or air
19. a prolonged low sound
20. on the outside

Related Meanings

1._____
2._____
3._____
4._____
5._____
6._____
7._____

Synonyms

8._____
9._____
10._____
11._____
12._____
13._____
14._____
15._____

Using the Dictionary

16._____
17._____
18._____
19._____
20._____

Spelling and Reading

rehearse	perfume	murmur	worth	external
circulate	service	disturb	world	internal
alert	search	further	current	burnt
worst	purpose	deserve	squirrel	conserve

Complete the Sentences   Write the spelling word that could best replace the underlined word or words.

1. One picture is <u>equal</u> to a thousand words.
2. This is the <u>most terrible</u> traffic jam I have ever seen.
3. We should <u>look</u> for a less crowded beach.
4. There is no need to investigate any <u>more</u>.
5. This light bulb has <u>worn</u> out.
6. Please <u>do not waste</u> water during this drought.
7. Do we need to <u>practice</u> the first act again?
8. Our mechanic understands the <u>inside</u> workings of the car's motor.
9. This <u>pleasant-smelling liquid</u> is made from lavender.
10. The <u>bushy-tailed rodent</u> raided the bird feeder.
11. Newly designed bills are beginning to <u>move</u> throughout the United States.
12. What is the <u>goal</u> of this club?
13. The new shutters improved the <u>outside</u> appearance of the house.

Complete the Story   Write the spelling words to complete the story.

From the quiet __14.__ of a pickup truck to the rumble of a tractor trailer, the motors of the trucking industry gear up each day.

Trucking is a demanding profession. Special schools teach __15.__ driving and safety regulations. Long-distance drivers must stay __16.__ through their long hours of work. They must also stop and start smoothly so they do not __17.__ the contents of their trucks.

Certainly, truck drivers __18.__ credit for their __19.__ of transporting goods in today's __20.__ of trade.

Complete the Sentences
1.
2.
3.
4.
5.
6.
7.
8.
9.
10.
11.
12.
13.

Complete the Story
14.
15.
16.
17.
18.
19.
20.

64

Spelling and Writing

Proofread Instructions

Six spelling words are not spelled correctly in the instructions below. Write the words correctly.

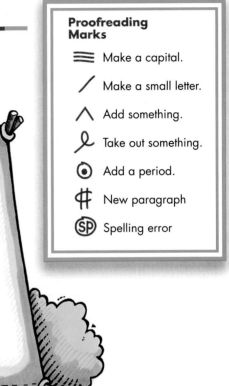

First, tie the extirnal tarp to branches above the site. Next, serch for the poles. Connect three long poles and four short poles. Stay alurt so that a squerrel does not get inside. Step into the tent and put the inturnal poles through the seams. Your perpose is to get shelter right away. You deserve it.

Proofreading Marks

≡	Make a capital.
/	Make a small letter.
∧	Add something.
ℓ	Take out something.
⊙	Add a period.
#	New paragraph
SP	Spelling error

Write Instructions

Expository Writing

Think of a process you know how to complete. Write a set of step-by-step instructions for someone to follow.

- Put the steps in order.
- Start each step with a verb.
- Use simple language.
- Warn your reader about any possible problems.

Use as many of the spelling words as you can.

Writing Process

Prewriting
⇩
Drafting
⇩
Revising
⇩
Editing
⇩
Publishing

Proofread Your Writing During → Editing

Proofread your writing for spelling errors as part of the editing stage in the writing process. Be sure to check each word carefully. Use a dictionary to check spelling if you are not sure.

VOCABULARY CONNECTIONS

Strategy Words

Review Words: r-Controlled Vowel /ûr/

Write the word from the box that completes each sentence.

burst	herd	person	thirst	verb

1. One _____ left the auditorium.
2. We both suddenly _____ into laughter.
3. The cowboys drove a thousand-head _____.
4. An exciting title might contain a _____.
5. Drink water to quench your _____.

Preview Words: r-Controlled Vowel /ûr/

Write the word from the box that could best replace the underlined word or words.

dirty	effort	operation	survey	worrisome

6. After lunch, the floor was <u>grimy</u>.
7. Please make an <u>attempt</u> to answer every question.
8. The storm clouds are <u>causing anxiety</u>.
9. First, the scout will <u>look over</u> the trail.
10. The nurse said we could cancel the <u>surgery</u>.

Review Words

1. _____
2. _____
3. _____
4. _____
5. _____

Preview Words

6. _____
7. _____
8. _____
9. _____
10. _____

Content Words

Language Arts: Prepositions

Write the word from the box that fits each clue.

against	along	among	behind	during

1. This means "in a line with; onward."
2. In this position, you are surrounded.
3. You may not see someone here.
4. This means "while."
5. This means "opposed to."

Language Arts: People

Write the words from the box that fit the meanings in the paragraph.

creative	mature	individual	society	mobile

Many people write to express their opinions because they believe that their own __6.__ views are important. Older people want __7.__ to benefit from their __8.__ experiences. Some writers try to broaden their understanding by becoming __9.__ and traveling frequently. They believe that new experiences make them more __10.__.

Apply the Spelling Strategy

Circle the letters that spell the /ûr/ sound in two of the Content Words you wrote.

Word Study

Collective Nouns

A **collective noun** is singular in form but plural in meaning. For example, a group of geese is a **gaggle,** and a group of lions is a **pride**. Write the Strategy Word that is a collective noun.

Language Arts: Prepositions
1. _____
2. _____
3. _____
4. _____
5. _____

Language Arts: People
6. _____
7. _____
8. _____
9. _____
10. _____

Collective Nouns
1. _____

Spelling and Thinking

READ THE SPELLING WORDS

	/âr/		
	1.	repair	*repair*	Chad can **repair** your bicycle wheel.
	2.	aware	*aware*	The fox is **aware** of people nearby.
	3.	carpet	*carpet*	We can sit in a circle on the **carpet**.
	4.	pardon	*pardon*	Please **pardon** me for being late.
	5.	guard	*guard*	My dog will **guard** the camp.
	6.	remark	*remark*	Your **remark** about Mars puzzled me.
	7.	scarce	*scarce*	Water is **scarce** in some places.
	8.	declare	*declare*	Ms. Fay will **declare** the bridge open.
	9.	argue	*argue*	Matt and Tanya **argue** about movies.
	10.	department	*department*	The **department** store has raincoats.
	11.	vary	*vary*	Some holidays have dates that **vary**.
	12.	prepare	*prepare*	Karen will **prepare** the fish.
	13.	flair	*flair*	Robin has a **flair** for acting.
	14.	article	*article*	One news **article** surprised him.
	15.	farther	*farther*	Venus is **farther** away than Mercury.
	16.	regard	*regard*	I have the highest **regard** for Grace.
	17.	area	*area*	One **area** of the garden is for herbs.
	18.	harvest	*harvest*	This year's pumpkin **harvest** is poor.
	19.	despair	*despair*	Do not **despair** about the lost cat.
	20.	flare	*flare*	The hiker carried a **flare**.

SORT THE SPELLING WORDS

1.–10. Write the words that have the /âr/ sound spelled **ar, are,** or **air**. Circle the letters that spell this vowel sound.

11.–20. Write the words that have the /är/ sound spelled **ar**.

REMEMBER THE SPELLING STRATEGY

Remember that the **r**-controlled vowel sound in **vary** (/âr/) can be spelled in different ways: **ar** in **vary, are** in **aware,** and **air** in **flair**. The **r**-controlled vowel sound in **carpet** (/är/) is often spelled **ar**.

Left margin word lists

/âr/

1.
2.
3.
4.
5.
6.
7.
8.
9.
10.

/är/

11.
12.
13.
14.
15.
16.
17.
18.
19.
20.

Spelling and Vocabulary

Word Meanings

Write the spelling word that matches each clue.

1. This is done in the fall on a farm.
2. When you are this, you are alert.
3. This is a brief statement.
4. This is a section of a business or a store.
5. When things change, they do this.
6. This means "get ready."
7. This might appear in a newspaper.
8. This means "respect" or "affection."
9. A region can be called this.
10. A soldier might do this.
11. When you make a mistake, you hope for this.
12. Some go wall-to-wall.

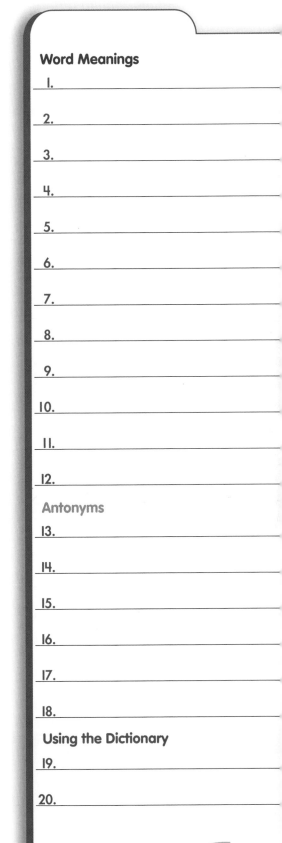

Antonyms

Write the spelling word that means the opposite of these words.

13. hope
14. nearer
15. break
16. plentiful
17. deny
18. agree

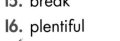
USING THE Dictionary

Two of the spelling words are **homophones**. Write the correct homophone for each definition.

19. to burn with a sudden flame
20. a natural talent

◆ ◆ ◆

Dictionary Check Be sure to check the definitions of the words in your **Spelling Dictionary**.

Word Meanings

1. _____
2. _____
3. _____
4. _____
5. _____
6. _____
7. _____
8. _____
9. _____
10. _____
11. _____
12. _____

Antonyms

13. _____
14. _____
15. _____
16. _____
17. _____
18. _____

Using the Dictionary

19. _____
20. _____

repair	aware	carpet	pardon	guard
remark	scarce	declare	argue	department
vary	prepare	flair	article	farther
regard	area	harvest	despair	flare

Complete the Paragraph   Write the spelling words that complete the paragraph.

Did you ever wonder how large stores choose the merchandise they sell? Each ___1.___ in a store has a buyer who makes those decisions. Certainly, the needs of people living in the ___2.___ are important. An ___3.___ of clothing popular in the city might not interest customers who live ___4.___ out in a rural area. Water skis would not be popular in places where rivers and lakes are ___5.___. Expensive, hand-woven ___6.___ might not sell in some communities. It takes a lot of planning for a buyer to ___7.___ a list of salable items. Good buyers must remain ___8.___ of the needs and trends in a community. They should have a ___9.___ for knowing what customers want to buy.

Complete the Sequences   Write the spelling word that belongs in each group.

10. discuss, debate, _____
11. plant, grow, _____
12. seriousness, sorrow, _____
13. say, state, _____
14. smolder, spark, _____
15. look, watch, _____

Finish the Rhymes   Write the spelling word that completes each rhyme.

16. After ruining Claire's garden, I sweetly asked for her _____.
17. Ben accomplishes tasks that are hard. His talents are held in high _____.
18. By the time we reached the park, we forgot Burt's rude _____.
19. Grandpa's car gets great care. It rarely needs _____.
20. Along the coast we get wary if the weather starts to _____.

Complete the Paragraph
1. _____
2. _____
3. _____
4. _____
5. _____
6. _____
7. _____
8. _____
9. _____

Complete the Sequences
10. _____
11. _____
12. _____
13. _____
14. _____
15. _____

Finish the Rhymes
16. _____
17. _____
18. _____
19. _____
20. _____

Spelling ᵃⁿᵈ Writing

Proofread a Story

Six spelling words are not spelled correctly in the story below. Write the words correctly.

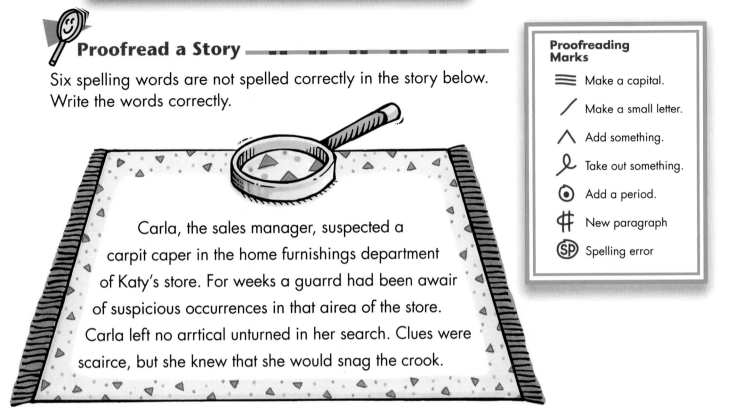

Carla, the sales manager, suspected a carpit caper in the home furnishings department of Katy's store. For weeks a guarrd had been awair of suspicious occurrences in that airea of the store. Carla left no arrtical unturned in her search. Clues were scairce, but she knew that she would snag the crook.

Proofreading Marks

≡	Make a capital.
/	Make a small letter.
∧	Add something.
ℓ	Take out something.
⊙	Add a period.
⌗	New paragraph
ⓈⓅ	Spelling error

Write a Story

Narrative Writing

Think of a simple, exciting story you can write in one paragraph.

- Begin with a surprising statement.
- Use vivid language.
- Connect one event to the next.
- Use active verbs.

Use as many spelling words as you can.

Writing Process

Prewriting
⇩
Drafting
⇩
Revising
⇩
Editing
⇩
Publishing

Proofread Your Writing During → **Editing**

Proofread your writing for spelling errors as part of the editing stage in the writing process. Be sure to check each word carefully. Use a dictionary to check spelling if you are not sure.

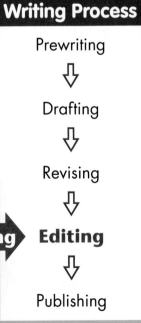

VOCABULARY CONNECTIONS

Strategy Words

Review Words
1. _____
2. _____
3. _____
4. _____
5. _____

Preview Words
6. _____
7. _____
8. _____
9. _____
10. _____

Review Words: r-Controlled Vowels /âr/, /är/

Write the word from the box that could best replace the underlined word or words.

cart	compare	march	stare	unfair

1. Janine says to <u>consider two or more</u> prices before buying.
2. Soldiers <u>walk with steady steps</u> in lines.
3. We can pull the children in the <u>wagon</u>.
4. I <u>look steadily</u> at a math problem for a while before trying to solve it.
5. Captain Bly's treatment of the sailors was cruel and <u>unjust</u>.

Preview Words: r-Controlled Vowels /âr/, /är/

Write the word from the box that fits each clue.

carton	garbage	paragraph	scarcely	temporary

6. This might contain milk, juice, or eggs.
7. This is often taken away by a truck.
8. A group of sentences about the same idea could be one of these.
9. This means "barely" or "hardly."
10. This is the opposite of **permanent**.

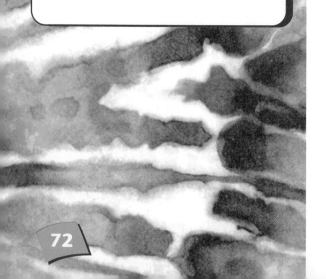

Content Words

Health: Nutrition

Write the word from the box that fits each clue.

| carbohydrate | protein | fiber | vitamins | minerals |

1. This comes from meat, eggs, and fish.
2. These are elements, such as iron and zinc, that plants and animals require for growth.
3. Examples of these are A, B, and C.
4. This starch or sugar gives your body energy.
5. This kind of food helps in digestion.

Fine Arts: Music

Write the word from the box that completes each sentence.

| carol | lullaby | folk song | lyrics | harmony |

6. You would hear a _____ at Christmastime.
7. A parent may sing a _____ at bedtime.
8. With three singers, you may sing in three-part _____.
9. The _____ to a song may tell a story.
10. A _____ usually comes from a specific country or region.

Apply the Spelling Strategy

Circle the letters that spell the /är/ sound in two of the Content Words you wrote. Draw a box around the letters that spell the /âr/ sound in one word you wrote.

Word Study

Clipped Words

A **clipped word** is a short, familiar form of a longer word. For example, **carbs** is short for **carbohydrates**. Write the Strategy Word whose clipped form is **temp**.

Health: Nutrition
1. _____
2. _____
3. _____
4. _____
5. _____

Fine Arts: Music
6. _____
7. _____
8. _____
9. _____
10. _____

Clipped Words
1. _____

Assessment and Review

Assessment — Units 7–11

Each Assessment Word in the box fits one of the spelling strategies you have studied over the past five weeks. Read the spelling strategies. Then write each Assessment Word under the unit number it fits.

Unit 7

1.–4. The /sh/ sound can be spelled in different ways: **sh** in **shelter, ti** in **patient,** and **ci** in **ancient.** The /ch/ sound can be spelled in different ways: **ch** in **cheap, tch** in **kitchen,** and **tu** in nature.

Unit 8

5.–8. The final **schwa-l** sound can be spelled in different ways: **le** in **angle, el** in **panel, il** in **civil,** and **al** in **final.**

Unit 9

9.–12. The **schwa-n** sound can be spelled in different ways: **en** in **oven, on** in **common,** and **ion** in **companion.** The **schwa-r** sound can be spelled in different ways: **er** in **copper** and **or** in **motor.**

Unit 10

13.–17. The **r**-controlled vowel sound you hear in **service** (/ûr/) can be spelled in different ways: **er** in **alert, ear** in **search, ir** in **circulate, ur** in **burnt,** and **or** in **world.**

Unit 11

18.–20. The **r**-controlled vowel sound you hear in **vary** (/âr/) can be spelled in different ways: **ar** in **vary, are** in **aware,** and **air** in **flair.** The **r**-controlled vowel sound you hear in **carpet** (/är/) is often spelled **ar.**

armor
stern
linen
morsel
attach
shallow
ample
vigor
worse
aircraft
welfare
burglar
modern
penalty
fixture
butcher
peril
prison
earnest
scarlet

Review — Unit 7: Consonant Sounds /sh/, /ch/

delicious	kitchen	picture	special	shadow
nature	shoulder	bunch	motion	chest

Write one /**sh**/ word and one /**ch**/ word to answer each riddle.

1.–2. a tasty group

3.–4. particular photograph

5.–6. body movement when you're breathing heavily

7.–8. shade caused by wild animal

Write the spelling words that have these meanings.

9. where your arm attaches to your body

10. a room where cooking is done

Review — Unit 8: Final /əl/

final	normal	general	angle	scramble
fossil	syllable	council	pupil	panel

Write the spelling word by adding the missing letters.

11. They found a **fo** __ __ **il** in the quarry.

12. Sue was elected to student **c** __ __ **nc** __ **l**.

13. We have a new __ **u** __ **il** in our class.

14. What was your time on the **fin** __ __ lap?

15. We walked our __ **orm** __ **l** route to school.

16. They looked in the **gen** __ **r** __ **l** direction of the teacher.

17. The two walls form a right __ **ng** __ __.

18. Do you know how to **scr** __ **mb** __ __ eggs?

19. Name the first **s** __ **lla** __ **le** of your word.

20. He decided to **pan** __ __ the walls in the den.

Unit 7

1. ____
2. ____
3. ____
4. ____
5. ____
6. ____
7. ____
8. ____
9. ____
10. ____

Unit 8

11. ____
12. ____
13. ____
14. ____
15. ____
16. ____
17. ____
18. ____
19. ____
20. ____

75

Unit 9

1. _____
2. _____
3. _____
4. _____
5. _____
6. _____
7. _____
8. _____
9. _____
10. _____

Unit 10

11. _____
12. _____
13. _____
14. _____
15. _____
16. _____
17. _____
18. _____
19. _____
20. _____

| remember | common | motor | governor | oven |
| dozen | mayor | section | solution | million |

Write the spelling word that completes each sentence.

1. The head of our state government is a wise _____.
2. She works well with the _____, who is head of our city.
3. There are many trees in our _____ of the block.
4. The council has a helpful _____ to the problem.
5. There are two _____ people in our large city.
6. Can you _____ when the Jeffersons moved here?
7. It was about a _____ years ago.
8. It is a _____ sight to see families picnicking in the parks.
9. I'll be just a minute, so keep the _____ running while I go back inside.
10. I want to make sure I turned the _____ off after baking the turkey.

Review Unit 10: r-Controlled Vowel /ûr/

| deserve | further | purpose | service | worth |
| worst | current | disturb | world | search |

Use the spelling words in the box and follow the directions.

11.–14. Write the one-syllable spelling words.

15. Write the word that has two consonants in the middle that are the same.

Write the spelling words that have these meanings.

16. more; extra
17. to be worthy of
18. to bother; interrupt
19. aim; plan
20. a help; an aid

Unit 11: r-Controlled Vowels /âr/, /är/

farther	article	guard	repair	declare
area	department	harvest	flare	prepare

Write a spelling word that means the same as the underlined words in each sentence.

1. We were too tired to go a <u>greater distance</u>.
2. Eating vegetables will help to <u>protect</u> you against getting sick.
3. Is this the <u>section</u> of town where you live?
4. It will take an hour to <u>get ready</u> for the show.
5. The campfire started with a bright <u>sudden light</u>.
6. Will the <u>crop</u> be large this year?
7. Corey works in the clothing <u>part</u> of the store.
8. This magazine has an interesting <u>piece of writing</u> about gardening.
9. I hope Dad can <u>fix</u> this broken lamp.
10. She should <u>state openly</u> that she is running for office.

Unit 11

1. _____
2. _____
3. _____
4. _____
5. _____
6. _____
7. _____
8. _____
9. _____
10. _____

WORD SORT **Spelling Study Strategy**

Sorting by Sounds

One good way to practice spelling is to place words into groups according to their spelling patterns. Here is a way to practice some of the words you studied in the past few weeks.

1. Make eight columns on a large piece of paper or on the chalkboard.

2. Write each of the following sounds at the head of each column: (1) **/sh/**, (2) **/ch/**, (3) **Final /əl/**, (4) **Final /ən/**, (5) **Final /ər/**, (6) **/ûr/**, (7) **/âr/**, (8) **/är/**.

3. Have a partner choose a spelling word from Units 7 through 11 and say the word aloud.

4. Write the spelling word under the heading for that sound. (Remember that the sounds can be spelled in different ways.)

WRITER'S

Grammar, Usage, and Mechanics

Sentences: Simple Subjects and Simple Predicates

Every sentence has a subject and a predicate. The simple subject is a noun or pronoun and tells whom or what the sentence is about.

The simple predicate is a verb. It may tell what the subject did or what was done to the subject. It may also be a form of the verb **be**.

The <u>team</u> in the red uniforms <u>won</u> both games.

     ↑   ↑

  simple subject   simple predicate

Practice
Activity

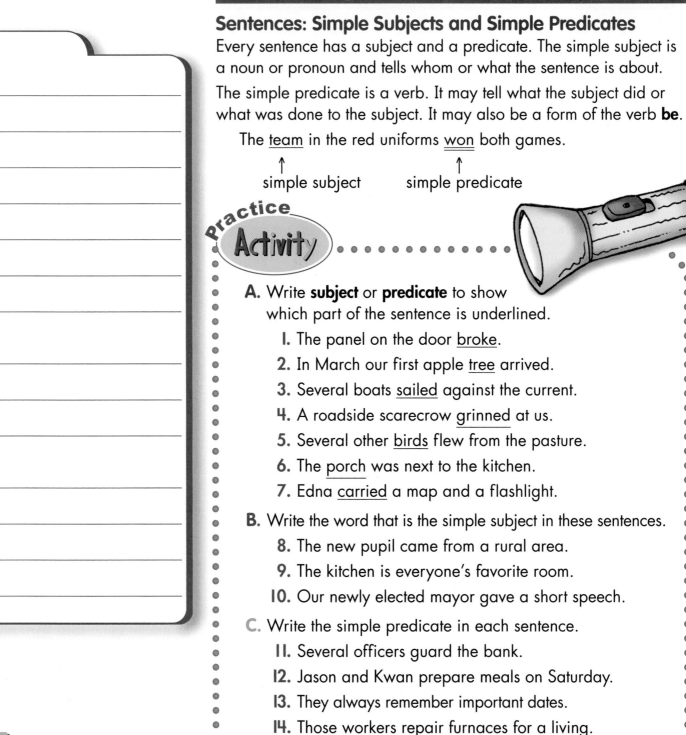

A. Write **subject** or **predicate** to show which part of the sentence is underlined.

  1. The panel on the door <u>broke</u>.

  2. In March our first apple <u>tree</u> arrived.

  3. Several boats <u>sailed</u> against the current.

  4. A roadside scarecrow <u>grinned</u> at us.

  5. Several other <u>birds</u> flew from the pasture.

  6. The <u>porch</u> was next to the kitchen.

  7. Edna <u>carried</u> a map and a flashlight.

B. Write the word that is the simple subject in these sentences.

  8. The new pupil came from a rural area.

  9. The kitchen is everyone's favorite room.

  10. Our newly elected mayor gave a short speech.

C. Write the simple predicate in each sentence.

  11. Several officers guard the bank.

  12. Jason and Kwan prepare meals on Saturday.

  13. They always remember important dates.

  14. Those workers repair furnaces for a living.

A.
  1. _____
  2. _____
  3. _____
  4. _____
  5. _____
  6. _____
  7. _____
B.
  8. _____
  9. _____
  10. _____
C.
  11. _____
  12. _____
  13. _____
  14. _____

Proofreading Strategy

Read it Backwards!

Good writers always proofread their writing for spelling errors. Here's a strategy that you can use to proofread your papers.

Instead of reading your paper from the first word to the last word, try reading it backwards. In other words, read it from the last word to the first. You would read the sentence **The dog barked twice**. like this: **twice barked dog The**.

It sounds funny, but reading your paper backward helps you think about the spelling of each word instead of the meaning of the sentence. Try it!

Electronic Spelling

Computer Words

Computers have changed our language. Today, we use many words that didn't even exist fifty years ago. We also use older words in new ways. For instance, once a **bookmark** was a piece of cloth or paper that you put in a book. Today, a **bookmark** is an electronic command. It is a way to find a place on the Internet.

Spell checkers may not recognize all these words, so you need to know how to spell them. Luckily, many are compound words—words made up of two shorter words. For example, **bookmark** is made from **book** and **mark**. To spell a compound word, just break it into two smaller words. Then spell each part.

Each word below has one of its parts misspelled. Write the word correctly.

Electronic Spelling
I.
2.
3.
4.
5.
6.

1. spreddsheet
2. hottlink
3. trubleshooting
4. bakkground
5. footnoet
6. Web syte

/ôr/

1. _____
2. _____
3. _____
4. _____
5. _____
6. _____
7. _____
8. _____
9. _____
10. _____
11. _____

/îr/

12. _____
13. _____
14. _____
15. _____
16. _____
17. _____
18. _____
19. _____
20. _____

Spelling and Thinking

READ THE SPELLING WORDS

1.	inform	*inform*	Kris will **inform** you of the date.
2.	ornament	*ornament*	Her hair **ornament** has shells on it.
3.	disappear	*disappear*	The cat seemed to **disappear** in the fog.
4.	pioneer	*pioneer*	Someday a **pioneer** may go to Mars.
5.	important	*important*	Clean oil is **important** for a car.
6.	warmth	*warmth*	All baby mammals need **warmth**.
7.	serious	*serious*	My brother is **serious** about art.
8.	forever	*forever*	The six-hour trip seemed to take **forever**.
9.	reward	*reward*	Di got a **reward** for returning the ring.
10.	appear	*appear*	Jaime will **appear** at six o'clock.
11.	perform	*perform*	A ballerina will **perform** today.
12.	force	*force*	You cannot **force** a parrot to speak.
13.	peer	*peer*	To see the cell, **peer** into the microscope.
14.	weary	*weary*	After the game, we were **weary**.
15.	pier	*pier*	A pelican rested on the **pier**.
16.	fortune	*fortune*	We were happy about their good **fortune**.
17.	career	*career*	An acting **career** might be exciting.
18.	pierce	*pierce*	We **pierce** the crust before baking it.
19.	formal	*formal*	The boys wore suits to the **formal** dance.
20.	enormous	*enormous*	An **enormous** elephant led the parade.

SORT THE SPELLING WORDS

1.–11. Write the words that have the /ôr/ sound spelled **or** or **ar**. Circle the letters that spell this vowel sound.

12.–20. Write the words that have the /îr/ sound spelled **eer, er, ear,** or **ier**. Circle the letters that spell this vowel sound.

REMEMBER THE SPELLING STRATEGY

Remember that the **r**-controlled vowel sound you hear in **force** (/ôr/) can be spelled **or** as in **force** or **ar** as in **warmth**. The **r**-controlled vowel sound you hear in **career** (/îr/) can be spelled **eer** as in **career, er** as in **serious, ear** as in **weary,** and **ier** as in **pierce**.

Spelling ^{and} Vocabulary

Prefixes

Add these prefixes to the roots or base words to write a spelling word.

1. dis + appear   3. per + form
2. in + form

Word Meanings

Write a spelling word that fits each clue.

4. A furnace could provide this.
5. You might get one if you return a valuable lost item.
6. To make a hole in something, you do this.
7. This is used to decorate something.
8. This means "power."
9. Wear your best for this kind of occasion.
10. This can mean "luck."
11.–12. These words are homophones.
13. It's a compound word.
14. This person is the first to do something.

USING THE Dictionary

Write the spelling word that is a synonym for each underlined word or words.

15. a <u>tired</u> traveler   18. an <u>influential</u> leader
16. a <u>solemn</u> expression   19. her teaching <u>profession</u>
17. a <u>huge</u> suitcase   20. A light will <u>show up</u>.

◆ ◆ ◆

Dictionary Check Be sure to check your answers in your **Spelling Dictionary**.

Prefixes

1. _____
2. _____
3. _____

Word Meanings

4. _____
5. _____
6. _____
7. _____
8. _____
9. _____
10. _____
11. _____
12. _____
13. _____
14. _____

Using the Dictionary

15. _____
16. _____
17. _____
18. _____
19. _____
20. _____

inform	ornament	disappear	pioneer	important
warmth	serious	forever	reward	appear
perform	force	peer	weary	pier
fortune	career	pierce	formal	enormous

Solve the Analogies Write a spelling word to solve each analogy.

1. **Hear** is to **listen** as **see** is to _____.
2. **Doctor** is to **profession** as **teacher** is to _____.
3. **Decorate** is to **decoration** as **adorn** is to _____.
4. **Deed** is to **do** as **experiment** is to _____.

Complete the Sentences Write a spelling word to complete each sentence.

5. For finding the puppy, Jamal was given a _____.
6. Martha's good _____ included wealth.
7.–8. The ice on the ground will _____ because of the _____ of the bonfire.
9. The anteater has an _____ nose.
10. The mansion had a _____ ballroom.
11.–12. When your cousins _____ at the door, I will be sure to _____ you.
13.–14. The nail can _____ the board with a little more _____ from the hammer.
15.–16. An _____ public figure will speak at the _____ before the ship leaves.
17.–18. The discoveries made by a _____ in medicine often affect humanity _____.
19.–20. The swimmer was so _____ that the doctor called her condition _____.

Have you seen Roscoe?

Reward upon return
Please call 555-7132.

Solve the Analogies

1. _____
2. _____
3. _____
4. _____

Complete the Sentences

5. _____
6. _____
7. _____
8. _____
9. _____
10. _____
11. _____
12. _____
13. _____
14. _____
15. _____
16. _____
17. _____
18. _____
19. _____
20. _____

Spelling and Writing

Proofread a Fairy Tale

Six words are not spelled correctly in this fairy tale. Write the words correctly.

There once was a princess whose father owned an enormus fortune in gold. Many serios young men from across the kingdom made formel requests to marry the princess, but the princess grew weery of them. She finally decided to infarm them that she was giving away her father's fortune. Little by little the young men began to disapear, all but one. The following year he and the princess married.

Proofreading Marks

≡	Make a capital.
/	Make a small letter.
∧	Add something.
ℓ	Take out something.
⊙	Add a period.
#	New paragraph
SP	Spelling error

Write a Fairy Tale

Narrative Writing

Base a humorous fairy tale on an unlikely hero or heroine. Include images that surprise the reader.

- Begin with a character description.
- Use comical images.
- Connect one event to the next.
- Use active verbs.

Use as many spelling words as you can.

Writing Process

Prewriting
⇩
Drafting
⇩
Revising
⇩
Editing
⇩
Publishing

Proofread Your Writing During → Editing

Proofread your writing for spelling errors as part of the editing stage in the writing process. Be sure to check each word carefully. Use a dictionary to check spelling if you are not sure.

VOCABULARY CONNECTIONS

Strategy Words

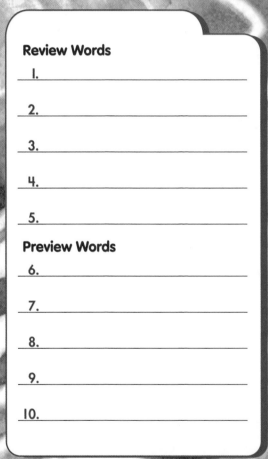

Review Words

1. _____
2. _____
3. _____
4. _____
5. _____

Preview Words

6. _____
7. _____
8. _____
9. _____
10. _____

Review Words: r-Controlled Vowels /ôr/, /îr/

Write the words from the box that complete the paragraph.

cheer	forest	near	record	sort

Birdwatchers can often be found in a __1.__ trying to get __2.__ as many birds as possible. They want to __3.__ out the different kinds of birds and __4.__ in their journals what each bird does. Finding a rare breed of bird must certainly __5.__ any birdwatcher.

Preview Words: r-Controlled Vowels /ôr/, /îr/

Write the word from the box that completes each sentence.

experience	ignore	ordinary	therefore	volunteer

6. Victor is a _____ in the Patient Records Department of the hospital.

7. Are you having an _____ day today?

8. You lost it; _____ you are the best person to find it.

9. Because of her years of _____, Charlene is the best leader.

10. Jamie tried to _____ the ringing of the alarm clock.

Content Words

Science: Eyes

Write the word from the box that fits each clue.

| cornea | membrane | image | retina | iris |

1. This is the inner lining around the inside of the eye.
2. This is the clear tissue over the front of the eye.
3. If you have brown eyes, this is brown.
4. You see this.
5. This is any thin, soft layer of tissue.

Fine Arts: Musical Instruments

Write the words from the box that complete the paragraph.

| brass | trumpet | cornet | tuba | trombone |

A marching band has ___6.___ instruments, which include several types of horns. One of these has a long bent tube that goes in and out. That is the slide ___7.___. The most familiar horn has three valves and a bell-shaped opening. That is the ___8.___. Similar to this familiar horn, but smaller, is the ___9.___. The largest of the horns is the ___10.___.

Apply the Spelling Strategy

Circle the letters that spell the /ôr/ sound in two of the Content Words you wrote.

Word Study

Word Roots

The root **corn** came from an old Latin word that meant "horn." A **unicorn** is an imaginary animal with one horn. Write the Content Word that has this root. It names an instrument that was often made from an animal horn in ancient times.

Science: Eyes

1. _____

2. _____

3. _____

4. _____

5. _____

Fine Arts: Musical Instruments

6. _____

7. _____

8. _____

9. _____

10. _____

Word Roots

1. _____

/oi/

1.

2.

3.

4.

5.

6.

7.

8.

9.

10.

/ou/

11.

12.

13.

14.

15.

16.

17.

18.

19.

20.

Spelling and Thinking

READ THE SPELLING WORDS

1. moisture — *moisture* — The **moisture** fogged up my glasses.
2. voyage — *voyage* — Their **voyage** began in New York.
3. employ — *employ* — Mandy will **employ** two assistants.
4. ounce — *ounce* — The dressing needs an **ounce** of olive oil.
5. mountain — *mountain* — There is a **mountain** near my town.
6. coward — *coward* — He is really a hero, not a **coward**.
7. allow — *allow* — My teacher will not **allow** mocking.
8. oyster — *oyster* — An **oyster** shell is flat and rough.
9. poise — *poise* — With great **poise,** the dancer bowed.
10. pronounce — *pronounce* — Please **pronounce** your words clearly.
11. avoid — *avoid* — A letter carrier cannot **avoid** dogs.
12. decoy — *decoy* — We might see a **decoy** on the lake.
13. couch — *couch* — That **couch** is Dad's favorite seat.
14. tower — *tower* — A snowy owl sat on top of the **tower**.
15. sour — *sour* — Lemons have a **sour** taste.
16. destroy — *destroy* — The storm did not **destroy** the shed.
17. bound — *bound* — Straw may be **bound** with string.
18. appoint — *appoint* — You may **appoint** your assistant.
19. allowance — *allowance* — Shara's **allowance** is more than mine.
20. annoy — *annoy* — The kitten began to **annoy** the parrot.

SORT THE SPELLING WORDS

1.–10. Write the words that have the /**oi**/ sound spelled **oi** or **oy**. Circle the letters that spell this sound.

11.–20. Write the words that have the /**ou**/ sound spelled **ou** or **ow**. Circle the letters that spell this sound.

REMEMBER THE SPELLING STRATEGY

Remember that the /**oi**/ sound can be spelled **oi** as in **poise** or **oy** as in **voyage**. The /**ou**/ sound can be spelled **ou** as in **sour** or **ow** as in **tower**.

Spelling and Vocabulary

Forms and Meaning

Write the spelling word from which these words were formed.

1. poised
2. unbound
3. moisturized
4. cowardly
5. towering

Word Meanings

Write the spelling word that fits into each group of words.

6. irritate, pester, bother
7. hire, use
8. completely ruin, wipe out
9. gram, pound
10. sofa, chair
11. sweet, bitter
12. journey, trip
13. clam, crab
14. hill, valley

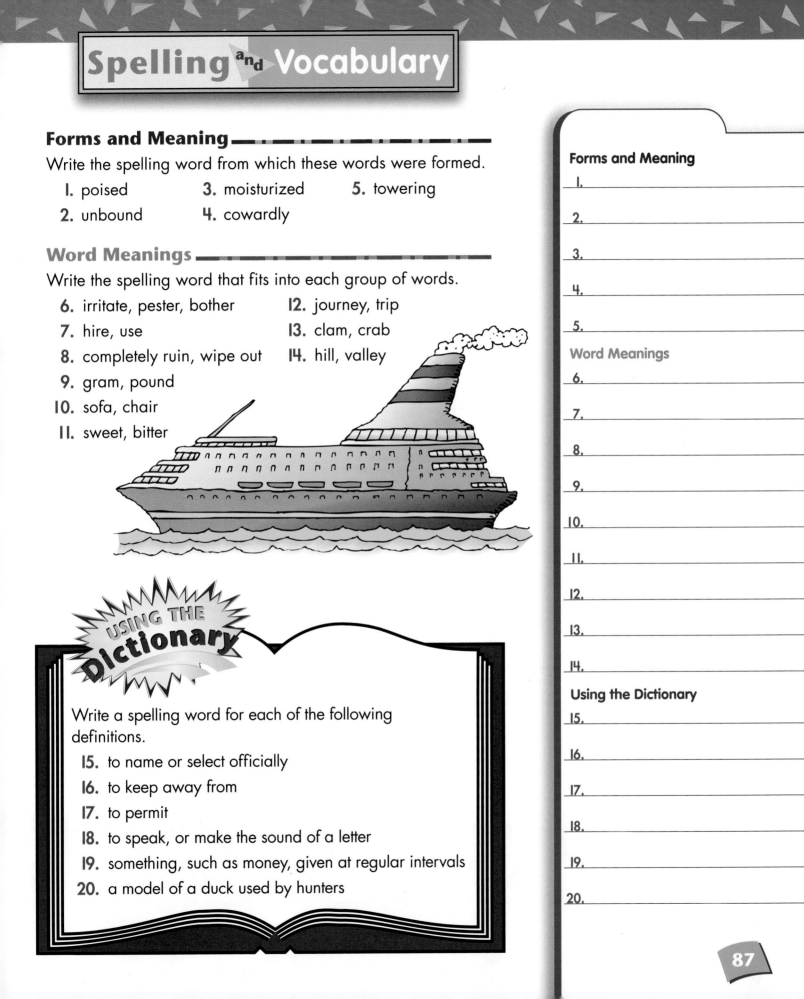

USING THE Dictionary

Write a spelling word for each of the following definitions.

15. to name or select officially
16. to keep away from
17. to permit
18. to speak, or make the sound of a letter
19. something, such as money, given at regular intervals
20. a model of a duck used by hunters

Forms and Meaning
1. _____
2. _____
3. _____
4. _____
5. _____

Word Meanings
6. _____
7. _____
8. _____
9. _____
10. _____
11. _____
12. _____
13. _____
14. _____

Using the Dictionary
15. _____
16. _____
17. _____
18. _____
19. _____
20. _____

Spelling and Reading

moisture	voyage	employ	ounce	mountain
coward	allow	oyster	poise	pronounce
avoid	decoy	couch	tower	sour
destroy	bound	appoint	allowance	annoy

Complete the Story Write the spelling words that complete this story of Pecos Bill.

Pecos Bill stood as high as a __1.__ over other cowpokes. No one could ever call him a __2.__. The only woman Bill loved, Sluefoot Sue, told him that he must __3.__ her to ride his wild horse. In order not to __4.__ her love for him, Bill made that one __5.__. With Sue on his back, the horse began to __6.__ up the slope of the __7.__. Sue was thrown off and landed on the moon.

Replace the Words Write the spelling word that could best replace the underlined word or words.

8.–9. She will <u>hire</u> the gymnast who has the most <u>balance</u>.

10.–11. A <u>carving of a duck</u> is on the table behind the <u>sofa</u>.

12.–13. Too much <u>dampness</u> in the sails slowed down our <u>trip</u>.

14.–15. When sand begins to <u>bother</u> the <u>sea mollusk</u>, it may create a pearl.

16.–17. Sharon tries to <u>stay away from</u> foods that are <u>tart</u>.

18. We <u>choose</u> you class president.

19. When you <u>speak</u> your words slowly, I understand you.

20. This pumpkin weighs no less than one <u>sixteenth of a pound</u> under fifteen pounds.

Complete the Story
1.
2.
3.
4.
5.
6.
7.

Replace the Words
8.
9.
10.
11.
12.
13.
14.
15.
16.
17.
18.
19.
20.

Spelling and Writing

Proofread a Description

Six words are not spelled correctly in this description. Write the words correctly.

Along the north ridge of a green mowntain, moysture glistens on the moss. Evergreen trees are bownd to the rough earth. Above stands a tawer of granite, the pale color of an oister shell, impossible to destroi. Its grace and poise suggest eternity.

Write a Description

Descriptive Writing

Write a description of a place that impressed you.

- Follow a logical spatial order, such as front to back or inside to outside.
- Use words to connect ideas, such as **within** or **beyond**.
- Use vivid comparisons.
- Use colorful adjectives.

Use as many spelling words as you can.

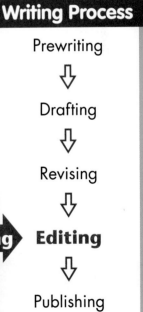

Writing Process

Prewriting

⇩

Drafting

⇩

Revising

⇩

Proofread Your Writing During ➤ **Editing**

⇩

Publishing

Proofread your writing for spelling errors as part of the editing stage in the writing process. Be sure to check each word carefully. Use a dictionary to check spelling if you are not sure.

VOCABULARY CONNECTIONS

Strategy Words

Review Words: Vowel Diphthongs /oi/, /ou/

Write the word from the box that completes each rhyme.

amount	coil	doubt	enjoy	powder

1. There are too many marbles for me to <u>count</u>. I did not expect such a large _____.
2. Dad begins his famous <u>chowder</u> with corn, potatoes, and garlic _____.
3. After slipping through the rich, black <u>soil</u>, the snake rolled up into a _____.
4. Manny and Greta have gone <u>out</u>; they will be back soon, I have no _____.
5. To dig in the mud like a little <u>boy</u> is just what Hector would _____.

Preview Words: Vowel Diphthongs /oi/, /ou/

Write the words from the box that complete the paragraph.

discount	drought	horsepower	loudness	voiced

With the ground so dry and hard after the __6.__, we needed a drill with plenty of __7.__ to find water. Neighbors at first __8.__ complaints about the __9.__ of the machine. To apologize, we gave them a __10.__ on a pipe to their well.

Review Words
1. _____
2. _____
3. _____
4. _____
5. _____

Preview Words
6. _____
7. _____
8. _____
9. _____
10. _____

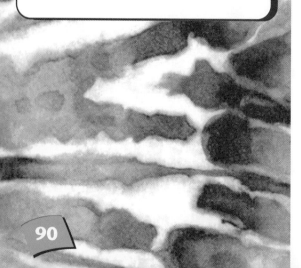

Content Words

Science: Space Exploration

Write the words from the box that fit the paragraph.

capsule	spacecraft	countdown	thrust	liftoff

The __1.__ had reached one minute. The __2.__ stood on the platform, ready for __3.__ . Inside the __4.__ sat the astronauts, preparing for the __5.__ of the rocket engines.

Math: Direction

Write the word from the box that matches each clue.

clockwise	horizontal	counterclockwise	vertical	flip

6. Watch hands go in this direction.
7. An acrobat can do this.
8. When you lie down, you are this.
9. A skyscraper is this.
10. This direction is the way the watch hands do not go.

Apply the Spelling Strategy

Circle the letters that spell the /**ou**/ sound in two of the Content Words you wrote. **Hint:** One word has the /**ou**/ sound twice.

Word Study

Coined Words

A **coined word** is made up to name something new. **Spacecraft** is a coined word that names a vehicle for traveling into space. Write the Content Word that was coined to name the launching of a spacecraft.

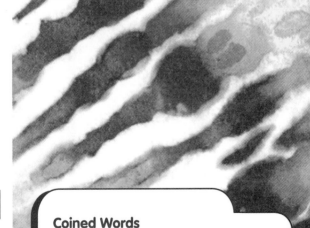

Science: Space Exploration

1. _____
2. _____
3. _____
4. _____
5. _____

Math: Direction

6. _____
7. _____
8. _____
9. _____
10. _____

Coined Words

1. _____

91

pre-
1. _____
2. _____
3. _____
4. _____
5. _____

re-
6. _____
7. _____
8. _____
9. _____
10. _____
11. _____
12. _____

post-
13. _____
14. _____
15. _____
16. _____

co-
17. _____
18. _____
19. _____
20. _____

Spelling and Thinking

READ THE SPELLING WORDS

1.	prerecorded	*prerecorded*	The radio show was **prerecorded**.
2.	reappear	*reappear*	Butterflies **reappear** in the spring.
3.	postscript	*postscript*	Her note has a **postscript** for you.
4.	cooperate	*cooperate*	Players **cooperate** on the field.
5.	prehistoric	*prehistoric*	The **prehistoric** egg was huge.
6.	posttest	*posttest*	The **posttest** has an essay question.
7.	coauthors	*coauthors*	We are **coauthors** of the article.
8.	recharge	*recharge*	Buy batteries that we can **recharge**.
9.	precaution	*precaution*	I took an umbrella as a **precaution**.
10.	postwar	*postwar*	Films showed a **postwar** rejoicing.
11.	rejoin	*rejoin*	Eartha can **rejoin** you after school.
12.	coexist	*coexist*	My fish cannot **coexist** with yours.
13.	prefix	*prefix*	A **prefix** is connected to a base word.
14.	coworker	*coworker*	His **coworker** came to Dad's party.
15.	reform	*reform*	We can **reform** the first plan.
16.	prepaid	*prepaid*	These **prepaid** tickets must be used.
17.	refresh	*refresh*	Let's **refresh** ourselves at the lake.
18.	postdate	*postdate*	You may **postdate** your letter.
19.	reenter	*reenter*	After a rest, **reenter** the pool.
20.	reclaim	*reclaim*	We must try to **reclaim** this forest.

SORT THE SPELLING WORDS

1.–5. Write the words that begin with the prefix **pre-**.

6.–12. Write the words that begin with the prefix **re-**.

13.–16. Write the words that begin with the prefix **post-**.

17.–20. Write the words that begin with the prefix **co-**.

REMEMBER THE SPELLING STRATEGY

Remember that prefixes, such as **pre-**, **re-**, **post-**, and **co-**, can be added to base words to form new words.

Spelling ᵃⁿᵈ Vocabulary

Prefixes and Meanings

Write a spelling word that means the following:

1. to appear again
2. after a war
3. to use a later date
4. a note added later
5. to exist together
6. paid in advance
7. recorded in advance
8. a test given after instruction
9. a group of letters added to the beginning of a word

Sentence Completion

Write a spelling word to complete each sentence.

10. We can _____ this land by draining it.
11. The two _____ shared credit for the book.
12. The mechanic can _____ the car's battery.
13. The criminal promised to _____.
14. After the fire drill, _____ the school.
15. The carpenter's _____ held the lumber steady.
16. A woolly mammoth is a _____ elephant.

USING THE Dictionary

Write the spelling word that would appear on a dictionary page with the following guide words.

17. continue • county
18. radiant • refund
19. regard • residue
20. post- • produce

◆ ◆ ◆

Dictionary Check Be sure to check the guide words in your **Spelling Dictionary**.

Prefixes and Meanings
1. _____
2. _____
3. _____
4. _____
5. _____
6. _____
7. _____
8. _____
9. _____

Sentence Completion
10. _____
11. _____
12. _____
13. _____
14. _____
15. _____
16. _____

Using the Dictionary
17. _____
18. _____
19. _____
20. _____

prerecorded	reappear	postscript	cooperate
prehistoric	posttest	coauthors	recharge
precaution	postwar	rejoin	coexist
prefix	coworker	reform	prepaid
refresh	postdate	reenter	reclaim

Solve the Analogies Write a spelling word to solve each analogy.

1. **Start** is to **restart** as **appear** is to _____.
2. **Risk** is to **chance** as **forethought** is to _____.
3. **Introduction** is to **conclusion** as **greeting** is to _____.
4. **Preserve** is to **maintain** as **improve** is to _____.
5. **Lose** is to **win** as **waste** is to _____.
6. **Opposition** is to **oppose** as **cooperation** is to _____.

Complete the Sequences Write the spelling word that belongs in each group.

7. pretest, test, _____
8. _____, base word, suffix
9. prewar, war, _____
10. predate, date, _____
11. _____, paid, postpaid
12. join, separate, _____

Complete the Paragraph Write the spelling words from the box to complete the paragraph.

Two scientists were __13.__ on a book about __14.__ creatures. Before the project, each __15.__ __16.__ her ideas on tape. The main idea was that some dinosaurs could __17.__ peacefully. For example, plant eaters would peacefully __18.__ themselves side by side at lakes and rivers. If they were attacked by predators, they could __19.__ the water. In this way, they could rest and __20.__ themselves to have energy for the next attack.

recharge
prehistoric
coexist
coauthors
reenter
coworker
refresh
prerecorded

Solve the Analogies
1.
2.
3.
4.
5.
6.

Complete the Sequences
7.
8.
9.
10.
11.
12.

Complete the Paragraph
13.
14.
15.
16.
17.
18.
19.
20.

94

Spelling and Writing

Proofread a Paragraph

Six words are not spelled correctly in this paragraph of advice for car trips. Write the words correctly.

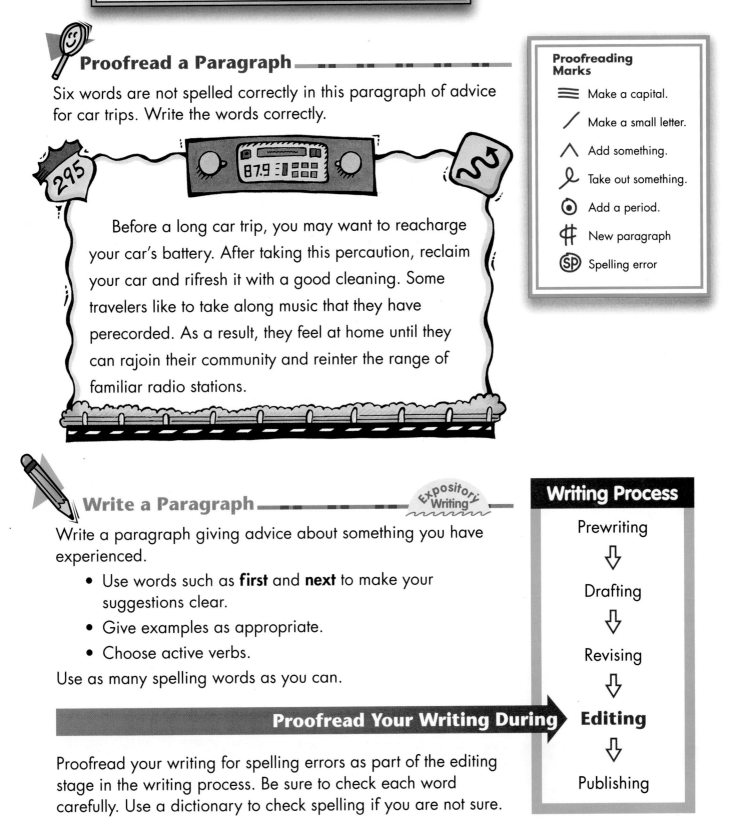

Before a long car trip, you may want to reacharge your car's battery. After taking this percaution, reclaim your car and rifresh it with a good cleaning. Some travelers like to take along music that they have perecorded. As a result, they feel at home until they can rajoin their community and reinter the range of familiar radio stations.

Proofreading Marks

≡	Make a capital.
/	Make a small letter.
∧	Add something.
ℓ	Take out something.
⊙	Add a period.
⌗	New paragraph
SP	Spelling error

Write a Paragraph

Expository Writing

Write a paragraph giving advice about something you have experienced.

- Use words such as **first** and **next** to make your suggestions clear.
- Give examples as appropriate.
- Choose active verbs.

Use as many spelling words as you can.

Writing Process

Prewriting
⇩
Drafting
⇩
Revising
⇩
Editing
⇩
Publishing

Proofread Your Writing During

Proofread your writing for spelling errors as part of the editing stage in the writing process. Be sure to check each word carefully. Use a dictionary to check spelling if you are not sure.

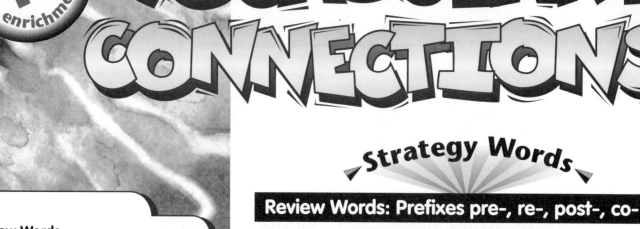

Unit 15 enrichment

VOCABULARY CONNECTIONS

▸Strategy Words◂

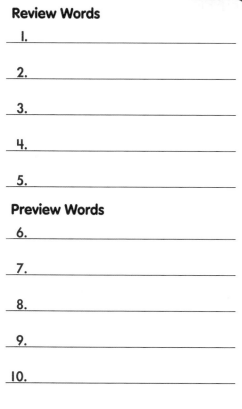

Review Words

1. _____
2. _____
3. _____
4. _____
5. _____

Preview Words

6. _____
7. _____
8. _____
9. _____
10. _____

Review Words: Prefixes pre-, re-, post-, co-

Write the word from the box that matches each clue.

pretest	preview	recover	reheat	rewrite

1. This helps you get ready for a test.
2. After an illness, you do this.
3. You do this to leftover food.
4. It is a way to improve an essay.
5. This shows you part of something that you will see later.

Preview Words: Prefixes pre-, re-, post-, co-

Write the word from the box that completes each sentence.

present	receive	reflect	refract	reverberate

6. My grandmother likes to _____ on her youth.
7. A liquid may bend or _____ an image.
8. Most people like to _____ a compliment.
9. We will _____ an award to the coach.
10. In a valley, your voice can _____.

96

Content Words

Social Studies: The Depression

Write the words from the box to complete the paragraph.

boxcar	fertile	dust bowl	renew	valley

Drought can cause green, __1.__ land in a river __2.__ to turn into a __3.__. During the Great Depression, many a farmer had to leave such dry land. Then he might travel in a train's __4.__ to try to __5.__ his life elsewhere.

Language Arts: Study Skills

Write the word that replaces the underlined word or words.

details	skim	main idea	topic	scan

6. When you just want an idea of what a piece of writing is about, you can <u>read quickly</u>.

7. When you are looking for a fact, you can <u>read quickly looking for particular words</u>.

8. The <u>subject</u> of a paragraph is what it is about.

9. Examples and reasons are <u>specific ideas</u>.

10. Try to understand the <u>general statement supported by examples and reasons</u> of the paragraph.

Apply the Spelling Strategy

Circle the prefix **re-** in one of the Content Words you wrote.

Word Study

Word Roots

The root **fract** comes from an old Latin word that meant "break." For example, a **fracture** is a broken bone. Write the Strategy Word that has this root and means "to bend or distort."

Social Studies: The Depression

1. _____
2. _____
3. _____
4. _____
5. _____

Language Arts: Study Skills

6. _____
7. _____
8. _____
9. _____
10. _____

Word Roots

1. _____

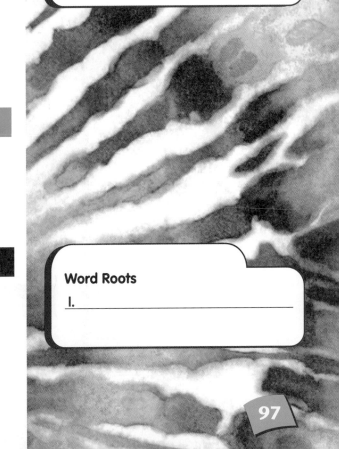

97

-er

1. _____
2. _____
3. _____
4. _____
5. _____

-est

6. _____
7. _____
8. _____
9. _____
10. _____

-ed

11. _____
12. _____
13. _____
14. _____
15. _____

-ing

16. _____
17. _____
18. _____
19. _____
20. _____

Spelling and Thinking

READ THE SPELLING WORDS

1.	calmer	*calmer*	The sea is **calmer** now than before.
2.	slimmest	*slimmest*	This is the **slimmest** pen I have seen.
3.	removed	*removed*	We **removed** our hats at the door.
4.	denying	*denying*	No one is **denying** that you won.
5.	sunnier	*sunnier*	Friday was **sunnier** than Saturday.
6.	wiser	*wiser*	I feel **wiser** since my trip to Africa.
7.	grayest	*grayest*	This is the **grayest** of the kittens.
8.	trimming	*trimming*	The barber was **trimming** Ed's hair.
9.	denied	*denied*	Marsha **denied** seeing the book.
10.	interesting	*interesting*	We had an **interesting** talk in class.
11.	sunniest	*sunniest*	This is the **sunniest** winter in years.
12.	trimmed	*trimmed*	Mary **trimmed** the rosebushes.
13.	wisest	*wisest*	Sam had the **wisest** solution.
14.	removing	*removing*	We will begin by **removing** the weeds.
15.	grayer	*grayer*	Lita's hair is **grayer** this year.
16.	calmest	*calmest*	Leonard was the **calmest** of us all.
17.	supplied	*supplied*	We **supplied** apricot bread and tea.
18.	slimmer	*slimmer*	Juan is **slimmer** and taller now.
19.	interested	*interested*	Are you **interested** in art?
20.	supplying	*supplying*	Marcus is **supplying** the plates.

SORT THE SPELLING WORDS

1.–5. Write the words that end with the suffix **-er**.

6.–10. Write the words that end with the suffix **-est**.

11.–15. Write the words that end with the suffix **-ed**.

16.–20. Write the words that end with the suffix **-ing**.

REMEMBER THE SPELLING STRATEGY

Remember that suffixes, such as **-er, -est, -ed,** and **-ing,** can be added to base words to form new words.

Spelling and Vocabulary

Word Structure

Write the spelling words that are formed by adding or subtracting the following letters.

1. gray + er
2. gray + est
3. slim + m + er
4. slim + m + est
5. sunny – y + i + er
6. sunny – y + i + est

Word Meanings

Write the spelling word that replaces the underlined base word in each sentence.

7. Of the twelve, Dana is the <u>calm</u> competitor.
8. Yesterday, they <u>trim</u> the fir trees.
9. We are <u>remove</u> snow from the skating pond.
10. There is an <u>interest</u> branch under the ice.
11. The figure skater seems <u>calm</u> than the racer.
12. Of all the judges, Abe seems the <u>wise</u>.
13. Of the two decisions, yours is the <u>wise</u> one.
14. The parents have <u>supply</u> hot chocolate.
15. No one is <u>deny</u> that it might be chilly.

USING THE Dictionary

Add the suffixes to the base words as shown below. Then look up the base word in your **Spelling Dictionary** to check the spelling.

16. supply + ing
17. deny + ed
18. remove + ed
19. trim + ing
20. interest + ed

Word Structure

1. _____
2. _____
3. _____
4. _____
5. _____
6. _____

Word Meanings

7. _____
8. _____
9. _____
10. _____
11. _____
12. _____
13. _____
14. _____
15. _____

Using the Dictionary

16. _____
17. _____
18. _____
19. _____
20. _____

calmer	slimmest	removed	denying	sunnier
wiser	grayest	trimming	denied	interesting
sunniest	trimmed	wisest	removing	grayer
calmest	supplied	slimmer	interested	supplying

Complete the Sentences

Complete the Sentences   Write the spelling word that best completes each sentence.

1. This is the most ____ book I have read.
2. On a ____ day, you should protect your skin.
3. After my hair is ____, it looks neater.
4. Your eyes look ____ than usual when you wear black.
5. Kate is ____ in astronomy.
6. Will you be ____ the hedges tomorrow?
7. Gino ____ his coat and sat down.
8. I am in the most relaxed, ____ mood I have been in all week.
9. You are breathing deeply and seem ____ now.
10. The ____ person in history may have been Solomon.
11. This is the brightest, ____ summer day I have ever seen.
12. This is the cloudiest, ____ day during our vacation.

Make Rhymes

Make Rhymes   Write the spelling word that completes each rhyme below.

13. That she had been crying, there was no ____.
14. Al's friend called him "miser"; of the two, Al was ____.
15. When the sun's bright light is high, the ____ shadows on the ground do lie.

Complete the Paragraph

Complete the Paragraph   Write the spelling words from the box to complete the paragraph.

Although running is a healthy way to have a <u>16.</u> body, good runners have never <u>17.</u> their bodies a proper diet. They need to continue <u>18.</u> themselves with energy food. Runners should be <u>19.</u> with water and should consider <u>20.</u> excess salt from their diet.

supplied
removing
slimmer
denied
supplying

Complete the Sentences

1. _____
2. _____
3. _____
4. _____
5. _____
6. _____
7. _____
8. _____
9. _____
10. _____
11. _____
12. _____

Make Rhymes

13. _____
14. _____
15. _____

Complete the Paragraph

16. _____
17. _____
18. _____
19. _____
20. _____

Spelling **and** Writing

Proofread a Paragraph

Six words are not spelled correctly in this paragraph about a race. Write the words correctly.

FINISH

The morning of the big race had arrived. Each runner had been supplyed with a racing number and a starting position. The runners had hoped that it would be a cool and cloudy day, but it was the sunnyest day of the week. They knew that the sunnyer the day, the more they would sweat. The skies, however, did not get any graer. It was intresting to watch the runners warm up with different exercises. There was no deniing the excitement in the air. Even the wisest among us could not predict who would win.

Proofreading Marks

≡ Make a capital.

/ Make a small letter.

∧ Add something.

℮ Take out something.

⊙ Add a period.

⌗ New paragraph

ⓈⓅ Spelling error

Write a Paragraph

Narrative Writing

Write a paragraph describing a competitive event that you have seen.

- Explain how and why things happened.
- Select active verbs.
- Pick colorful adjectives.
- Try to keep your reader interested.

Use as many of the spelling words as you can.

Proofread Your Writing During

Proofread your writing for spelling errors as part of the editing stage in the writing process. Be sure to check each word carefully. Use a dictionary to check spelling if you are not sure.

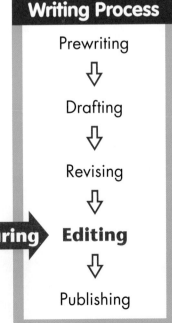

Writing Process

Prewriting

⇩

Drafting

⇩

Revising

⇩

Editing

⇩

Publishing

VOCABULARY CONNECTIONS

►Strategy Words◄

Review Words: Suffixes -er, -est, -ed, -ing

Write the word from the box that could best replace the underlined word or words.

happiest	kinder	passed	quicker	safest

1. Matt is the <u>cheeriest</u> player on the team.
2. I feel <u>most secure</u> after the plane lands.
3. This runner is <u>faster</u> on his feet than that one.
4. You can be <u>more considerate</u> than this.
5. Finally, she <u>went by</u> the lead rider.

Preview Words: Suffixes -er, -est, -ed, -ing

Write the word from the box that best completes each sentence.

admitted	directed	excelling
obtaining	resulting	

6. The coach _____ us to do sit-ups.
7. I will be _____ a new backpack for carrying my books this year.
8. Shel is _____ in math this term.
9. Judy _____ that she forgot to call.
10. Your hard work is _____ in a beautiful vegetable garden.

Review Words

1. _____
2. _____
3. _____
4. _____
5. _____

Preview Words

6. _____
7. _____
8. _____
9. _____
10. _____

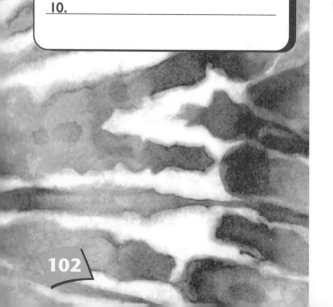

Content Words

Social Studies: Anthems

Write the words from the box to complete the beginning of "The Star Spangled Banner."

| anthem | gleaming | hailed | proudly | twilight |

Our National ___1.___

Oh, say, can you see by the dawn's early light,
What so ___2.___ we ___3.___ at the ___4.___'s last ___5.___?

Math: Multiplication

Write the word from the box that matches each clue.

| composite | multiple | factors | prime | greatest |

6. This type of number can be divided only by the number one and by itself.

7. It means "largest."

8. This is the number that results from multiplying a particular number with any other number.

9. These are numbers that can be multiplied together to get a particular product.

10. This type of number can be divided by a number other than itself and the number one.

Apply the Spelling Strategy

Circle the suffix **-est, -ed,** or **-ing** in three words you wrote.

Word Study

Related Words

Words such as **daylight, moonlight,** and **lightning** are related by the word part **light.** Write the Content Word that is related to these words.

Social Studies: Anthems

1. _____
2. _____
3. _____
4. _____
5. _____

Math: Multiplication

6. _____
7. _____
8. _____
9. _____
10. _____

Related Words

1. _____

Spelling and Thinking

READ THE SPELLING WORDS

1. chorus	*chorus*	I remember the **chorus** of that song.
2. create	*create*	Uncle Bob can **create** a tiny railroad.
3. suitcase	*suitcase*	Bring the big gray **suitcase**.
4. cereal	*cereal*	Odessa likes **cereal** with berries.
5. recent	*recent*	The **recent** storm blew down our tree.
6. practice	*practice*	I want to **practice** the piano now.
7. company	*company*	We have **company** this evening.
8. expect	*expect*	Akela did not **expect** a party.
9. jacket	*jacket*	I like that blue denim **jacket**.
10. frantic	*frantic*	Ken was **frantic** when he lost the watch.
11. choir	*choir*	The whole **choir** applauded Marie.
12. grocery	*grocery*	Phil bought corn at the **grocery** store.
13. recite	*recite*	Kim can **recite** poetry from memory.
14. celebrate	*celebrate*	We will **celebrate** Mario's arrival.
15. exercise	*exercise*	When I **exercise,** I grow stronger.
16. correct	*correct*	All of your answers are **correct**.
17. comic	*comic*	A successful **comic** writes many jokes.
18. select	*select*	Kay will **select** wood for her project.
19. plastic	*plastic*	Use this **plastic** to wrap the food.
20. stomach	*stomach*	Strawberries upset Kwami's **stomach**.

SORT THE SPELLING WORDS

1. Write the word that has both a **/k/** sound spelled **c** and an **/s/** sound spelled **c** before **e**.
2.–14. Write the other words with a **/k/** sound spelled **c, ck,** or **ch**.
15.–20. Write the words with an **/s/** sound spelled **c** before **e** or **i**.

REMEMBER THE SPELLING STRATEGY

Remember that the **/k/** sound can be spelled in different ways: **c** in **company, ck** in **jacket,** and **ch** in **chorus**. The **/s/** sound in **cereal** and **recite** is spelled **c**. The **c** is followed by **e (cereal)** or **i (recite)**.

/k/, /s/
1. _____

/k/
2. _____
3. _____
4. _____
5. _____
6. _____
7. _____
8. _____
9. _____
10. _____
11. _____
12. _____
13. _____
14. _____

/s/
15. _____
16. _____
17. _____
18. _____
19. _____
20. _____

Spelling and Vocabulary

Word Groups

Write the spelling word that belongs in each group.

1. practice, workout, _____
2. department, hardware, _____
3. toast, eggs, _____
4. excited, nervous, _____

Word Meanings

Write the spelling word that matches each clue.

5. You carry one when you go on a trip.
6. This is the song verse that repeats.
7. It means "of a time not long ago."
8. You would do this at a party.
9. It means "to repeat out loud."
10. This could be a group or a business.
11. When you do it, you change from wrong to right.
12. You believe something is going to occur.
13. You do this to improve any skill.
14. This is someone who tells jokes.
15. This material is waterproof.
16. It means "to choose."

USING THE Dictionary

Write the spelling words for the following dictionary respellings.

17. /kwîr/
18. /jăk′ ĭt/
19. /krē āt′/
20. /stŭm′ ək/

◆ ◆ ◆

Dictionary Check Be sure to check the words and their respellings in your **Spelling Dictionary**.

Word Groups
1. _____
2. _____
3. _____
4. _____

Word Meanings
5. _____
6. _____
7. _____
8. _____
9. _____
10. _____
11. _____
12. _____
13. _____
14. _____
15. _____
16. _____

Using the Dictionary
17. _____
18. _____
19. _____
20. _____

Spelling and Reading

chorus	create	suitcase	cereal	recent
practice	company	expect	jacket	frantic
choir	grocery	recite	celebrate	exercise
correct	comic	select	plastic	stomach

Complete the Paragraph

1.
2.
3.
4.
5.
6.
7.
8.
9.
10.

Complete the Sentences

11.
12.
13.
14.
15.
16.
17.
18.
19.
20.

Complete the Paragraph Write spelling words to complete the paragraph.

A hundred years ago, Americans could not __1.__ among numerous television channels for entertainment. They had to __2.__ their own fun. Sometimes, a __3.__ of actors, an amusing __4.__, or an unusual form of entertainment called a medicine show would travel through town. At the medicine show, a salesperson would __5.__ to all present the wonders of a liquid or pill that might __6.__ every ill. A free show would entertain the crowd, and the salesperson would __7.__ the people to buy the medicine. The performers would __8.__ their acts between stops. It was quite a __9.__ life because everyone lived out of a __10.__.

Complete the Sentences Write the spelling word that completes each sentence.

11. There are several kinds of oat ____ here.
12. Jack's ____ was full after a turkey dinner.
13. We plan to ____ your performance with a huge party.
14. My ____ has a corduroy collar.
15. A ____ sheet keeps the dew off our tent.
16. I will send a ____ photograph of myself.
17. Have you bought any food in the new ____ store?
18. The ____ of the song is about a train.
19. I have one more math ____ to do in order to finish my homework.
20. Chanisse sings in the school ____.

106

Spelling and Writing

Proofread a Paragraph

Six words are not spelled correctly in this paragraph about singing groups. Write the words correctly.

> When a kwire sings joyfully, everyone wants to selebrate. Long afterward, the audience remembers the corus of its favorite song. In resent years, we have learned that singing is good for our physical health. When we praktise singing, we breathe fully, and our circulation improves. For these reasons, I believe our school should select a musical director and kreate a singing group.

Proofreading Marks

≡	Make a capital.
/	Make a small letter.
∧	Add something.
ℓ	Take out something.
⊙	Add a period.
⌗	New paragraph
⑤Ⓟ	Spelling error

Write a Paragraph  Persuasive Writing

Write a paragraph giving reasons for starting a certain class or activity at your school.

- Begin with a strong statement.
- Support your statement, or main idea, with reasons and examples.
- Close with a statement of what you want to happen.

Use as many spelling words as you can.

Proofread Your Writing During

Proofread your writing for spelling errors as part of the editing stage in the writing process. Be sure to check each word carefully. Use a dictionary to check spelling if you are not sure.

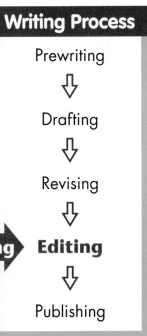

Writing Process

Prewriting
⇩
Drafting
⇩
Revising
⇩
Editing
⇩
Publishing

VOCABULARY CONNECTIONS

►Strategy Words◄

Review Words: Consonant Sounds /k/, /s/

Write the words from the box that complete the paragraph.

cattle	certain	coaches	coast	icicle

A group of hikers filled up three __1.__ on a train. They were traveling to the California __2.__. The hikers were __3.__ to use up a lot of energy later, so they rested first. A few looked out the window and saw __4.__ grazing on the plains. It was so cold that a shimmering __5.__ hung outside the window.

Preview Words: Consonant Sounds /k/, /s/

Write the word from the box that could best replace the underlined word or words.

ceiling	central	chord	contribute	license

6. There is a crack across the <u>top of this room</u>.
7. We <u>give</u> to charities that help those in need.
8. A single <u>combination of notes</u> calmed her.
9. Huge storms cross the <u>middle</u> plains.
10. To drive a truck, he needs a <u>legal document</u>.

Review Words
1. _____
2. _____
3. _____
4. _____
5. _____

Preview Words
6. _____
7. _____
8. _____
9. _____
10. _____

Content Words

Fine Arts: Music

Write the word from the box that completes each sentence.

compose orchestra evening program musical

1. Sarah will _____ a song for her mother.
2. In a _____, actors sing their lines in addition to talking.
3. An _____ always includes stringed instruments.
4. The performers' names are in the _____.
5. The first concert will be performed on Saturday _____.

Math: Decimals

Write the word from the box that completes each sentence.

decimal tenths hundredths thousandths zeros

6. There are two _____ in 100.
7. 1.68 is a _____ number.

For the number 2.534

8. the digit 3 is in the _____ place.
9. the digit 4 is in the _____ place.
10. the digit 5 is in the _____ place.

Apply the Spelling Strategy

Circle the Content Word you wrote that spells the /**k**/ sound **ch**. Circle the Content Word you wrote that spells the /**s**/ sound **c**.

Word Study

Greek Spellings

In the Greek language, the letters **ch** are pronounced /**k**/. That is why **chord,** a word that came from Greek, is pronounced /**kord**/. Write the Content Word that also has a **ch** pronounced /**k**/.

Fine Arts: Music

1. _____
2. _____
3. _____
4. _____
5. _____

Math: Decimals

6. _____
7. _____
8. _____
9. _____
10. _____

Greek Spellings

1. _____

Assessment and Review

Assessment Units 13–17

Each Assessment Word in the box fits one of the spelling strategies you have studied over the past five weeks. Read the spelling strategies. Then write each Assessment Word under the unit number it fits.

Unit 13 _____

1.–4. The **r**-controlled vowel sound you hear in **force** (/ôr/) can be spelled **or** as in **force** or **ar** as in **warmth**. The **r**-controlled vowel sound you hear in **career** (/îr/) can be spelled **eer** as in **career, er** as in **serious, ear** as in **weary,** and **ier** as in **pierce**.

Unit 14 _____

5.–8. The /oi/ sound can be spelled **oi** as in **poise** or **oy** as in **voyage**. The /ou/ sound can be spelled **ou** as in **sour** or **ow** as in **tower**.

Unit 15 _____

9.–12. Prefixes, such as **pre-, re-, post-,** and **co-,** can be added to base words to form new words.

Unit 16 _____

13.–16. Suffixes, such as **-er, -est, -ed,** and **-ing,** can be added to base words to form new words.

Unit 17 _____

17.–20. The /k/ sound can be spelled in different ways: **c** in **company, ck** in **jacket,** and **ch** in **chorus.** The /s/ sound in **cereal** and **recite** is spelled **c**. The **c** is followed by **e** (**cereal**) or **i** (**recite**).

clearing
noisy
refuel
beginning
chrome
sheer
convoy
rethink
continued
cucumber
warning
fountain
co-owner
friendliest
conceal
cinema
earlier
drown
lore
prepackage

Review — Unit 13: r-Controlled Vowels /ôr/, /îr/

important	perform	disappear	reward	force
peer	appear	forever	serious	enormous

Write the spelling word that is the opposite.

1. appear
2. disappear
3. tiny
4. punish

Write the word that completes each sentence.

5. It is quite ____ that you get here on time.
6. I am very ____ about learning a foreign language.
7. If you ____ through the window, you might see the bus coming.
8. Sue and Stu like to ____ for audiences by playing duets on the piano.
9. If the plug doesn't fit into the socket, don't ____ it.
10. You can't stay young ____, but you can enjoy youth while it lasts.

Review — Unit 14: Vowel Diphthongs /oi/, /ou/

mountain	avoid	appoint	ounce	allowance
pronounce	bound	allow	destroy	tower

Write the spelling word that belongs in each group.

11. cash, spending money, ____
12. hill, valley, ____
13. speak, say, ____
14. ton, pound, ____
15. elect, choose, ____
16. leap, jump, ____
17. castle, drawbridge, ____
18. ruin, wipe out, ____
19. stay away, escape, ____
20. give permission, let, ____

Unit 13
1. _____
2. _____
3. _____
4. _____
5. _____
6. _____
7. _____
8. _____
9. _____
10. _____

Unit 14
11. _____
12. _____
13. _____
14. _____
15. _____
16. _____
17. _____
18. _____
19. _____
20. _____

Review — Unit 15: Prefixes pre-, re-, post-, co-

cooperate	reappear	postscript	prehistoric	prefix
postdate	coworker	precaution	posttest	refresh

Write the spelling word that matches each meaning.

1. message written at the end of a letter
2. to put a day, month, or year on a document that is later than the actual date
3. a test given after instruction has been given

Follow the directions below to write the other spelling words.

4.–5. Write the spelling words that begin with the prefix that means "with" or "together."

6.–8. Write the spelling words that begin with the prefix that means "before."

9.–10. Write the spelling words that begin with the prefix that means "back" or "again."

Review — Unit 16: Suffixes -er, -est, -ed, -ing

interesting	denied	supplying	sunnier	wisest
removed	slimmer	grayer	removing	calmest

Use words from the box and follow the directions below.

11.–12. Write the spelling words in which -ing was added to a base word without changing the spelling.

13. Write the spelling word in which a final **e** was dropped before **-ing** was added.

14.–16. Write the spelling words that have the same suffix as **happier**.

17.–18. Write the spelling words that have the same suffix as **funniest**.

19.–20. Write the spelling words that have the same suffix as **played**.

| exercise | company | create | grocery | correct |
| practice | expect | stomach | jacket | celebrate |

Write the spelling words by adding the missing letters.

1. comp __ n __
2. __ reat __
3. co __ __ ect
4. pr __ cti __ __
5. gro __ __ ry

6. __ __ lebrat __
7. ex __ __ cise
8. ja __ __ et
9. e __ pect
10. st __ ma __ __

GAME **Spelling Study Strategy**

Spelling Questions

Practicing spelling words can be fun if you make it into a game. Play this game with a partner.

1. Write the spelling words you and your partner want to study on index cards or slips of paper. Each of you will keep half of the cards.

2. Choose a word from your pile and have your partner try to guess the word by asking questions that can be answered by "yes" or "no." For example, "Does it start with a **c**?" or "Is it an action word?"

3. Make a mark on scrap paper for each time your partner asks a question. After your partner guesses the word, he or she must spell it correctly out loud. Then give the word card to your partner.

4. Now it is your turn to try to guess the word your partner draws from his or her pile. Keep track of how many guesses you make, too. After you guess the word, spell it for your partner and keep the card.

5. After you have practiced all the words, see who guessed the most words and asked the fewest questions.

Unit 5

1. _____
2. _____
3. _____
4. _____
5. _____
6. _____
7. _____
8. _____
9. _____
10. _____

WRITER'S

Grammar, Usage, and Mechanics

Nouns: Plurals and Possessives

A plural noun names more than one person, place, thing, or idea. Most nouns add **-s** or **-es** to form the plural. Some change in other ways, and some are spelled the same in the singular and plural.

one **pet**   two **pets**   one **dish**   two **dishes**

one **child**   several **children**   one **fish**   many **fish**

A possessive noun shows ownership. Most singular nouns add an apostrophe and **s** (**'s**) to form the possessive. Plural nouns ending in **s** add just an apostrophe (**s'**) to form the possessive. Plurals that don't end in **s** add apostrophe and **s** (**'s**) to show possession.

the **boy's** ball   the **girls'** shoes   the **men's** van

Practice Activity

A. Write the plural form of these nouns.

1. dog   4. woman
2. deer   5. cucumber
3. watch   6. gentleman

B. Write the possessive form of the underlined noun.

7. the shell of the <u>oyster</u>; the _____ shell

8. the wagons of the <u>pioneers</u>; the _____ wagons

9. the hard drive of the <u>computer</u>; the _____ hard drive

10. the coat of the <u>man</u>; the _____ coat

11. the chrome of the <u>car</u>; the _____ chrome

12. the food of the <u>cats</u>; the _____ food

A.
1.
2.
3.
4.
5.
6.
B.
7.
8.
9.
10.
11.
12.

WORKSHOP

Circle and Check

Good writers always proofread their writing for spelling errors. Here's a strategy you can use to proofread your papers.

Instead of reading your paper the regular way, look at just the first three or four words. Are they spelled correctly? If you know that they are all correct, go on and check the next three or four words. If you are unsure about a word, circle it and keep going. Look at your whole paper this way—one group of words at a time.

When you have looked at your whole paper, get a dictionary and check the spelling of all words that you circled. You will find that it's easy and fast to look up several words at once. Try it!

Electronic Spelling

Spell Checkers

Computers often have special programs that can help you proofread. Many have spell checkers that alert you to misspelled words. But even the best spell checker cannot find every mistake.

Sometimes you may misspell a word by typing letters that spell a different word. For example, you might type **tow** when you meant to type **two**. Both words are spelled correctly, so a spell checker would not catch the mistake.

Look at the underlined words below. Which are misspelled? Write those words correctly. Write **OK** if a word is correct.

Electronic Spelling

1. _____
2. _____
3. _____
4. _____
5. _____
6. _____

1. Try not to <u>loose</u> your new pen.
2. May I <u>sue</u> your pencil for a minute?
3. You have to be <u>quite</u> in a library.
4. This <u>pear</u> is very juicy!
5. Dry your <u>hare</u> when you finish swimming.
6. Did you <u>accept</u> the invitation?

Spelling and Thinking

READ THE SPELLING WORDS

1.	Ohio	Ohio	Lake Erie borders **Ohio**.
2.	Maine	Maine	River rafting is fun in **Maine**.
3.	Alaska	Alaska	Summer is best in **Alaska**.
4.	Iowa	Iowa	Corn grows well in **Iowa**.
5.	Texas	Texas	Davy Crockett is a **Texas** hero.
6.	Nevada	Nevada	Explore the desert in **Nevada**.
7.	Montana	Montana	Horse ranches are in **Montana**.
8.	Florida	Florida	**Florida** has unusual wildlife.
9.	Alabama	Alabama	Cotton grows in **Alabama**.
10.	Maryland	Maryland	Eat crab cakes in **Maryland**.
11.	South Carolina	South Carolina	In **South Carolina** there are ocean resorts.
12.	California	California	**California** was rich in gold.
13.	Washington	Washington	Big apples grow in **Washington**.
14.	New York	New York	**New York** is in the Northeast.
15.	North Dakota	North Dakota	Winter comes early in **North Dakota**.
16.	Colorado	Colorado	Mountains rise in **Colorado**.
17.	Massachusetts	Massachusetts	Fall is pretty in **Massachusetts**.

18.–20. Name three other states.

end in vowel sound

1.
2.
3.
4.
5.
6.
7.
8.
9.
10.
11.

end in consonant or silent vowel

12.
13.
14.
15.
16.
17.

Write three other states here.

18.
19.
20.

SORT THE SPELLING WORDS

1.–11. Write the spelling words that end in a vowel sound. Circle the letter that spells the final vowel sound.

12.–17. Write the spelling words that end in a silent vowel or in a consonant. Circle the silent vowel or consonant.

REMEMBER THE SPELLING STRATEGY

Remember that it is important to be able to spell the names of the states correctly.

Spelling and Vocabulary

Word Clues

Write the spelling word that matches each clue.

1. Its capital is Denver.
2. Polar bears live here.
3. Its capital is Carson City.
4. Baltimore is its largest city.
5. Augusta is its capital.
6. Birmingham is its big city.

Word Structure

Write the state name for each state nickname.

7. Evergreen State   W __ sh __ ngt __ n
8. Lone Star State   T __ x __ s
9. Hawkeye State   __ __ w __
10. Sunshine State   Fl __ r __ d __
11. Buckeye State   __ h __ __
12. Empire State   N __ w Y __ rk
13. Bay State   M __ ss __ ch __ s __ tts
14. Golden State   C __ l __ f __ rn __ __

USING THE Dictionary

Unscramble the letters to write the spelling words that fit the facts. Capitalize the first letter of each word.

15. It comes from the name **Carolus,** Latin name for Charles.   **utohs iaalcorn**
16. It comes from the Latin or Spanish word meaning "mountainous."   **naotnam**
17. It comes from the Native American word meaning "friend" or "ally."   **rhton odtaak**

Word Clues
1.
2.
3.
4.
5.
6.

Word Structure
7.
8.
9.
10.
11.
12.
13.
14.

Using the Dictionary
15.
16.
17.

Complete the Paragraph

1. _____
2. _____
3. _____
4. _____
5. _____
6. _____
7. _____
8. _____
9. _____
10. _____
11. _____

Complete the Sentences

12. _____
13. _____
14. _____
15. _____
16. _____
17. _____

Ohio	Maine	Alaska	Iowa
Texas	Nevada	Montana	Florida
Alabama	Maryland	South Carolina	California
Washington	New York	North Dakota	Colorado
	Massachusetts		

Complete the Paragraph   One letter is given for each spelling word in the paragraph. Write the state name correctly.

The largest wheat farms in the world are on the Great Plains from **1.** T __ __ __ __ in the South to **2.** __ __ r __ __ __ __ __ __ __ __ and **3.** __ __ n __ __ __ __ in the North. One of the most important livestock states is **4.** __ o __ __. Oranges and grapefruits are grown in the four warm states: **5.** __ __ __ r __ __ __ , **6.** C __ __ __ __ __ __ __ __ __ , Arizona, and Texas. The largest apple-growing state is **7.** __ __ __ h __ __ __ __ __ __ , followed by **8.** __ __ __ Y __ __ __ and Michigan. The newest source of oil in the United States is found in the northern part of **9.** __ l __ __ __ __. The largest deposits of coal in the world are in the Appalachian Mountains from **10.** __ __ __ b __ __ __ north into Pennsylvania. The computer industry is centered both south of San Francisco, California, and near Boston, **11.** __ __ __ __ __ __ __ __ __ __ __ __ s.

Complete the Sentences   Write the spelling word that completes each sentence.

12. Washington, D.C., is a small piece of land between Virginia and _____.
13. The western boundary of _____ directly borders California.
14. The easternmost state in the United States is _____.
15. The state of _____ is directly east of Georgia.
16. The United States Postal Service abbreviation for _____ is OH.
17. The United States Postal Service abbreviation for _____ is CO.

Spelling and Writing

Proofread a Paragraph

Six words are not spelled correctly in this paragraph about a road trip. Write the words correctly.

GO-MOBILE

If you plan to travel to the West during the summer, you might want to take a northern route. Otherwise, you might find the heat uncomfortable. For example, you could head west from Masachusets, through New Youk and Ohayo. From Chicago, you could go through Iowa and continue north toward North Dacota. You could continue west to Mountana. Eventually, you would get to Washinton.

Proofreading Marks

- ≡ Make a capital.
- / Make a small letter.
- ∧ Add something.
- ℓ Take out something.
- ⊙ Add a period.
- ⌗ New paragraph.
- ⓢⓟ Spelling error

Write a Paragraph

Expository Writing

Write a paragraph describing the best route to somewhere. Include some interesting information about the journey or the destination.

- Use direction words such as **east** and **west** or **left** and **right**.
- Consult an atlas or a map if necessary.
- Use logical order.

Use as many state names from the spelling list as you can.

Proofread Your Writing During ➤

Writing Process

Prewriting
⬇
Drafting
⬇
Revising
⬇
Editing
⬇
Publishing

Proofread your writing for spelling errors as part of the editing stage in the writing process. Be sure to check each word carefully. Use a dictionary to check spelling if you are not sure.

119

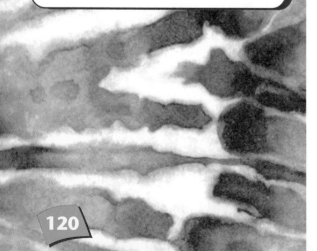
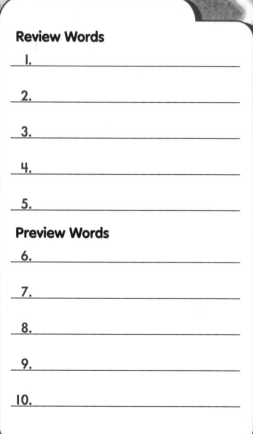

VOCABULARY CONNECTIONS

Strategy Words

Review Words: Geography Names

Write the word from the box that matches each clue.

| Africa | America | Asia | Canada | Europe |

1. China is on this continent, which is the world's largest.
2. Ontario and Alberta are provinces in this North American country.
3. This is the world's second largest continent. Countries on it include Ghana and Nigeria.
4. France and Italy are on this continent.
5. This has both a north continent and a south continent.

Preview Words: Geography Names

Write the word from the box that could best complete each sentence.

| Caribbean | District | eastward |
| geography | province | |

6. The water is clear and blue in the _____.
7. Sara is interested in travel and _____.
8. The _____ of Quebec borders Vermont.
9. Head _____ from Missouri to Illinois.
10. We can visit the _____ of Columbia and see the National Zoo.

Review Words
1. _____
2. _____
3. _____
4. _____
5. _____

Preview Words
6. _____
7. _____
8. _____
9. _____
10. _____

Content Words

Science: Fuel

Write the word from the box that matches each clue.

anthracite	lignite	bituminous	peat	coal

1. partly decayed plant matter, used as fuel or fertilizer
2. a general term for a solid form of fuel composed mainly of carbon and found underground
3. burns with little smoke; hard coal, mined in Pennsylvania
4. having to do with a grade of coal that contains tarry substances and smokes as it burns
5. a low-quality brownish coal

Social Studies: American West

Write the word from the box that matches each clue.

cavalry	oppress	command	plains	westward

6. opposite of **eastward**
7. a large stretch of flat land
8. a group of soldiers who used to fight on horseback
9. to give orders; to direct
10. to govern cruelly

Apply the Spelling Strategy

Circle one word you wrote that spells the /s/ sound with a **c**.

Word Study

Eponyms

An **eponym** is a word that comes from someone's name. A **sandwich** was named after the **Earl of Sandwich,** who asked for a quick meal of some meat between two slices of bread. Write the Strategy Word that may have come from the name of the Italian explorer, **Amerigo Vespucci.**

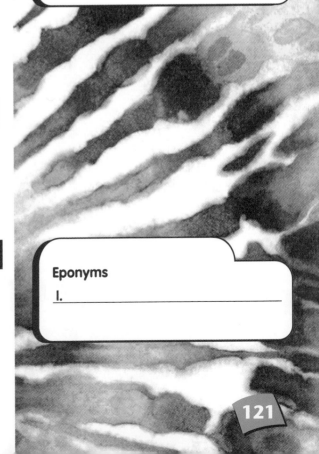

Science: Fuel
1. _____
2. _____
3. _____
4. _____
5. _____

Social Studies: American West
6. _____
7. _____
8. _____
9. _____
10. _____

Eponyms
1. _____

consonant

1. _____
2. _____
3. _____
4. _____
5. _____
6. _____
7. _____
8. _____

vowel

9. _____
10. _____
11. _____
12. _____
13. _____
14. _____
15. _____
16. _____
17. _____
18. _____
19. _____
20. _____

Spelling and Thinking

READ THE SPELLING WORDS

1. dishonest — *dishonest* — That was a **dishonest** answer.
2. incomplete — *incomplete* — Laura's drawing is **incomplete**.
3. imperfect — *imperfect* — The gem was **imperfect** but beautiful.
4. nonfiction — *nonfiction* — A biography is a work of **nonfiction**.
5. unequal — *unequal* — The chair legs are **unequal** in length.
6. incorrect — *incorrect* — The spelling of my name is **incorrect**.
7. dislike — *dislike* — Claire and Matt **dislike** anchovies.
8. nonstop — *nonstop* — I prefer a **nonstop** flight.
9. unsure — *unsure* — Miguel was **unsure** of the directions.
10. disagree — *disagree* — If you **disagree,** tell me what you think.
11. inactive — *inactive* — The volcano had long been **inactive**.
12. nonviolent — *nonviolent* — Fasting can be a **nonviolent** protest.
13. unbutton — *unbutton* — Jim began to **unbutton** his jacket.
14. impolite — *impolite* — An **impolite** reply would be rude.
15. disobey — *disobey* — I try not to **disobey** my parents.
16. impatient — *impatient* — Jeannie is **impatient** for the answer.
17. nonsense — *nonsense* — This song sounds like **nonsense** to me.
18. unknown — *unknown* — The writer of this story is **unknown**.
19. impossible — *impossible* — Nothing seems **impossible** to her.
20. informal — *informal* — We can have an **informal** meeting now.

SORT THE SPELLING WORDS

1.–8. Write the words that have a prefix beginning with a consonant. Circle the prefix.

9.–20. Write the words that have a prefix beginning with a vowel. Circle the prefix.

REMEMBER THE SPELLING STRATEGY

Remember that the prefixes **dis-, im-, in-, non-,** and **un-** can be added to base words. These new words mean the opposite of the base words. For example, **disagree** means the opposite of **agree**.

Spelling and Vocabulary

Word Meanings

Write the spelling word that best replaces the underlined word or words.

1. I try not to be <u>rude</u> even if I am annoyed.
2. The rhyme was <u>not perfect</u>, which made the poem even funnier.
3. I think your watch is <u>wrong</u>.
4. Susan is <u>confused</u> about what to do next.
5. I do <u>not agree</u> with the group's opinion.
6. It is <u>not possible</u> for us to arrive on time.
7. The words are <u>without logic</u> unless you know the code.
8. The rehearsal was <u>without formality</u>; no one was in costume.

Word Structure

Write spelling words by adding the missing letters.

9. u __ b __ t __ o __
10. __ m __ ati __ __ __
11. __ n __ c __ i __ e
12. u __ k __ o __ n
13. d __ s __ be __
14. __ o __ s __ o __

USING THE Dictionary

Write the spelling words that are antonyms for these words. Then use your **Spelling Dictionary** to write the abbreviation that tells the part of speech of each spelling word.

15. like
16. complete
17. fiction
18. equal
19. honest
20. violent

Word Meanings
1. _____
2. _____
3. _____
4. _____
5. _____
6. _____
7. _____
8. _____

Word Structure
9. _____
10. _____
11. _____
12. _____
13. _____
14. _____

Using the Dictionary
15. _____
16. _____
17. _____
18. _____
19. _____
20. _____

Spelling and Reading

dishonest	incomplete	imperfect	nonfiction	unequal
incorrect	dislike	nonstop	unsure	disagree
inactive	nonviolent	unbutton	impolite	disobey
impatient	nonsense	unknown	impossible	informal

Solve the Analogies Write the spelling word that completes each analogy.

1. **Wisdom** is to **foolishness** as **sense** is to ____.
2. **Submit** is to **rebel** as **obey** is to ____.
3. **Considerate** is to **inconsiderate** as **polite** is to ____.
4. **Calm** is to **restless** as **patient** is to ____.
5. **True** is to **untrue** as **fiction** is to ____.

Complete the Sentences Write the spelling word that completes each sentence.

6. Ann and Lou ____ about the meaning of the movie.
7. The ____ flight should take six hours.
8. Karl is ____ about when the race begins.
9. The vase is ____ because of a scratch near the top.
10. The sloth moves so slowly, it seems ____.
11. Will you help your brother ____ his coat?
12. Without a tail, the Manx cat looks ____.
13. The amounts of water in the cups are ____.
14. Everyone voted in favor of a ____ protest against the new laws.
15. If you ____ snow and cold weather, you might enjoy living in Florida.
16. Although the logic is sound, the answer is ____.
17. We all wore shorts to the ____ party.
18. It is ____ for an inexperienced swimmer to cross that river on such a windy day.
19. The new principal's name is ____ to us.
20. To cheat on a test is ____.

Solve the Analogies
1.
2.
3.
4.
5.

Complete the Sentences
6.
7.
8.
9.
10.
11.
12.
13.
14.
15.
16.
17.
18.
19.
20.

Spelling and Writing

Proofread a Paragraph

Six words are not spelled correctly in this paragraph about a plane trip. Write the words correctly.

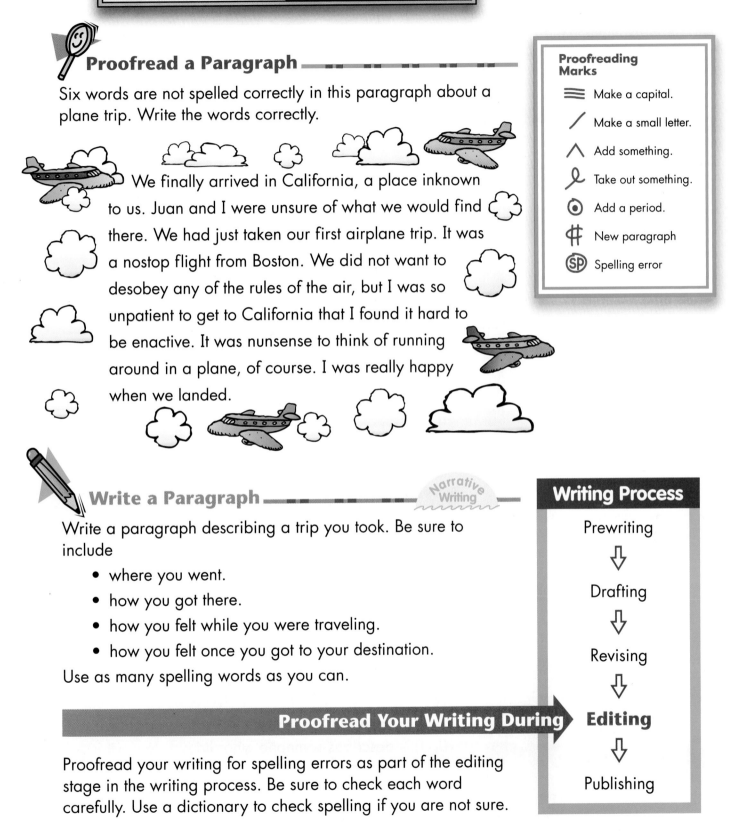

We finally arrived in California, a place inknown to us. Juan and I were unsure of what we would find there. We had just taken our first airplane trip. It was a nostop flight from Boston. We did not want to desobey any of the rules of the air, but I was so unpatient to get to California that I found it hard to be enactive. It was nunsense to think of running around in a plane, of course. I was really happy when we landed.

Proofreading Marks

≡	Make a capital.
/	Make a small letter.
∧	Add something.
ℓ	Take out something.
⊙	Add a period.
⌗	New paragraph
SP	Spelling error

Write a Paragraph

Narrative Writing

Write a paragraph describing a trip you took. Be sure to include

- where you went.
- how you got there.
- how you felt while you were traveling.
- how you felt once you got to your destination.

Use as many spelling words as you can.

Writing Process

Prewriting
⇩
Drafting
⇩
Revising
⇩
Editing
⇩
Publishing

Proofread Your Writing During ➤

Proofread your writing for spelling errors as part of the editing stage in the writing process. Be sure to check each word carefully. Use a dictionary to check spelling if you are not sure.

▸Strategy Words◂

Review Words:
Prefixes dis-, im-, in-, non-, un-

Write the word from the box that completes each sentence.

discover	uncover	unhappy	unpack	untie

1. Can you _____ this knot in my shoe?
2. Chloe will be _____ if it rains today.
3. We might _____ a new route home.
4. When you _____, you will find a note from me.
5. Jayne removed the cloth to _____ the new statue.

Preview Words:
Prefixes dis-, im-, in-, non-, un-

Write the word from the box that matches each clue.

indifference	nonfat	nonproductive
	nonprofit nonreturnable	

6. If milk is this, it is skim milk.
7. If you do not care, you are feeling this.
8. Making money is not the purpose.
9. This means that it is yours forever.
10. This describes someone who did not do anything useful today.

Review Words

1. _____
2. _____
3. _____
4. _____
5. _____

Preview Words

6. _____
7. _____
8. _____
9. _____
10. _____

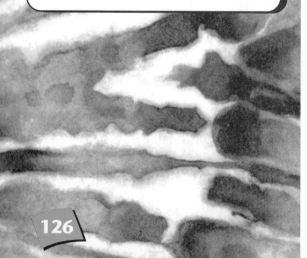

126

Content Words

Social Studies: Business

Write the words from the box to complete the sentences.

| billboard | refund | brand | slogan | disappoint |

I.–2. The manager wrote a catchy _____ and had it printed on a _____.

3. Which is your favorite _____ of cereal?

4. The store will give you a _____ if you are not happy with your new computer game.

5. The company does not want to _____ its customers.

Language Arts: Shades of Meaning

Write the word that best names each example below.

| antonym | homophone | synonym |
| homograph | homonym | |

6. happy/joyful

7. content (meaning "happy")/content (meaning "what's inside")

8. for/four; ring/ring/wring

9. in/out

10. here/hear (**Hint:** This is a kind of homonym.)

Apply the Spelling Strategy

Circle the prefix **dis-** in one of the Content Words you wrote.

Word Study

Anagrams

Anagrams are words that have all the same letters. **Below** and **elbow** are anagrams. Write the Strategy Word that is an anagram of **unite**.

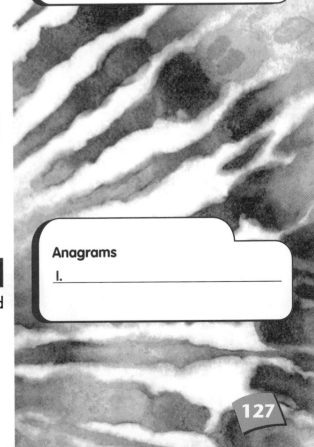

Social Studies: Business

1. _____
2. _____
3. _____
4. _____
5. _____

Language Arts: Shades of Meaning

6. _____
7. _____
8. _____
9. _____
10. _____

Anagrams

1. _____

Spelling and Thinking

READ THE SPELLING WORDS

1. broken	*broken*	Two of the eggs are **broken**.
2. frighten	*frighten*	Storms **frighten** some children.
3. specialize	*specialize*	We **specialize** in finding treasure.
4. organize	*organize*	I would like to **organize** my books.
5. shaken	*shaken*	Sue was a little **shaken** by the news.
6. fertilize	*fertilize*	Fish bones can **fertilize** soil.
7. awaken	*awaken*	Grandmother will **awaken** at ten.
8. realize	*realize*	I did not **realize** that Tara was here.
9. loosen	*loosen*	We can **loosen** your boot laces.
10. summarize	*summarize*	I will **summarize** my long message.
11. criticize	*criticize*	I must **criticize** that TV ad.
12. forgotten	*forgotten*	We have not **forgotten** your birthday.
13. modernize	*modernize*	The city will **modernize** its railway.
14. stolen	*stolen*	A famous painting was **stolen**.
15. generalize	*generalize*	Do not **generalize** about people.
16. memorize	*memorize*	Dan will **memorize** this long poem.
17. frozen	*frozen*	A **frozen** lemonade would taste good.
18. civilize	*civilize*	One cannot **civilize** some animals.
19. flatten	*flatten*	The baker will **flatten** the dough.
20. straighten	*straighten*	Robin will **straighten** the books.

-en

1. _____
2. _____
3. _____
4. _____
5. _____
6. _____
7. _____
8. _____
9. _____
10. _____

-ize

11. _____
12. _____
13. _____
14. _____
15. _____
16. _____
17. _____
18. _____
19. _____
20. _____

SORT THE SPELLING WORDS

1.–10. Write the spelling words that have the ending **-en**. Circle the ending.

11.–20. Write the spelling words that have the ending **-ize**. Circle the ending.

REMEMBER THE SPELLING STRATEGY

Remember that the endings **-en** and **-ize** can be added to base words to form new words.

Spelling and Vocabulary

Word Meanings

Write the spelling word that matches each definition.

1. provide a summary
2. make modern
3. commit to memory
4. put in order
5. state in a general way
6. come to a realization
7. evaluate; be critical
8. educate
9. scare
10. have a specialty

Word Groups

Write the spelling word that fits into each word group.

11. freeze, froze, _____
12. forget, forgot, _____
13. break, broke, _____
14. steal, stole, _____
15. shake, shook, _____
16. awake, _____, awakened

USING THE Dictionary

Write the spelling words for the dictionary respellings.

17. /strāt′ n/
18. /flăt′ n/
19. /loo′ sən/
20. /fûr′ tl īz′/

◆ ◆ ◆

Dictionary Check Use your **Spelling Dictionary** to check the respelling of each word.

Word Meanings

1. _____
2. _____
3. _____
4. _____
5. _____
6. _____
7. _____
8. _____
9. _____
10. _____

Word Groups

11. _____
12. _____
13. _____
14. _____
15. _____
16. _____

Using the Dictionary

17. _____
18. _____
19. _____
20. _____

Spelling and Reading

broken	frighten	specialize	organize	shaken
fertilize	awaken	realize	loosen	summarize
criticize	forgotten	modernize	stolen	generalize
memorize	frozen	civilize	flatten	straighten

Solve the Analogies Write the spelling word that completes each analogy.

1. **Animal** is to **feed** as **plant** is to _____.
2. **Approve** is to **disapprove** as **praise** is to _____.
3. **Squeeze** is to **release** as **tighten** is to _____.
4. **Amusement** is to **amuse** as **fear** is to _____.
5. **Heat** is to **melted** as **cold** is to _____.
6. **Take** is to **taken** as **steal** is to _____.
7. **Found** is to **missing** as **whole** is to _____.
8. **Soothe** is to **calm** as **tame** is to _____.

Complete the Sentences Write the spelling word that best completes each sentence.

9. Cable car workers will _____ the outdated track system.
10. I wish they could _____ out crooked Lombard Street.
11. Did the clatter on the Golden Gate Bridge _____ you?
12. Does Grandma _____ it is time for lunch?
13. I will relax and _____ my thoughts.
14. Dad wants to _____ the directions to Golden Gate Park.
15. Our memories of San Francisco won't be _____.
16. Do not _____ about the weather in California from the weather in San Francisco.
17. To briefly _____, San Francisco is foggy.
18. In April 1906, people were _____ when they learned about the earthquake in San Francisco.
19. Some people worry that another earthquake will _____ the city again some day.
20. People who _____ in the study of earthquakes are always watching San Francisco.

Solve the Analogies
1. _____
2. _____
3. _____
4. _____
5. _____
6. _____
7. _____
8. _____

Complete the Sentences
9. _____
10. _____
11. _____
12. _____
13. _____
14. _____
15. _____
16. _____
17. _____
18. _____
19. _____
20. _____

130

Spelling and Writing

Proofread a Paragraph

Six words are not spelled correctly in this paragraph about an unusual event. Write the words correctly.

Last night I saw something that would frightin most people. I saw a frozin trout in the bathroom sink. I had to jump back and flatten myself against the wall. My brother had come home late from a fishing trip and forgottin to put the fish in the freezer. Now I realise what happened, and I am no longer shakun. However, it is difficult not to criticise my brother.

Write a Paragraph

Narrative Writing

Write a paragraph about a funny or unusual event that has occurred in your life.

- Connect events with words that show the passage of time.
- Use colorful adjectives.
- Use specific words to describe your feelings.
- Use active verbs.

Use as many spelling words as possible.

Proofread Your Writing During

Writing Process

Prewriting

⇩

Drafting

⇩

Revising

⇩

Editing

⇩

Publishing

Proofread your writing for spelling errors as part of the editing stage in the writing process. Be sure to check each word carefully. Use a dictionary to check spelling if you are not sure.

VOCABULARY CONNECTIONS

Strategy Words

Review Words: Endings -en, -ize

Write the word from the box that matches each of these definitions.

blacken	dampen	harden	soften	tighten

1. to make black
2. to make soft
3. to make damp
4. to make tight
5. to make hard

Preview Words: Endings -en, -ize

Write the word from the box that completes each sentence.

categorize	mechanize	capitalization
	fertilizer	national

6. When you capitalize letters, you follow the rules of _____.
7. If we put _____ on the beans, they will grow faster.
8. The word that relates to **nationalize** is _____.
9. The farmer bought a milking machine to _____ his dairy business.
10. We can _____ these books by subject.

Review Words

1. _____
2. _____
3. _____
4. _____
5. _____

Preview Words

6. _____
7. _____
8. _____
9. _____
10. _____

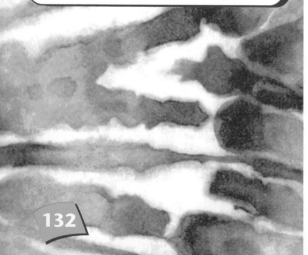

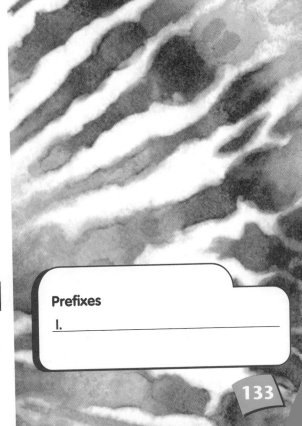

Content Words

Language Arts: Mechanics

Write a word from the box to replace the underlined words.

capitalize	indent	draft	punctuate	edit

1. We use <u>uppercase for</u> the first letter in a sentence.
2. First, you write a <u>rough version</u> of a report.
3. You should use commas, apostrophes, end marks, <u>semicolons, and colons</u> correctly in your final report.
4. It is usual to <u>insert several spaces</u> when you write the first line of a paragraph.
5. When you <u>check for errors</u>, you usually improve your writing.

Language Arts: Taking Notes

Write the word from the box that best matches each clue.

note taking	summarizing	outlining
underlining	subhead	

6. This means drawing a line under some words.
7. This heading explains the main heading.
8. When you do this, you are saying something briefly but including all the main ideas.
9. This means writing a list of main ideas and details.
10. This means jotting down what you hear or read.

Apply the Spelling Strategy

Circle the ending **-ize** in one of the Content Words you wrote.

Word Study

Prefixes

The prefix **sub-** means "under." A **subway** runs underground. A **submarine** travels underwater. Write the Content Word that means "a heading that comes under a main head in text."

Language Arts: Mechanics
1. _____
2. _____
3. _____
4. _____
5. _____

Language Arts: Taking Notes
6. _____
7. _____
8. _____
9. _____
10. _____

Prefixes
1. _____

133

one word

1.
2.
3.
4.
5.
6.
7.
8.

hyphenated

9.
10.
11.
12.
13.
14.
15.
16.

two words

17.
18.
19.
20.

Spelling and Thinking

READ THE SPELLING WORDS

1. outline	outline	First, make an **outline**.
2. home run	home run	Pedro hit a **home run**.
3. full-time	full-time	I have a **full-time** job.
4. up-to-date	up-to-date	Buy an **up-to-date** hat.
5. homework	homework	Robin does **homework**.
6. peanut butter	peanut butter	Dan likes **peanut butter**.
7. waterproof	waterproof	I need **waterproof** boots.
8. make-believe	make-believe	Play a **make-believe** game.
9. downstairs	downstairs	We painted **downstairs**.
10. themselves	themselves	They washed **themselves**.
11. merry-go-round	merry-go-round	The **merry-go-round** is old.
12. underline	underline	I will **underline** the word.
13. part of speech	part of speech	A noun is a **part of speech**.
14. sweatshirt	sweatshirt	Wear your **sweatshirt**.
15. forty-four	forty-four	There are **forty-four** pens.
16. good-bye	good-bye	We said **good-bye**.
17. double-header	double-header	I saw a **double-header**.
18. itself	itself	The monkey washes **itself**.
19. twenty-seven	twenty-seven	We need **twenty-seven** cups.
20. parcel post	parcel post	Send the box **parcel post**.

SORT THE SPELLING WORDS

1.–8. Write the spelling words that are written as one word. Draw a line between the two parts of the compound.

9.–16. Write the spelling words that are hyphenated compounds.

17.–20. Write the spelling words that are made of two or more separate words.

REMEMBER THE SPELLING STRATEGY

Remember that a compound word is formed from two or more smaller words that make a new word or group of words: **homework, peanut butter, up-to-date**.

Spelling ᵃⁿᵈ Vocabulary

Word Structure

Replace each underlined word part to write a spelling word.

1. hitch<u>ing</u> post
2. <u>part</u>-time
3. up<u>stairs</u>
4. <u>under</u>ground
5. out<u>side</u>
6. <u>wood</u>work
7. seventy-<u>four</u>
8. <u>fire</u>proof
9. <u>figure</u> of speech
10. make-<u>do</u>

Word Clues

Write the spelling word that matches each clue.

11. It can mean "their usual selves."
12. It can mean "its own self."
13. Some people like to wear this when they run or jog.
14. Most batters want to hit one of these.
15. Many people eat this in a sandwich with jelly.

USING THE Dictionary

Write the spelling word for each dictionary respelling.

16. /twĕn′tē sĕv′ən/
17. /ŭp′ tə dāt′/
18. /gŏŏd bī′/
19. /mĕr′ē gō round′/
20. /dŭb′əl hĕd′ər/

◆ ◆ ◆

Dictionary Check Be sure to check your answers in your **Spelling Dictionary**.

Word Structure
I. ___
2. ___
3. ___
4. ___
5. ___
6. ___
7. ___
8. ___
9. ___
10. ___

Word Clues
II. ___
12. ___
13. ___
14. ___
15. ___

Using the Dictionary
16. ___
17. ___
18. ___
19. ___
20. ___

Spelling and Reading

outline
up-to-date
waterproof
themselves
part of speech
good-bye
twenty-seven

home run
homework
make-believe
merry-go-round
sweatshirt
double-header
parcel post

full-time
peanut butter
downstairs
underline
forty-four
itself

Complete the Sentences

Complete the Sentences Write the spelling word that best completes each sentence.

1. The teacher asked the students to seat _____ quietly.
2. A washer and a dryer are _____ in the basement.
3. Sandy has finished her social studies and her math _____.
4. I will label each _____ in this sentence.
5. Cal rode on a _____ that included a six-foot rabbit.
6. You need _____ gloves to build a snowman.
7. Mr. Robins works as a _____ librarian.
8. The dog bounded out of the pond and shook _____.
9. Use the red marker to _____ important facts.
10. We will send this box of clothes by _____.
11. When I make an _____, I refer to my text and class notes.
12. Multiply eleven times four to get _____.
13. Mother wants an _____ computer for her work.
14. A young child may have a _____ friend.
15. Multiply nine times three to get _____.

Complete the Paragraph Write the spelling words from the box that complete the paragraph.

Today was the last day of our team's baseball season. We won the second game of a __16.__. I hit a __17.__. After the game, we had __18.__ cookies and lemonade. The coach gave each of us a __19.__ with our team's name on it. When we all said __20.__, it was sad. I know I will play again next year.

sweatshirt
good-bye
double-header
home run
peanut butter

Complete the Sentences
1.
2.
3.
4.
5.
6.
7.
8.
9.
10.
11.
12.
13.
14.
15.

Complete the Paragraph
16.
17.
18.
19.
20.

Spelling and Writing

Proofread a Paragraph

Six words are not spelled correctly in this descriptive paragraph about souvenirs. Write the words correctly.

Jorge and Susanna recommend buying up to date souvenirs on vacation. In California, they bought the following items: a sweat shirt from Disneyland, some delicious peanutbutter from the Farmer's Market, a photograph of the winning homerun at a Dodgers game, a funny snapshot of them-selves by the Pacific Ocean, and a waterproof cap from the boardwalk. When they said goodbye to California, they had twice the luggage they had brought with them.

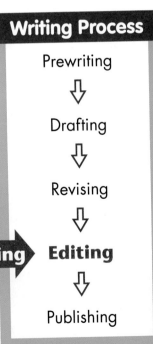

Write a Paragraph

Descriptive Writing

Write a paragraph telling about objects you have collected. Try to recall special details.

- Begin with a main idea.
- Then organize the details logically.
- Select colorful adjectives.
- End with a sentence that concludes your paragraph.

Use as many spelling words as possible.

Proofread Your Writing During

Writing Process

Prewriting

⇩

Drafting

⇩

Revising

⇩

Editing

⇩

Publishing

Proofread your writing for spelling errors as part of the editing stage in the writing process. Be sure to check each word carefully. Use a dictionary to check spelling if you are not sure.

VOCABULARY CONNECTIONS

Strategy Words

Review Words: Compound Words

Write a word from the box to complete each sentence.

basketball	flashlight	mailbox
newspaper	weekend	

1. The season for watching professional _____ is winter.
2. A boy threw the daily _____ onto their porch.
3. Last _____, I visited the Berkshire Hills.
4. We keep batteries and a _____ in the car.
5. We went to the _____, hoping her letter was there.

Preview Words: Compound Words

Write the words from the box that complete the paragraph.

background	campfire	cross-country
thunderstorm	wristwatch	

My dad decided we would take a __6.__ trip and do some camping on the way. One night, we set up a roaring __7.__ where we could see a waterfall in the __8.__. Later, there was a heavy __9.__, so we slept in a nearby cave. In the morning, we found a gold __10.__. Someone who had also taken shelter in that cave must have left the watch there.

Review Words

1. _____
2. _____
3. _____
4. _____
5. _____

Preview Words

6. _____
7. _____
8. _____
9. _____
10. _____

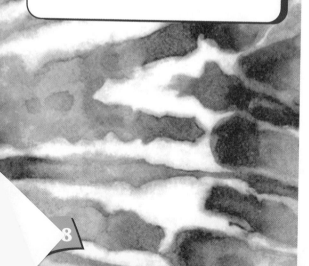

Content Words

Health: Teeth

Write the word from the box that matches each clue.

bicuspid	molar	cuspid	toothbrush	incisor

1. You use this to keep your teeth clean.
2. This is a tooth with two points on it.
3. It is called a canine tooth and has one point.
4. This is one of the eight front teeth.
5. Located behind the bicuspids, this is a grinding tooth.

Social Studies: Pioneers

Write the words by unscrambling the letters in the paragraph.

chimney	hearth	fireplace	hollow	floor

6.
A **acerifpel** is a source of warmth and beauty in a home. It is
7. **8.**
usually built around a **owlolh** opening in a wall with a **nichyme**
9.
extending toward the sky. The **orfol** outside the fireplace is usually
10.
covered with stone so that sparks from the fire in the **tarheh** cannot

reach flammable material. Pioneers and others used to cook and

bake in a fireplace.

Health: Teeth
1. _____
2. _____
3. _____
4. _____
5. _____
Social Studies: Pioneers
6. _____
7. _____
8. _____
9. _____
10. _____

Apply the Spelling Strategy

Circle the two words you wrote that are compound words.

Word Study

Word Roots

The root **bi** comes from old Greek and Latin words that meant
"two" or "twice." A **biathlon** is a contest involving two sports.
Write the Content Word that has this root and means "a two-
pointed tooth that helps to bite and grind food."

Word Roots
1. _____

Spelling and Thinking

READ THE SPELLING WORDS

1.	vane	*vane*	The **vane** turns as the wind blows.
2.	principal	*principal*	The school **principal** is a quiet man.
3.	country	*country*	The **country** will elect a new president.
4.	weight	*weight*	The **weight** of my cat is nine pounds.
5.	kernel	*kernel*	There is a corn **kernel** on your tie.
6.	vein	*vein*	A **vein** carries blood to the heart.
7.	county	*county*	This **county** includes Redwood City.
8.	coarse	*coarse*	Claire's dog has **coarse** white fur.
9.	invent	*invent*	Did Edison **invent** the microphone?
10.	except	*except*	Everyone **except** Sal came to the game.
11.	colonel	*colonel*	A **colonel** ranks above a lieutenant.
12.	dairy	*dairy*	Cheese and yogurt are **dairy** products.
13.	capitol	*capitol*	State officials meet in the **capitol**.
14.	accept	*accept*	Please **accept** my apology.
15.	vain	*vain*	The **vain** girl keeps brushing her hair.
16.	principle	*principle*	On **principle,** I will not gossip.
17.	event	*event*	The final **event** is the long jump.
18.	capital	*capital*	Which city is the **capital** of your state?
19.	diary	*diary*	I enjoy writing in my **diary**.
20.	course	*course*	Which **course** is better to follow?

homophone for wait
1. _____

homophones
2. _____

3. _____

4. _____

5. _____

6. _____

7. _____

8. _____

9. _____

10. _____

11. _____

12. _____

similar words
13. _____

14. _____

15. _____

16. _____

17. _____

18. _____

19. _____

20. _____

SORT THE SPELLING WORDS

1. Write the spelling word that is a homophone for **wait**.

2.–12. Write each group of homophones.

13.–20. Write the pairs of spelling words that are similar but not identical in sound or spelling.

REMEMBER THE SPELLING STRATEGY

Remember that when words sound similar to each other or when they are homophones, their spellings can be easily confused.

Spelling ᵃⁿᵈ Vocabulary

Word Meanings

Write the spelling word that fits each clue.

1. You keep a daily record of your experiences in it.
2. This means "to take something offered."
3. It means "other than."
4. This means "rough; not smooth."
5. This is a room or building where milk is stored.
6. A sport may be played on this land.

Word Structure

Decide which letters are missing and write the spelling words.

7. i __ v __ n __
8. co __ n __ r __
9. w __ i __ ht
10. e __ e __ t
11. __ ou __ t __

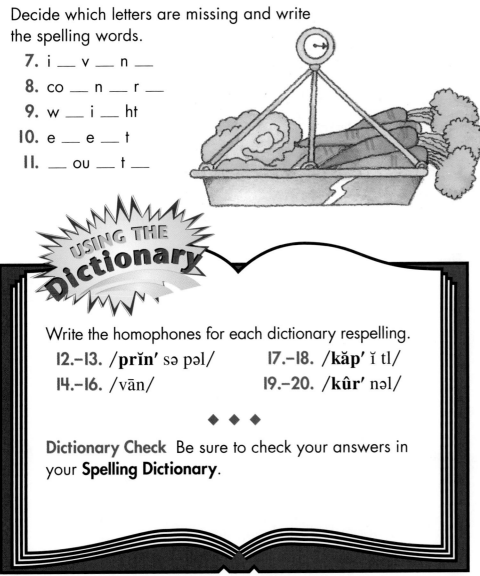

USING THE Dictionary

Write the homophones for each dictionary respelling.

12.–13. /prĭn′ sə pəl/   17.–18. /kăp′ ĭ tl/
14.–16. /vān/   19.–20. /kûr′ nəl/

◆ ◆ ◆

Dictionary Check Be sure to check your answers in your **Spelling Dictionary**.

Word Meanings
1.
2.
3.
4.
5.
6.

Word Structure
7.
8.
9.
10.
11.

Using the Dictionary
12.
13.
14.
15.
16.
17.
18.
19.
20.

Spelling and Reading

vane	principal	country	weight	kernel
vein	county	coarse	invent	except
colonel	dairy	capitol	accept	vain
principle	event	capital	diary	course

Complete the Paragraph

1. _____
2. _____
3. _____
4. _____
5. _____
6. _____
7. _____
8. _____
9. _____
10. _____

Replace the Words

11. _____
12. _____
13. _____
14. _____
15. _____
16. _____
17. _____
18. _____
19. _____
20. _____

Complete the Paragraph   Write the spelling words that complete the paragraph.

Shane plans to __1.__ an invitation to see Joe's grandfather's __2.__ and egg farm. Both boys prefer the __3.__ to the city and would __4.__ any excuse to be outdoors. Joe once put off going inside for breakfast by feeding corn to the chickens one __5.__ at a time! Shane likes everything about farming __6.__ getting up early. Joe's grandfather, who is a retired army __7.__, wakes the boys at five in the morning for chores. This weekend, he will have them choose a new __8.__ to show the direction the wind blows. He wants one large enough to be visible from the next __9.__. The one he has now says MILK in __10.__ letters.

Replace the Words   Write the spelling word that could best replace the underlined word or words.

11. This <u>rough</u> fabric is water resistant.
12. I keep my <u>personal journal</u> hidden.
13. The <u>head of the school</u> declared a holiday.
14. Karyn does not borrow money out of <u>a strong guiding rule</u>.
15. The veterinarian looked for a <u>blood vessel</u> in the horse's shoulder.
16. Compare the <u>heaviness</u> of an elephant with that of a car.
17. He is so <u>conceited</u> that he even keeps a mirror in his backpack.
18. The <u>occurrence</u> we are celebrating is your birthday.
19. The <u>building that houses the government</u> is in Springfield.
20. Rob took a Spanish <u>class</u> during the summer.

Spelling and Writing

Proofread a Paragraph

Six words are not spelled correctly in this paragraph about Washington, D.C. Write the words correctly.

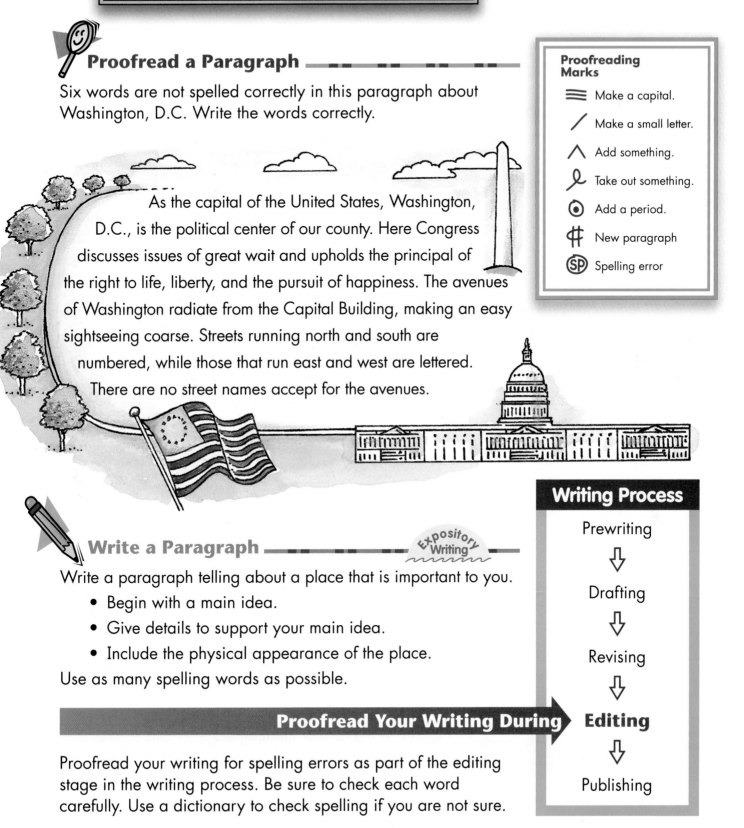

As the capital of the United States, Washington, D.C., is the political center of our county. Here Congress discusses issues of great wait and upholds the principal of the right to life, liberty, and the pursuit of happiness. The avenues of Washington radiate from the Capital Building, making an easy sightseeing coarse. Streets running north and south are numbered, while those that run east and west are lettered. There are no street names accept for the avenues.

Proofreading Marks

≡ Make a capital.

/ Make a small letter.

∧ Add something.

℮ Take out something.

⊙ Add a period.

New paragraph

SP Spelling error

Write a Paragraph — Expository Writing

Write a paragraph telling about a place that is important to you.

- Begin with a main idea.
- Give details to support your main idea.
- Include the physical appearance of the place.

Use as many spelling words as possible.

Proofread Your Writing During

Writing Process

Prewriting

⇩

Drafting

⇩

Revising

⇩

Editing

⇩

Publishing

Proofread your writing for spelling errors as part of the editing stage in the writing process. Be sure to check each word carefully. Use a dictionary to check spelling if you are not sure.

VOCABULARY CONNECTIONS

Strategy Words

Review Words

1. _____
2. _____
3. _____
4. _____
5. _____
6. _____

Preview Words

7. _____
8. _____
9. _____
10. _____
11. _____
12. _____

Review Words: Easily Confused Words

Write the word from the box to complete each sentence.

brake	break	steal	steel	waist	waste

1. On a whim, the player decided to try to _____ second base.
2. The dancer wore a sash around her _____.
3. In the desert, we do not _____ water.
4. Railroad tracks are made of _____.
5. Be sure to _____ your bike as you approach an intersection.
6. Darren would never _____ a promise.

Preview Words: Easily Confused Words

Write the word from the box that matches each clue.

cession	palate	pallet	session	verses	versus

7. This is the surrender of something, such as rights or property.
8. These are groups of lines in a poem.
9. It means "against."
10. This is the roof of the mouth.
11. This is a hard bed or mattress.
12. This can mean "a meeting of a group."

Content Words

Health: Injuries

Write a word from the box to complete each sentence.

fracture	blister	bruise	injury	frostbite

1. Dress warmly for skiing; you can get _____ .
2. Do not fall off your bike and _____ a bone.
3. If you _____ your arm, it turns black and blue.
4. Running in the wrong shoes can create a _____.
5. As you can see, almost any sport can cause an _____.

Science: Computers

Write the words from the box that complete the paragraph.

byte	silicon	debug	software	modem

The smallest amount of information a computer can store is called a __6.__. A __7.__ allows computers to communicate over telephone lines. A computer chip is made of a substance called __8.__. Programs that control a computer's functions are called __9.__. If something goes wrong, we must __10.__ the system.

Apply the Spelling Strategy

Circle the Content Word you wrote that is a homophone for **bite**. Underline the Content Word that is a homophone for **brews**.

Word Study

Word History

The first "computer bug" was a real bug—a moth flew into the Mark II computer! Since then, when a computer program has a flaw or a defect, someone must find the problem and fix it. Write the Content Word that describes this adjustment.

Health: Injuries

1. _____
2. _____
3. _____
4. _____
5. _____

Science: Computers

6. _____
7. _____
8. _____
9. _____
10. _____

Word History

1. _____

145

Assessment and Review

Assessment Units 19–23

Each Assessment Word in the box fits one or more of the spelling strategies you have studied over the past five weeks. Read the spelling strategies. Then write each Assessment Word under the unit number it fits.

Unit 19

1.–4. It is important to be able to spell the names of the states correctly.

Unit 20

5.–9. The prefixes **dis-, im-, in-, non-,** and **un-** can be added to base words. The new words mean the opposite of the base words. For example, **disagree** means the opposite of **agree**.

Unit 21

10.–12. The endings **-en** and **-ize** can be added to base words to form new words.

Unit 22

13.–16. A compound word is formed from two or more smaller words that make a new word or group of words: **homework, peanut butter, up-to-date**.

Unit 23

17.–20. When words sound similar to each other or when they are homophones, their spellings can be easily confused.

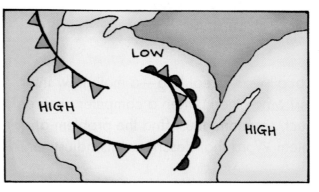

Word Box
proven
Wisconsin
disgrace
horseback
ally
unfasten
weather map
nonsmoker
device
sharpen
Arkansas
unlisted
close-up
magnetize
Wyoming
impure
devise
pocketbook
Arizona
alley

Unit 19
1.
2.
3.
4.

Unit 20
5.
6.
7.
8.
9.

Unit 21
10.
11.
12.

Unit 22
13.
14.
15.
16.

Unit 23
17.
18.
19.
20.

Unit 19: State Names

California	Massachusetts	North Dakota	Texas	Alaska
Florida	New York	Washington	Maine	Ohio

Write the spelling word that answers each riddle.

1. This state name has two sets of double letters.

2.–3. Each of these names begins and ends with the same letter.

4. This state name has one syllable.

5. The letter **X** marks the middle of this state name.

6.–7. Each of these states has two words in its name.

8. This state is the southernmost state.

9. This state has the same name as the country's capital city.

10. This state name ends with the letters **ia**.

Review **Unit 20: Prefixes dis-, im-, in-, non-, un-**

unsure	dislike	impossible	unknown	disagree
impatient	nonfiction	disobey	dishonest	nonsense

Write a spelling word by adding a prefix to each word.

11. sure
12. like
13. known
14. patient
15. obey
16. sense
17. possible
18. agree
19. fiction
20. honest

Unit 19
1. _____
2. _____
3. _____
4. _____
5. _____
6. _____
7. _____
8. _____
9. _____
10. _____

Unit 20
11. _____
12. _____
13. _____
14. _____
15. _____
16. _____
17. _____
18. _____
19. _____
20. _____

147

Review — Unit 21: Endings -en, -ize

loosen	frighten	organize	criticize	awaken
realize	broken	forgotten	frozen	stolen

Write a spelling word that means the opposite of each clue.

1. praise
2. go to sleep
3. fixed
4. remembered
5. melted
6. tighten

Write a spelling word that means the same as each clue.

7. scare
8. understand
9. taken away
10. arrange

Review — Unit 22: Compound Words

home run	forty-four	good-bye	up-to-date	homework
themselves	waterproof	downstairs	outline	itself

Add the missing part of these compound words to write a spelling word.

11. them
12. run
13. work
14. self
15. forty
16. out

Write the spelling word that means the opposite of the underlined word.

17. Always try to wear <u>leaky</u> clothes when walking in the rain.
18. Everyone must come <u>upstairs</u> for breakfast no later than eight o'clock.
19. As he left for school, Benito waved <u>hello</u>.
20. Every school needs an <u>old</u> set of encyclopedias.

country	accept	except	principal	principle
course	event	invent	weight	capital

Write the spelling word to complete each sentence.

1. Ms. Ormsby, the school _____, will open the assembly.
2. Step on the scale and check your _____.
3. Charleston is the _____ of West Virginia.
4. Alaska is the largest state in our _____.
5. I am happy to _____ your invitation.
6. Everyone _____ Rosie is going to the game.
7. The Golden Rule is a _____ many choose to live by.
8. Please call home in the _____ you expect to be late.
9. Salad was the first _____ of the meal.
10. In what year did Alexander Graham Bell _____ the telephone?

Unit 23

1. _____
2. _____
3. _____
4. _____
5. _____
6. _____
7. _____
8. _____
9. _____
10. _____

WORD SORT Spelling Study Strategy

Sorting by Prefixes and Suffixes

Sorting words is a good way to practice your spelling words. Here is a fun way to sort spelling words by their prefixes and suffixes.

1. Write each of these prefixes on a card: **dis-, im-, in-, non-,** and **un-**.
2. Write each of the words from Unit 20 on a card. Turn the cards facedown.
3. Pick a card and then place it under the prefix it matches. Spell the word to yourself as you place it.
4. Continue until you have used all the words. You might want to think of some new words with these prefixes and add them to the word sort, too.
5. Try the same word sort with the words from Unit 21 and the suffixes **-en** and **-ize**.

dis- im- im- un- non- -en -ize

149

Grammar, Usage, and Mechanics

Pronouns: Personal and Possessive

A pronoun can take the place of a noun. Use the personal pronouns **I, me, we,** and **us** to speak or write about yourself. Use **she, her, it, he, him, you, they,** and **them** to refer to other people and things.

Papa said that **he** and **I** can give **you** a ride.

The possessive pronouns **his, its, our, her, their, my,** and **your** show ownership.

Lisa already handed in **her** paper.

The class gave a gift to **our** teacher.

Practice Activity

A. Write the pronoun in each sentence. Circle any possessive pronouns.

1. Ask the boys if they want a peanut butter sandwich.
2. The drawing that I made is hanging in the hall.
3. Where is my magazine about Alaska?
4. Make sure that you lock the door.
5. They disagree about the homework assignment.
6. Kim will organize our facts into an outline.

B. Write the pronoun that could replace the underlined word or words.

7. Alice took <u>Alice's</u> list to the store.
8. Both teachers wrote <u>the teachers'</u> names on the board.
9. <u>Shawn and I</u> disagree on the answer to the question.
10. Those kittens seem to like <u>that girl</u>!
11. Kevin found out <u>Kevin's</u> bike had been repaired.
12. The dog wagged <u>the dog's</u> tail to say good-bye.

A.
  1.
  2.
  3.
  4.
  5.
  6.
B.
  7.
  8.
  9.
  10.
  11.
  12.

WORKSHOP

Proofreading Strategy

One at a Time!

Good writers always proofread their writing for spelling mistakes. Here's a strategy that you can use to proofread your papers.

Focus on one kind of mistake at a time. First, skim your paper and look for one kind of problem, such as word endings. Then, look for another kind of problem, such as contractions or capitalization.

Each time you look will take only a few minutes. You'll be surprised by how easy it is to spot problems when you look only for one kind. Try it!

Electronic Spelling

Techtalk

Computers have created a whole new language of their own. Spell checkers may not recognize all this techtalk, or technical language. Much of it is new. So you might keep a personal dictionary of techtalk that you use. Some of the terms are the initial letters of longer words.

Here are some translations of techtalk.

CAD   **C**omputer **A**ided **D**esign   URL   **U**niform **R**esource **L**ocator
CPU   **C**entral **P**rocessing **U**nit   RAM   **R**andom **A**ccess **M**emory
ISP   **I**nternet **S**ervice **P**rovider   ROM   **R**ead **O**nly **M**emory

Use the list above to decide which of the following techtalk terms is misspelled. Write those terms correctly. Write **OK** if a term is correct.

1. CUP
2. CAD
3. IPS
4. RAM
5. RMO
6. LUR

Electronic Spelling
1. _____
2. _____
3. _____
4. _____
5. _____
6. _____

-or

1. _____
2. _____
3. _____
4. _____
5. _____
6. _____
7. _____
8. _____

-er

9. _____
10. _____
11. _____
12. _____
13. _____
14. _____

-ist

15. _____
16. _____
17. _____
18. _____
19. _____
20. _____

Spelling and Thinking

READ THE SPELLING WORDS

1.	director	*director*	The **director** of the play is Arnie.
2.	pitcher	*pitcher*	The **pitcher** threw with his left hand.
3.	commander	*commander*	They saluted their **commander**.
4.	colonist	*colonist*	A **colonist** settled in Jamestown.
5.	typist	*typist*	A **typist** will prepare this letter.
6.	scientist	*scientist*	The **scientist** studied sea life.
7.	editor	*editor*	An **editor** spots story problems.
8.	homemaker	*homemaker*	A **homemaker** manages the home.
9.	operator	*operator*	The phone **operator** speaks clearly.
10.	professor	*professor*	Hans's mother is a college **professor**.
11.	creditor	*creditor*	A **creditor** expects to be paid.
12.	instructor	*instructor*	Meg's gym **instructor** teaches well.
13.	artist	*artist*	The sidewalk **artist** draws with chalk.
14.	passenger	*passenger*	A **passenger** boards the bus.
15.	inventor	*inventor*	Thomas Edison was an **inventor**.
16.	tourist	*tourist*	The **tourist** visited a historic house.
17.	cyclist	*cyclist*	Every **cyclist** needs a helmet.
18.	actor	*actor*	The **actor** bowed and left the stage.
19.	publisher	*publisher*	A **publisher** makes and sells books.
20.	gardener	*gardener*	That **gardener** is fond of roses.

SORT THE SPELLING WORDS

1.–8. Write the words with the suffix **-or**. Circle the suffix.

9.–14. Write the words with the suffix **-er**. Circle the suffix.

15.–20. Write the words with the suffix **-ist**. Circle the suffix.

REMEMBER THE SPELLING STRATEGY

Remember that the suffixes **-or, -er,** and **-ist** mean "one who."
An **editor** is "one who edits." A **pitcher** is "one who pitches."
A **tourist** is "one who tours."

Spelling and Vocabulary

Word Meanings

Write a spelling word to match each clue.

1. an early American settler
2. a naval rank
3. one who cares for flowers
4. prints and sells books
5. one who creates new devices
6. one who studies the world around us
7. a pedaler
8. found on the stage

Word Parts

Follow the directions to write a spelling word.

9. catcher – ca + pi = _____
10. homework – work + maker = _____
11. stylist – styl + typ = _____
12. creator – crea + edi = _____
13. stranger – stra + passe = _____
14. confessor – con + pro = _____

USING THE Dictionary

Two **guide words** appear on the top of every page in your **Spelling Dictionary**. These two words are the first and last words on the dictionary page. Write the spelling words that appear on the page with each set of guide words.

15. deny • dis-
16. Ohio • palace
17. course • cyclone
18. argue • badge
19. include • internal
20. thrust • typewriter

Word Meanings

1. _____
2. _____
3. _____
4. _____
5. _____
6. _____
7. _____
8. _____

Word Parts

9. _____
10. _____
11. _____
12. _____
13. _____
14. _____

Using the Dictionary

15. _____
16. _____
17. _____
18. _____
19. _____
20. _____

Spelling and Reading

director   pitcher   commander   colonist   typist
scientist   editor   homemaker   operator   professor
creditor   instructor   artist   passenger   inventor
tourist   cyclist   actor   publisher   gardener

Solve the Analogies

1.

2.

3.

4.

Complete the Sentences

5.

6.

7.

8.

9.

10.

11.

12.

13.

14.

15.

16.

17.

18.

19.

20.

Solve the Analogies   Write the spelling word that completes each analogy.

1. **Shop** is to **shopkeeper** as **home** is to _____.
2. **Cake** is to **baker** as **flower** is to _____.
3. **Chemistry** is to **chemist** as **science** is to _____.
4. **Boat** is to **sailor** as **stage** is to _____.

Complete the Sentences   Write the spelling word that completes each sentence.

5. The _____ watches the signal from the catcher.
6. My dance _____ wants me to practice an hour a day.
7. A _____ usually asks a debtor to sign a document.
8. The story was about an early _____ in Virginia.
9. An _____ must have a good imagination.
10. The ambitious _____ wanted to pedal from Denver to San Francisco.
11. A watercolor _____ may paint on wet paper.
12. A college _____ usually has spent years studying a particular subject.
13. This company is the _____ of many atlases and maps.
14. Every airline _____ must pass through a security check.
15. The _____ suggested that the author drop a chapter that was boring.
16. A film _____ might say "Cut" or "Quiet on the set."
17. My brother is a forklift _____ at the lumber mill.
18. A _____ may develop a wrist injury from repeating the same movements over and over.
19. Sharon's _____ in the navy had a voice like gravel being shoveled.
20. Simone wants to be a lifetime _____ and see the world.

Spelling and Writing

Proofread an Ad

Six words are not spelled correctly in these job advertisements. Write the words correctly.

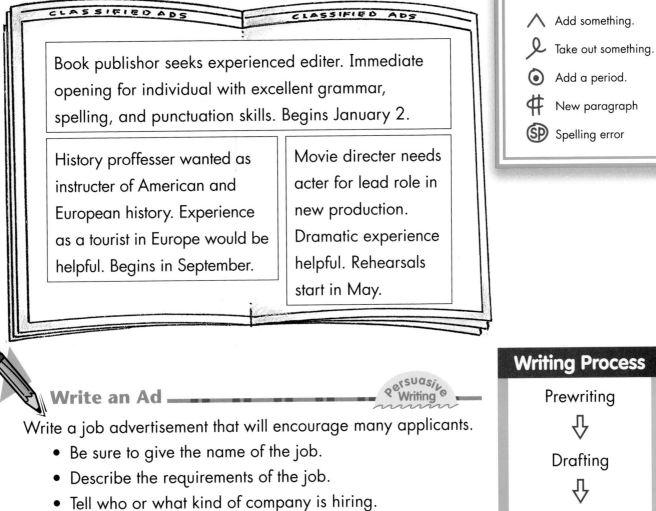

CLASSIFIED ADS   CLASSIFIED ADS

Book publishor seeks experienced editer. Immediate opening for individual with excellent grammar, spelling, and punctuation skills. Begins January 2.

History proffesser wanted as instructer of American and European history. Experience as a tourist in Europe would be helpful. Begins in September.

Movie directer needs acter for lead role in new production. Dramatic experience helpful. Rehearsals start in May.

Proofreading Marks

≡ Make a capital.

/ Make a small letter.

∧ Add something.

℮ Take out something.

⊙ Add a period.

⌗ New paragraph

ⓢⓟ Spelling error

Write an Ad

Persuasive Writing

Write a job advertisement that will encourage many applicants.

- Be sure to give the name of the job.
- Describe the requirements of the job.
- Tell who or what kind of company is hiring.
- Say when the opening is available.

Use as many spelling words as possible.

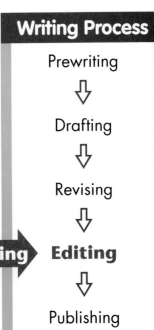

Writing Process

Prewriting

⇩

Drafting

⇩

Revising

⇩

Editing

⇩

Publishing

Proofread Your Writing During Editing

Proofread your writing for spelling errors as part of the editing stage in the writing process. Be sure to check each word carefully. Use a dictionary to check spelling if you are not sure.

VOCABULARY CONNECTIONS

Strategy Words

Review Words: Suffixes -or, -er, -ist

Write the word from the box that could best replace the underlined word or words.

camper	farmer	leader	listener	speaker

1. A speaker always enjoys a <u>person who quietly pays attention</u>.
2. The next <u>lecturer</u> is an animal trainer.
3. <u>A person who raises food crops</u> appreciates fertile land.
4. <u>A person sleeping outdoors away from houses</u> should have a compass and a first-aid kit.
5. <u>A person whom others readily follow</u> usually has charm and appears confident.

Preview Words: Suffixes -or, -er, -ist

Write a word from the box to complete each sentence.

autobiographer	geographer	geologist
oceanographer	visitor	

6. The ____ collected stones and crystals.
7. An ____ would probably learn how to scuba-dive.
8. Joe has a ____ from Indonesia.
9. This ____ draws maps of places all over the world.
10. An ____ may review diaries and letters he or she has written.

Review Words

1. _____
2. _____
3. _____
4. _____
5. _____

Preview Words

6. _____
7. _____
8. _____
9. _____
10. _____

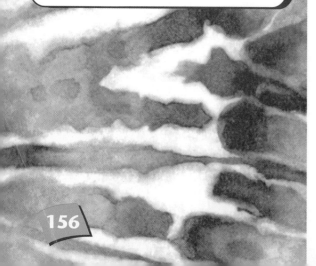

Content Words

Language Arts: Television

Write the word from the box that matches each clue.

| comedy | telecast | episode | writer | studio |

1. It is intended to make you laugh.
2. This is one part of a show.
3. Someone who prepares scripts is one.
4. In this place, a show is filmed.
5. This is a television broadcast.

Fine Arts: Entertainment

The scrambled words in this paragraph are from the box.
Unscramble the letters and write the words.

| jester | mandolin | lute | minstrel | recorder |

A type of drama that was very popular at the royal courts during the sixteenth century was comedy of art. Two performers were the **rlnsteim** 6. and the **etsrej** 7. The minstrel played the **olnadinm** 8. and the **etul** 9. A court **decorerr** 10. sometimes wrote down an account of the event.

Apply the Spelling Strategy

Circle the suffix **-er** in three of the Content Words you wrote.

Word Study

Word Roots

The root **tele** comes from an old Greek word that meant "far." A **telephone** carries voices over long distances. Write the Content Word that has this root and means "a picture sent from far away."

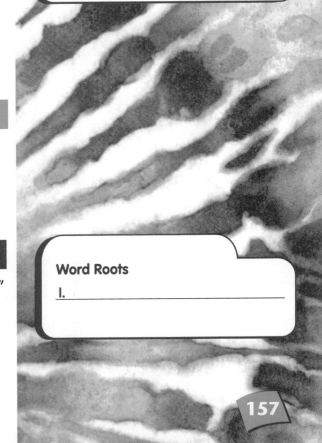

Language Arts: Television

1. _____
2. _____
3. _____
4. _____
5. _____

Fine Arts: Entertainment

6. _____
7. _____
8. _____
9. _____
10. _____

Word Roots

1. _____

Spelling and Thinking

READ THE SPELLING WORDS

1.	soldiers	*soldiers*	Many **soldiers** defended the country.
2.	pianos	*pianos*	These **pianos** need to be tuned.
3.	essays	*essays*	Sam enjoys **essays** about nature.
4.	chiefs	*chiefs*	Four fire **chiefs** got awards.
5.	treaties	*treaties*	The **treaties** were signed in 1918.
6.	countries	*countries*	The two **countries** made peace.
7.	luggage	*luggage*	Karla's **luggage** is green plaid.
8.	skis	*skis*	We should wax these **skis**.
9.	characters	*characters*	These **characters** will wear masks.
10.	badges	*badges*	Lars has **badges** for good deeds.
11.	valleys	*valleys*	The sheep graze in the **valleys**.
12.	palaces	*palaces*	Most French **palaces** have fountains.
13.	beliefs	*beliefs*	Your **beliefs** may change some day.
14.	gentlemen	*gentlemen*	These **gentlemen** have had dinner.
15.	latches	*latches*	Release the **latches** on that door.
16.	envelopes	*envelopes*	Robin needs six **envelopes**.
17.	loaves	*loaves*	The round **loaves** are wheat bread.
18.	groceries	*groceries*	We need **groceries** from the store.
19.	heroes	*heroes*	Legends usually have brave **heroes**.
20.	diaries	*diaries*	One day my **diaries** may be published.

no change

1. _____

add -s or -es

2. _____
3. _____
4. _____
5. _____
6. _____
7. _____
8. _____
9. _____
10. _____
11. _____
12. _____
13. _____
14. _____

change form

15. _____
16. _____
17. _____
18. _____
19. _____
20. _____

SORT THE SPELLING WORDS

1. Write the word that stays the same in the plural form.

2.–14. Write the words that form the plural with **-s** or **-es**.

15.–20. Write the words that form the plural in other ways. Circle the letters that change or are added.

REMEMBER THE SPELLING STRATEGY

Remember that plural nouns name more than one person, place, or thing. Plurals are formed in various ways: by adding **-s** (**envelopes**); by adding **-es** (**latches**); or by changing final **y** to **i** and adding **-es** (**diaries**). Some plurals are exceptions.

Spelling and Vocabulary

Word Meanings

Write a spelling word to match each clue.

1. some suitcases
2. some reports
3. food items
4. buildings for royal families
5. people whom you admire
6. big instruments with keys

Word Structure

Follow the directions to write a spelling word.

7. leaves – ea + oa =
8. ledges – le + ba =
9. matches – m + l =
10. antelopes – ant + env =
11. canaries – can + di =

Write the plural form of each word in parentheses. You will be writing the spelling word that completes each sentence.

12. We visited three _____ on our trip. (country)
13. Those two _____ want tea. (gentleman)
14. Some of the _____ have no lines. (character)
15. He held two _____ about gardening. (belief)
16. All of the police _____ came to the meeting. (chief)

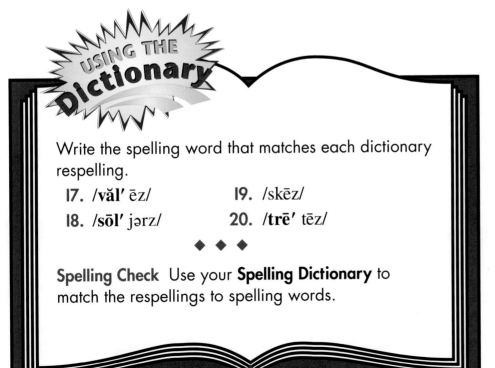

USING THE Dictionary

Write the spelling word that matches each dictionary respelling.

17. /văl′ ēz/
18. /sōl′ jərz/
19. /skēz/
20. /trē′ tēz/

◆ ◆ ◆

Spelling Check Use your **Spelling Dictionary** to match the respellings to spelling words.

Word Meanings

1. _____
2. _____
3. _____
4. _____
5. _____
6. _____

Word Structure

7. _____
8. _____
9. _____
10. _____
11. _____
12. _____
13. _____
14. _____
15. _____
16. _____

Using the Dictionary

17. _____
18. _____
19. _____
20. _____

Spelling ᴬⁿᵈ Reading

soldiers	pianos	essays	chiefs	treaties
countries	luggage	skis	characters	badges
valleys	palaces	beliefs	gentlemen	latches
envelopes	loaves	groceries	heroes	diaries

Replace the Words Write the spelling word that best replaces the underlined word or words.

1. Kings and queens live in huge mansions.
2. The president travels to many nations.
3. When wars end, leaders sign agreements.
4. What are your ideas about right and wrong?
5. Make sure that all the door hooks work.
6. Mom and Seth write in their journals every night.

Complete the Sentences Write the spelling word that completes each of the following sentences.

7. The baker sold six _____ of French bread.
8. Naomi's _____ and ski poles are here.
9. The _____ of the Iroquois Nation attended the ceremony.
10. When we shop, we wheel our _____ around in carts.
11. There are four major _____ in this play.
12. All _____ must wear suits and ties.
13. We hope all of our _____ fits in the trunk of the car.
14. We call them _____ because they faced danger for us.
15. Chad has three _____ for his woodland skills.
16. We can seal these _____ by using a damp sponge.
17. In these river _____, there are bridges.
18. All _____ have to learn to follow orders.
19. The musician earns a living by tuning _____.
20. We wrote three _____ on the Civil War.

Replace the Words
1.
2.
3.
4.
5.
6.

Complete the Sentences
7.
8.
9.
10.
11.
12.
13.
14.
15.
16.
17.
18.
19.
20.

160

Spelling and Writing

Proofread a Paragraph

Six words are not spelled correctly in this paragraph. Write the words correctly.

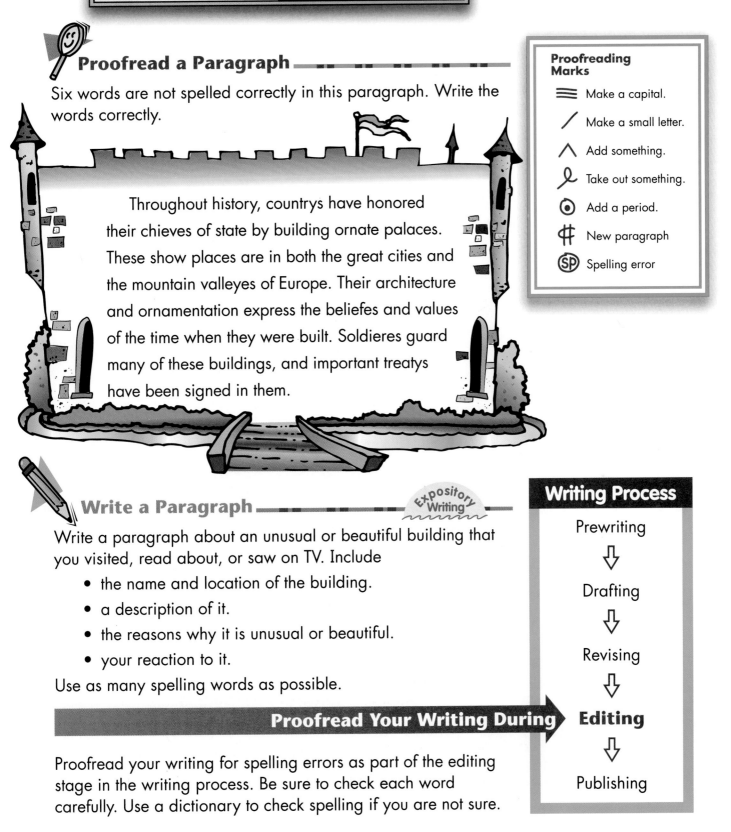

Throughout history, countrys have honored their chieves of state by building ornate palaces. These show places are in both the great cities and the mountain valleyes of Europe. Their architecture and ornamentation express the beliefs and values of the time when they were built. Soldieres guard many of these buildings, and important treatys have been signed in them.

Proofreading Marks

≡	Make a capital.
/	Make a small letter.
∧	Add something.
ℓ	Take out something.
⊙	Add a period.
#	New paragraph
SP	Spelling error

Write a Paragraph

Expository Writing

Write a paragraph about an unusual or beautiful building that you visited, read about, or saw on TV. Include

- the name and location of the building.
- a description of it.
- the reasons why it is unusual or beautiful.
- your reaction to it.

Use as many spelling words as possible.

Proofread Your Writing During

Proofread your writing for spelling errors as part of the editing stage in the writing process. Be sure to check each word carefully. Use a dictionary to check spelling if you are not sure.

Writing Process

Prewriting
⇩
Drafting
⇩
Revising
⇩
Editing
⇩
Publishing

Unit 26 enrichment

VOCABULARY CONNECTIONS

▸Strategy Words◂

Review Words: Plurals

Write the word from the box that completes each sentence.

babies	clothes	monkeys	pennies	teams

1. Human _____ are very dependent on adults.
2. Howler _____ have a memorable cry.
3. Both _____ have new quarterbacks.
4. The huge jar contained more than thirty dollars in _____.
5. It is time to put our summer _____ away in boxes and store them in the attic.

Preview Words: Plurals

Write the word from the box that matches each clue.

castanets	ceramics	linguistics
multiples		tropics

6. It is the art of making clay pottery.
7. This is the study of language.
8. This part of the earth lies just north and south of the equator.
9. When these numbers are divided by another number, there is no remainder.
10. They are hollowed pieces of wood held in each hand and clicked with the fingers.

Review Words
1. _____
2. _____
3. _____
4. _____
5. _____

Preview Words
6. _____
7. _____
8. _____
9. _____
10. _____

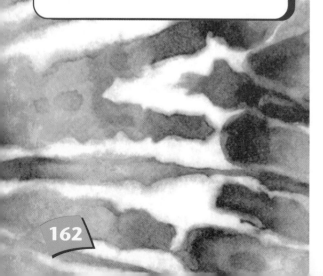

Content Words

Science: Research

Write a word from the box that fits each definition.

| research | tundra | reside | wolves | rodent |

1. cold, arctic region
2. careful study; experimentation
3. doglike animals that travel in packs
4. to live in a place
5. a type of animal that has large front teeth used for gnawing; the group includes mice, rats, squirrels, and beavers

Math: Angles

Write the word from the box that matches each clue.

| measures | rays | degrees | vertex | obtuse |

6. These are units of distance used to measure angles.
7. This angle measures greater than ninety degrees.
8. They are lines that radiate from a center.
9. It is the point where the two sides of an angle meet.
10. These are standards for determining weight, length, or other dimensions.

Apply the Spelling Strategy

Circle the letter that forms the plural in four of the Content Words you wrote.

Word Study

Words From Other Languages

This Strategy Word names small finger cymbals. It comes from a Spanish word, **castañeta**. Write the word.

Science: Research

1. _____
2. _____
3. _____
4. _____
5. _____

Math: Angles

6. _____
7. _____
8. _____
9. _____
10. _____

Words From Other Languages

1. _____

Spelling and Thinking

bi- or tri-

1. _____
2. _____
3. _____
4. _____
5. _____
6. _____
7. _____
8. _____

mid- or semi-

9. _____
10. _____
11. _____
12. _____
13. _____
14. _____
15. _____
16. _____
17. _____
18. _____
19. _____
20. _____

READ THE SPELLING WORDS

1.	bimonthly	*bimonthly*	I write a **bimonthly** bulletin.
2.	midday	*midday*	By **midday,** the bud had opened.
3.	semicircle	*semicircle*	We sat in a **semicircle**.
4.	trisect	*trisect*	I **trisect** the angle into parts.
5.	bicycle	*bicycle*	Miguel's **bicycle** is metallic red.
6.	midterm	*midterm*	Gina passed her **midterm** exam.
7.	semifinal	*semifinal*	Amir won the **semifinal** meet.
8.	midair	*midair*	An eagle dived in **midair**.
9.	semiannual	*semiannual*	It's a **semiannual** sale!
10.	midafternoon	*midafternoon*	The rain came in **midafternoon**.
11.	semicolon	*semicolon*	A **semicolon** connects sentences.
12.	bisect	*bisect*	To **bisect** the circle, draw a line.
13.	tricycle	*tricycle*	The **tricycle** was his favorite gift.
14.	midnight	*midnight*	At **midnight,** a new year begins.
15.	bifocals	*bifocals*	She stared over her **bifocals**.
16.	semisweet	*semisweet*	Taste this **semisweet** chocolate.
17.	triangle	*triangle*	The flag is folded into a **triangle**.
18.	biweekly	*biweekly*	He does gymnastics **biweekly**.
19.	midland	*midland*	The **midland** has no seashore.
20.	semiformal	*semiformal*	Her **semiformal** dress is velvet.

SORT THE SPELLING WORDS

1.–8. Write the spelling words that begin with the prefix **bi-** or **tri-**. Circle the prefixes.

9.–20. Write the spelling words that begin with the prefix **mid-** or **semi-**. Circle the prefixes.

REMEMBER THE SPELLING STRATEGY

Remember that the prefixes **bi-, mid-, semi-,** and **tri-** relate to number or position; **bi-** means "two"; **tri-** means "three"; **semi-** means "half" or "partly"; and **mid-** means "middle."

Spelling and Vocabulary

Word Structure

Add a prefix to each word below to make a spelling word.

1. angle
2. night
3. term
4. monthly
5. afternoon
6.–7. cycle
8. focals

Word Meanings

Write the spelling word that best replaces each underlined word or phrase.

9. I will divide into two equal parts the pie.

10. We like to have our noon meal outdoors.

11. The photo caught Jean in a point above solid ground as he jumped for the ball.

12. I enjoy art class twice a week with Ms. Plum.

13. Arthur lives in the center of the state and has never seen the ocean.

14. Mr. Cohen showed us how to use lines to divide into three parts a right angle.

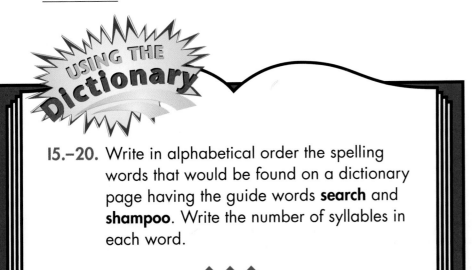

USING THE Dictionary

15.–20. Write in alphabetical order the spelling words that would be found on a dictionary page having the guide words **search** and **shampoo**. Write the number of syllables in each word.

◆ ◆ ◆

Dictionary Check Look in your **Spelling Dictionary** to see if you placed the words in the correct order.

Word Structure
1. ___
2. ___
3. ___
4. ___
5. ___
6. ___
7. ___
8. ___

Word Meanings
9. ___
10. ___
11. ___
12. ___
13. ___
14. ___

Using the Dictionary
15. ___
16. ___
17. ___
18. ___
19. ___
20. ___

Spelling and Reading

bimonthly	midday	semicircle	trisect	bicycle
midterm	semifinal	midair	semiannual	midafternoon
semicolon	bisect	tricycle	midnight	bifocals
semisweet	triangle	biweekly	midland	semiformal

Complete the Sentences

1. ___
2. ___
3. ___
4. ___
5. ___
6. ___
7. ___
8. ___
9. ___

Match the Clues

10. ___
11. ___
12. ___
13. ___
14. ___
15. ___
16. ___
17. ___
18. ___
19. ___
20. ___

Complete the Sentences Write the spelling words to complete these sentences.

1. The passenger quietly switched to the empty seat when the airplane was in ___.
2. One of the two tires on my ___ was mysteriously flattened.
3. He could not find his ___, so he could not read the note.
4. At ___, Mr. Alvarez saw a red full moon.
5. Ms. Green makes ___ trips, on New Year's Day and the Fourth of July, to some unknown place.
6. When we returned to school from our ___ vacation, some books were missing.
7. At exactly ___, the sun was bright and cast no shadow.
8. A ___ was drawn on the sidewalk with an **X** marked at each of the three angles.
9. We were dismissed from school that day in ___, an hour earlier than usual.

Match the Clues Write a spelling word to match each clue.

10. This means "every two weeks."
11. This means "every two months."
12. This punctuation mark connects two sentences.
13. This means "somewhat formal."
14. This means "partially sweet."
15. This means "half a circle."
16. You do this if you split a figure three ways.
17. It has three wheels.
18. This contest comes before the final competition.
19. When you do this, you divide something in two.
20. If you live in the middle of a region, you live here.

Spelling and Writing

Proofread a Paragraph

Six words are not spelled correctly in this paragraph. Write the words correctly.

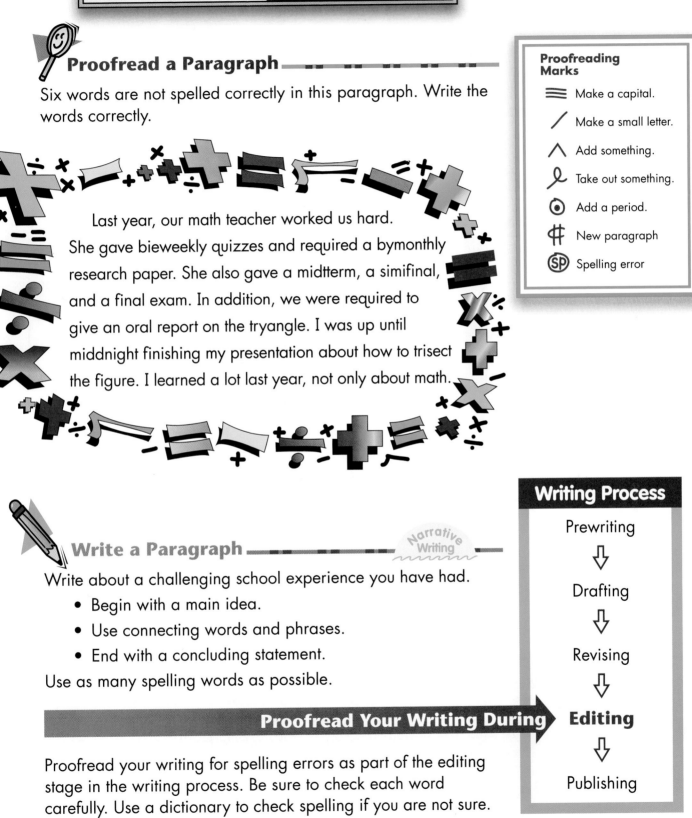

Last year, our math teacher worked us hard. She gave bieweekly quizzes and required a bymonthly research paper. She also gave a midtterm, a simifinal, and a final exam. In addition, we were required to give an oral report on the tryangle. I was up until middnight finishing my presentation about how to trisect the figure. I learned a lot last year, not only about math.

Proofreading Marks

≡ Make a capital.

/ Make a small letter.

∧ Add something.

℘ Take out something.

⊙ Add a period.

⌗ New paragraph

(SP) Spelling error

Write a Paragraph — Narrative Writing

Write about a challenging school experience you have had.

- Begin with a main idea.
- Use connecting words and phrases.
- End with a concluding statement.

Use as many spelling words as possible.

Proofread Your Writing During → Editing

Proofread your writing for spelling errors as part of the editing stage in the writing process. Be sure to check each word carefully. Use a dictionary to check spelling if you are not sure.

Writing Process

Prewriting

⇩

Drafting

⇩

Revising

⇩

Editing

⇩

Publishing

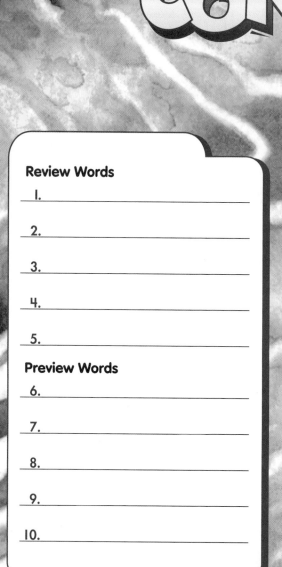

Review Words

1. _____
2. _____
3. _____
4. _____
5. _____

Preview Words

6. _____
7. _____
8. _____
9. _____
10. _____

Unit 27 enrichment

VOCABULARY CONNECTIONS

Strategy Words

Review Words: Prefixes bi-, mid-, semi-, tri-

Write the word that matches each clue. You will use one word from the box and write four new words by adding the prefix **bi-, mid-,** or **semi-** to the four other words.

| trio | buoyant | glare | April | level |

1. It could include April 14, 15, and 16. (**Hint:** Because **April** is a proper noun, you need to put a hyphen between the prefix and the noun.)
2. It means "floats under some conditions."
3. It can mean "having two floors."
4. It means "a somewhat strong light."
5. This word does not take a prefix. The Latin root meaning "three" is already part of the word.

Preview Words: Prefixes bi-, mid-, semi-, tri-

Write the word from the box to complete each sentence.

| bilingual | midsummer | midway | trilogy | tripod |

6. In our _____ family, we speak Spanish and English.
7. Balancing the camera on the _____, Mr. Pappas took a picture of the whole family.
8. We set the marker _____ on the rope and began the tug-of-war contest.
9. Nathan has read all three books in the _____.
10. We usually go on a _____ camping trip.

Content Words

Math: Angles

Write the words from the box that complete the paragraph.

edges	rectangular	faces	triangular	prism

This clear, shiny __1.__ has five flat __2.__ or sides. The three long __3.__ faces are joined by two short __4.__ bases. The __5.__ are sharp.

Math: Geometry

Write the word from the box that completes each sentence.

diagonal	octagon	hexagon	pentagon	perimeter

6. Shape **a** is a _____.
7. The distance around a polygon is called its _____.
8. Shape **b** is an _____.
9. Line **c** is the _____ of the rectangle.
10. Shape **d** is a _____.

Apply the Spelling Strategy

Circle the prefix that means "three" in one of the Content Words you wrote.

Word Study

Word Roots

The root **logy** comes from an old Greek word, **logos,** which meant "story." An **anthology** is a collection of stories or poems. Write the Strategy Word that has this root and means "a group of three related stories or books."

Math: Angles

1. _____
2. _____
3. _____
4. _____
5. _____

Math: Geometry

6. _____
7. _____
8. _____
9. _____
10. _____

Word Roots

1. _____

Spelling and Thinking

READ THE SPELLING WORDS

1.	generous	*generous*	Mark made **generous** contributions.
2.	message	*message*	She left a **message** for us.
3.	stranger	*stranger*	A **stranger** walked into the café.
4.	grudge	*grudge*	Martha is not holding a **grudge**.
5.	margin	*margin*	Leave a **margin** of at least an inch.
6.	energy	*energy*	Exercise gives you more **energy**.
7.	oxygen	*oxygen*	We need to breathe nitrogen and **oxygen**.
8.	genius	*genius*	Albert Einstein was a **genius**.
9.	college	*college*	We have a small **college** in our town.
10.	lodge	*lodge*	The **lodge** is halfway up the mountain.
11.	imagine	*imagine*	I cannot **imagine** you with gray hair.
12.	stingy	*stingy*	Scrooge was known as a **stingy** man.
13.	apology	*apology*	The speaker made a public **apology**.
14.	gentleman	*gentleman*	Above all, a **gentleman** must be kind.
15.	arrange	*arrange*	Can you **arrange** a special meeting?
16.	pledge	*pledge*	The brothers made a **pledge** of loyalty.
17.	region	*region*	Water is scarce in that **region**.
18.	damage	*damage*	There was little **damage** to the car.
19.	ledger	*ledger*	A bookkeeper keeps an accurate **ledger**.
20.	average	*average*	He is about **average** in height.

SORT THE SPELLING WORDS

1.–4. Write the words that spell the /j/ sound **dge**.

5.–14. Write the words that spell the /j/ sound **g** followed by **e**.

15.–20. Write the words that spell the /j/ sound **g** followed by **i** or **y**.

REMEMBER THE SPELLING STRATEGY

Remember that the /j/ sound can be spelled in different ways: **dge** in **lodge**, **g** followed by **e** in **damage**, **g** followed by **i** in **imagine**, and **g** followed by **y** in **energy**.

dge

1. ___
2. ___
3. ___
4. ___

g followed by e

5. ___
6. ___
7. ___
8. ___
9. ___
10. ___
11. ___
12. ___
13. ___
14. ___

g followed by i or y

15. ___
16. ___
17. ___
18. ___
19. ___
20. ___

Spelling and Vocabulary

Word Meanings

Write the spelling word that matches each clue.

1. This is the empty border around the writing on a page.
2. Do this if you want to invent something.
3. When you schedule and plan an event, you do this.
4. This describes someone who gives to benefit others.
5. This is someone who is extremely intelligent.
6. This is lasting anger about an injury suffered.
7. This is a geographical area.

Word Clues

Write a spelling word for each of these clues.

8. delivered by a messenger
9. after high school
10. breakage
11. promise

12. strength and vigor
13. opposite of generous
14. saying you are sorry

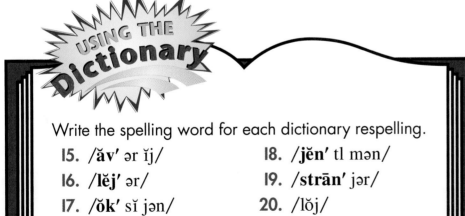

USING THE Dictionary

Write the spelling word for each dictionary respelling.

15. /ăv′ ər ĭj/
16. /lĕj′ ər/
17. /ŏk′ sĭ jən/

18. /jĕn′ tl mən/
19. /strān′ jər/
20. /lŏj/

◆ ◆ ◆

Dictionary Check Look in your **Spelling Dictionary** to match the respellings to spelling words.

Word Meanings
1. _____
2. _____
3. _____
4. _____
5. _____
6. _____
7. _____

Word Clues
8. _____
9. _____
10. _____
11. _____
12. _____
13. _____
14. _____

Using the Dictionary
15. _____
16. _____
17. _____
18. _____
19. _____
20. _____

generous	message	stranger	grudge	margin
energy	oxygen	genius	college	lodge
imagine	stingy	apology	gentleman	arrange
pledge	region	damage	ledger	average

Solve the Analogies

Solve the Analogies Write the spelling word that completes each analogy.

1. **Great** is to **good** as **excellent** is to _____.
2. **Girl** is to **lady** as **boy** is to _____.
3. **Paint** is to **canvas** as **pencil** is to _____.
4. **Comedian** is to **funny** as **miser** is to _____.
5. **Dull** is to **boring** as **unselfish** is to _____.
6. **Cottage** is to **house** as **cabin** is to _____.

Complete the Sentences

Complete the Sentences Write the spelling words that complete each sentence.

7.–8. June tried to _____ the name and occupation of the _____ on the train.

9.–10. The young boy made a _____ to his mother that he would go to _____ to study.

11.–12. Until I offered him an _____, Jamie held a _____ against me.

13.–14. Our bodies require _____ for life and good nutrition for _____.

15.–16. We are going to this eastern _____, which you see near the right _____ of the map.

17.–18. Generally, it would be better not to ignore a _____ from a scientific _____.

19.–20. If we _____ the furniture carefully, there will be no _____ to it on the trip.

Solve the Analogies
1.
2.
3.
4.
5.
6.

Complete the Sentences
7.
8.
9.
10.
11.
12.
13.
14.
15.
16.
17.
18.
19.
20.

Spelling and Writing

Proofread a Letter

Six words are not spelled correctly in this letter. Write the words correctly.

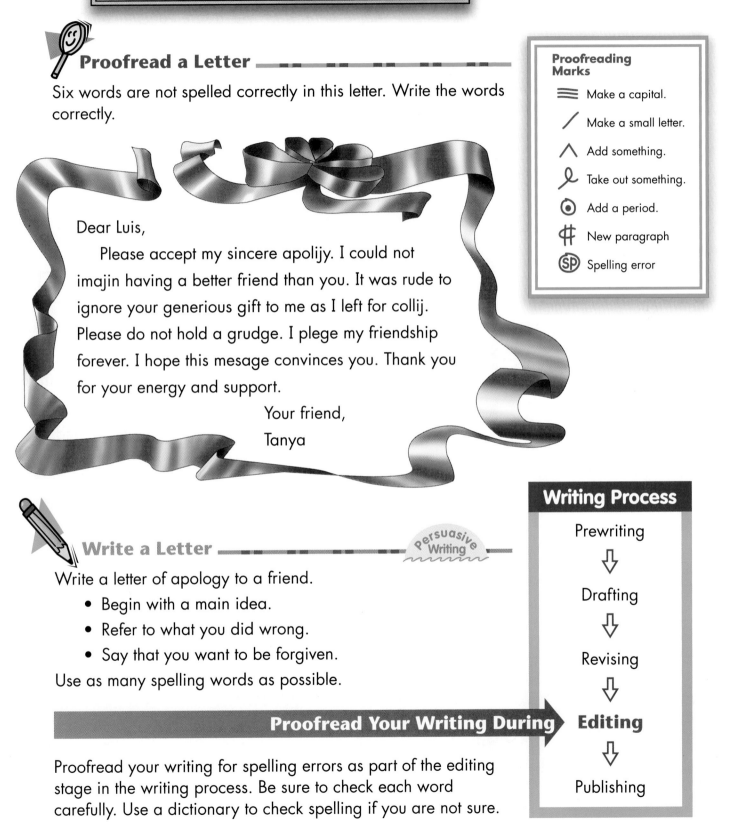

Dear Luis,

Please accept my sincere apolijy. I could not imajin having a better friend than you. It was rude to ignore your generious gift to me as I left for collij. Please do not hold a grudge. I plege my friendship forever. I hope this mesage convinces you. Thank you for your energy and support.

Your friend,

Tanya

Proofreading Marks

≡ Make a capital.

/ Make a small letter.

∧ Add something.

ℓ Take out something.

⊙ Add a period.

New paragraph

SP Spelling error

Write a Letter

Persuasive Writing

Write a letter of apology to a friend.

- Begin with a main idea.
- Refer to what you did wrong.
- Say that you want to be forgiven.

Use as many spelling words as possible.

Writing Process

Prewriting

⇩

Drafting

⇩

Revising

⇩

Editing

⇩

Publishing

Proofread Your Writing During → Editing

Proofread your writing for spelling errors as part of the editing stage in the writing process. Be sure to check each word carefully. Use a dictionary to check spelling if you are not sure.

VOCABULARY CONNECTIONS

►Strategy Words◄

Review Words
1. _____
2. _____
3. _____
4. _____
5. _____

Preview Words
6. _____
7. _____
8. _____
9. _____
10. _____

Review Words: Consonant Sound /j/

Write words from the box to complete the paragraph.

engine	gem	gentle	hedge	village

As we drove out of the small New England __1.__, the car __2.__ sputtered. Our __3.__, relaxed mood turned to annoyance. Sean got out of the car and pulled his tools from the trunk. We got out, too, and sat in the shade of a tall __4.__. Suddenly, I spotted something shiny lying on the ground. I yelped, "I have found a __5.__!"

Preview Words: Consonant Sound /j/

Write the word from the box that completes each sentence.

agent	geometry	knowledge	imaginary	smudge

6. Maureen plays a secret _____ in the school play.
7. Janine's _____ of fabrics makes her an excellent clothing shopper.
8. Sara whisked her _____ cape across her shoulders and pranced out of the room.
9. You may need some soap to get the _____ off your collar.
10. Matt is interested in building, so he enjoys _____.

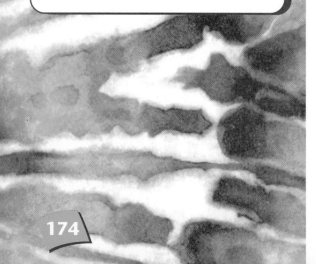

Content Words

Math: Decimals

Write the words from the box that complete the sentences.

billion	expanded	digit	place value	standard

1. (5 – 1,000,000,000) + 1 is an _____ numeral.
2. 5,000,000,001 is a _____ numeral.
3.–5. In the number 5,000,000,001, the _____ 5 has a _____ of five _____.

Social Studies: Elections

Write words from the box to complete the paragraph.

ballots	ratify	legislate	veto	municipal

The mayor is the head of a city or __6.__ government. Voters cast their __7.__ for the person best suited for the job. In some cities, it is the job of the city council to __8.__, or create new laws, for that city. The mayor has the power to reject, or __9.__, those laws. If the mayor approves of a law, the city council can then __10.__, or adopt, the new law.

Apply the Spelling Strategy

Circle the letters that combine to spell the /**j**/ sound in two of the Content Words you wrote.

Word Study

Words in Context

Write the one Strategy Word that can complete all of the following phrases:

- real estate _____
- chemical _____
- double _____

Math: Decimals

1. _____
2. _____
3. _____
4. _____
5. _____

Social Studies: Elections

6. _____
7. _____
8. _____
9. _____
10. _____

Words in Context

1. _____

-ty or -ity

1. _____
2. _____
3. _____
4. _____
5. _____
6. _____
7. _____
8. _____
9. _____

-ness, -ment, or -ive

10. _____
11. _____
12. _____
13. _____
14. _____
15. _____
16. _____
17. _____
18. _____
19. _____
20. _____

Spelling and Thinking

READ THE SPELLING WORDS

1.	vanity	*vanity*	The actress displays **vanity**.
2.	humanity	*humanity*	A doctor can help **humanity**.
3.	sickness	*sickness*	The baby's **sickness** lasted a week.
4.	amusement	*amusement*	A playground provides **amusement**.
5.	detective	*detective*	A **detective** looks for evidence.
6.	loyalty	*loyalty*	Her **loyalty** is to her family.
7.	majority	*majority*	The **majority** of us wanted a party.
8.	gentleness	*gentleness*	She admires the doe's **gentleness**.
9.	argument	*argument*	The **argument** is about politics.
10.	humidity	*humidity*	This **humidity** curls my hair.
11.	ability	*ability*	Tim's singing **ability** is exceptional.
12.	blindness	*blindness*	Saul's **blindness** began at birth.
13.	activity	*activity*	An art **activity** would be fun.
14.	relative	*relative*	I have a **relative** who is famous.
15.	employment	*employment*	Rosa needs summer **employment**.
16.	specialty	*specialty*	Angel food cake is Ali's **specialty**.
17.	creativity	*creativity*	With **creativity,** we can improve it.
18.	arrangement	*arrangement*	The flower **arrangement** goes here.
19.	swiftness	*swiftness*	The cheetah is known for **swiftness**.
20.	tardiness	*tardiness*	This note will explain my **tardiness**.

SORT THE SPELLING WORDS

1.–9. Write the spelling words that end with the suffix **-ty** or **-ity**. Circle each suffix.

10.–20. Write the spelling words that end with the suffix **-ness, -ment,** or **-ive**. Circle each suffix.

REMEMBER THE SPELLING STRATEGY

Remember that the suffixes **-ty, -ity, -ness, -ment,** and **-ive** can be added to base words to form nouns.

Spelling and Vocabulary

Word Structure

Write the spelling word that goes with each base word.

1. human
2. relate
3. detect
4. amuse
5. sick
6. special

Word Meanings

Write the spelling word that matches each clue.

7. state of being active
8. action or process of being arranged
9. action or process of being employed
10. quality of being gentle
11. state of being blind
12. quality of being creative
13. state of being tardy
14. state of being vain
15. quality of being able

USING THE Thesaurus

Write the spelling word that is an antonym for each word. To check your answers, look up each spelling word (or base word) in your **Writing Thesaurus**.

16. agreement
17. dryness
18. faithlessness
19. minority
20. slowness

Word Structure
1.
2.
3.
4.
5.
6.
Word Meanings
7.
8.
9.
10.
11.
12.
13.
14.
15.
Using the Thesaurus
16.
17.
18.
19.
20.

vanity	humanity	sickness	amusement
detective	loyalty	majority	gentleness
argument	humidity	ability	blindness
activity	relative	employment	specialty
creativity	arrangement	swiftness	tardiness

Solve the Analogies

1.
2.
3.
4.

Complete the Paragraph

5.
6.
7.
8.
9.
10.
11.
12.
13.
14.

Complete the Sentences

15.
16.
17.
18.
19.
20.

Solve the Analogies   Write the spelling word that completes each analogy.

1. **Local** is to **locality** as **humid** is to _____.
2. **Sad** is to **sadness** as **tardy** is to _____.
3. **Thread** is to **tailor** as **clue** is to _____.
4. **Ill** is to **illness** as **amuse** is to _____.

Complete the Paragraph   Write the spelling words that complete the paragraph.

A childhood __5.__ left Helen Keller blind and deaf. Her teacher, Anne Sullivan, broke through the child's anger with patience and __6.__. Sullivan's __7.__ always kept her at Helen's side. Sullivan used imagination and __8.__ to teach Helen, and the child began to show great __9.__ in school. She mastered her subjects with amazing __10.__. As an adult, Helen Keller found __11.__ as an author and lecturer. Her life was filled with joy and __12.__. Helen Keller overcame more hardships than the __13.__ of people. She became an inspiration to all __14.__.

Complete the Sentences   Write the spelling word that completes each sentence.

15. That is a beautiful _____ of flowers.
16. In spite of his _____, he traveled everywhere.
17. The dictionary will settle this _____ about words!
18. Jess has a _____ who lives in India.
19. Her _____ spoiled the effect of her beauty.
20. This artist's _____ is portraits of children.

Spelling and Writing

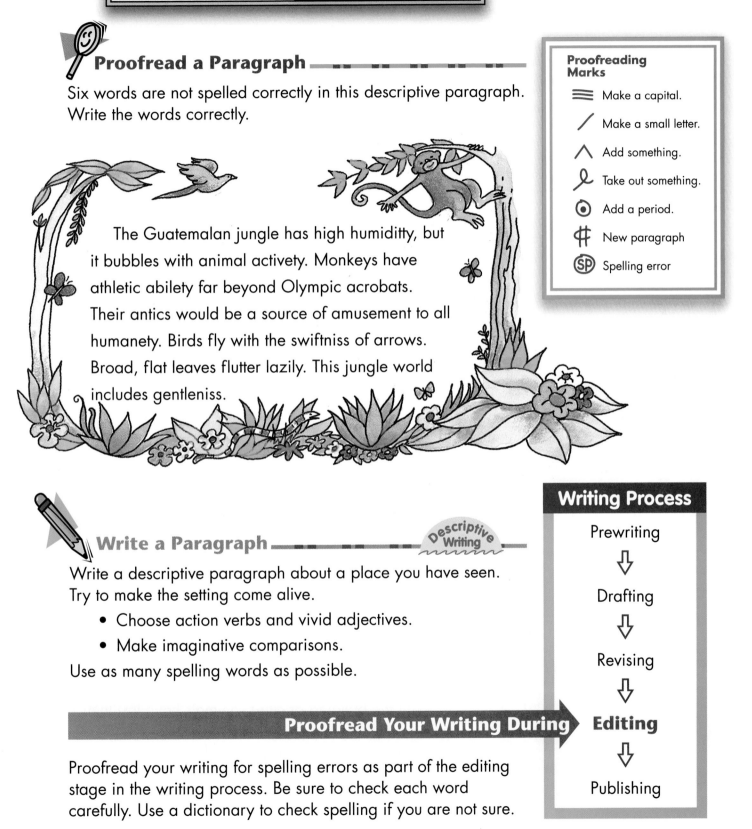

Proofread a Paragraph

Six words are not spelled correctly in this descriptive paragraph. Write the words correctly.

The Guatemalan jungle has high humiditty, but it bubbles with animal activety. Monkeys have athletic abilety far beyond Olympic acrobats. Their antics would be a source of amusement to all humanety. Birds fly with the swiftniss of arrows. Broad, flat leaves flutter lazily. This jungle world includes gentleniss.

Proofreading Marks

≡ Make a capital.
/ Make a small letter.
∧ Add something.
℮ Take out something.
⊙ Add a period.
New paragraph
(SP) Spelling error

Write a Paragraph — *Descriptive Writing*

Write a descriptive paragraph about a place you have seen. Try to make the setting come alive.

- Choose action verbs and vivid adjectives.
- Make imaginative comparisons.

Use as many spelling words as possible.

Writing Process

Prewriting
⇩
Drafting
⇩
Revising
⇩
Proofread Your Writing During ▶ Editing
⇩
Publishing

Proofread your writing for spelling errors as part of the editing stage in the writing process. Be sure to check each word carefully. Use a dictionary to check spelling if you are not sure.

VOCABULARY CONNECTIONS

Strategy Words

Review Words

1. _____
2. _____
3. _____
4. _____
5. _____

Preview Words

6. _____
7. _____
8. _____
9. _____
10. _____

Review Words:
Suffixes -ty, -ity, -ness, -ment, -ive

Write the word from the box that matches each clue.

agreement	boldness	fitness	sadness	treatment

1. If you have this, you are not meek.
2. One example would be ice for a bruise.
3. Exercise contributes to this.
4. This occurs when people make a decision together.
5. You might feel this if your friend moved away.

Preview Words:
Suffixes -ty, -ity, -ness, -ment, -ive

Write the word from the box that best replaces the underlined word or words.

assignment	authority	development
document	opportunity	

6. The Declaration of Independence is a <u>written statement</u> prepared by American leaders.
7. With the <u>building</u> of cities, animals have lost their homes.
8. Karla has the <u>chance</u> to work for a veterinarian.
9. I will complete this <u>job</u> before vacation.
10. Juan is respectful of his father's <u>control</u>.

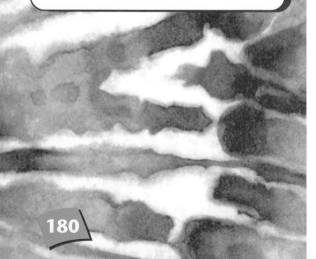

Content Words

Science: Electricity

Write the word from the box that matches each definition.
One letter is given.

ampere	volt	electricity	watt	kilowatt

1. unit measuring electric power: __ __ t __
2. unit measuring electric current moving in one direction:
   a __ __ __ __ __
3. the movement of electric current to create power:
   __ __ __ __ __ __ __ __ __ __ y
4. unit measuring the attraction of positive and negative
   charges: __ o __ __
5. 1000 watts: __ i __ __ __ __ __ __

Social Studies: Pioneers

Write the words from the box that complete the paragraph.

equip	journey	fort	stockade	guide

When a group of pioneers planned a __6.__ to the West, they
would __7.__ themselves with wagons and supplies. Then they
would find a __8.__ to lead them. This person would know where
to find each fenced-in area, or __9.__. Sometimes the pioneers
would stay inside a cavalry __10.__ for protection.

Apply the Spelling Strategy

Circle the suffix **-ity** in one of the Content Words you wrote.

Word Study

Eponyms

An **eponym** is a word that comes from someone's name. The
volt was named after **Alessandro Volta,** a pioneer in electricity.
Write the Content Word that came from the name of another
scientist, **James Watt.**

Science: Electricity

1. _____
2. _____
3. _____
4. _____
5. _____

Social Studies: Pioneers

6. _____
7. _____
8. _____
9. _____
10. _____

Eponyms

1. _____

Unit 25
1.
2.
3.
4.

Unit 26
5.
6.
7.
8.

Unit 27
9.
10.
11.
12.

Unit 28
13.
14.
15.
16.

Unit 29
17.
18.
19.
20.

Each Assessment Word in the box fits one of the spelling strategies you have studied over the past five weeks. Read the spelling strategies. Then write each Assessment Word under the unit number it fits.

Unit 25

1.–4. The suffixes **-or, -er,** and **-ist** mean "one who." An **editor** is "one who edits." A **pitcher** is "one who pitches." A **tourist** is "one who tours."

Unit 26

5.–8. Plural nouns name more than one person, place, or thing. Plurals are formed in various ways: by adding **-s** (**envelopes**); by adding **-es** (**latches**); or by changing final **y** to **i** and adding **-es** (**diaries**). Some plurals are exceptions.

Unit 27

9.–12. The prefixes **bi-, mid-, semi-,** and **tri-** relate to number or position: **bi-** means "two"; **tri-** means "three"; **semi-** means "half" or "partly"; and **mid-** means "middle."

Unit 28

13.–16. The /j/ sound can be spelled in different ways: **dge** in **lodge**, **g** followed by **e** in **damage**, **g** followed by **i** in **imagine**, and **g** followed by **y** in **energy**.

Unit 29

17.–20. The suffixes **-ty, -ity, -ness, -ment,** and **-ive** can be added to base words to form nouns.

captive
register
semidarkness
ourselves
organist
density
wedge
biplane
radios
drummer
counselor
batteries
triweekly
gently
loneliness
juggler
ranches
midstream
ginger
installment

Review

Unit 25: Suffixes -or, -er, -ist

creditor	director	passenger	scientist	actor
professor	editor	artist	tourist	pitcher

Write a spelling word to replace the underlined words.

1. We paid the <u>one who gives us credit</u> on time.
2. I was a <u>person who rides</u> on the early train.
3. Mr. Kaul is a mathematics <u>person who teaches</u>.
4. This <u>person who paints</u> has a great reputation.
5. Have you written a letter to the newspaper <u>person who edits</u>?
6. A <u>person trained in science</u> is working on a cure.
7. Has the <u>one who directs</u> assigned parts yet?
8. The <u>one who pitches</u> signaled the catcher.
9. I am a frequent <u>person who tours</u> in the summer.
10. The <u>one who acts</u> began the play by giving a dramatic opening speech.

Review

Unit 26: Plurals

skis	beliefs	envelopes	heroes	countries
soldiers	chiefs	pianos	valleys	characters

Write a spelling word by making each word plural.

11. valley
12. character
13. piano
14. hero
15. country
16. chief
17. envelope
18. ski
19. belief
20. soldier

Unit 25

1. _____
2. _____
3. _____
4. _____
5. _____
6. _____
7. _____
8. _____
9. _____
10. _____

Unit 26

11. _____
12. _____
13. _____
14. _____
15. _____
16. _____
17. _____
18. _____
19. _____
20. _____

Review Unit 27: Prefixes bi-, mid-, semi-, tri-

| midday | bicycle | triangle | semicircle | midair |
| semisweet | biweekly | midnight | tricycle | midland |

Write a spelling word for each clue.

1. the middle of the day
2. the middle section of land
3. two-wheeler
4. three-wheeler
5. middle of the night
6. every two weeks
7. figure with three angles
8. half a circle
9. only partly sweet
10. the middle of the air

Review Unit 28: Consonant Sound /j/

| margin | average | apology | ledger | energy |
| imagine | message | stranger | college | arrange |

Find the misspelled word. Write it correctly.

11. Can you arange to be here by noon?
12. My brother goes to colledge in Ohio.
13. If anyone calls for me, please take a mesage.
14. We keep a record of sales in this lejer.
15. Regular exercise gives me enerjy.
16. The teacher wrote notes in the margine.
17. What is the averedge age of the class?

Write a spelling word for each clue.

18. It has four syllables. Two syllables have just one letter.
19. It has three syllables. The first and last syllables have a **short i** sound.
20. It begins with three consonants. It can be a noun or an adjective.

Unit 29: Suffixes -ty, -ity, -ness, -ment, -ive

relative	specialty	argument	arrangement	detective
ability	sickness	amusement	vanity	activity

Change these verbs into nouns by adding a suffix.

1. argue
2. arrange
3. detect

4. amuse
5. relate

Change these adjectives into nouns by adding a suffix.

6. vain
7. special
8. active

9. able
10. sick

Unit 29

1. _____
2. _____
3. _____
4. _____
5. _____
6. _____
7. _____
8. _____
9. _____
10. _____

GAME — Spelling Study Strategy

Circle Dot

Practicing your spelling words can be fun if you make it into a game. Here's an idea you can try with a friend.

1. Find a partner to trade spelling lists with. Be sure that you both can read all the words on your lists.

2. Ask your partner to read the first word on your list. Write the word on a piece of scrap paper.

3. Now ask your partner to spell that word out loud—one letter at a time.

4. As your partner says each letter, draw a dot under every correct letter. If you wrote a letter that is not correct, or if you left out a letter, draw a little circle. Use the circles to see the parts of the word that gave you trouble.

5. Write the word again. Check your spelling with your partner.

6. Keep going until you have tried every word on your list.

Grammar, Usage, and Mechanics

Adjectives

Adjectives describe nouns and pronouns. Some adjectives tell what kind. Others, such as **many** and **six,** tell how many. The adjectives **this, that, these,** and **those** tell which one. The articles **a, an,** and **the** are also adjectives.

> **Those four** players can ride in **the red** van.
>
> **An** artist does **remarkable** things with **a simple** brush.
>
> **The kind** gentleman brought **colorful** bicycles for **those** children.

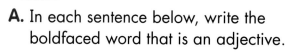

A. In each sentence below, write the boldfaced word that is an adjective.

   1. Every day, our **garden** provided us with **fresh** beans.

   2. **Don't** touch my sister's **new** luggage!

   3. Did **many** people **answer** your newspaper ad?

   4. Put your groceries **in this** bag.

   5. **Do** you read the **biweekly** newspaper?

   6. Leave a **wide** margin on your **paper**.

B. Write the word that is described by the underlined adjective.

   7. I loved those <u>silly</u> characters at the end.

   8. Put them in the <u>long</u> envelopes and mail them.

   9. Will you ride your <u>new</u> bicycle to school?

  10. Perhaps you will be a <u>famous</u> scientist some day!

  11. The <u>tired</u> detective wrote a report.

  12. The glacier carved <u>deep</u> valleys.

A.

  1.

  2.

  3.

  4.

  5.

  6.

B.

  7.

  8.

  9.

  10.

  11.

  12.

WORKSHOP

Pair Up With a Partner!

Good writers always proofread their writing for spelling errors. Here's a strategy that you can use to proofread your papers.

Pair up with a partner, instead of proofreading all alone. Ask your partner to read your work aloud slowly. Meanwhile, you look at each word as it is read. Is it spelled correctly?

This strategy really works. Hearing each word read aloud helps you focus on the word instead of the sentence. And a partner can help you fix misspellings. Try it.

Electronic Spelling

1. _____
2. _____
3. _____
4. _____
5. _____
6. _____

Graphics

Computers allow you to make attractive and colorful diagrams easily. Such diagrams can illustrate a report or story or provide useful information such as the location of fire exits.

A diagram contains both a picture or other graphic and labels. Often, you create those labels in a computer art program, which may have no spell checker. Check your labels carefully to be sure that you have spelled them correctly. They are an important part of any diagram.

Look at the diagram labels below. Which have misspelled words? Write the words correctly. Write **OK** if a label is correct.

1. chair for directer
2. pasenger cars
3. early tricycle
4. different kinds of enerjy
5. turist bureau
6. U.S. heros

Spelling and Thinking

READ THE SPELLING WORDS

1.	diamond	*diamond*	She wore a **diamond** ring.
2.	handsome	*handsome*	Morris is a **handsome** boy.
3.	truly	*truly*	Sara **truly** enjoys doing math.
4.	camera	*camera*	We will not forget the **camera**.
5.	language	*language*	His first **language** is Filipino.
6.	beautiful	*beautiful*	Look at the **beautiful** bird.
7.	government	*government*	The city **government** approved the tax.
8.	umbrella	*umbrella*	We sat under the beach **umbrella**.
9.	thorough	*thorough*	That house painter is very **thorough**.
10.	judgment	*judgment*	He always tries to use good **judgment**.
11.	separate	*separate*	I can **separate** the coins from the bills.
12.	suppose	*suppose*	Do you **suppose** they got lost?
13.	chocolate	*chocolate*	Kai had a **chocolate** birthday cake.
14.	route	*route*	This **route** goes across the river.
15.	cousin	*cousin*	My **cousin** Melvin plays basketball.
16.	sincerely	*sincerely*	I **sincerely** hope he arrives early.
17.	address	*address*	Our new **address** is 12 Spring Lane.
18.	poison	*poison*	The skull symbolizes **poison**.
19.	although	*although*	Lib is here, **although** he looks sick.
20.	skiing	*skiing*	Neesa likes cross-country **skiing**.

SORT THE SPELLING WORDS

1. Write the spelling word that has one syllable.
2.–5. Write the words that can be pronounced as two or three syllables.
6.–16. Write the words that are always two syllables.
17.–20. Write the words that are always three syllables.

REMEMBER THE SPELLING STRATEGY

Remember that it is important to know the correct spellings of words that are often misspelled.

one syllable

1. _____

two or three syllables

2. _____

3. _____

4. _____

5. _____

two syllables

6. _____

7. _____

8. _____

9. _____

10. _____

11. _____

12. _____

13. _____

14. _____

15. _____

16. _____

three syllables

17. _____

18. _____

19. _____

20. _____

Spelling and Vocabulary

Word Meanings

Write the spelling word that belongs in each group.

1. laws, taxes, politicians, _____
2. decision, evaluation, ruling, _____
3. lovely, pretty, stunning, _____
4. skating, sledding, _____
5. attractive, good-looking, _____
6. guess, presume, surmise, _____
7. path, road, way, _____
8. truly, honestly, _____

Word Structure

The consonants or the vowels are missing in the following spelling words. Write the words correctly.

9. l _ ng _ _ g _
10. p _ _ s _ n
11. u _ _ _ e _ _ a
12. a _ _ _ e _ _
13. c _ _ s _ n
14. tr _ l _

USING THE Dictionary

Write the spelling word for each dictionary respelling.

15. /ôl *thō′*/
16. /chô′ kə lĭt/
17. /sĕp′ ə rāt′/
18. /kăm′ ər ə/
19. /dī′ mənd/
20. /thûr′ ō/

♦ ♦ ♦

Dictionary Check Be sure to check the respellings in your **Spelling Dictionary**.

Word Meanings

1. _____
2. _____
3. _____
4. _____
5. _____
6. _____
7. _____
8. _____

Word Structure

9. _____
10. _____
11. _____
12. _____
13. _____
14. _____

Using the Dictionary

15. _____
16. _____
17. _____
18. _____
19. _____
20. _____

diamond	handsome	truly	camera	language
beautiful	government	umbrella	thorough	judgment
separate	suppose	chocolate	route	cousin
sincerely	address	poison	although	skiing

Complete the Sentences
1.
2.
3.
4.
5.
6.
7.
8.
9.
10.

Use the Clues
11.
12.
13.
14.
15.
16.
17.
18.
19.
20.

Complete the Sentences Write the spelling word that completes each sentence.

1. A _____ rainbow appeared after the storm.
2. After the marathon, I _____ you were tired.
3. He is so _____, he will wash every window.
4. A _____ forms from a combination of coal, pressure, and a long period of time.
5. This _____ will take you to San Antonio.
6. An _____ can turn inside out in a high wind.
7. Some islanders speak a _____ unique to them.
8. Marcia likes _____ with nuts.
9. I have a first _____ who lives in Sicily.
10. Can you _____ the yolk from the white of the egg?

Use the Clues Write the spelling word that matches each clue.

11. It contains two smaller words and means "pleasing in appearance."
12. Ours has three branches: a president, a congress, and a supreme court.
13. One kind makes videos; another, snapshots.
14. This sport can be done on snow or on water.
15. Making a good one requires careful thinking.
16. This includes a number, a street name, a city, a state, and a ZIP code.
17. If you consume this, you become very ill.
18. This means "even though."
19. This means "with sincerity."
20. This means "really" or "truthfully."

Spelling and Writing

Proofread a Paragraph

Six words are not spelled correctly in this paragraph. Write the words correctly.

The snow-capped mountain shone like a dimond in the dawn light. We looked forward to skiying down its powdery slopes someday. The sightseeing roote took us to a rest stop with a beautiful view. We took some pictures with my new camura. By then it had started to rain. No one had an ombrella, so we went inside and drank hot choclit until the shower was over.

Proofreading Marks

≡	Make a capital.
/	Make a small letter.
∧	Add something.
ℓ	Take out something.
⊙	Add a period.
⌗	New paragraph
⑤⑭	Spelling error

Write a Paragraph

Expository Writing

Write a paragraph about a problem or conflict you solved.

- Begin with a strong image.
- Use words that indicate the order of events.
- Explain how you solved the problem or conflict.

Use as many spelling words as you can.

Proofread Your Writing During ➤

Writing Process

Prewriting
⬇
Drafting
⬇
Revising
⬇
Editing
⬇
Publishing

Proofread your writing for spelling errors as part of the editing stage in the writing process. Be sure to check each word carefully. Use a dictionary to check spelling if you are not sure.

VOCABULARY CONNECTIONS

Strategy Words

Review Words: Words Writers Use

Write the word from the box that best replaces the underlined word or words.

alive	everyday	enough	surprise	trouble

1. Walking after dinner is part of our <u>daily</u> routine.
2. Do you have <u>a satisfactory supply of</u> pencils?
3. We had <u>difficulty</u> opening that new jar of spaghetti sauce.
4. The sudden snowstorm was a <u>shock</u> to everyone in our town.
5. The bored children came <u>to life</u> when the puppet act began.

Preview Words: Words Writers Use

Write words from the box to complete the sentences.

beyond	all right	favorite	finally	information

6. I have the _____ I need to make a decision.
7. Marny _____ finished choosing a gift.
8. Pluto lies _____ the other eight planets.
9. Zach's _____ color is yellow.
10. It will be _____ for you to borrow that book, even though I haven't read it yet.

Review Words
1. _____
2. _____
3. _____
4. _____
5. _____

Preview Words
6. _____
7. _____
8. _____
9. _____
10. _____

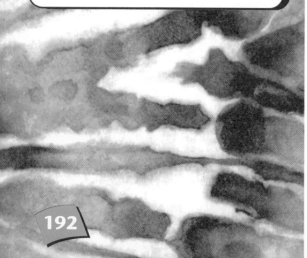

Content Words

Science: Animals

Write words from the box to complete the paragraph.

amphibian	**salamander**	**dolphin**
	vertebrate	**mammal**

Every member of the ___1.___ and the ___2.___ class is a
___3.___. An example of the warm-blooded class is the ___4.___.
An example of the cold-blooded class is the ___5.___.

Fine Arts: Music

Write words from the box to complete the paragraph.

alto	**sections**	**soprano**	**key**	**woodwind**

The community chamber orchestra has been rehearsing for
its concert. The orchestra is made up of three ___6.___: brass,
string, and ___7.___. This year's concert features a trio written
in the ___8.___ of A major from Mozart's opera, *The Magic Flute*.
The trio is sung by three boys. One sings ___9.___, another sings
mezzo-soprano, and the third sings ___10.___.

Apply the Spelling Strategy

Circle the consonant digraph in two of the Content Words
you wrote. Draw a box around the Content Words you wrote
in which a /**k**/ sound is spelled **c** or **k**.

Word Study

Compound Words

A **compound word** is made of two or more smaller words.
Compound words can be open, as in **peanut butter,** or closed,
as in **homework**. Write the Strategy Word that is an open
compound.

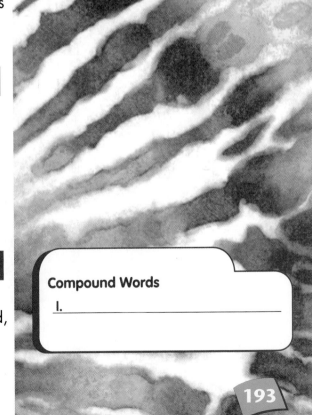

Science: Animals

1. _____
2. _____
3. _____
4. _____
5. _____

Fine Arts: Music

6. _____
7. _____
8. _____
9. _____
10. _____

Compound Words

1. _____

Spelling ^{and} Thinking

-ous
1. _____
2. _____
3. _____
4. _____
5. _____
6. _____
7. _____
8. _____

-ish
9. _____
10. _____
11. _____
12. _____
13. _____

-ant
14. _____
15. _____
16. _____

-ic
17. _____
18. _____
19. _____
20. _____

READ THE SPELLING WORDS

1. childish	*childish*	His **childish** actions made us laugh.
2. joyous	*joyous*	Singing can be a **joyous** experience.
3. energetic	*energetic*	Hayley is an active, **energetic** girl.
4. bluish	*bluish*	My lips turned **bluish** in the icy sea.
5. pleasant	*pleasant*	A springtime stroll is **pleasant**.
6. basic	*basic*	We will start with **basic** algebra.
7. humorous	*humorous*	The **humorous** book made me laugh.
8. stylish	*stylish*	That hat was **stylish** in the Fifties.
9. cubic	*cubic*	The jar's volume is a **cubic** meter.
10. dramatic	*dramatic*	The **dramatic** scenes were moving.
11. marvelous	*marvelous*	Mom and I had a **marvelous** time.
12. famous	*famous*	The Mona Lisa is a **famous** painting.
13. adventurous	*adventurous*	A sailor needs an **adventurous** spirit.
14. vacant	*vacant*	This garden was once a **vacant** lot.
15. dangerous	*dangerous*	Toys on stairs are **dangerous**.
16. radiant	*radiant*	The bride and groom are **radiant**.
17. vigorous	*vigorous*	He is a **vigorous** man, full of life.
18. foolish	*foolish*	It is **foolish** to destroy a friendship.
19. mysterious	*mysterious*	A **mysterious** ship appeared at night.
20. selfish	*selfish*	They were **selfish** not to offer help.

SORT THE SPELLING WORDS

1.–8. Write the spelling words that have the suffix **-ous**.

9.–13. Write the spelling words that have the suffix **-ish**.

14.–16. Write the spelling words that have the suffix **-ant**.

17.–20. Write the spelling words that have the suffix **-ic**.

REMEMBER THE SPELLING STRATEGY

Remember that the suffixes **-ous, -ish, -ant,** and **-ic** can be added to base words or roots to form adjectives.

Spelling and Vocabulary

Word Meanings

Write the spelling word that matches each clue.

1. disregarding others; concerned only with oneself
2. hard to understand; puzzling
3. fashionable; in style
4. empty; not occupied
5. bold; daring; willing to try new experiences and take risks
6.–7. very active; full of energy

Word Structure

Combine the base word and suffix to form a spelling word. Write the word. You may need to change the spelling of the base word.

8. child + ish
9. danger + ous
10. marvel + ous
11. cube + ic
12. base + ic
13. blue + ish

USING THE Thesaurus

Write the spelling word that is a synonym for each word. Use your **Writing Thesaurus** to check your answers.

14. comical
15. theatrical
16. well-known
17. silly
18. merry
19. agreeable
20. brilliant

Word Meanings
1.
2.
3.
4.
5.
6.
7.

Word Structure
8.
9.
10.
11.
12.
13.

Using the Thesaurus
14.
15.
16.
17.
18.
19.
20.

Spelling and Reading

childish   joyous   energetic   bluish
pleasant   basic   humorous   stylish
cubic   dramatic   marvelous   famous
adventurous   vacant   dangerous   radiant
vigorous   foolish   mysterious   selfish

Solve the Analogies   Write the spelling word that completes each analogy.

1. **Cone** is to **conic** as **cube** is to _____.
2. **Glory** is to **glorious** as **marvel** is to _____.
3. **Red** is to **reddish** as **blue** is to _____.
4. **Piety** is to **pious** as **adventure** is to _____.
5. **Sweet** is to **sour** as **anonymous** is to _____.
6. **Allergy** is to **allergic** as **energy** is to _____.
7. **Kind** is to **cruel** as **generous** is to _____.
8. **Pomp** is to **pompous** as **joy** is to _____.
9. **Exciting** is to **dull** as **wise** is to _____.
10. **Defying** is to **defiant** as **pleasing** is to _____.
11. **Luster** is to **lustrous** as **vigor** is to _____.

Complete the Sentences   Write the spelling word that best completes each sentence.

12. Maybe we can use the _____ field for our fair.
13. He is a _____ coach; his players often laugh.
14. The actor looked _____ with joy as he bowed again and again.
15. Top hats were _____ in the nineteenth century.
16. Watch out for that _____ ledge!
17. My brother is a very funny comedian, but he wants to act in _____ plays.
18. Her _____ disappearance surprised everyone.
19. A _____ person would sulk about losing.
20. Its _____ shape is triangular.

Solve the Analogies
1.
2.
3.
4.
5.
6.
7.
8.
9.
10.
11.

Complete the Sentences
12.
13.
14.
15.
16.
17.
18.
19.
20.

Spelling and Writing

Proofread an Introduction

Six words are not spelled correctly in this introduction to a play. Write the words correctly.

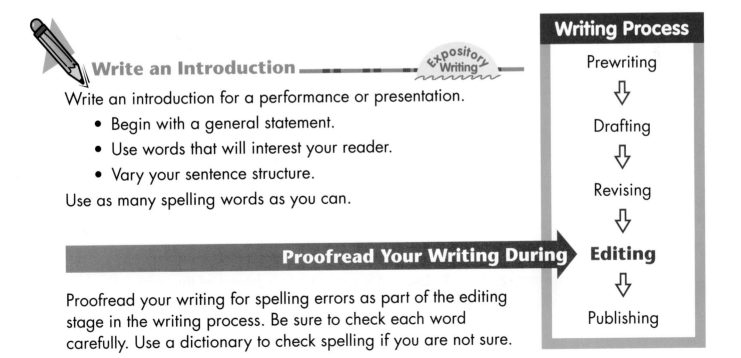

We have a marvelis performance for you this evening. The famous dramatik actor Paul Conway will star in this humoris play about a stylesh gentleman. The basik plot is that this gentleman meets a female electrician. For some mysterius reason, the two fall in love.

Proofreading Marks

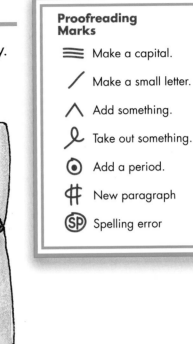

≡ Make a capital.

/ Make a small letter.

∧ Add something.

℮ Take out something.

⊙ Add a period.

New paragraph

SP Spelling error

Write an Introduction

Expository Writing

Write an introduction for a performance or presentation.

- Begin with a general statement.
- Use words that will interest your reader.
- Vary your sentence structure.

Use as many spelling words as you can.

Writing Process

Prewriting
⇩
Drafting
⇩
Revising
⇩
Editing
⇩
Publishing

Proofread Your Writing During ▶ Editing

Proofread your writing for spelling errors as part of the editing stage in the writing process. Be sure to check each word carefully. Use a dictionary to check spelling if you are not sure.

VOCABULARY CONNECTIONS

►Strategy Words◄

Review Words:
Suffixes -ous, -ish, -ant, -ic

Write the word from the box that completes each sentence.

gigantic	arctic	arithmetic	clinic	British

1. Mr. Soledad, our _____ teacher, certainly loves numbers!
2. The original thirteen states were once _____ colonies.
3. Naomi Cohen is a nurse at the neighborhood _____.
4. Polar bears and reindeer can thrive in _____ conditions.
5. The *H.M.S. Queen Elizabeth II* is a _____ ship.

Preview Words:
Suffixes -ous, -ish, -ant, -ic

Write the word from the box that best replaces the underlined word or words.

applicant	curious	mountainous
participant	tremendous	

6. Nico is <u>inquisitive</u> about weather.
7. Peru has some <u>extremely hilly</u> countryside.
8. Every <u>group member</u> is proud of the work.
9. One <u>person seeking a job opening</u> is here.
10. The roar of the crowd was <u>overpowering</u>.

Review Words
1. _____
2. _____
3. _____
4. _____
5. _____

Preview Words
6. _____
7. _____
8. _____
9. _____
10. _____

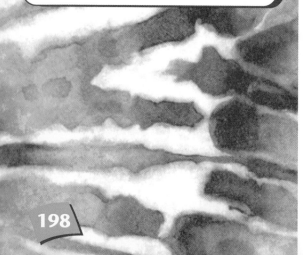

198

Content Words

Social Studies: The Spanish Armada

Write the words from the box to complete the paragraph. You will need to make one word plural.

armada	harbor	cannon	historic	defeat

    In 1588 Spain sent an __1.__ of ships to attack England. The English were able to __2.__ the Spanish fleet by firing __3.__ to protect each __4.__ . After this __5.__ conquest, England became the most powerful naval force in the world.

Science: Genetics

Write the word from the box that matches each clue.

gene	instinct	heredity	reflex	relate

6. an unlearned, immediate response to something
7. the passing down of physical and mental traits from parents to children
8. an inborn tendency to act in a certain way
9. a verb that can mean to "show a connection between"
10. a tiny part of a cell that determines the characteristics to be passed on to offspring

Apply the Spelling Strategy

Circle the suffix **-ic** in one of the Content Words you wrote.

Word Study

Shades of Meaning

When words mean almost but not quite the same thing, we say they have different **shades of meaning. Inquiring, interested,** and **nosy** all are ways of being **curious**. Write the Strategy Word that fits with the meaning of these words: **huge, big, giant, ____ .**

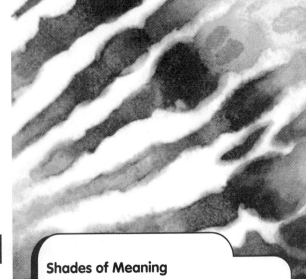

Social Studies: The Spanish Armada
1. _____
2. _____
3. _____
4. _____
5. _____

Science: Genetics
6. _____
7. _____
8. _____
9. _____
10. _____

Shades of Meaning
1. _____

synonyms

1. _____
2. _____
3. _____
4. _____
5. _____
6. _____
7. _____
8. _____
9. _____
10. _____

antonyms

11. _____
12. _____
13. _____
14. _____
15. _____
16. _____
17. _____
18. _____
19. _____
20. _____

Spelling and Thinking

READ THE SPELLING WORDS

#			
1.	delight	*delight*	Puppet shows **delight** the children.
2.	exit	*exit*	Watch for the **exit** sign, please.
3.	public	*public*	You may not wear that hat in **public**.
4.	increase	*increase*	Was there an **increase** in the toll?
5.	freedom	*freedom*	I enjoy **freedom** of speech.
6.	lengthen	*lengthen*	In the evening, shadows **lengthen**.
7.	backward	*backward*	Can you say the alphabet **backward**?
8.	liberty	*liberty*	In a free land, you have **liberty**.
9.	narrow	*narrow*	The road is too **narrow** for the truck.
10.	eastern	*eastern*	I live in **eastern** Tennessee.
11.	entire	*entire*	This **entire** estate is his.
12.	western	*western*	The seacoast is in **western** Oregon.
13.	decrease	*decrease*	We should **decrease** the ticket price.
14.	private	*private*	They had a **private** conversation.
15.	whole	*whole*	This **whole** day has been wonderful.
16.	extend	*extend*	Firefighters will **extend** a ladder.
17.	forward	*forward*	Go **forward** to the chalkboard.
18.	pleasure	*pleasure*	With **pleasure**, I will help you.
19.	entrance	*entrance*	This **entrance** has double doors.
20.	slender	*slender*	A **slender** gazelle nibbled grass.

SORT THE SPELLING WORDS

1.–10. Write the pairs of synonyms from the spelling list.

11.–20. Write the pairs of antonyms from the spelling list.

REMEMBER THE SPELLING STRATEGY

Remember that **synonyms** are words that have the same, or a similar, meaning: **freedom, liberty**. **Antonyms** are words that have an opposite meaning: **western, eastern**.

Spelling and Vocabulary

Word Meanings

Write the spelling word that fits each clue.

1. You enter this way.
2. This coast of Ireland is on the Irish Sea.
3. We do not like prices to do this.
4. We usually walk this way.
5. This means that everyone is welcome.
6. You go out through this.
7. This means "confidential."

Word Structure

8.–10. Mix and match a syllable from each column to create spelling words. Write the words.

de	crease
back	ern
west	ward

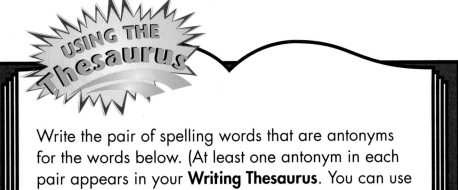

USING THE Thesaurus

Write the pair of spelling words that are antonyms for the words below. (At least one antonym in each pair appears in your **Writing Thesaurus**. You can use those words to check your answers.)

11.–12. confinement; denial   17.–18. displeasure

13.–14. incomplete   19.–20. shorten

15.–16. broad

Word Meanings

1. _____
2. _____
3. _____
4. _____
5. _____
6. _____
7. _____

Word Structure

8. _____
9. _____
10. _____

Using the Thesaurus

11. _____
12. _____
13. _____
14. _____
15. _____
16. _____
17. _____
18. _____
19. _____
20. _____

Spelling and Reading

delight	exit	public	increase	freedom
lengthen	backward	liberty	narrow	eastern
entire	western	decrease	private	whole
extend	forward	pleasure	entrance	slender

Complete the Story   Write the spelling words that complete the story. The first letter of each word is given.

Anne stowed away on a ship headed for the Massachusetts Bay Colony. Anxious to find f___**1.**___ in the new world, she could not wait for the ship to e___**2.**___ the English harbor and head out to sea. As the ship moved f___**3.**___ into the open sea, it began to i___**4.**___ its speed. As Anne glanced b___**5.**___, she could see the boat's wake e___**6.**___ far behind her. Ahead there was nothing but miles and miles of ocean. The sun set in the w___**7.**___ sky. Anne took great p___**8.**___ in dreaming about her new home. She imagined with d___**9.**___ a w___**10.**___ new life.

Complete the Sentences   Write the spelling word that completes each sentence. The first letter of each word is given.

11. Has there been a d_____ in the price of gasoline in recent weeks?
12. It was Patrick Henry who said, "Give me l_____, or give me death."
13. That dog ate the e_____ cherry pie.
14. They are having a p_____ conversation.
15. This waterway is too n_____ for that boat.
16. The pianist has s_____ fingers.
17. Sam enjoyed the free p_____ concert.
18. Please l_____ the seat belt for Charlie.
19. Many apple orchards have been established in e_____ Washington.
20. Go into the stadium through this e_____.

Complete the Story
1.
2.
3.
4.
5.
6.
7.
8.
9.
10.

Complete the Sentences
11.
12.
13.
14.
15.
16.
17.
18.
19.
20.

202

Spelling and Writing

Proofread a Paragraph

Six words are not spelled correctly in this paragraph. Write the words correctly.

New York Harbor is the major shipping port in the estern United States. Huge ocean liners and small privte sailboats are greeted by the Statue of Liberty as they make their entrence and move foreward into the harbor. In the wistern United States is San Francisco Bay. Because of the increase in San Francisco's population, it has become the largest public port on the West Coast.

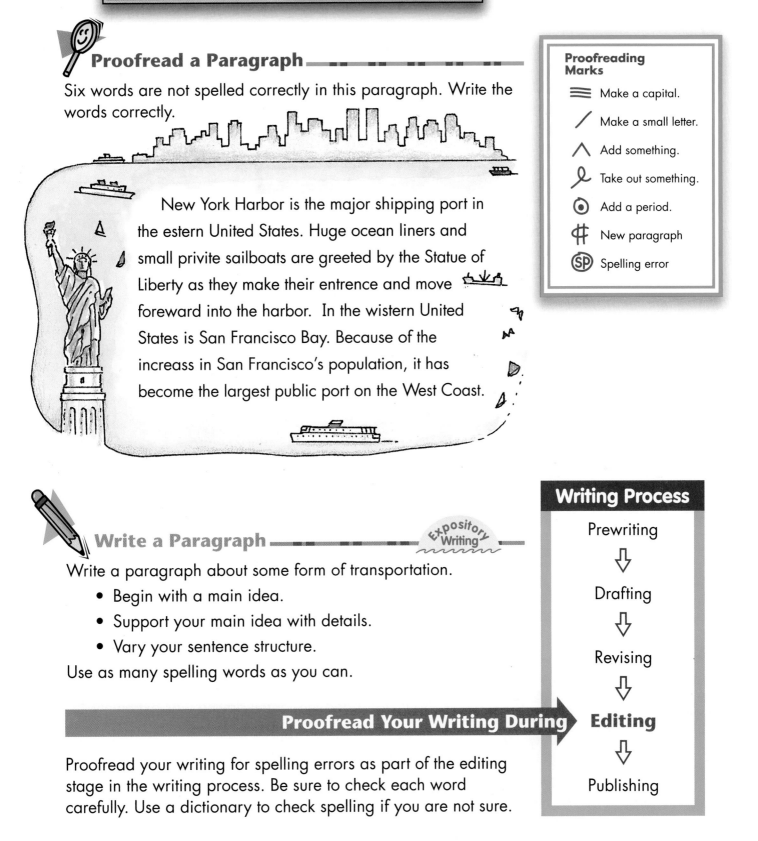

Write a Paragraph

Expository Writing

Write a paragraph about some form of transportation.

- Begin with a main idea.
- Support your main idea with details.
- Vary your sentence structure.

Use as many spelling words as you can.

Writing Process

Prewriting
⇩
Drafting
⇩
Revising
⇩
Proofread Your Writing During ▶ **Editing**
⇩
Publishing

Proofread your writing for spelling errors as part of the editing stage in the writing process. Be sure to check each word carefully. Use a dictionary to check spelling if you are not sure.

VOCABULARY CONNECTIONS

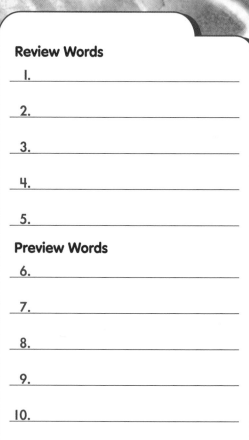

Review Words

1. _____
2. _____
3. _____
4. _____
5. _____

Preview Words

6. _____
7. _____
8. _____
9. _____
10. _____

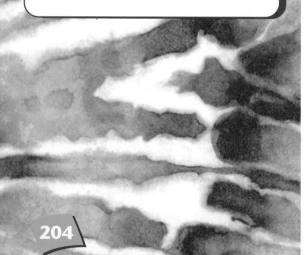

Strategy Words

Review Words: Synonyms & Antonyms

Write the word from the box that best replaces the underlined word or words.

helpful	helpless	powerful	powerless	often

1. Mrs. Soledad frequently brushes her cat.
2. Joan is useful to her fellow actors.
3. We felt without power against the hurricane.
4. An infant is unable to care for itself.
5. Though slow, the ox is very strong.

Preview Words: Synonyms & Antonyms

Write the word from the box that best completes each sentence.

valuable	worthless	optimism	pessimism	success

6. With _____, you are more likely to succeed.
7. In A. A. Milne's famous stories, Eeyore is known for his _____.
8. That ring is a _____ fake.
9. Your good and thoughtful advice was extremely _____ to me.
10. Jay did not let _____ go to his head.

Content Words

Science: Bones

Write words from the box to complete the paragraph.

backbone	spine	calcium	vertebrae	skeleton

The __1.__, also called the __2.__, is a series of jointed bones called __3.__. These bones are found in the middle of the back. This spinal column supports the entire human __4.__. We need __5.__ in our diet because it helps us grow strong bones and teeth.

Social Studies: The Civil War

Write words from the box to complete the paragraph.

abolish	slave	antislavery	southern	northern

There were many __6.__ citizens and some __7.__ citizens who wanted to __8.__ slavery. They did not believe that any human being should be a __9.__. Therefore, many joined the __10.__ movement.

Apply the Spelling Strategy

Circle the two Content Words you wrote that are synonyms. Underline the two Content Words you wrote that are antonyms.

Word Study

Suffixes

The suffix **-ism** means "act or practice of" or "quality or condition of." **Heroism** is the act or practice of being heroic. **Patriotism** is the quality or condition of being patriotic. Write the Strategy Word that means "the quality of being optimistic."

Science: Bones
1. _____
2. _____
3. _____
4. _____
5. _____

Social Studies: The Civil War
6. _____
7. _____
8. _____
9. _____
10. _____

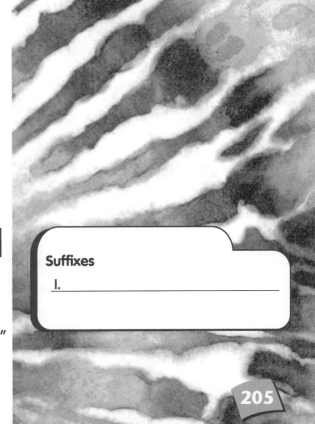

Suffixes
1. _____

European

1. _____
2. _____
3. _____
4. _____
5. _____
6. _____
7. _____
8. _____
9. _____
10. _____
11. _____
12. _____
13. _____
14. _____

Asian, Australian, Native American

15. _____
16. _____
17. _____
18. _____
19. _____
20. _____

Spelling and Thinking

READ THE SPELLING WORDS

1.	haiku	*haiku*	The **haiku** describes falling snow.
2.	macaroni	*macaroni*	Vic likes **macaroni** with tomatoes.
3.	karate	*karate*	Opponents bow in a **karate** match.
4.	chipmunk	*chipmunk*	A **chipmunk** ran across the porch.
5.	alligator	*alligator*	They saw an **alligator** in a swamp.
6.	knapsack	*knapsack*	He put a flashlight in the **knapsack**.
7.	boomerang	*boomerang*	The **boomerang** came flying back.
8.	plaza	*plaza*	People are dancing in the **plaza**.
9.	kimono	*kimono*	Her **kimono** is yellow satin.
10.	plaid	*plaid*	This **plaid** jacket is from Scotland.
11.	robot	*robot*	I wish a **robot** could clean my room.
12.	waffle	*waffle*	We have an old **waffle** iron.
13.	crochet	*crochet*	I can **crochet** a scarf or a hat.
14.	yogurt	*yogurt*	Marvin likes **yogurt** and honey.
15.	shampoo	*shampoo*	My hair **shampoo** smells good.
16.	beret	*beret*	Your blue **beret** matches my coat.
17.	burro	*burro*	Alex rode his **burro** to town.
18.	guitar	*guitar*	This **guitar** is fifty years old.
19.	hammock	*hammock*	I like to nap in a **hammock**.
20.	yodel	*yodel*	Learning to **yodel** takes practice.

SORT THE SPELLING WORDS

1.–14. Write the words that come from European languages. Check your **Spelling Dictionary** for word histories.

15.–20. Write the words that come from Asian, Australian, or Native American languages.

REMEMBER THE SPELLING STRATEGY

Remember that the English language includes many words that come from other languages.

Spelling and Vocabulary

Word Meanings

Write the spelling words that come from the following translations of foreign words. Use your **Spelling Dictionary** if you need help identifying the nation where each spelling word originated.

1. This German word means "an eating bag."
2. This Spanish word means "broad street."
3. This Japanese word means "empty" and "hand."
4. This German word means "sing."
5. This Czechoslovakian word means "work."
6. This Japanese word means "amusement" and "sentence."

Word Structure

7.–10. Write the spelling words that have double consonants.

11.–12. Write the spelling words that have double vowels.

13.–14. Write the spelling words that end in **-et**.

USING THE Dictionary

Write the spelling word that fits each definition. Write the part of speech for each word.

15. a long, loose Japanese robe
16. a creamy food made from milk
17. pasta in the shape of hollow tubes
18. a pattern of squares formed by stripes
19. a small animal resembling a squirrel
20. a stringed instrument played by plucking

Word Meanings

1. _____
2. _____
3. _____
4. _____
5. _____
6. _____

Word Structure

7. _____
8. _____
9. _____
10. _____
11. _____
12. _____
13. _____
14. _____

Using the Dictionary

15. _____
16. _____
17. _____
18. _____
19. _____
20. _____

haiku	macaroni	karate	chipmunk
alligator	knapsack	boomerang	plaza
kimono	plaid	robot	waffle
crochet	yogurt	shampoo	beret
burro	guitar	hammock	yodel

Complete the Paragraphs

I.

2.

3.

4.

5.

6.

7.

8.

Complete the Sentences

9.

10.

II.

12.

13.

14.

15.

16.

17.

18.

19.

20.

Complete the Paragraphs   Write spelling words to complete the paragraphs.

Enrique lives in the Mexican countryside. Every morning he sees a local farmer leading his __1.__ to market. The farmer sells his produce in the __2.__. After school, Enrique relaxes in his rope __3.__ and practices strumming his __4.__.

Miyako lives in Japan. When she goes to school, she carries her books in a __5.__. At home she sometimes wears a traditional __6.__ for celebrations. For her __7.__ class, she wears an exercise uniform called a **gi**. Miyako likes to write __8.__.

Complete the Sentences   Write the spelling word that best completes each sentence.

9. We saw a tiny _____ eating acorns.
10. An _____ wrestler held the animal's jaws shut.
II. We mixed the creamy _____ with strawberries.
12. If you throw a _____, prepare for its return.
13. Sheila likes to eat _____ and cheese.
14. Calvin can _____ songs he learned in Switzerland.
15. We saw a _____ capping bottles in a factory.
16. Margot can _____ beautiful place mats for your dining room table.
17. I had a _____ with maple syrup.
18. The red blouse matches the red _____ skirt.
19. After the game, Nate needed to _____ his hair.
20. I would not wear a _____ on my head on a windy day.

Spelling and Writing

Proofread a Paragraph

Six words are not spelled correctly in this paragraph. Write the words correctly.

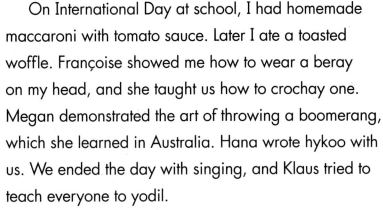

On International Day at school, I had homemade maccaroni with tomato sauce. Later I ate a toasted woffle. Françoise showed me how to wear a beray on my head, and she taught us how to crochay one. Megan demonstrated the art of throwing a boomerang, which she learned in Australia. Hana wrote hykoo with us. We ended the day with singing, and Klaus tried to teach everyone to yodil.

Write a Paragraph

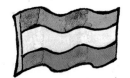 *Expository Writing*

Write a paragraph about a special event.

- Identify the event.
- Organize your ideas in chronological order.
- Use words that indicate the order of events.

Use as many spelling words as you can.

Writing Process

Prewriting

⇩

Drafting

⇩

Revising

⇩

Proofread Your Writing During ▶ **Editing**

⇩

Publishing

Proofread your writing for spelling errors as part of the editing stage in the writing process. Be sure to check each word carefully. Use a dictionary to check spelling if you are not sure.

VOCABULARY CONNECTIONS

Strategy Words

Review Words: Words From Other Languages

Write words from the box to complete the paragraph.

cottage	island	steak	blue jeans	orchard

Last summer my family took a ferry to an __1.__ off the coast of Maine. We stayed in a small __2.__ and wore __3.__ every day. One afternoon we had a picnic in an apple __4.__ and ate grilled __5.__.

Preview Words: Words From Other Languages

Write a word from the box to complete each sentence.

barbecue	buffet	garage	marimba	restaurant

6. A ____ player strikes that musical instrument with wooden mallets.

7. Please put your bikes in the ____ before the storm begins.

8. Delicious smells are coming from the Italian ____ across the street.

9. There were three dessert tables at the festive ____ lunch.

10. My mother uses lemon, brown sugar, and fennel in her ____ sauce.

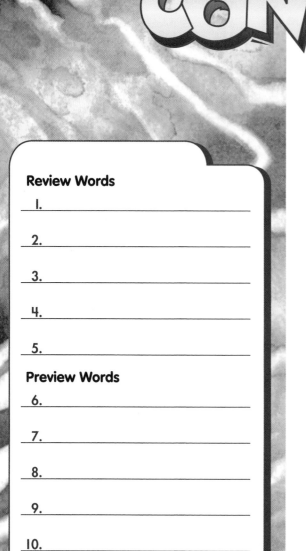

Review Words

1. _____
2. _____
3. _____
4. _____
5. _____

Preview Words

6. _____
7. _____
8. _____
9. _____
10. _____

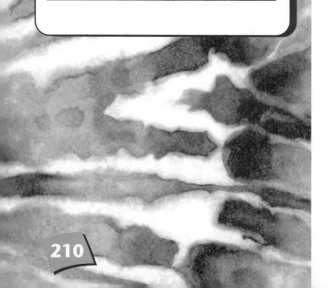

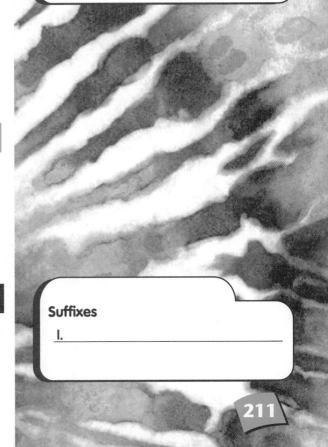

Content Words

Fine Arts: Performances

Write the word from the box that best replaces the underlined word or words in each sentence.

ballet	opera	concert	gallery	theater

1. We saw my aunt's paintings in a <u>place for exhibiting art</u>.
2. Eric's band played a benefit <u>musical performance</u>.
3. The old-fashioned <u>movie hall</u> had a player piano.
4. *Rigoletto* is a very sad <u>musical drama</u> by the nineteenth-century Italian composer Giuseppe Verdi.
5. *Swan Lake* is a famous <u>classical dance</u>.

Science: Sound

Write the word from the box that matches each clue.

amplifier	static	cassette	turntable	reverse

6. This is a tape recording in a plastic case.
7. You can rotate a recording on this circular platform.
8. This is backward, as in a recording played backward.
9. A recorded sound that is not clear has this.
10. To increase the strength of a signal, you use this.

Apply the Spelling Strategy

Circle the double consonants in three of the Content Words you wrote.

Word Study

Suffixes

The suffix **-ette** means "little." A **dinette** is a little dining area. Write the Content Word that came from the French word for "little box."

Fine Arts: Performances
1. _____
2. _____
3. _____
4. _____
5. _____

Science: Sound
6. _____
7. _____
8. _____
9. _____
10. _____

Suffixes
1. _____

211

Spelling ᴬᴺᴰ Thinking

READ THE SPELLING WORDS

1.	apt.	*apt.*	The abbreviation **apt.** means apartment.
2.	no.	*no.*	The abbreviation **no.** means number.
3.	qt.	*qt.*	The abbreviation **qt.** means quart.
4.	in.	*in.*	The abbreviation **in.** means inch.
5.	gal.	*gal.*	The abbreviation **gal.** means gallon.
6.	oz.	*oz.*	The abbreviation **oz.** means ounce.
7.	yd.	*yd.*	The abbreviation **yd.** means yard.
8.	lb.	*lb.*	The abbreviation **lb.** means pound.
9.	sq.	*sq.*	The abbreviation **sq.** means square.
10.	Gen.	*Gen.*	The abbreviation **Gen.** means General.
11.	ave.	*ave.*	The abbreviation **ave.** means avenue.
12.	wt.	*wt.*	The abbreviation **wt.** means weight.
13.	yr.	*yr.*	The abbreviation **yr.** means year.
14.	co.	*co.*	The abbreviation **co.** means company.
15.	doz.	*doz.*	The abbreviation **doz.** means dozen.
16.	pkg.	*pkg.*	The abbreviation **pkg.** means package.
17.	amt.	*amt.*	The abbreviation **amt.** means amount.
18.	pt.	*pt.*	The abbreviation **pt.** means pint.
19.	hr.	*hr.*	The abbreviation **hr.** means hour.
20.	ft.	*ft.*	The abbreviation **ft.** means foot.

first two or three letters

1. ____
2. ____
3. ____
4. ____
5. ____
6. ____
7. ____

first and last letters

8. ____
9. ____
10. ____
11. ____
12. ____
13. ____
14. ____

three other letters

15. ____
16. ____
17. ____

letters not all in word

18. ____
19. ____
20. ____

SORT THE SPELLING WORDS

Write the abbreviations formed from

   1.–7. the first two or three letters of the word.

   8.–14. the first and last letters of the word.

  15.–17. three other letters in the word.

18.–20. letters that are not all in the word.

REMEMBER THE SPELLING STRATEGY

Remember that abbreviations are formed in various ways.

Spelling ^{and} Vocabulary

Word Structure

Write the abbreviations for the following words.

1. General
2. avenue
3. apartment
4. gallon
5. weight
6. year
7. company
8. foot
9. yard

Word Meanings

Replace the words in boldface with abbreviations from the spelling list.

10.–17. Almost Quick Apple–Walnut Cake
(Enough for 3 **dozen** servings)
I **quart** milk   3 cups flour   I **pint** apple juice
I cup sugar   I teaspoon baking powder
2 eggs   I small **package** chopped walnuts
Bake in two **square** nine-**inch** cake pans for one **hour** in 350-degree oven. Adjust **amount** of ingredients for desired quantity.

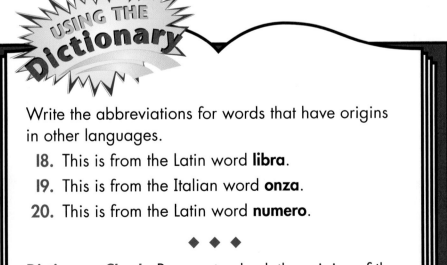

USING THE Dictionary

Write the abbreviations for words that have origins in other languages.

18. This is from the Latin word **libra**.
19. This is from the Italian word **onza**.
20. This is from the Latin word **numero**.

◆ ◆ ◆

Dictionary Check Be sure to check the origins of the words in your **Spelling Dictionary**.

Word Structure

1. ___
2. ___
3. ___
4. ___
5. ___
6. ___
7. ___
8. ___
9. ___

Word Meanings

10. ___
11. ___
12. ___
13. ___
14. ___
15. ___
16. ___
17. ___

Using the Dictionary

18. ___
19. ___
20. ___

apt.	no.	qt.	in.	gal.
oz.	yd.	lb.	sq.	Gen.
ave.	wt.	yr.	co.	doz.
pkg.	amt.	pt.	hr.	ft.

Use the Clues Write the abbreviation that matches each clue.

1. It is the title of a high-ranking soldier.
2. This is the same as sixty minutes.
3. It is a business operation.
4. This abbreviates a word for a wide road.
5. This is a home that is part of a building.
6. It means "two cups."
7. This means "four cups."
8. This is "sixteen cups."

Complete the Forms Replace the underlined words in these forms with abbreviations from the spelling list.

9.–15.

∞ **Form Number 2** ∞

Name: _Androc Levotzsky_

Date of Birth: _10_   _16_   _1971_
              month   day   year

Height: _6 feet_   _1 inch_

Weight: _200 pounds_   _1 ounce_

16.–20.

CLOONEY'S FABRICS
Order Form

1 yard blue cotton

1 package knitting needles

1 square quilting

1 bag beads; equal amount shells

1 dozen yarn skeins

Use the Clues
1.
2.
3.
4.
5.
6.
7.
8.

Complete the Forms
9.
10.
11.
12.
13.
14.
15.
16.
17.
18.
19.
20.

Spelling and Writing

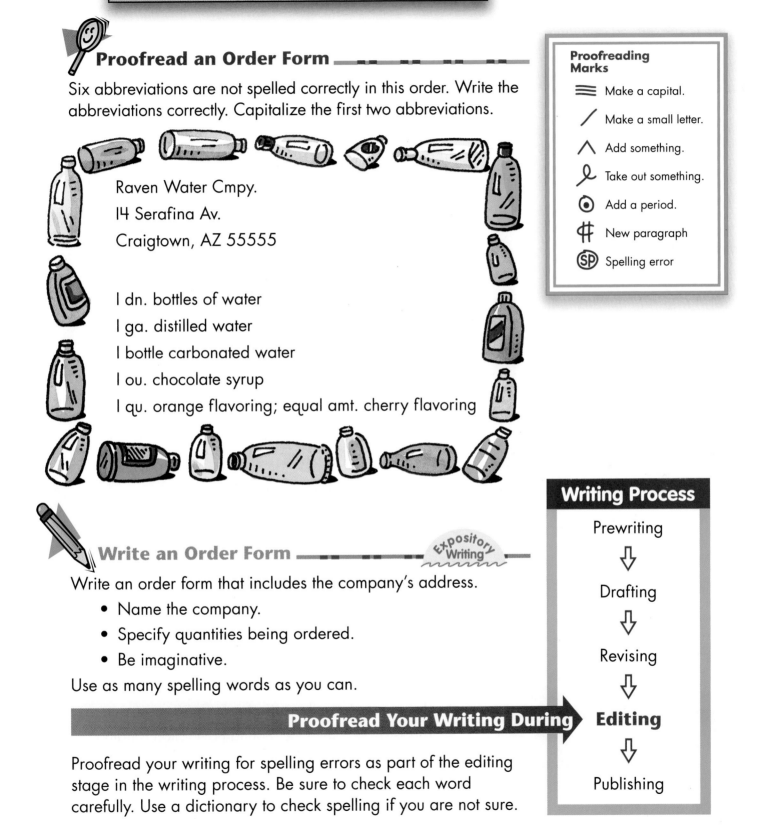

Proofread an Order Form

Six abbreviations are not spelled correctly in this order. Write the abbreviations correctly. Capitalize the first two abbreviations.

Raven Water Cmpy.
14 Serafina Av.
Craigtown, AZ 55555

1 dn. bottles of water
1 ga. distilled water
1 bottle carbonated water
1 ou. chocolate syrup
1 qu. orange flavoring; equal amt. cherry flavoring

Proofreading Marks

≡	Make a capital.
/	Make a small letter.
∧	Add something.
ℓ	Take out something.
⊙	Add a period.
#	New paragraph
SP	Spelling error

Write an Order Form

Expository Writing

Write an order form that includes the company's address.

- Name the company.
- Specify quantities being ordered.
- Be imaginative.

Use as many spelling words as you can.

Writing Process

Prewriting
⇩
Drafting
⇩
Revising
⇩
Editing
⇩
Publishing

Proofread Your Writing During → **Editing**

Proofread your writing for spelling errors as part of the editing stage in the writing process. Be sure to check each word carefully. Use a dictionary to check spelling if you are not sure.

VOCABULARY CONNECTIONS

Strategy Words

Review Words: Abbreviations

Write the abbreviation from the box that matches the underlined word.

Apr.	Dec.	Feb.	Fri.	Nov.

1. <u>April</u> 7, 2001
2. <u>November</u> 1, 1998
3. <u>December</u> 20, 2003
4. <u>February</u> 14, 1956
5. <u>Friday</u>, Sept. 15

Preview Words: Abbreviations

Write the word or abbreviation from the box that matches each clue.

A.M.	mph	P.M.	scuba	sonar

6. This is an acronym (a word made from the first letters or syllables of other words) for "<u>s</u>elf-<u>c</u>ontained <u>u</u>nderwater <u>b</u>reathing <u>a</u>pparatus."
7. It stands for "miles per hour."
8. This comes from the Latin for "after noon."
9. This is an acronym for "<u>so</u>und <u>n</u>avigation <u>r</u>anging."
10. This comes from the Latin for "before noon."

Review Words
1. _____
2. _____
3. _____
4. _____
5. _____

Preview Words
6. _____
7. _____
8. _____
9. _____
10. _____

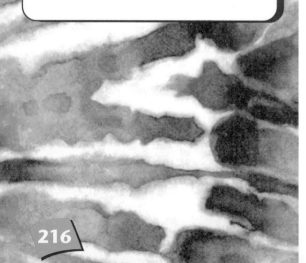

Content Words

Science: Insects

Write the word that best replaces the underlined words.

| aphid | millipede | centipede | termite | cricket |

1. A <u>wood-eating insect</u> can damage a house.
2. The <u>chirping insect</u> creates a quiet mood.
3. Despite its name, a <u>poison-jawed arthropod</u> does not actually have a hundred legs.
4. A <u>many-legged arthropod</u> does not actually have a thousand legs.
5. A <u>small soft-bodied insect</u> can harm crops.

Math: Division

Write a word from the box to complete each sentence.

| cross-multiply | simplify | divisible | terms | reduce |

6. To find the product of two fractions, you need to _____.
7. Both 4 and 8 are _____ by 4.
8.–10. To _____ the fraction $^4/_8$, we _____ it to its lowest _____.

Apply the Spelling Strategy

Circle the Content Word you wrote that is formed from the word **simple**. Underline the Content Word you wrote that is formed from the word **divide**.

Word Study

Antonyms

Antonyms are words with opposite meanings. **Minimum** and **maximum** are antonyms. Write the Content Word that is an antonym for **increase** and **expand**.

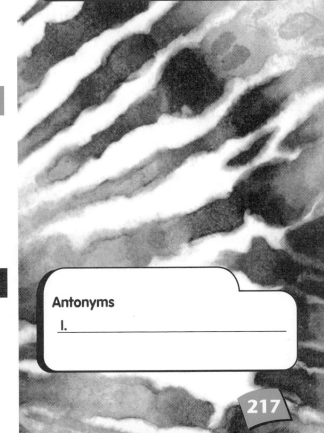

Science: Insects

1. _____
2. _____
3. _____
4. _____
5. _____

Math: Division

6. _____
7. _____
8. _____
9. _____
10. _____

Antonyms

1. _____

Unit 36
Review Units 31–35

Unit 32

1. _____
2. _____
3. _____
4. _____
5. _____

Unit 33

6. _____
7. _____
8. _____
9. _____
10. _____
11. _____

Unit 34

12. _____
13. _____
14. _____
15. _____
16. _____

Unit 35

17. _____
18. _____
19. _____
20. _____

Assessment and Review

Assessment / Units 31–35

Each Assessment Word in the box fits one of the spelling strategies you have studied over the past five weeks. Read the spelling strategies. Then write each Assessment Word under the unit number it fits. You will not write any words from Unit 31.

Unit 31 _____
It is important to know the correct spellings of words that are often misspelled.

Unit 32 _____
1.–5. The suffixes **-ous, -ish, -ant,** and **-ic** can be added to base words or roots to form adjectives.

Unit 33 _____
6.–11. **Synonyms** are words that have the same, or a similar, meaning: **freedom, liberty**. **Antonyms** are words that have an opposite meaning: **western, eastern**.

Unit 34 _____
12.–16. The English language includes many words that come from other languages.

Unit 35 _____
17.–20. Abbreviations are formed in various ways.

envious
clamor
barrette
ignorant
tsp.
domestic
uproar
poncho
min.
vibrant
exhibit
mustache
tbsp.
patio
sheepish
display
mi.
horrible
ukulele
dreadful

address	beautiful	separate	sincerely	umbrella
language	government	suppose	cousin	although

Find the word that is misspelled in each sentence. Write it correctly.

1. Do you supose we can get tickets at this late date?
2. What is your street adress?
3. You have on a buetiful coat.
4. I keep my homework in a seperate place in my room.
5. I sinserely hope you can come to the party.
6. I will be there, altho I will be late.
7. What is the langage spoken in Brazil?
8. You'd better take your umbella.
9. The goverment offices are in the capitol.
10. My aunt's daughter is my cuzin.

Review Unit 32: Suffixes -ous, -ish, -ant, -ic

energetic	humorous	mysterious	pleasant	vacant
marvelous	selfish	foolish	famous	dangerous

Write a spelling word by adding a suffix to each base word. You may need to change the spelling of the base word.

11. energy
12. humor
13. fool
14. danger
15. mystery
16. please
17. marvel
18. self
19. vacate
20. fame

Unit 31
1. _____
2. _____
3. _____
4. _____
5. _____
6. _____
7. _____
8. _____
9. _____
10. _____

Unit 32
11. _____
12. _____
13. _____
14. _____
15. _____
16. _____
17. _____
18. _____
19. _____
20. _____

219

Review — Unit 33: Synonyms & Antonyms

entrance	lengthen	private	whole	freedom
public	narrow	delight	forward	entire

Write the spelling word that is an antonym for each of these words.

1. shorten
2. private
3. wide
4. backward
5. exit
6. captivity

Write a spelling word that could replace the underlined word in each sentence.

7. The child's face beamed with <u>pleasure</u>.
8. One should never ask a friend about his or her <u>personal</u> matters.
9. Did you eat the <u>entire</u> pizza?
10. The <u>whole</u> class participated in the science fair.

Review — Unit 34: Words From Other Languages

guitar	macaroni	plaid	shampoo	chipmunk
robot	alligator	kimono	burro	karate

Write the spelling word that fits the meaning.

11. a musical stringed instrument
12. a pattern of checks or squares
13. a small donkey
14. a loose outer garment
15. liquid for washing hair
16. a kind of pasta
17. a reptile
18. a squirrel-like animal
19. a machine
20. a method of self-defense

Unit 35: Abbreviations

co.	hr.	lb.	pkg.	yr.
in.	wt.	yd.	sq.	ft.

Write the abbreviation for each underlined word.

1.–2. In one <u>hour</u> we will receive a <u>package</u>.

3.–4. It has a <u>weight</u> of one <u>pound</u>.

5.–6. Our <u>company</u> was founded in the <u>year</u> 1985.

7.–8. The space is one <u>square</u> <u>foot</u>.

9.–10. I ordered cloth that is one <u>yard</u> and one <u>inch</u> wide.

Unit 35

1. _____
2. _____
3. _____
4. _____
5. _____
6. _____
7. _____
8. _____
9. _____
10. _____

WORD SORT

Spelling Study Strategy

Sorting by Parts of Speech

One good way to practice spelling words is to place words into groups. Here is a way to practice some of the spelling words you have been studying in the past few weeks.

1. Make four columns across a large piece of paper.

2. Write one of these parts of speech at the top of each column: **Nouns, Verbs, Adjectives, Adverbs**.

3. Have a partner choose a spelling word from Units 31 through 35 and say it aloud.

4. Write the spelling word in the column under the correct heading. If you disagree about the part of speech, use the word in a sentence to decide which is correct. (Some words can be used as more than one part of speech.)

Unit 36 enrichment

WRITER'S

Grammar, Usage, and Mechanics

Adverbs

Adverbs describe verbs or adjectives. They tell how, when, where, or to what extent (how much). Many adverbs end in **-ly**. Other common adverbs are **fast, very, often, again, sometimes,** and **soon**.

Let's eat **first** and **then** finish this project.

Practice Activity

A.
  1. _____
  2. _____
  3. _____
  4. _____
  5. _____
  6. _____
B.
  7. _____
  8. _____
  9. _____
  10. _____
  11. _____
  12. _____

A. Write the adverb in each sentence below.

1. If we leave now, we will have plenty of time.
2. The phone often rings at dinnertime.
3. This building looks awfully familiar.
4. The diver climbed the ladder and dove again.
5. Have you seen an art exhibit recently?
6. I will return your barrette then.

B. Some words from your spelling lists have been turned into adverbs. Use the adverbs to fill in the blanks.

| foolishly | privately | entirely |
| selfishly | publicly | dangerously |

7. When the news was announced _____, the world cheered.
8. You are sitting _____ close to that fire!
9. It rained, and I _____ left my book outside.
10. It snowed so much that the car was _____ covered.
11. He explained it to me _____.
12. She _____ kept all the money herself.

WORKSHOP

Sentence by Sentence

Good writers always proofread their work for spelling errors. Here's a strategy you can use to proofread your papers.

Instead of reading in the regular way, look at one sentence at a time. Pay close attention to the first and last word. Make sure that the first word starts with a capital letter. Then make sure that the last word is followed by a punctuation mark.

This way of looking at a paper helps you focus on details, such as capital letters and punctuation, instead of ideas. It may sound funny, but it works. Try it!

Electronic Spelling

1. _____
2. _____
3. _____
4. _____
5. _____
6. _____

Electronic Spelling

Computer Language

Computers are changing language and bringing new words into use. Some of these words are so new that they may not be listed in older dictionaries.

Luckily, many of these new words are easy to spell. Several begin with **inter-** or end with **-ware**. Knowing this can help you spell them correctly.

Look at these words. Which have spelling mistakes? Write those words correctly. Write **OK** if a word is correct.

1. intrenet
2. hardwear
3. software
4. interactive
5. interfase
6. sharewhere

Challenge Activities

replace	Braille	lease
outweigh	delete	marine

A. Each row has three words with the same vowel spelling pattern. Write the word that does not follow that pattern.

1. outweigh, neighbor, Braille, freight
2. lease, scary, memory, foggy
3. police, delete, gasoline, marine
4. operate, outweigh, replace, populate
5. feature, beneath, marine, lease
6. trait, detain, replace, complain

B. Write a challenge word for each clue.

1. a type of print in books for the blind
2. to be heavier than
3. to substitute
4. of the sea
5. to take out
6. agreement signed by an owner and a tenant

C. Pretend that some creatures from the sea were suddenly able to write and communicate with other marine life. You are one of these creatures. In fact, you are a reporter for *Land, Sea, and Sky News.* Write an account of some families you have observed who have leased cottages nearby. Use challenge words if you can.

A.
1. _____
2. _____
3. _____
4. _____
5. _____
6. _____

B.
1. _____
2. _____
3. _____
4. _____
5. _____
6. _____

Challenge Activities

lotion	grocer	horizon
sorrow	retire	dynamite

A. Unscramble the letters and write the challenge words. Circle the letters that spell the **long i** sound or the **long o** sound in each word.

1. c r o e r g
2. i n z o o r h
3. a t m i y n d e

4. i o t o n l
5. i e t r e r
6. r o o s r w

B. Write a challenge word that relates to each group.

1. ointment, balm, _____
2. skyline, vista, _____
3. gunpowder, TNT, _____
4. grief, sadness, _____
5. withdraw, retreat, _____
6. storekeeper, merchant, _____

C. You own a grocery store. However, you have decided to retire. You have mixed emotions about this. On the one hand, you will miss being a grocer. On the other hand, you look forward to broadening your horizons with new experiences and interests. Write a paragraph telling about your feelings right now and your plans for the future. Use some challenge words or forms of challenge words.

A.
1. _____
2. _____
3. _____
4. _____
5. _____
6. _____

B.
1. _____
2. _____
3. _____
4. _____
5. _____
6. _____

Challenge Activities

butte	pollute	nuisance
utensil	junior	substitute

A.
1.
2.
3.
4.
5.
6.

B.
1.
2.
3.
4.
5.
6.

A. **1.–5.** Five challenge words can be used as nouns. Write the plural forms of those words.

     6. One of the challenge words is a verb. Change that word to a noun by adding the **-ion** suffix. Write the new word.

B. Write a challenge word to complete each analogy.

    1. Calm is to **turbulent** as **cleanse** is to _____.

    2. Older is to **senior** as **younger** is to _____.

    3. Eternal is to **permanent** as **replacement** is to _____.

    4. Helper is to **pest** as **convenience** is to _____.

    5. Hammer is to **tool** as **fork** is to _____.

    6. Forest is to **tree** as **mountain range** is to _____.

C. People think very differently about the care and use of rivers, lakes, and oceans. They are influenced by whether they fish, sail, own factories, study wildlife, and so forth. Choose any two people. Write a persuasive paragraph from one person's point of view about the use of our water supply. Then choose a person who might have entirely different ideas. Write a paragraph expressing that person's point of view. Use as many challenge words as possible.

Challenge Activities

| coffee | auburn | falter |
| faucet | awkward | alternate |

A. The letters that spell the /ô/ sound are missing in the challenge words. Write the words correctly.

1. __ __ kward
2. f __ __ ter
3. c __ ffee
4. f __ __ cet
5. __ __ burn
6. __ __ ternate

B. Write a challenge word to complete each sentence.

1. Due to the heavy traffic, Dad took an _____ route home.
2. Don't try to memorize every word in your speech or you might get nervous and _____.
3. Her _____ hair was the color of autumn leaves.
4. Because the package was large and _____, it would not fit in the trunk of the car.
5. A major export of Brazil is _____.
6. The plumber came to unclog the drain and tighten the _____.

C. Here is your chance to make your own invention. It could be an alternate way of doing something that people presently find awkward. It could be something entirely new. Perhaps you can invent a faucet that never leaks or a fantasy faucet that produces any kind of drink you name. Write about your invention and describe it as fully as you can. Add drawings or a diagram if you wish. Use challenge words when you can.

A.
1.
2.
3.
4.
5.
6.
B.
1.
2.
3.
4.
5.
6.

227

Challenge Activities

secretary	treasurer	senate
cashier	summon	vanish

A. Match a syllable from Column A with a syllable from Column B to form challenge words. Write the words.

	A	B
1.	van	ier
2.	sen	mon
3.	cash	ate
4.	sum	ish

B. **1.–2.** Write the challenge words that have more than two syllables.

C. Write challenge words to complete the paragraphs. Remember to capitalize a word used as a proper noun. You will have to add **-ed** to one word.

We have a very well-organized system of government in the United States. The House of Representatives and the __1.__ are the two branches of Congress. Both branches of Congress and every department in the government have people performing certain functions that are necessary for the government to operate smoothly. At a store, you pay a __2.__ for your purchases. However, in our government all funds and finances are handled by a __3.__. A __4.__ organizes files, delivers important messages, and keeps the department in order.

Government employees must be loyal and dedicated. They may be __5.__ at any hour of the night to handle important crisis situations. They know that problems will not __6.__ but must be straightened out to ensure an effective system.

D. Write a mystery story. At the start of your story, tell about a secret message that has vanished. What was in the message? Who is suspected of the crime? Add details and clues. Be sure to tell how the crime was solved.

Sidebar answer column:

A.
1.
2.
3.
4.

B.
1.
2.

C.
1.
2.
3.
4.
5.
6.

Challenge Activities

champion	scorching	situated
eruption	suction	extinguish

A. The **sh** and **ch** sounds are spelled incorrectly in the challenge words below. Write the words correctly.

1. erupcion 3. sichuated 5. extinguich
2. shampion 4. sucshion 6. scorshing

B. Write the challenge word that is a synonym for each clue.

1. a drawing in by removing part of the air
2. put out
3. burning
4. winner
5. violent outburst
6. located

C. In diaries people often reveal more about their views and feelings than they would share with others in a conversation. Imagine that you have recently experienced the eruption of a volcano nearby. Write a diary entry about what you saw and how you felt about it. Write it as if you were an eyewitness. Use challenge words when you can.

A.
1.
2.
3.
4.
5.
6.
B.
1.
2.
3.
4.
5.
6.

Challenge Activities

mussel	freckle	arrival
stencil	possible	additional

A. Unscramble the underlined challenge word in each question. Write the word correctly. Then answer the question with either **Yes** or **No**.

1. Is it <u>silopebs</u> for a person to climb a beanstalk?
2. Does an airline sometimes have a late <u>iralavr</u> of a flight?
3. If you are learning something new, do you often have to spend <u>tdianaidol</u> time in practice?
4. Would you rather eat pickled <u>sumsle</u> than fresh lobster?
5. Do you have a <u>kleefrc</u> on your foot?
6. Is a <u>stnecil</u> the same as a pencil?

B. Pretend that your challenge words can speak. Write the words that would say the following sentences.

1. "Forever on your skin I will stay,
   Never able to be washed away."
2. "Follow my outline with a pencil,
   And many different shapes you can _____."
3. "I sound like **muscle,**
   But my spelling can be a puzzle."

C. Write the challenge word that is an antonym for each underlined word.

1. <u>departure</u> schedule
2. <u>fewer</u> chores
3. <u>unworkable</u> solution

A.
1.
2.
3.
4.
5.
6.

B.
1.
2.
3.

C.
1.
2.
3.

Challenge Activities

| latter | escalator | specimen |
| elevator | cinnamon | suspicion |

A. The letters in each word below are hiding in a challenge word. Write each challenge word.

1. cannon   3. coins   5. castle
2. voter   4. late   6. piece

B. Write a challenge word to complete each sentence.

1. Between the written book report and the oral speech, I have chosen the ＿＿＿.

2. We added both nutmeg and ＿＿＿ to our hot chocolate.

3. Please remember to lift your feet as you step off the ＿＿＿.

4. The ＿＿＿ will surely be the quickest way to reach the tenth floor.

5. Did you remember to bring your rock ＿＿＿ for today's science class?

6. One character was above ＿＿＿ in the movie mystery.

C. Someone has entered the spice factory during the night and mixed up all the spices. The cinnamon is now in pepper containers. The cloves were put in parsley containers. How did the culprit get into the packaging area? Who might be responsible for switching the spices? You are Monsieur or Mademoiselle Toufaux, a famous detective. Write a paragraph in which you explain what you believe happened, step by step. Tell why you think it happened. If you have a solution to the mysterious happenings, include it. Use as many challenge words as you can.

A.
1. _____
2. _____
3. _____
4. _____
5. _____
6. _____
B.
1. _____
2. _____
3. _____
4. _____
5. _____
6. _____

Challenge Activities

girth	birthmark	furnish
stirrups	hurdles	swerve

A.
1.
2.
3.
4.
5.
6.

B.
1.
2.
3.
4.
5.
6.

A. 1.–2. Write the singular noun form of the two plural challenge words. Circle the letters that spell the /ûr/ sound.

3.–4. Write the plural noun form of the two singular challenge words. Circle the letters that spell the /ûr/ sound.

5.–6. Write the past tense form of the two challenge words that are verbs in their most common usage. Circle the letters that spell the /ûr/ sound.

B. Write the challenge word that matches each definition.

1. barriers or obstacles used in races
2. to supply or give
3. the distance around something
4. to turn aside from a straight course
5. foot supports that are hung from a horse's saddle to support the rider's feet
6. a mark present on the body from birth

C. Imagine you are a commentator giving an account of a horse show. Bring it alive for the listener or reader. Be a commentator who feels what it is like to be the rider and who catches the excitement of the crowd. Write your commentary. Use as many challenge words as you can to describe the riders, horses, the course, and the crowd.

Challenge Activities

wary	aquarium	harmonica
solitaire	carnival	pharmacy

A. Unscramble the letters and write the challenge words.

1. n a r a c l i v
2. i m o c a n r a h
3. r a y w
4. a r u u i q a m
5. r h m a p c y a
6. i l t a i r e s o

B. Write the challenge word that completes each group.

1. cautious, apprehensive, _____
2. tambourine, castanets, _____
3. tank, bowl, _____
4. single, lone, _____
5. circus, amusement show, _____
6. drugstore, apothecary, _____

C. The diamond merchants are trying to persuade people that everyone should own a diamond. They want to convince people that diamonds add sparkle to life whether a person wears them to a carnival or on a shopping trip to a pharmacy. What ideas do you have for an advertising campaign? Try to convince people that diamonds make a person attractive, fashionable, and happy. Write a persuasive advertisement for a full page in a major magazine. Use an illustration to accompany your ad.

A.
1. _____
2. _____
3. _____
4. _____
5. _____
6. _____

B.
1. _____
2. _____
3. _____
4. _____
5. _____
6. _____

Challenge Activities

| florist | corporal | sincere |
| boardwalk | eerie | ordinance |

A. Match a syllable from Column A with a syllable from Column B to form challenge words. Write the words.

	A	**B**
1.	ee	walk
2.	board	cere
3.	flo	rie
4.	sin	rist

B. Write a challenge word to answer each question.

1. Which challenge word has the /ən/ sound?
2. Which challenge word has the /əl/ sound?

C. Write a challenge word to complete each analogy.

1. **Captain** is to **lieutenant** as **sergeant** is to _____.
2. **Secure** is to **safe** as **mysterious** is to _____.
3. **Foodstuff** is to **grocer** as **bouquet** is to _____.
4. **Suggestion** is to **proposal** as **command** is to _____.
5. **Honest** is to **truthful** as **genuine** is to _____.
6. **Street** is to **sidewalk** as **beach** is to _____.

D. Create a comic strip. Use a resort that has a boardwalk along the ocean. You might make the central character a florist because both residents and visitors buy flowers for various reasons. Make notes to describe the florist and some of the people who enter the shop. Make other notes about the boardwalk and the people and things you might put in your comic strip. Draw your comic strip and put in speech balloons. Use some of the challenge words in the dialogue. If you prefer, write a paragraph instead of developing a comic strip.

A.
1.
2.
3.
4.

B.
1.
2.

C.
1.
2.
3.
4.
5.
6.

Challenge Activities

lounge	trousers	loiter
foundation	corduroy	asteroid

A. The /**oi**/ sound and the /**ou**/ sound are spelled incorrectly in the challenge words below. Write the words correctly.

1. trowsers
2. lownge
3. fowndation
4. corduroi
5. loyter
6. asteroyd

B. Write a challenge word to complete each sentence.

1. On weekends, I try to find a little time to _____ in a comfortable chair.
2. The engineer will tell us if the building's _____ is strong and solid.
3. My father's new _____ have a blue and white checkered print.
4. I will wear my red _____ skirt to the party.
5. Please do not _____ on your way to the dentist.
6. We saw photographs of a comet and an _____ at the science museum.

C. Imagine a hotel lounge. There are various people in it. For example, one young man is casually dressed in corduroy trousers and a sweatshirt. Some people are more formally dressed. Suddenly a waiter carrying a tray with dishes of ice cream slips, and the ice cream hits one of the people. Put yourself in the situation. Take the part of one of the onlookers. Write what happened next. Use some of the challenge words in your description.

A.
1. _____
2. _____
3. _____
4. _____
5. _____
6. _____

B.
1. _____
2. _____
3. _____
4. _____
5. _____
6. _____

Challenge Activities

preface	redirect	co-anchor
preamble	recuperate	post meridiem

A. The prefixes are incorrectly attached. Change the prefixes. Write the challenge words correctly.

1. reface
2. reamble
3. postanchor
4. predirect
5. precuperate
6. comeridiem

B. A challenge word is used incorrectly in each sentence. Write the correct word.

1. An author often writes a redirect, which is placed at the beginning of a book to introduce the text.
2. A post meridiem is one member of a team of news reporters who work together to broadcast the news.
3. People who have had operations need time to preamble before they can get back on their feet.
4. In the co-anchor to the Declaration of Independence, our founding fathers set forth the purpose of that very important document.
5. The initialization P.M. represents the word **preface,** meaning "after midday."
6. Due to the sudden storm at sea, the captain had to recuperate the ship's course.

C. Use the prefixes **pre-, re-, post-,** and **co-** as headings for four columns. List each challenge word under the appropriate heading. Then list other words that begin with these prefixes. Choose any six of the words you listed and purposely misuse them in sentences, as in Activity B. Exchange papers and have a classmate complete the exercise by writing the correct word for each sentence.

A.
1.
2.
3.
4.
5.
6.
B.
1.
2.
3.
4.
5.
6.

Challenge Activities

| laughed | hiccupped | fluffier |
| laughing | hiccupping | fluffiest |

A. Write challenge words to complete the two columns of related forms. Remember to use the rules for adding suffixes.

	-ed		**-ing**
laugh	1. ___		2. ___
hiccup	3. ___		4. ___
	-er		**-est**
fluffy	5. ___		6. ___

B. Examine the structure of the two words given. Write the challenge word that fits with the group.

1. interested, contained, ___
2. trimmed, planned, ___
3. swimming, trimming, ___
4. counseling, interesting, ___
5. sunniest, funniest, ___
6. easier, sunnier, ___

C. Answer each question below. Try to develop a plot for a story as suggested by the questions and the answers you wrote. Write your story using some of the challenge words, or forms of them.

1. What could be fluffy?
2. What are some things that make people laugh?
3. When would it be embarrassing to have a bad case of the hiccups?

A.
1.
2.
3.
4.
5.
6.
B.
1.
2.
3.
4.
5.
6.

Challenge Activities

recipe	crackers	coconut
juicy	scallop	broccoli

A.
1.
2.
3.
4.
5.
6.

B.
1.
2.
3.
4.
5.
6.

A. The letters that spell the /**s**/ sound and the /**k**/ sound are incorrect in the words below. Write the challenge words correctly. Circle the letters that spell the /**s**/ or /**k**/ sound in each word.

1. k r a c e r s
2. j u i s y
3. b r o c k o l i
4. s k a l l o p
5. k o k o n u t
6. r e s i p e

B. Write the challenge words to complete the paragraph. You will have to add an **-s** to two words.

   If you are going to cook a meal, the wisest thing to do is to plan a menu. Look in cookbooks to find several interesting ___1.___. A light soup with ___2.___ might be served as an appetizer. For the main course you might choose a meat, such as ___3.___ steaks, or a seafood, such as ___4.___. One green vegetable you might serve is ___5.___. Fresh fruit topped with shredded ___6.___ might be a perfect ending for your meal.

C. Pretend you just received word that you won a contest. As your prize, you can have dinner at any restaurant in the world. All transportation and expenses will be paid! Write an imaginary diary entry as if you have just received the news. Add details. For example, tell what kind of contest you entered and what you did to win. Write a second diary entry, pretending you have chosen the restaurant and location. Make up names if you wish. In your final entry, pretend you have made the trip and are now back home. Tell about the elegant meal you had. Use some of the challenge words.

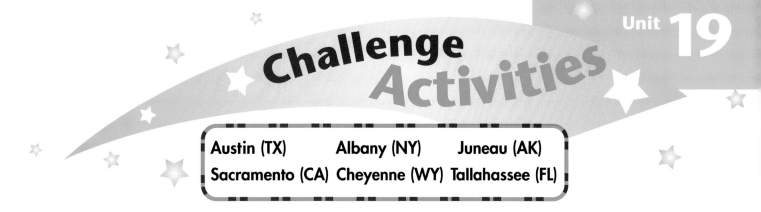

Challenge Activities

Austin (TX) Albany (NY) Juneau (AK)
Sacramento (CA) Cheyenne (WY) Tallahassee (FL)

A. The challenge words name the capital cities of six states. Write the challenge word for each dictionary respelling. Remember to capitalize all proper nouns.

1. /săk′ rə **měn′** tō/
2. /**jōō′** nō′/
3. /tăl′ ə **hăs′** ē/
4. /**ô′** stən/
5. /shī **ăn′**/
6. /**ôl′** bə nē/

B. Write the name of the state capital that is indicated by the • in each state outline. Use a map of the United States if you need help.

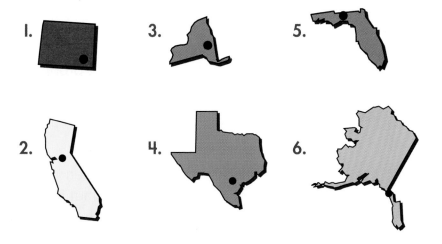

1. 2. 3. 4. 5. 6.

A.
1. _____
2. _____
3. _____
4. _____
5. _____
6. _____
B.
1. _____
2. _____
3. _____
4. _____
5. _____
6. _____

C. We all have ideas about places we have never been to and know very little about. Write three or four sentences telling your ideas about any city on the challenge list. Then look up the facts about the city and write four or five sentences based on facts that seem important about the city.

Challenge Activities

unlikely	immature	nondairy
uncommon	insincere	discontinue

A. The prefixes **un-, im-, in-, non-,** and **dis-** are missing from the challenge words. Write the words correctly.

1. __ __ mature
2. __ __ __ dairy
3. __ __ likely
4. __ __ __ continue
5. __ __ sincere
6. __ __ common

B. Write the challenge word that is the antonym for the underlined word in the phrase. You will have to add the **-ed** suffix to one word.

1. the <u>mature</u> decision
2. the <u>common</u> problem
3. the <u>likely</u> choice
4. the <u>dairy</u> product
5. the <u>continued</u> item
6. the <u>sincere</u> letter

C. Imagine that a new nondairy drink has just been introduced on the market. The makers claim that it will replace milk. Of course, the dairy farmers are unhappy about the situation and believe this claim is unfounded. Take the farmers' side and write a persuasive report about why it is unlikely that the new product will replace milk. Use as many challenge words as you can in your report.

A.
1. _____
2. _____
3. _____
4. _____
5. _____
6. _____

B.
1. _____
2. _____
3. _____
4. _____
5. _____
6. _____

Challenge Activities

quicken	strengthen	dramatize
broaden	colonize	plagiarize

A. Write a challenge word to complete each equation.

1. colony – y + ize = _____
2. dramatic – ic + ize = _____
3. quibble – bble + ck + en = _____
4. plague – ue + iar + ize = _____
5. strenuous – uous + g + then = _____
6. broccoli – ccoli + ad + en = _____

B. Write a challenge word to complete each sentence.

1. To _____ is to make wider or larger.
2. To _____ is to make or become powerful.
3. To _____ is to make into a play or a screenplay.
4. To _____ is to establish a settlement.
5. To _____ is to make or become rapid.
6. To _____ is to take ideas or written passages from another.

C. Imagine that your class has decided to dramatize a scene about early colonization in the United States. Unfortunately, someone has plagiarized material from another play rather than writing original material. Write an explanation of the situation. Then tell what you can do now to produce a successful play. Use the challenge words or forms of them when you can.

A.
1. _____
2. _____
3. _____
4. _____
5. _____
6. _____
B.
1. _____
2. _____
3. _____
4. _____
5. _____
6. _____

Unit 22

Challenge Activities

| eyeglasses | field goal | decimal point |
| cheerleader | time zone | daylight-saving time |

A.
1.
2.
3.
4.
5.
6.

B.
1.
2.
3.
4.
5.
6.

A. Write each challenge word correctly by rearranging the mixed-up parts.

1. eyetime
2. cheerglasses
3. field zone
4. time goal
5. decimal leader
6. daylight-saving point

B. Write challenge words to complete the paragraph. You will have to add **-s** to one word.

Everyone was excited about the first football game of the season. The game was scheduled to begin at 8 P.M., but for those in the Pacific __1.__, live television coverage would begin three hours later. My family had great seats, and I remembered to bring my __2.__ so I wouldn't miss a single play. We could see the stadium lights from miles away because __3.__ had just ended and it became dark very early. We arrived in time to see a group of __4.__ performing for the spectators. During the first play, the quarterback threw a pass that was short of a first down by what seemed to be a __5.__! The team scored three points when they made a __6.__ three plays later.

C. Some sports are played in only one country. When people from another country see these sports, they may not have any idea what is going on. What do you think a person from another country would say about American football? Imagine that you are someone watching your very first game of football. Which football terms and which actions might seem strange to you? Perhaps you can imagine that you are from Australia, Japan, or Spain. If so, compare and contrast football with your country's game of Rugby, kemari, or soccer. Use the challenge words when you can.

242

navel	burrow	bridal
naval	borough	bridle

A. 1.–2. Write the challenge words that have the **long i** sound. Circle the letter in each word that spells the sound.

3.–4. Write the words that have the **long a** sound. Circle the letter in each word that spells the sound.

5.–6. Write the words that have the **long o** sound. Circle the letters in each word that spell the sound.

B. Write a challenge word to complete each sentence.

1. Moles _____ through fields in search of earthworms.
2. Her _____ gown was made of ivory satin.
3. Brooklyn is a _____ in New York City.
4. The United States is a great _____ power.
5. The jockey held the horse's _____ at the starting gate.
6. I have a delicious _____ orange in my lunch box.

C. Many people in Washington, DC, keep their ears open for information. What if they overhear these statements?

An important-looking, older gentleman is saying to another, "I'm very worried. We're having trouble with the (nā′ vəl) section. We may have to cancel the whole operation."

A city planner is telling her assistant, "That (bûr′ ō) is popular. Many people want to live there."

What is it that each speaker is referring to? Write some sentences of your own. Use challenge words or other words with homophones. Exchange papers with someone. Write the most likely meaning of the homophone.

A.
1. ___
2. ___
3. ___
4. ___
5. ___
6. ___
B.
1. ___
2. ___
3. ___
4. ___
5. ___
6. ___

Challenge Activities

aviator	discoverer	cartoonist
commentator	adventurer	specialist

A.
1.
2.
3.
4.
5.
6.

B.
1.
2.
3.
4.
5.
6.

A. Unscramble the letters and write the challenge words. Circle the letters that spell the suffix that means "one who" in each word.

1. n e m o a m c r o t t
2. t e e u r r n v d a
3. t o r i a c o s n t
4. i o t a r v a
5. s i v e e r d o r c
6. p a i c t s i e l s

B. Complete the challenge words. Some letters have been filled in as clues.

1. _ _ _ _ _ _ _ _ _ or
2. _ i _ _ _ _ _ _ er
3. _ a _ _ _ _ _ ist
4. _ _ _ _ _ _ _ _ rer
5. _ _ _ _ _ _ _ r
6. _ _ e _ _ _ _ ist

C. Do the careers suggested by the challenge words above sound interesting? What might the cartoonist do? What might the specialist do? Make some prewriting notes. Write phrases that begin like this: an aviator who. . . . Then tell something about the person's situation. For example, you might write:

- an aviator who tries to beat the world record for the most transatlantic crossings
- an aviator who is a captain for a commercial airline

Do the same with the other challenge words. After you have completed your prewriting notes, use one idea and write a short story. You may wish to put yourself in the role of the main character.

Challenge Activities

oboes	orchids	galleries
tactics	teenagers	secretaries

A. Study the structure of each word given in the singular and plural. Complete the analogies by writing the singular and plural of a challenge word that has a similar structure.

   1.–2. tiptoe : tiptoes :: _____ : _____

   3.–4. picnic : picnics :: _____ : _____

   5.–6. aphid : aphids :: _____ : _____

   7.–8. family : families :: _____ : _____

   9.–10. passenger : passengers :: _____ : _____

 11.–12. biography : biographies :: _____ : _____

B. Write a challenge word to complete each analogy.

   1. Flutes are to **piccolos** as **bassoons** are to _____.

   2. Trees are to **oaks** as **flowers** are to _____.

   3. Courts are to **lawyers** as **offices** are to _____.

   4. Plays are to **theaters** as **paintings** are to _____.

   5. Children are to **infants** as **adults** are to _____.

   6. Objectives are to **strategies** as **goals** are to _____.

C. In a magic kingdom by the sea, the musicians presented the queen with an acrostic poem based on the word **oboes**.

Oh how
Beautiful
Our silver sounds
Echoing still through the
Silence of memory.

Choose another challenge word and use the letters and the ideas suggested by the word to write an acrostic poem.

A.
1. _____
2. _____
3. _____
4. _____
5. _____
6. _____
7. _____
8. _____
9. _____
10. _____
11. _____
12. _____

B.
1. _____
2. _____
3. _____
4. _____
5. _____
6. _____

Challenge Activities

bilateral	midfield	tricornered
bicoastal	midsection	semiweekly

A. Add the prefixes **bi-, mid-, tri-,** or **semi-** to the following words to form challenge words. Write the challenge words.

1. field
2. section
3. lateral
4. coastal
5. weekly
6. cornered

B. A challenge word is misused in each sentence. Write the correct challenge word.

1. The United States is tricornered because it has the Atlantic Ocean on the east and the Pacific Ocean on the west.
2. A midfield agreement affects two sides.
3. We have tickets for seats in the bicoastal of the stadium.
4. His new geometric desk is semiweekly.
5. Our local newspaper is published tricornered.
6. At the start of the game, the ball was placed midsection.

C. Did you ever put opposites, or "somewhat" opposites, together to make nonsense? For example, can you put on "a round tricornered hat"? This week's challenge words are especially good for nonsense opposites because the prefix indicates number or position. All you have to do is use them to describe something with a different number or position. You can say, for example, that you read your semiweekly Sunday paper. Have some fun with nonsense opposites. Write a story or a rhyme using some of the challenge words.

A.
1.
2.
3.
4.
5.
6.

B.
1.
2.
3.
4.
5.
6.

Challenge Activities

fidget	**sledgehammer**	**gesture**
misjudge	**gender**	**refrigerator**

A. The /**j**/ sound is spelled incorrectly in the following words. Write the challenge words correctly.

1. figet
2. jesture
3. misjuge
4. jender
5. slegehammer
6. refridgerator

B. Write the challenge word for each clue.

1. masculine or feminine
2. long, heavy hammer
3. to move nervously
4. to evaluate incorrectly
5. a motion used to express meaning
6. a box used for storing food at low temperature

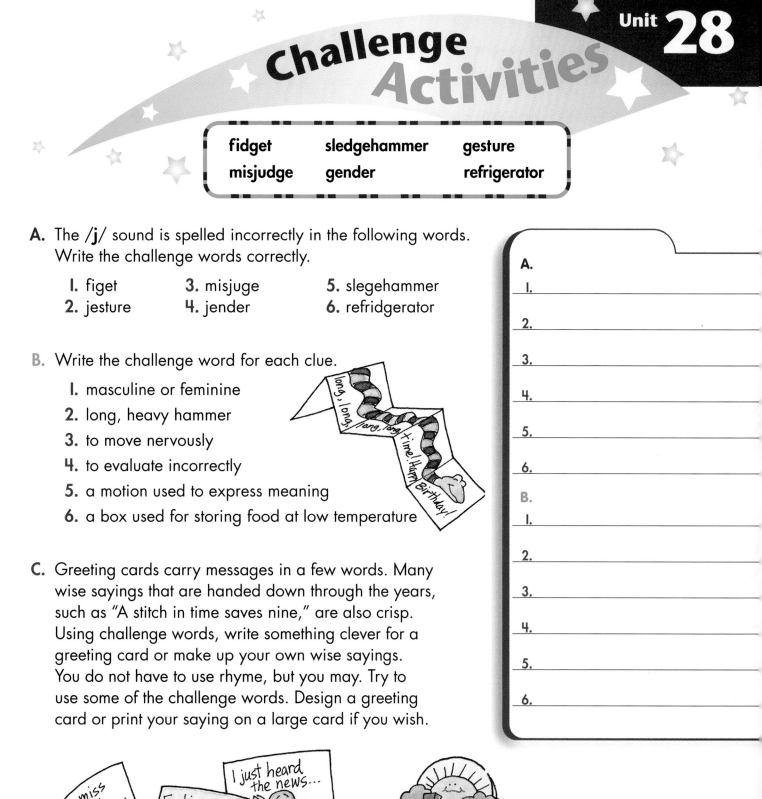

C. Greeting cards carry messages in a few words. Many wise sayings that are handed down through the years, such as "A stitch in time saves nine," are also crisp. Using challenge words, write something clever for a greeting card or make up your own wise sayings. You do not have to use rhyme, but you may. Try to use some of the challenge words. Design a greeting card or print your saying on a large card if you wish.

A.
1. _____
2. _____
3. _____
4. _____
5. _____
6. _____
B.
1. _____
2. _____
3. _____
4. _____
5. _____
6. _____

Challenge Activities

replacement	promptness	mobility
refreshment	usefulness	maturity

A. Write a challenge word to complete each equation.

1. replace + ment = _____
2. prompt + ness = _____
3. mobile − e + ity = _____
4. refresh + ment = _____
5. mature − e + ity = _____
6. useful + ness = _____

B. Write a challenge word to complete each sentence.

1. The invention of the automobile provided greater _____ for people.
2. A computer is valued more for its _____ than its beauty.
3. Have they found a _____ for the injured quarterback?
4. Being responsible is a sign of _____.
5. A glass of spring water with a little lemon juice is a popular summer _____.
6. _____ is necessary when meeting deadlines.

C. You see how the suffixes **-ity, -ness,** and **-ment** often make a word that stands for an idea rather than something concrete. When two people talk about an abstract idea, they cannot be sure that the word used means quite the same thing to both of them. Do you think, for example, that fifth-graders and adults have the same idea when they mention the word **maturity**? What about the word **usefulness**? Do you and your friends necessarily think of the same thing when you hear that word?

Write what each of the challenge words means to you. Then write what it might mean to someone else.

A.
1.
2.
3.
4.
5.
6.

B.
1.
2.
3.
4.
5.
6.

Challenge Activities

| waive | croquet | sergeant |
| gradual | acquire | poinsettia |

A. Unscramble the letters and write the challenge words.

1. v e i w a
2. s n t e a t i o p i
3. t n g r e e a s
4. u t r q c o e
5. d u r a a g l
6. q r c u i e a

B. Three of the challenge words are nouns. Write a challenge word for each clue below.

1. a person   2. a plant   3. a game

C. Write a challenge word to complete each sentence.

1. To get something is to _____ it.
2. To give up something is to _____ it.
3. A slow but continuous change is a _____ one.

D. The best way to remember what you learn is to understand it thoroughly and make links with other things you know. A good way to remember commonly misspelled words is to know their meanings thoroughly and then make some links to help you remember the spellings. These linking devices to help you remember are called **mnemonics,** from the Greek word for mindful. They can be stories, jingles, or anything else that helps. For example, for the word **waive** this sentence might be helpful: If I wave my hand, **I** can **waive** it. Write mnemonics for the challenge words.

A.
1.
2.
3.
4.
5.
6.
B.
1.
2.
3.
C.
1.
2.
3.

Challenge Activities

reluctant	periodic	thunderous
terrific	ticklish	simultaneous

A. The suffixes **-ous, -ish, -ant,** and **-ic** are incorrectly attached. The result is a list of nonsense words. Choose the correct suffixes and write the challenge words correctly.

1. terrifish
2. ticklant
3. simultaneish
4. reluctic
5. periodous
6. thunderant

B. Each underlined word in the sentences below is an antonym for a challenge word. Write the challenge word that goes with each antonym.

1. She was feeling <u>awful</u> on the day of the big race.
2. They had a <u>different</u> broadcast on the radio station.
3. She was very <u>willing</u> to take on the new responsibilities.
4. His lateness was becoming a <u>continual</u> problem.
5. She was very <u>insensitive</u> about the subject of women's rights.
6. The actors received <u>quiet</u> applause after the finale.

C. Through the ages, playwrights and writers for television comedies have amused their audiences with characters that have one exaggerated trait. Most of the challenge words could describe exaggerated characters. Make up a comedy skit for a television show. Write a scene or two using some challenge words to describe traits or actions of characters. The setting can be in the past or in the present. You might even use an existing plot and re-create the characters. *Goldilocks and the Three Bears,* for example, would probably be quite funny if you used exaggerations.

A.
1.
2.
3.
4.
5.
6.

B.
1.
2.
3.
4.
5.
6.

Challenge Activities

deflate	worried	incident
inflate	distressed	happening

A. Write a challenge word that follows the same spelling pattern as the words in each group.

   1. tried, hurried, _____

   2. depressed, pressed, _____

   3. president, accident, _____

   4. delete, degrade, _____

   5. inscribe, inspect, _____

   6. walking, eating, _____

B. Follow the directions to write the challenge words.

   1.–2. Write the challenge words that are nouns meaning "event."

   3.–4. Write the challenge words that can be used as adjectives meaning "agonized."

   5. Write the challenge word that is a verb meaning "to fill up."

   6. Write the challenge word that is a verb meaning "to make smaller."

C. Imagine that you are in a harbor witnessing a sailboat race. Write an eyewitness report about what is happening. You might include an incident that caused the concern of the contest participants as well as the onlookers. Use as many challenge words as possible in your eyewitness report. Try to use other words that are synonyms or antonyms in your report.

A.
1. _____
2. _____
3. _____
4. _____
5. _____
6. _____

B.
1. _____
2. _____
3. _____
4. _____
5. _____
6. _____

251

Challenge Activities

chowder	safari	kayak
goulash	llama	verandah

A. Write the challenge word for each following dictionary respelling.

1. /kī′ ăk′/
2. /sə fä′ rē/
3. /chou′ dər/
4. /go͞o′ läsh′/
5. /lä′ mə/
6. /və răn′ də/

B. Write the challenge word that fits each word history.

1. From the African word **safariy** meaning "trip."
2. From the Hindi word **verandā** meaning "railing."
3. From the Inuit word **qajaq** meaning "canoe."
4. From the Hungarian word **gulyas** meaning "herdsman's meat."
5. From the French word **chaudière** meaning "stew pot."
6. From the Quechua word that means "cud-chewing mammal."

C. Your imagination can let you travel around the world without moving an inch. This week's challenge words suggest a number of beautiful, exciting places. Picture the kayak, for example, in its home setting. Close your eyes and bring the scene to life. Put yourself in the kayak. Can you hear the quiet splash and feel the tug of the water as you dip in your paddle? How does the air feel on your skin? Is it summer or winter? Are you alone under the northern skies? Choose any of the challenge words and go traveling. Then write about where you have been.

A.
1.
2.
3.
4.
5.
6.

B.
1.
2.
3.
4.
5.
6.

| Jr. | adj. | ht. |
| Sr. | adv. | etc. |

A. Think of the word that each challenge abbreviation stands for. Then follow each direction.

    1.–3. Write the abbreviations that are formed from the first and last letters of words.

    4.–5. Write the abbreviations that are formed from the first three letters of words.

    6. Write the abbreviation that comes from the Latin **et cetera** meaning "and so forth."

B. The challenge abbreviations in the following are written incorrectly. Rewrite each abbreviation correctly.

    1. Mr. Jeffrey J. Johnson, jr.

    2. tomatoes, corn, peas, etc

    3. com•i•cal (**kôm′** ĭ kəl) Aj.

    4. Dr. Ross Sintu, SR.

    5. hap•pi•ly (**hăp′** ə lē) ADV.

    6. Peter—age 11, hgt. 55 in., wt. 84 lbs.

C. Abbreviations are very useful at times. The key to success in writing, however, is using language that is appropriate for your purpose. Make a list of different kinds of writing in which it would be suitable to use abbreviations. For example, should you use abbreviations when you take notes? What about in ads? After you have completed your list, select several types of writing and write examples with abbreviations in them. Use some of the challenge words as well as other abbreviations.

A.
1. _____
2. _____
3. _____
4. _____
5. _____
6. _____
B.
1. _____
2. _____
3. _____
4. _____
5. _____
6. _____

253

WRITER'S HANDBOOK
Contents

The first step in learning your spelling words is correcting your pretest. Follow these steps with your teacher.

These tips will help you do better on your spelling tests and remember how to spell words when you are writing.

Spelling is for writing. Learning these steps in the writing process will help you become a better writer.

These ideas will help you practice the four basic types of writing: narrative, descriptive, expository, and persuasive.

Spelling Strategy
When You Take a Test

 Get ready for the test. Make sure your paper and pencil are ready.

 Listen carefully as your teacher says each word and uses it in a sentence. Don't write before you hear the word **and** the sentence.

Write the word carefully. Make sure your handwriting is easy to read. If you want to print your words, ask your teacher.

 Use a pen to correct your test. Look at the word as your teacher says it.

Say the word aloud. Listen carefully as your teacher spells the word. Say each letter aloud. Check the word one letter at a time.

 Circle any misspelled parts of the word.

 Look at the correctly written word. Spell the word again. Say each letter out loud.

 Write any misspelled word correctly.

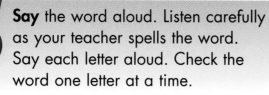

Spelling Strategy
When You Write a Paper

1 **Think** of the exact word you want to use.

2 **Write** the word, if you know how to spell it.

3 **Say** the word to yourself, if you are not sure how to spell it.

4 **Picture** what the word looks like when you see it written.

5 **Write** the word.

6 **Ask** yourself whether the word looks right.

7 **Check** the word in a dictionary if you are not sure.

SPELLING AND THE Writing Process

Writing anything—a friendly letter, a paper for school—usually follows a process. The writing process has five steps. It might look like this if you tried to draw a picture of it:

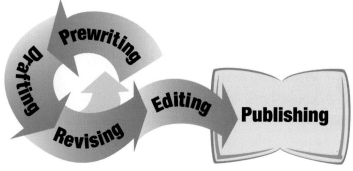

Part of that writing process forms a loop. That is because not every writing task is the same. It is also because writers often jump back and forth between the steps as they change their minds and think of new ideas.

Here is a description of each step:

Prewriting This is thinking and planning ahead to help you write.

Drafting This means writing your paper for the first time. You usually just try to get your ideas down on paper. You can fix them later.

Revising This means writing your final draft. Here is where you rewrite, change, and add words.

Editing This is where you feel you have said all you want to say. Now you proofread your paper for spelling errors and errors in grammar and punctuation.

Publishing This is making a copy of your writing and sharing it with your readers. Put your writing in a form that your readers will enjoy.

Confident spellers are better writers. Confident writers understand better their own writing process. Know the five steps. Know how they best fit the way you write.

SPELLING AND Writing Ideas

Being a good speller can help make you a more confident writer. Writing more can make you a better writer. Here are some ideas to get you started.

Ideas for Descriptive Writing

You might…

- describe something very, very small and something very, very big.
- describe something from the point of view of an insect.
- describe your most prized possession.

Ideas for Narrative Writing

You might…

- write a story about your first visit to someplace new.
- write a story about an event that helped you "grow up."
- write a story about a bad day or a best day playing your favorite sport.

Ideas for Persuasive Writing

You might…

- try to persuade your classmates to read a book you like.
- try to persuade your parents to let you have a pet.
- try to persuade your teacher to change a class rule.

Ideas for Expository Writing

You might…

- write how to prepare your favorite dish.
- inform your classmates how to create a craft object.
- write instructions on how to care for a lawn mower or carpentry tool.

More Ideas for Expository Writing

You might…

- find out how your local government works and write a report.
- interview an animal caregiver and write a report about the job.
- choose a career you might like and write a report about it.

Manuscript Handwriting Models

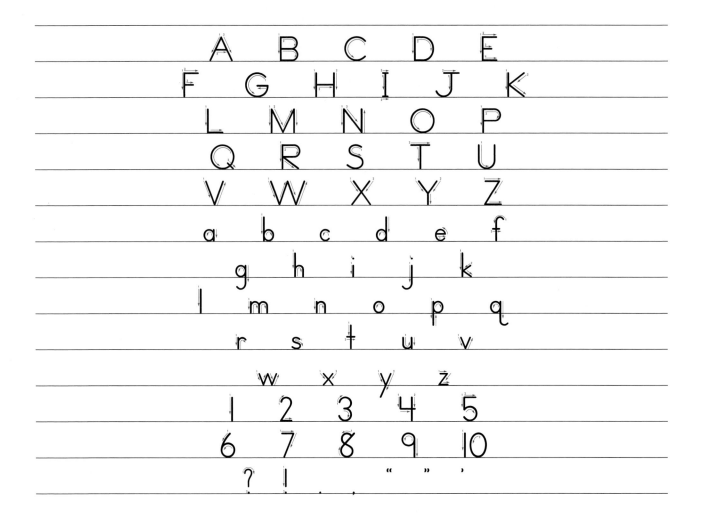

Cursive Handwriting Models

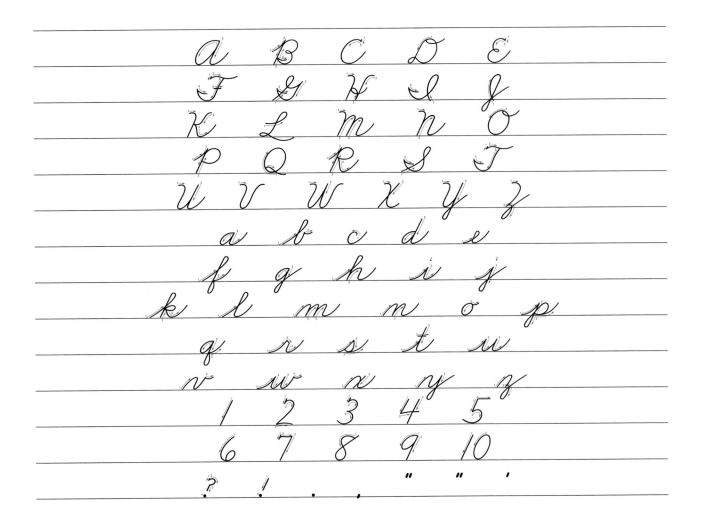

High Frequency Writing Words

A

a
about
afraid
after
again
air
all
almost
also
always
am
America
an
and
animal
animals
another
any
anything
are
around
as
ask
asked
at
ate
away

B

baby
back
bad
ball
balloons

baseball
basketball
be
bear
beautiful
because
become
bed
been
before
being
believe
best
better
big
bike
black
boat
book
books
both
boy
boys
bring
broke
brother
build
bus
but
buy
by

C

call
called
came

can
candy
can't
car
care
cars
cat
catch
caught
change
charge
children
Christmas
circus
city
class
clean
clothes
come
comes
coming
could
couldn't
country
cut

D

Dad
day
days
decided
did
didn't
died
different
dinner

do
does
doesn't
dog
dogs
doing
done
don't
door
down
dream

E

each
earth
eat
eighth
else
end
enough
even
every
everybody
everyone
everything
except
eyes

F

family
fast
father
favorite
feel
feet
fell

few
field
fight
finally
find
fire
first
fish
five
fix
food
football
for
found
four
free
Friday
friend
friends
from
front
fun
funny
future

G

game
games
gas
gave
get
gets
getting
girl
girls
give

go
God
goes
going
good
got
grade
grader
great
ground
grow

H

had
hair
half
happened
happy
hard
has
have
having
he
head
heard
help
her
here
he's
high
hill
him
his
hit
home
homework

hope
horse
horses
hot
hour
house
how
hurt

I

I
I'd
if
I'm
important
in
into
is
it
its
it's

J

job
jump
just

K

keep
kept
kids
killed
kind
knew
know

L

lady
land
last
later
learn
leave
left
let
let's
life
like
liked
likes
little
live
lived
lives
long
look
looked
looking
lost
lot
lots
love
lunch

M

mad
made
make
making
man
many
math

may
maybe
me
mean
men
might
miss
Mom
money
more
morning
most
mother
mouse
move
Mr.
Mrs.
much
music
must
my
myself

N

name
named
need
never
new
next
nice
night
no
not
nothing
now

O

of
off
oh
OK
old
on
once
one
only
or
other
our
out
outside
over
own

P

parents
park
party
people
person
pick
place
planet
play
played
playing
police
president
pretty
probably
problem
put

High Frequency Writing Words (continued)

R

ran
read
ready
real
really
reason
red
responsibilities
rest
ride
riding
right
room
rules
run
running

S

said
same
saw
say
scared
school
schools
sea
second
see
seen
set
seventh
she
ship
shot

should
show
sick
since
sister
sit
sleep
small
snow
so
some
someone
something
sometimes
soon
space
sport
sports
start
started
states
stay
still
stop
stopped
store
story
street
stuff
such
sudden
suddenly
summer
sure
swimming

T

take
talk
talking
teach
teacher
teachers
team
tell
than
Thanksgiving
that
that's
the
their
them
then
there
these
they
they're
thing
things
think
this
thought
three
through
throw
time
times
to
today
together
told
too
took

top
tree
trees
tried
trip
trouble
try
trying
turn
turned
TV
two

U

united
until
up
upon
us
use
used

V

very

W

walk
walked
walking
want
wanted
war
was
wasn't
watch
water
way
we

week
weeks
well
went
were
what
when
where
which
while
white
who
whole
why
will
win
winter
wish
with
without
woke
won
won't
work
world
would
wouldn't

Y

yard
year
years
yes
you
your
you're

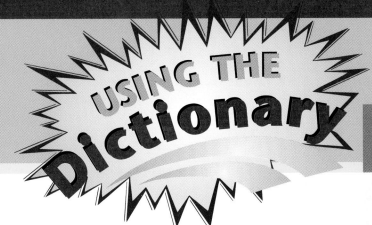

USING THE Dictionary

- Practice using guide words in a dictionary. Think of words to spell. Then use the guide words to find each word's entry. Do this again and again until you can use guide words easily.

- Some spellings are listed with the base word. To find **easiest,** you would look up **easy.** To find **remaining,** you would look up **remain.** To find **histories,** you would look up **history.**

- If you do not know how to spell a word, guess the spelling before looking it up. Try to find the first three letters of the word. (If you just use the first letter, you will probably take too long.)

- If you can't find a word, think of how else it might be spelled. For example, if a word starts with the **/k/ sound,** the spelling might begin with **k, c,** or even **ch.**

Guide Words

The **guide words** at the top of each dictionary page can help you find the word you want quickly. The first guide word tells you the first word on that page. The second guide word tells you the last word on that page. The entries on the page fall in alphabetical order between these two guide words.

Entries

Words you want to check in the dictionary are called **entries**. Entries provide a lot of information besides the correct spelling. Look at the sample entry below.

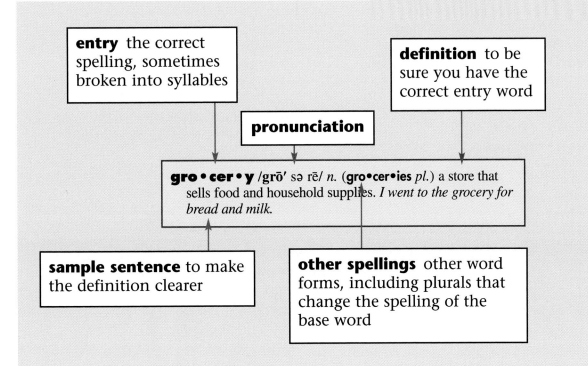

entry the correct spelling, sometimes broken into syllables

definition to be sure you have the correct entry word

pronunciation

gro•cer•y /grō′ sə rē/ *n.* (**gro•cer•ies** *pl.*) a store that sells food and household supplies. *I went to the grocery for bread and milk.*

sample sentence to make the definition clearer

other spellings other word forms, including plurals that change the spelling of the base word

a • bil • i • ty /ə bĭl′ ĭ tē/ *n.* (**a•bil•i•ties** *pl.*) the power to do something well. *A pilot has the ability to fly a plane through a storm.*

a • bol • ish /ə bŏl′ ĭsh/ *v.* to put an end to. *The speaker urged us to abolish poverty.*

ac • cept /ăk sĕpt′/ *v.* **a.** to take something given or offered. *You should accept gifts with a smile and a polite "thank you."* **b.** to agree to; to consent to. *She accepted the idea.*

ac • tive /ăk′ tĭv/ *adj.* **a.** moving about; lively. *Rabbits are more active than turtles.* **b.** working; functioning: *an active volcano.*

ac • tiv • i • ty /ăk tĭv′ ĭ tē/ *n.* (**ac•tiv•i•ties** *pl.*) **a.** action; being active. *Athletes enjoy physical activity.* **b.** an organized thing to do. *Our school has many music, science, and art activities.*

ac • tor /ăk′ tər/ *n.* a person who acts on the stage, in motion pictures, on radio, or on television. *A good actor can make people laugh or cry.*

ad • dress /ə drĕs′/ or /ăd′ rĕs/ *n.* (**ad•dress•es** *pl.*) **a.** a speech or writing: *Lincoln's Gettysburg Address.* **b.** a direction on a piece of mail that tells where it is to be sent and to whom. *Write the address in permanent ink.*

ad • ven • ture /ăd vĕn′ chər/ *n.* **a.** a bold and dangerous trip. *The mountain-climbing trip was a daring adventure.* **b.** an unusual, exciting experience. *Going to the zoo is an adventure for young children.*

ad • ven • tur • ous /ăd vĕn′ chər əs/ *adj.* **a.** fond of new adventures; willing to take risks: *an adventurous explorer.* **b.** full of risk or danger: *an adventurous voyage.*

a • gainst /ə gĕnst′/ *prep.* **a.** in opposition to. *I like to watch the Bears play football against the Giants.* **b.** next to. *In the photo the houses looked dark against the red sunset.* **c.** in contact with; on. *I left the ladder leaning against the house.*

Al • a • bam • a /ăl′ ə băm′ ə/ *n.* a southern state in the United States. *Alabama is a farming state.*

A • las • ka /ə lăs′ kə/ *n.* a state of the United States. *Alaska is our largest state.*

a • lert /ə lûrt′/ *adj.* watchful; attentive; wide awake. *A good night's sleep helps you stay alert the next day.*

al • li • ga • tor /ăl′ ĭ gā′ tər/ *n.* a large reptile with a narrow body, short legs, long tail, and thick skin. *Alligators live in warm, swampy areas.* [Spanish *el lagarto*, the lizard.]

alligator

al • low /ə lou′/ *v.* to let; to permit. *Our parents allow us to watch TV if we have finished our homework.*

al • low • ance /ə lou′ əns/ *n.* a definite amount of money given regularly for spending. *Chang is saving his allowance to buy a basketball.*

a • long¹ /ə lông′/ or /ə lŏng′/ *prep.* in a line with. *Houses stretched along the river for miles.*

a • long² /ə lông′/ or /ə lŏng′/ *adv.* **a.** onward. *Move along!* **b.** with one. *Bring a friend along.*

al • though /ôl thō′/ *conj.* though. *I went to the beach, although there were clouds in the sky.*

al • to¹ /ăl′ tō/ *n.* the low part in music sung by a woman or a boy. *The song is written for soprano and alto.*

al • to² /ăl′ tō/ *adj.* for an alto: *the alto section.*

a • mong /ə mŭng′/ *prep.* **a.** in the midst of; surrounded by: *among the trees.* **b.** with a portion to each of. *Distribute the party favors among the guests.*

a • mount /ə mount′/ *n.* **a.** total; sum. *The amount of your bill is $13.98.* **b.** quantity. *The recipe calls for a small amount of milk.*

am•pere /ăm′ pîr′/ *n.* the unit used in measuring the strength of an electric current. *How many amperes does a light bulb use?* [After the French scientist, André Maria Ampère, 1775–1836.]

am•phib•i•an /ăm′ fĭb′ ē ən/ *n.* a cold-blooded animal that has gills and lives in water when young but develops lungs and breathes air when mature. *Frogs, toads, and salamanders are amphibians.*

amphibian

am•pli•fi•er /ăm′ plə fī′ ər/ *n.* a device that increases the strength of electric waves or impulses. *Amplifiers are used in radio and television sets.*

amt. amount.

a•muse /ə myōōz′/ *v.* **a.** to entertain. *Parents can amuse their children by reading them stories.* **b.** to cause to laugh or smile. *The monkey's antics amused the passers-by.*

a•muse•ment /ə myōōz′ mənt/ *n.* **a.** being amused. *Val's amusement was evident from her smile.* **b.** entertainment; sport; pastime. *Chess is his favorite amusement.*

an•cient /ān′ shənt/ *adj.* belonging to times long ago. *There are many ancient temples in Greece, Italy, and Egypt.* [Latin *ante*, before.]

an•gel /ān′ jəl/ *n.* an immortal, spiritual being. *According to tradition, angels are messengers from heaven.*

an•gle /ăng′ gəl/ *n.* the figure formed by two lines that come together in a point. *The teacher drew an angle on the chalkboard.*

an•noy /ə noi′/ *v.* to bother; to irritate; to disturb. *Flies often annoy picnickers.*

an•nu•al /ăn′ yōō əl/ *adj.* coming once a year; occurring once a year. *Most workers get an annual vacation of two weeks.*

-ant a suffix used with verbs: **a.** to form adjectives that mean "having the quality of": *resistant.* **b.** to form nouns that mean "person or thing that accomplishes something": *assistant.*

Pronunciation Key

ă	pat	ŏ	pot	th	**th**in
ā	pay	ō	toe	*th*	**th**is
âr	care	ô	paw, for	hw	**wh**ich
ä	father	oi	noise	zh	vision
ĕ	pet	ou	out	ə	about,
ē	be	ŏŏ	took		item,
ĭ	pit	ōō	boot		pencil,
ī	pie	ŭ	cut		gallop,
îr	pier	ûr	urge		circus

an•them /ăn′ thəm/ *n.* a song of praise or devotion. *The choir sang a stirring anthem.*

an•thra•cite /ăn′ thrə sīt′/ *n.* coal that burns with little smoke; hard coal. *Anthracite is mined in Pennsylvania.*

an•ti•slav•e•ry /ăn′ tē slā′ və rē/ *adj.* opposed to slavery. *The antislavery movement gained strength during the Civil War.*

an•to•nym /ăn′ tə nĭm′/ *n.* a word that means the opposite of another word. *"Hot" and "cold" are antonyms.*

a•part•ment /ə pärt′ mənt/ *n.* a group of rooms to live in, usually in a large building called an apartment house. *Our apartment is on the fourth floor.*

a•phid /ā′ fĭd/ *n.* a tiny insect that sucks juices from plants. *Aphids can damage tomato plants.*

a•pol•o•gy /ə pŏl′ ə jē/ *n.* (**a•pol•o•gies** *pl.*) words saying one is sorry; asking pardon. *Please accept my apology for coming so late; I was delayed by heavy traffic.*

ap•pear /ə pîr′/ *v.* **a.** to show up; to be seen. *He appeared for breakfast promptly at seven o'clock.* **b.** to seem; to give an appearance. *She appeared to like the suggestion.*

ap•point /ə point′/ *v.* to select; to choose; to assign. *Ms. Farrell appointed Mr. Kowalski to head the committee.*

apt. apartment.

ar•e•a /âr′ ē ə/ *n.* **a.** an amount of space or surface. *How do you find the area of a triangle?* **b.** a region or section. *The cabin is in a forested area.*

ar • gue /är′ gyoō/ *v.* (**ar•gues, ar•gued, ar•gu•ing**) **a.** to disagree; to dispute; to quarrel. *Tanya often argues with Michael.* **b.** to give reasons for or against. *The lawyer argued her case effectively.*

ar • gu • ment /är′ gyə mənt/ *n.* **a.** a quarrel or disagreement. *Rob had an argument with his coach.* **b.** a statement that is supposed to prove a point. *Carmen's last argument was the most convincing.*

ar • ma • da /är mä′ də/ *n.* a large fleet of armed ships. *Spain sent an armada to invade England in 1588.*

ar • range /ə rānj′/ *v.* (**ar•rang•es, ar•ranged, ar•rang•ing**) **a.** to organize; to put in order. *Everything is arranged for the party.* **b.** to plan; to prepare. *I can arrange to go tonight.*

ar • range • ment /ə rānj′ mənt/ *n.* **a.** an establishment of order; a fixing of position. *We haven't yet decided about the furniture arrangement.* **b.** the order in which things appear: *an alphabetical arrangement of last names.* **c.** preparation. *What arrangements have been made for the party?*

ar • rive /ə rīv′/ *v.* (**ar•rives, ar•rived, ar•riv•ing**) **a.** to come to a particular place; to reach a destination. *When will you arrive at the airport?* **b.** to come. *The big day finally arrived.*

ar • ti • cle /är′ tĭ kəl/ *n.* **a.** a piece of writing in a book, newspaper, or magazine. *I read an interesting article about whales.* **b.** an object; a thing: *an article of clothing.* **c.** one of three words (*a, an, the*) used before nouns.

art • ist /är′ tĭst/ *n.* **a.** a person who is skilled in any of the fine arts, especially painting or music. *Picasso was a great artist.* **b.** any skillful or creative person. *A gourmet cook is an artist in the kitchen.*

as • tro • naut /ăs′ trə nôt′/ *n.* a person who is trained to travel in outer space in a spaceship. *Only extremely capable people are selected as astronauts.*

au • di • ence /ô′ dē əns/ *n.* **a.** a number of people who come together to see or hear something: *the audience in the theater.* **b.** all of the persons who can see or hear something: *television audience.* [Latin *audire*, to hear.]

au • thor /ô′ thər/ *n.* the writer of a book, story, article, etc.; a writer. *The author sent us a copy of her book.*

au • to • mo • bile /ô′ tə mə bēl′/ or /ô′ tə mō′ bēl′/ *n.* a four-wheeled passenger vehicle, usually with a gasoline engine, for driving on roads and streets; car. *Automobiles require regular maintenance.*

automobile

ave. avenue.

av • e • nue /ăv′ ə noō′/ or /-nyoō′/ *n.* a wide street or road, especially one lined with trees. *The shop was located on one side of a shady avenue.*

av • er • age[1] /ăv′ ər ĭj/ or /ăv′ rĭj/ *n.* the result obtained when the sum of two or more figures is divided by the total number of figures. *The average of 10, 4, 7, and 3 is 6.*

av • er • age[2] /ăv′ ər ĭj/ or /ăv′ rĭj/ *adj.* **a.** determined by averaging. *The average score on the test was 75.* **b.** common; ordinary; usual: *an average day.*

a • void /ə void′/ *v.* to stay away from; to keep from meeting. *I avoided him when he had the measles.*

a • wak • en /ə wā′ kən/ *v.* to wake up; to rouse. *A loud noise awakened her in the middle of the night.*

a • ware /ə wâr′/ *adj.* alert to; knowing; conscious of. *Are you aware that you are late to school?*

aw • ful /ô′ fəl/ *adj.* very bad; very ugly; unpleasant. *That was an awful movie.*

back • bone /băk′ bōn′/ *n.* the system of bones that runs down the center of the back; the spine. *Every vertebrate has a backbone.*

back • ward /băk′ wərd/ *adv.* toward the rear; in a direction away from the front. *Drive the car backward into the garage.*

badge /băj/ *n.* an emblem worn to show membership in an organization or as an award. *Firefighters and police officers wear badges.*

bal•let /bă lā′/ or /băl′ ā′/ *n.* **a.** a formal, traditional way of dancing, using precise, graceful movements. *Football players often take classes in ballet to increase their agility.* **b.** a theatrical dance performed by a group. *Have you seen the ballet Swan Lake?*

bal•lot /băl′ ət/ *n.* the act or method of voting. *This election will be by secret ballot.*

ball•room¹ /bôl′ rōōm′/ or /-rŏŏm′/ *n.* a large room for dancing. *Ballrooms usually have polished wooden floors.*

ball•room² /bôl′ rōōm′/ or /-rŏŏm′/ *adj.* having to do with social dances such as the waltz, tango, and foxtrot. *Women often wear dresses with full skirts for ballroom dancing.*

ba•sic /bā′ sĭk/ *adj.* (**ba•si•cal•ly** *adv.*) forming the foundation or base; fundamental. *The procedure may vary slightly, but the basic pattern remains the same.*

beak•er /bē′ kər/ *n.* a glass container used in laboratories and usually having a flat bottom and a small lip for pouring. *Handle the beakers and test tubes carefully.*

beau•ti•ful /byōō′ tə fəl/ *adj.* having beauty; pleasing to the eye, ear, or mind; lovely: *a beautiful painting.*

beau•ty /byōō′ tē/ *n.* (**beau•ties** *pl.*) the quality that makes a person or thing pleasing to the senses. *The beauty of the music made us forget everything else.*

be•hind¹ /bĭ hīnd′/ *prep.* **a.** in back of; at the rear of: *behind the house.* **b.** later than; slower than: *behind schedule.*

be•hind² /bĭ hīnd′/ *adv.* to the rear; in the rear. *We left him behind.*

be•lief /bĭ lēf′/ *n.* **a.** the acceptance of something as true or real: *belief in life on other planets.* **b.** confidence; faith. *You must have belief in your own ability.*

be•neath¹ /bĭ nēth′/ *adv.* in a lower place. *The water fell to the rocks beneath.*

be•neath² /bĭ nēth′/ *prep.* under; lower than. *I sat beneath the tree.*

be•ret /bə rā′/ *n.* a round, soft, flat cap of wool or felt. *She wore her beret tilted at a jaunty angle.* [French *béret.*]

bi- a prefix that means: **a.** two: *bicycle.* **b.** every two; twice during: *biweekly.*

Pronunciation Key

ă	pat	ŏ	pot	th	**th**in
ā	pay	ō	toe	*th*	**th**is
âr	care	ô	paw, for	hw	**wh**ich
ä	father	oi	noise	zh	vision
ě	pet	ou	out	ə	about,
ē	be	ŏŏ	took		item,
ĭ	pit	ōō	boot		pencil,
ī	pie	ŭ	cut		gallop,
îr	pier	ûr	urge		circus

bi•cus•pid /bī kŭs′ pĭd/ *n.* a tooth that has two points or cusps. *Adults usually have eight bicuspids.*

bi•cy•cle /bī′ sĭk′ əl/ or /-sĭ kəl/ *n.* a vehicle having two wheels mounted on a light metal frame with a seat for the rider, a bar for steering, and pedals turned by the feet. *Riding a bicycle requires a good sense of balance.*

bicycle

bi•foc•al /bī fō′ kəl/ or /bī′ fō′-/ *adj.* having two different points of focus: *a bifocal lens.*

bi•foc•als /bī fō′ kəlz/ *n. pl.* a pair of glasses designed to improve both close and distant vision. *Mrs. Rodriguez wears bifocals so she won't have to change glasses for reading.*

bill•board /bĭl′ bôrd′/ or /-bōrd′/ *n.* a large board, usually outdoors, on which advertisements or notices are pasted. *Billboards along the highway advertise places to eat or sleep.*

bil•lion /bĭl′ yən/ *n.* one thousand million; 1,000,000,000. *The earth is over four billion years old.*

bi•month•ly¹ /bī mŭnth′ lē/ *adj.* **a.** occurring once every two months: *a bimonthly magazine.* **b.** occurring twice a month: *bimonthly meetings.*

bi•month•ly² /bī mŭnth′ lē/ *adv.* **a.** every two months. *Issues appear bimonthly.* **b.** twice a month. *We meet bimonthly.*

bi • og • ra • phy /bī ŏg′ rə fē/ *n.* (**bi•og•ra•phies** *pl.*) an account of a person's life. *I read a biography of Thomas Edison.* [Greek *bios,* life + *graphein,* to write.]

bi • sect /bī sĕkt′/ or /bī′ sĕkt′/ *v.* to divide into two equal parts. *Use your compass to bisect this angle.*

bi • tu • mi • nous /bĭ tōō′ mə nəs/ or /-tyōō′-/ *adj.* having to do with a grade of coal that contains tarry substances and smokes as it burns. *Most coal in the United States is bituminous.*

bi • week • ly¹ /bī wēk′ lē/ *adj.* **a.** occurring once every two weeks: *a biweekly paycheck.* **b.** occurring twice a week: *biweekly classes.*

bi • week • ly² /bī wēk′ lē/ *adv.* **a.** every two weeks. *We are paid biweekly.* **b.** twice a week. *The class meets biweekly, on Tuesdays and Thursdays.*

blind • ness /blīnd′ nĭs/ *n.* the state of being unable to see. *Regular eye checkups can prevent some conditions that might cause blindness.*

blis • ter /blĭs′ tər/ *n.* a soft raised place on the skin that is filled with fluid. *A burn can cause a blister.*

bliz • zard /blĭz′ ərd/ *n.* a storm with snow and strong winds. *The blizzard lasted four days.*

blu • ish /blōō′ ĭsh/ *adj.* somewhat blue. *When you are cold, your skin may look bluish.*

boo • mer • ang /bōō′ mə răng′/ *n.* a curved piece of wood or other material that can be thrown so it returns to the thrower. *Boomerangs are used as hunting weapons.* [Native Australian *boomerang.*]

both • er¹ /bŏ*th*′ ər/ *n.* something that troubles or worries. *Mosquitoes are a bother during the summer.*

both • er² /bŏ*th*′ ər/ *v.* **a.** to give trouble to. *Don't bother me while I'm writing.* **b.** to take the time and trouble. *Don't bother to wash the dishes now.*

bound¹ /bound/ *v.* past tense and past participle of **bind**.

bound² /bound/ *adj.* **a.** certain; sure. *You're bound to win.* **b.** obliged; required: *bound by an oath.* **c.** in a cover or binding: *a bound book.*

bound³ /bound/ *adj.* ready to go; going; on the way. *We are bound for Minnesota.*

bowl /bōl/ *n.* a round, deep dish. *Soup is usually served in a bowl.*

bowl

box • car /bŏks′ kär′/ *n.* a railroad freight car with sides and a roof. *The boxcar was loaded with crates.*

brand /brănd/ *n.* a particular kind of product. *Advertisers persuade you to buy their brands.*

brass /brăs/ *n.* a yellowish metal made by melting copper and zinc together. *Many band instruments are made of brass.*

break /brāk/ *v.* (**breaks, broke, bro•ken, break•ing**) to come apart; to separate into pieces. *The dish will break if it falls.*

broad /brôd/ *adj.* **a.** wide; large from side to side. *The West contains broad stretches of forests.* **b.** plain; easy to understand: *a broad hint.* **c.** of wide range; not small. *My father has a broad view of life.*

bro • ken¹ /brō′ kən/ *v.* past participle of **break**.

bro • ken² /brō′ kən/ *adj.* split into pieces; shattered: *a broken window.*

broth /brôth/ or /brŏth/ *n.* a clear, thin soup. *Mother used beef broth in the casserole.*

bruise¹ /brōōz/ *v.* to injure, as from a fall or a blow, by causing blood vessels to break and discolor the skin. *Did you bruise yourself when you fell?*

bruise² /brōōz/ *n.* an injury in which the skin is tender and discolored. *A bruise turns black and blue.*

buf • fa • lo /bŭf′ ə lō/ *n.* (**buf•fa•los** or **buf•fa•loes** *pl.*) a large animal with a hump on its back and a large head; a bison. *We saw a herd of buffalo in the park.*

build • ing /bĭl′ dĭng/ *n.* a structure such as a house, school, factory, etc. *Our new building is larger than the old one.*

bunch /bŭnch/ *n.* (**bunch•es** *pl.*) a group of things of the same kind, growing together or put together. *We took a bunch of flowers to Edward when he was in the hospital.*

burn /bûrn/ *v.* (**burns, burned** or **burnt, burn•ing**) to be on fire; to affect by or as if by fire. *I burned my hand on the hot stove.*

bur•ro /bûr′ ō/ or /boŏr′ ō/ *n.* a small donkey. *Burros can carry heavy packs.* [Spanish *borrico,* donkey.]

busi•ness /bĭz′ nĭs/ *n.* (**busi•ness•es** *pl.*) **a.** the work a person does to earn a living; an occupation. *Both an editor and a reporter are in the newspaper business.* **b.** trade; buying and selling; commercial dealings. *Have you considered a career in business?*

byte /bīt/ *n.* a small unit for measuring information stored in a computer; memory space available for storage. *A byte is a sequence of eight binary digits, or bits.*

cal•ci•um /kăl′ sē əm/ *n.* a mineral found in some rocks and foods. *Foods such as milk, fish, and cereal are high in calcium.*

cal•cu•late /kăl′ kyə lāt′/ *v.* (**cal•cu•lates, cal•cu•lat•ed, cal•cu•lat•ing**) to find out by using mathematics; to compute. *Can you calculate the sum of these numbers?*

cal•cu•la•tor /kăl′ kyə lā′ tər/ *n.* a machine that calculates. *Using a calculator makes it easier to solve long or complicated math problems.*

Cal•i•for•nia /kăl′ ə fôr′ nyə/ or /-fôr′ nē ə/ *n.* a state in the southwestern United States. *California borders on the Pacific Ocean; its capital is Sacramento.*

calm /käm/ *adj.* quiet; still; peaceful. *After the wind died down, the surface of the lake grew calm.*

cam•er•a /kăm′ ər ə/ or /kăm′ rə/ *n.* a machine for taking photographs or motion pictures. *Is there film in your camera?*

can•non /kăn′ ən/ *n.* (**can•nons** or **can•non** *pl.*) a big gun, often one on wheels or fixed to the ground. *Cannons are heavy and difficult to transport.*

camera

Pronunciation Key

ă	pat	ŏ	pot	th	thin
ā	pay	ō	toe	th	this
âr	care	ô	paw, for	hw	which
ä	father	oi	noise	zh	vision
ĕ	pet	ou	out	ə	about,
ē	be	oŏ	took		item,
ĭ	pit	oō	boot		pencil,
ī	pie	ŭ	cut		gallop,
îr	pier	ûr	urge		circus

cap•i•tal /kăp′ ĭ tl/ *n.* **a.** the city or town where the government of a country or a state is located. *Washington, D.C., is the capital of the United States.* **b.** an uppercase letter in writing or printing. *You begin a sentence with a capital.*

▶ **Capital** sounds like **capitol.**

cap•i•tal•ize /kăp′ ĭ tl īz′/ *v.* (**cap•i•tal•iz•es, cap•i•tal•ized, cap•i•tal•iz•ing**) to write using a capital letter. *Remember to capitalize the first letters of important words in titles.*

cap•i•tol /kăp′ ĭ tl/ *n.* a building in which the representatives and senators of a state or country meet. *A committee of senators and representatives met in the capitol to discuss the tax plan.*

▶ **Capitol** sounds like **capital.**

cap•sule /kăp′ səl/ or /-soōl/ *n.* **a.** a small case or container, especially one for medicine. *Take one capsule before every meal.* **b.** an enclosed front section that can be separated from the rest of a spacecraft. *The astronauts rode in the space capsule.*

car•bo•hy•drate /kär′ bō hī′ drāt′/ *n.* a substance, such as sugar or starch, that is composed of carbon, hydrogen, and oxygen. *Foods such as bread and potatoes are rich in carbohydrates.*

ca•reer /kə rîr′/ *n.* a profession; a chosen occupation. *She hopes to pursue a career in marine biology.*

car•ol[1] /kăr′ əl/ *n.* a song of joy or praise. *The choir sang a cheerful carol.*

car•ol[2] /kăr′ əl/ *v.* to sing carols. *Our class went caroling at a nursing home.*

car•pet¹ /kär′ pĭt/ *n.* a thick, heavy fabric for covering a floor. *I have a new carpet in my room.*

car•pet² /kär′ pĭt/ *v.* to cover with carpet. *This year we carpeted the bedrooms.*

cas•sette /kə sĕt′/ *n.* a small case containing magnetic tape for recording sound or other information. *Let's listen to the songs on your new cassette.*

cau•tion /kô′ shən/ *n.* **a.** being careful; taking care. *Cross streets with caution.* **b.** a warning. *Did you read the caution on the label?* [Latin *cautio,* from *cavere,* to take care.]

cav•al•ry /kăv′ əl rē/ *n.* a group of soldiers trained to fight on horseback or in armored vehicles such as tanks. *My grandfather served in the cavalry during World War II.*

cel•e•brate /sĕl′ ə brāt′/ *v.* (**cel•e•brates, cel•e•brat•ed, cel•e•brat•ing**) to honor a special time or event. *How would you like to celebrate your birthday?*

cen•ti•pede /sĕn′ tə pēd′/ *n.* a small wormlike animal with many pairs of legs, a pair to a segment. *Centipedes feed at night and destroy harmful insects.*

ce•re•al /sîr′ ē əl/ *n.* a food made from grain. *For breakfast my favorite cereal is oatmeal.* [Latin *Ceres,* the goddess of agriculture.]

char•ac•ter /kăr′ ək tər/ *n.* **a.** a person in a play or book. *The character of Pinocchio appeals to children.* **b.** a way of behaving, thinking, and feeling. *Her character changed when she became a success.* **c.** a letter; a sign. *Chinese and Japanese writing and printing have characters completely different from ours.*

cheap /chēp/ *adj.* **a.** costing only a little money. *Oranges are cheap in the spring.* **b.** of poor quality. *Those cheap tires will wear out quickly.*

chem•i•cal¹ /kĕm′ ĭ kəl/ *n.* any substance used in chemistry or made by chemistry. *Some chemicals are poisonous.*

chem•i•cal² /kĕm′ ĭ kəl/ *adj.* having to do with chemistry: *a chemical experiment.*

chest /chĕst/ *n.* **a.** a piece of furniture having drawers; a bureau. *My socks are in the top drawer of the chest.* **b.** a large box with a lid on it: *toy chest.* **c.** the upper front part of the body. *I have a cold in my chest.*

chest

chief¹ /chēf/ *n.* a leader; the head of a tribe or group; the person who is in charge. *The police chief reviewed the case.*

chief² /chēf/ *adj.* main; most important. *Hal's chief aim was a good education.*

child•ish /chīl′ dĭsh/ *adj.* **a.** of a child; like a child: *a high childish voice.* **b.** silly; foolish; not proper for an adult: *a childish desire to show off.*

chim•ney /chĭm′ nē/ *n.* a tall, hollow structure with an outside opening for smoke from a fireplace, stove, or furnace. *We could smell the smoke coming from the chimney.*

chip•munk /chĭp′ mŭngk′/ *n.* a small squirrel-like animal with stripes on its back. *Chipmunks live in holes in the ground.* [from *chitmunk,* from Algonquian *ajidamoon*, squirrel.]

choc•o•late¹ /chô′ kə lĭt/ or /chŏk′ ə-/ or /chôk′ lĭt/ *n.* **a.** a food made by roasting and grinding the beans of a cacao tree. *Bitter chocolate is used in cooking.* **b.** a candy made from chocolate: *a box of chocolates.*

choc•o•late² /chô′ kə lĭt/ or /chŏk′ ə-/ or /chôk′ lĭt/ *adj.* made or flavored with chocolate: *chocolate ice cream.*

choir /kwīr/ *n.* a group of people who sing together. *Meg sings alto in the choir.*

choose /chōōz/ *v.* (**choos•es, chose, cho•sen, choos•ing**) **a.** to select; to pick out. *He didn't know which sweater to choose.* **b.** to decide. *Grandmother chose to join an exercise class.*

cho•rus /kôr′ əs/ or /kōr′-/ *n.* **a.** group of people singing together. *The chorus gave a concert.* **b.** the part of a song that is repeated. *Most songs have verses before the chorus.*

Spelling Dictionary

cho•sen¹ /chō′ zən/ *v.* past participle of **choose.**

cho•sen² /chō′ zən/ *adj.* picked out by choice: *a chosen group.*

cir•cu•late /sûr′ kyə lāt′/ *v.* (**cir•cu•lates, cir•cu•lat•ed, cir•cu•lat•ing**) to move in a regular path back to a starting point. *The blood circulates throughout the body and returns to the heart.*

cit•i•zen /sĭt′ ĭ zən/ *n.* a member of a nation who has rights, such as voting, and who also has the duty of being loyal to the nation. *Any person born in this country is a citizen of the United States.*

civ•il /sĭv′ əl/ *adj.* **a.** having to do with a citizen or citizens: *civil rights.* **b.** not military or religious: *a civil marriage.* **c.** polite; courteous: *a civil answer.*

civ•i•lize /sĭv′ ə līz′/ *v.* (**civ•i•liz•es, civ•i•lized, civ•i•liz•ing**) to change from a primitive state to a more highly developed way of life; to educate. *The Romans tried to civilize the tribes they conquered.*

claim¹ /klām/ *v.* **a.** to ask for the return of something that one owns: *to claim a suitcase.* **b.** to declare; to assert. *He claimed he had never been there.*

claim² /klām/ *n.* a demand for something as rightful or due. *The airline was quick to process our claim for the lost baggage.*

clause /klôz/ *n.* a sentence or part of a sentence having both a subject and a predicate. *"When they came" is a dependent clause because it cannot stand alone.*

clock•wise /klŏk′ wīz′/ *adv.* in the direction in which the hands of a clock turn. *The plane circles clockwise in the sky.*

clockwise

co- a prefix that means "with" or "together": *coexist.*

co. company.

coal /kōl/ *n.* a dark-colored mineral composed mainly of carbon, found underground and used as a fuel. *This furnace burns coal.*

Pronunciation Key

ă	pat	ŏ	pot	th	**thin**
ā	pay	ō	toe	*th*	**this**
âr	care	ô	paw, for	hw	**which**
ä	father	oi	noise	zh	vision
ĕ	pet	ou	out	ə	about,
ē	be	ŏŏ	took		item,
ĭ	pit	ōō	boot		pencil,
ī	pie	ŭ	cut		gallop,
îr	pier	ûr	urge		circus

coarse /kôrs/ or /kōrs/ *adj.* **a.** composed of large particles. *Our driveway is made of coarse gravel.* **b.** of poor quality. *The prisoners were fed coarse food.*

▶ **Coarse** sounds like **course.**

co•au•thor /kō ô′ thər/ *n.* joint author; one of two or more who write together. *Scientific articles may have coauthors.*

co•ex•ist /kō′ ĭg zĭst′/ *v.* to exist together in the same time or place. *Nations can coexist in peace if they agree to resolve their problems through compromise.*

col•lege /kŏl′ ĭj/ *n.* a school that is more advanced than a high school. *Students who plan to go to college often study at least one foreign language.*

colo•nel /kûr′ nəl/ *n.* an army officer who ranks just below a general. *The insignia of a colonel is a silver eagle.*

▶ **Colonel** sounds like **kernel.**

col•o•nist /kŏl′ ə nĭst/ *n.* Someone who lives in a colony; a settler. *The Pilgrims were among the first American colonists.*

Col•o•ra•do /kŏl′ ə rä′ dō/ or /kŏl′ ə răd′ ə/ *n.* a state in the western United States. *Colorado is in the heart of the Rocky Mountains.*

com•e•dy /kŏm′ ĭ dē/ *n.* (**com•e•dies** *pl.*) **a.** a funny movie or play. *The audience laughed at the comedy.* **b.** any funny happening: *a comedy of errors.*

com•ic¹ /kŏm′ ĭk/ *adj.* funny. *The comic actions of the clown make me laugh.*

com•ic² /kŏm′ ĭk/ *n.* a person who does or says funny things to make people laugh. *The comic told a funny joke.*

Spelling Dictionary

com • ics /kŏm′ ĭks/ *n. pl.* funny pictures; cartoons. *Some Sunday papers have the comics in color.*

com • mand¹ /kə mănd′/ *v.* to tell what to do; to give an order to. *The general commanded the soldiers to remain and fight.*

com • mand² /kə mănd′/ *n.* an order; a direction. *Follow the commands of the officer directing traffic.*

com • mand • er /kə măn′ dər/ *n.* a person who commands. *The superintendent of police is the commander of the police force.*

com • ment¹ /kŏm′ ĕnt′/ *n.* a brief remark expressing an opinion. *My teacher wrote an encouraging comment about my book report.*

com • ment² /kŏm′ ĕnt′/ *v.* to remark; to express an opinion. *The reporters asked the senator to comment on the news story.*

com • merce /kŏm′ ərs/ *n.* the buying and selling of goods. *There are laws that regulate interstate commerce.*

com • mon /kŏm′ ən/ *adj.* **a.** frequent; usual. *Temperatures of ninety degrees are common in the summer.* **b.** belonging to more than one person or company. *The city parks are common property.*

com • pan • ion /kəm păn′ yən/ *n.* **a.** a friend; a comrade. *We have been companions since first grade.* **b.** anything that matches another. *We must buy a companion to that lamp.*

com • pa • ny /kŭm′ pə nē/ *n.* (**com•pan•ies** *pl.*) **a.** a group of people joined together for a common purpose; especially, a business. *Mr. Steel's company makes tractors.* **b.** friendship; society; association. *We enjoy each other's company.* **c.** guests. *We are having company for dinner.*

com • plete¹ /kəm plēt′/ *v.* (**com•pletes, com•plet•ed, com•plet•ing**) to finish. *The new building was completed in June.*

com • plete² /kəm plēt′/ *adj.* **a.** having no parts lacking; full: *a complete set.* **b.** ended; finished. *The report will be complete tomorrow.* **c.** thorough; perfect: *a complete surprise.*

com • pose /kəm pōz′/ *v.* (**com•pos•es, com•posed, com•pos•ing**) **a.** to make by putting different things together. *Concrete is composed of cement, sand, gravel, and water.* **b.** to make up; to create; to write. *Mozart composed many symphonies.*

com • pos • ite /kəm pŏz′ ĭt/ *adj.* made up of various parts. *A collage is a composite picture.*

com • po • si • tion /kŏm′ pə zĭsh′ ən/ *n.* **a.** something made up or composed. *Our teacher assigned a one-page composition.* **b.** a piece of music. *My piano teacher gave me a new composition to practice.*

com • pute /kəm pyo͞ot′/ *v.* (**com•putes, com•put•ed, com•put•ing**) to work out using mathematics; to calculate. *Use these numbers to compute the average cost.*

con • cert /kŏn′ sûrt′/ or /-sərt/ *n.* a program of music in which one or more players perform. *The musicians performed at the concert.*

concert

con • serve /kən sûrv′/ *v.* (**con•serves, con•served, con•serv•ing**) to protect from loss or harm; to preserve. *We were all asked to conserve water during the drought.*

con • sti • tu • tion /kŏn′ stĭ to͞o′ shən/ *n.* the rules, laws, and principles by which a nation, state, club, etc., is governed. *The constitution of our club states that we must have a new president every year.*

con • sume /kən so͞om′/ *v.* (**con•sumes, con•sumed, con•sum•ing**) **a.** to eat or drink. *She consumed the cracker in a single bite.* **b.** to buy for use. *Americans consume large quantities of shoes every year.*

con • tain /kən tān′/ *v.* **a.** to have or include as contents. *Each box of dishes contains four bowls.* **b.** to have as a capacity; to be able to hold. *A quart contains thirty-two ounces.*

con • test /kŏn′ tĕst′/ *n.* a test, struggle, game, etc., to determine a winner. *Who won the prize in the art contest?*

con•tin•ue /kən tĭn′ yōo/ *v.* (**con•tin•ues, con•tin•ued, con•tin•u•ing**) **a.** to go on without stopping. *We continued walking until we reached the camp.* **b.** to go on again after stopping; to resume. *The story will be continued next week.*

coon•skin[1] /kōon′ skĭn/ *n.* a raccoon pelt: *a coonskin coat.*

coon•skin[2] /kōon′ skĭn/ *adj.* made of coonskin: *a coonskin cap.*

co•op•er•ate /kō ŏp′ ə rāt′/ *v.* (**co•op•er•ates, co•op•er•at•ed, co•op•er•at•ing**) to work together to get something done. *If everyone cooperates, we will soon finish.*

cop•per[1] /kŏp′ ər/ *n.* a soft, reddish-brown metal. *Copper is used to make pennies.*

cop•per[2] /kŏp′ ər/ *adj.* made of copper. *We polished the copper pots until they shone.*

cor•ne•a /kôr′ nē ə/ *n.* the transparent outside layer of the eyeball. *The cornea covers the iris and the pupil of the eye.*

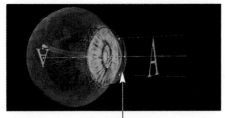

cornea

cor•net /kôr nĕt′/ *n.* a brass instrument similar to the trumpet but having a softer sound. *Jan is keen to learn how to play the cornet.*

cor•rect[1] /kə rĕkt′/ *adj.* having no mistakes; right. *Gary was sure he had the correct answer to the problem.*

cor•rect[2] /kə rĕkt′/ *v.* to remove errors from; to make right. *Please correct the spelling on your papers.*

cos•tume /kŏs′ tōom′/ or /-tyōom′/ *n.* **a.** a characteristic style of dress. *People around the world wear different costumes.* **b.** the particular clothing worn to imitate a person or animal. *He wore a lion costume for the play.*

couch /kouch/ *n.* (**couch•es** *pl.*) a piece of furniture that can seat several people; a sofa. *My friends and I sit on the couch to watch TV.*

Pronunciation Key

ă	pat	ŏ	pot	th	**th**in
ā	pay	ō	toe	*th*	**th**is
âr	care	ô	paw, for	hw	**wh**ich
ä	father	oi	noise	zh	vision
ĕ	pet	ou	out	ə	about,
ē	be	ŏŏ	took		item,
ĭ	pit	ōō	boot		pencil,
ī	pie	ŭ	cut		gallop,
îr	pier	ûr	urge		circus

coun•cil /koun′ səl/ *n.* **a.** a group of people who meet to decide on plans or a course of action or to give advice: *a council of property owners.* **b.** a small group of people elected by the citizens to decide on the laws and general management of a city or organization: *the city council.*

▶ **Council** sounds like **counsel.**

coun•sel[1] /koun′ səl/ *n.* **a.** advice. *He listens to counsel from people he likes.* **b.** a lawyer or lawyers who are handling a case: *the counsel for the defense.*

▶ **Counsel** sounds like **council.**

coun•sel[2] /koun′ səl/ *v.* to give counsel or advice to. *The principal counseled us to resolve our quarrel.*

▶ **Counsel** sounds like **council.**

count•down /kount′ doun′/ *n.* the counting backwards to zero to show how long before something will begin. *We watched the countdown to the space shuttle's liftoff.*

coun•ter•clock•wise /koun′ tər klŏk′ wīz′/ *adv.* in a direction opposite from the way the hands of a clock move. *Move your piece counterclockwise around the game board.*

coun•try /kŭn′ trē/ *n.* (**coun•tries** *pl.*) **a.** a nation. *Switzerland is a small country.* **b.** the land outside the city; a rural area of small towns and farms. *Every summer we go to the country.*

coun•ty[1] /koun′ tē/ *n.* (**coun•ties** *pl.*) a part of a state in the United States. *In Louisiana a county is called a parish.*

coun•ty[2] /koun′ tē/ *adj.* of a county. *Who won the county elections?*

Spelling Dictionary

course /kôrs/ or /kōrs/ *n.* **a.** a direction; a way; a path. *The fallen tree lay directly in our course.* **b.** a part of a meal. *The third course was roast beef.* **c.** a series of lessons or classes. *Li took an art course last year.*

▶ Course sounds like **coarse**.

cous•in /kŭz′ ĭn/ *n.* a son or daughter of an aunt or uncle. *I have seven cousins.*

cow•ard /kou′ ərd/ *n.* a person who cannot control fear or who won't face danger. *The lion in the story was a coward.*

co•work•er /kō′ wûr′ kər/ *n.* a fellow worker. *Juanita's coworkers took her out to lunch on her birthday.*

coy•o•te /kī ō′ tē/ or /kī′ ōt/ *n.* a small wild wolf found mainly in western North America. *The coyote howled at the moon.*

cre•ate /krē āt′/ *v.* (**cre•ates, cre•at•ed, cre•at•ing**) **a.** to make a thing that has not been made before; to form. *The artist created a painting.* **b.** to cause; to produce. *It takes only one loud person to create a disturbance.*

cre•a•tive /krē ā′ tĭv/ *adj.* able to create; inventive; expressive; imaginative. *It takes a creative writer to write an exciting story.*

cre•a•tiv•i•ty /krē ā′ tĭv′ ĭ tē/ *n.* the quality of being creative. *The teacher said my poster showed great creativity.*

cred•it /krĕd′ ĭt/ *n.* **a.** recognition; favorable regard. *He deserves credit for his work.* **b.** a system of buying goods by charging the amount and paying the bill, with interest, later. *Using credit is convenient but expensive.*

cred•i•tor /krĕd′ ĭ tər/ *n.* a person or business to whom money is owed. *If you pay your creditors promptly, you will have a good credit rating.*

crick•et /krĭk′ ĭt/ *n.* a small hopping insect somewhat like a grasshopper. *A male cricket chirps by rubbing its wings together.*

cricket

crit•i•cal /krĭt′ ĭ kəl/ *adj.* **a.** marked by careful analysis and judgment: *a critical essay.* **b.** judging severely or unfavorably. *Critical comments can hurt a person's feelings.* **c.** important; crucial: *the critical moment.*

crit•i•cize /krĭt′ ĭ sīz′/ *v.* (**crit•i•ciz•es, crit•i•cized, crit•i•ciz•ing**) **a.** to evaluate or judge as a critic. *Melanie was asked to criticize the poem.* **b.** to judge unfavorably. *Dad criticized me for not keeping my room clean.*

cro•chet /krō shā′/ *v.* to make by looping yarn or thread into links with a hooked needle. *My aunt crocheted a sweater for the baby.* [French *crochet*, a hook.]

cross-mul•ti•ply /krôs′ mŭl′ tə plī′/ or /krŏs′-/ *v.* to find the product of two fractions by multiplying the numerator of one by the denominator of the other and vice versa. *You can save time by canceling before you cross-multiply.*

cu•bic /kyōō′ bĭk/ *adj.* **a.** shaped like a cube. *The sculpture was composed of cubic forms.* **b.** having length, width, and depth; three-dimensional. *A cubic inch is the volume of a cube whose edges measure one inch.*

cur•rent[1] /kûr′ ənt/ *n.* **a.** the movement of water or air in a definite direction; a flow. *The canoe tipped over because of the strong current.* **b.** the movement or flow of electricity in a wire. *The current was cut off when the fuse blew.*

cur•rent[2] /kûr′ ənt/ *adj.* belonging to the present. *What is the current price?*

cus•pid /kŭs′ pĭd/ *n.* a tooth with one point or cusp; canine tooth. *Cuspids are used to tear food.*

cy•clist /sī′ klĭst/ *n.* a person who rides a bicycle or motorcycle. *An American cyclist won the bicycle race.*

cy•clone /sī′ klōn′/ *n.* a severe storm with high-speed winds blowing around a relatively calm center. *A cyclone may be as large as a thousand miles across.*

dai • ly¹ /dā′ lē/ *adj.* appearing, done, or occurring every day. *He takes a daily walk in the park.*

dai • ly² /dā′ lē/ *adv.* each day; every day. *She delivers newspapers daily.*

dair • y /dâr′ ē/ *n.* (**dair•ies** *pl.*) a building or a part of a building in which milk is stored or processed. *The farmers bring their milk to the dairy every morning.*

dam • age¹ /dăm′ ĭj/ *n.* an injury, harm, or break that lowers the worth or usefulness of something. *The storm caused severe damage.*

dam • age² /dăm′ ĭj/ *v.* (**dam•ag•es, dam•aged, dam•ag•ing**) to break, injure, or harm something. *The accident damaged their car.*

dan • ger • ous /dān′ jər əs/ *adj.* **a.** perilous; risky; full of danger: *a dangerous sport.* **b.** likely to cause injury, harm, or damage: *a dangerous criminal.*

de • bug /dē bŭg′/ *v.* (**de•bugs, de•bugged, de•bug•ging**) to locate and correct errors or malfunctioning parts in a system. *If your computer program doesn't work, you'll have to debug it.*

de • cay¹ /dĭ kā′/ *v.* to rot; to become rotten. *Most fruits will decay if they are not kept in a cool, dry place.*

de • cay² /dĭ kā′/ *n.* a gradual rotting or loss of strength, beauty, etc. *The decay of the Roman Empire led to its destruction.*

de • cide /dĭ sīd′/ *v.* (**de•cides, de•cid•ed, de•cid•ing**) to reach a decision; to make up one's mind. *I decided to tell them.*

dec • i • mal¹ /dĕs′ ə məl/ *n.* any number that contains a fraction of ten. *The number 87.75 is a decimal.*

dec • i • mal² /dĕs′ ə məl/ *adj.* based on ten; counted by tens. *The metric system is a decimal system.*

de • clare /dĭ klâr′/ *v.* (**de•clares, de•clared, de•clar•ing**) **a.** to announce publicly and formally; to make known to others. *Only Congress can declare war.* **b.** to say positively and surely; to state openly. *Mark declared he would never again be late for school.*

Pronunciation Key

ă	pat	ŏ	pot	th	thin
ā	pay	ō	toe	th	this
âr	care	ô	paw, for	hw	which
ä	father	oi	noise	zh	vision
ĕ	pet	ou	out	ə	about,
ē	be	ŏŏ	took		item,
ĭ	pit	ōō	boot		pencil,
ī	pie	ŭ	cut		gallop,
îr	pier	ûr	urge		circus

de • coy /dē′ koi′/ *n.* a wooden bird used by hunters to fool other birds. *When the ducks got near the decoy, the hunter fired.*

decoy

de • crease¹ /dĭ krēs′/ *v.* (**de•creas•es, de•creased, de•creas•ing**) to become less; to diminish. *The noise decreased sharply when the window was closed.*

de • crease² /dē′ krēs′/ *n.* a growing less; a decline; a reduction. *There was a sharp decrease in interest after we lost seven games in a row.*

de • feat¹ /dĭ fēt′/ *v.* **a.** to conquer; to win over; to beat. *The team defeated their opponents.* **b.** to cause to fail; to produce failure. *The rain defeated our plans.*

de • feat² /dĭ fēt′/ *n.* an overcoming; a conquering. *The defeat of the army brought an end to the war.*

de • gree /dĭ grē′/ *n.* **a.** a level, step, or stage in a process or series. *He worked his way up by degrees.* **b.** a unit used to measure temperature. *Water freezes at thirty-two degrees Fahrenheit.* **c.** a unit used to measure the arc of a circle and the size of an angle. *A circle contains 360 degrees.*

de • li • cious /dĭ lĭsh′ əs/ *adj.* pleasing in taste or smell; tasting good; delightful. *We had a delicious meal at the restaurant.*

de • light¹ /dĭ līt′/ *v.* to give pleasure to; to please. *The new game delighted the children.*

de • light² /dĭ līt′/ *n.* enjoyment; pleasure; joy; something delightful. *Her sense of humor is a delight.*

Spelling Dictionary

de•ny /dĭ nī′/ *v.* (**de•nies, de•nied, de•ny•ing**) **a.** to state that something is untrue or incorrect. *The prisoner denied that she had robbed the store.* **b.** to refuse to give or allow. *The court denied his request for a new trial.*

de•part•ment /dĭ pärt′ mənt/ *n.* a section or part of something; a division of an organization, government, etc.: *the police department; the sporting-goods department.*

de•pos•it¹ /dĭ pŏz′ ĭt/ *v.* **a.** to lay down and leave. *The river deposits soil at the delta.* **b.** to put away for safety; to put money in a bank. *He deposited a check in his account.*

de•pos•it² /dĭ pŏz′ ĭt/ *n.* **a.** something put down and left behind: *a muddy deposit.* **b.** money put in a bank. *There was no record of my deposit.*

de•scribe /dĭ skrīb′/ *v.* (**de•scribes, de•scribed, de•scrib•ing**) to tell about in detail with words or pictures. *He described the movie so completely that I didn't even want to see it.*

de•serve /dĭ zûrv′/ *v.* (**de•serves, de•served, de•serv•ing**) to be worthy of; to have earned as a reward, punishment, right, etc. *Your suggestion deserves further consideration.*

de•sign¹ /dĭ zīn′/ *v.* to draw or sketch something to be done; to plan the details. *The builder designed a new shopping center.*

de•sign² /dĭ zīn′/ *n.* **a.** a drawing or plan. *The design for the building called for an elevator.* **b.** a pattern or arrangement of colors, materials, etc. *The blanket was woven in an intricate design.*

de•spair¹ /dĭ spâr′/ *n.* a feeling that hope is gone. *Greg was in despair because his dog had been lost for five days.*

de•spair² /dĭ spâr′/ *v.* to give up. *Don't despair—we might still win.*

de•stroy /dĭ stroi′/ *v.* to put an end to; to ruin; to tear down; to wreck completely. *The fire destroyed the beautiful cathedral.*

de•tail /dĭ tāl′/ *n.* a small part of something. *Your schoolwork will look neater if you pay attention to the details.*

de•tec•tive /dĭ tĕk′ tĭv/ *n.* a person, often a law officer, who finds information and solves crimes. *The detective waited in her car until the suspect arrived.*

di•ag•on•al¹ /dī ăg′ ə nəl/ *n.* a line joining opposite corners of a rectangle or other polygon. *A diagonal splits a rectangle into two equal triangles.*

di•ag•on•al² /dī ăg′ ə nəl/ *adj.* slanting: *a diagonal path.*

dia•mond /dī′ mənd/ or /dī′ ə mənd/ *n.* a brilliant precious stone formed of crystallized carbon. *Mrs. Rinaldi has a diamond in her wedding ring.*

diamond

di•a•ry /dī′ ə rē/ *n.* (**di•a•ries** *pl.*) a written record of the things that the writer has done or thought day by day. *Ricardo kept a travel diary of his trip to New York.*

dif•fer /dĭf′ ər/ *v.* to be unlike. *The two nations differ in their languages and customs.*

dig•it /dĭj′ ĭt/ *n.* the numeral for any number from 1 to 9 and usually the numeral for 0. *The numeral 150 has three digits.*

di•lute¹ /dĭ lōōt′/ or /dī-/ *v.* (**di•lutes, di•lut•ed, di•lut•ing**) to make weaker or thinner by adding more liquid. *Adding water will dilute a chemical solution.*

di•lute² /dĭ lōōt′/ or /dī-/ *adj.* weak; thin: *a dilute acid.*

di•rect¹ /dĭ rĕkt′/ *v.* **a.** to point out the way to a place. *The usher directed us to our seats.* **b.** to be in charge of; to manage. *The police directed traffic.*

di•rect² /dĭ rĕkt′/ *adj.* straight; not roundabout: *a direct route.*

di•rec•tor /dĭ rĕk′ tər/ or /dī-/ *n.* a person who directs or manages the work done by other people. *He became the director of sales.*

dis- a prefix that means "not" or "the opposite of": *dishonest.*

dis•a•gree /dĭs′ ə grē′/ *v.* (**dis•a•grees, dis•a•greed, dis•a•gree•ing**) to differ in opinion. *The children disagreed about the rules of the game.*

dis•ap•pear /dĭs′ ə pîr′/ *v.* to go out of sight; to vanish. *The train disappeared in the distance.*

dis•ap•point /dĭs′ ə point′/ *v.* to fail to satisfy the wish or hope of. *The movie disappointed me; I thought it would be much better.*

dis•cuss /dĭ skŭs′/ *v.* to talk seriously about. *The committee discussed possible solutions to the traffic problem.*

dis•hon•est /dĭs ŏn′ ĭst/ *adj.* not honest; not fair; lying or cheating. *Copying someone else's answers is dishonest.*

dis•like /dĭs līk′/ *v.* (**dis•likes, dis•liked, dis•lik•ing**) to have a feeling against; to object to. *At first I disliked him but now we are friends.*

dis•o•bey /dĭs′ ə bā′/ *v.* to refuse or fail to obey. *Soldiers learn never to disobey orders.*

dis•turb /dĭ stûrb′/ *v.* **a.** to bother; to interrupt. *When we go to the library, we try not to disturb people who are reading.* **b.** to upset; to worry. *We were disturbed to hear that Mr. O'Brien was ill.* **c.** to put into disorder; to mess up. *Don't disturb anything in my room.*

di•vis•i•ble /dĭ vĭz′ ə bəl/ *adj.* capable of being divided. *The number 100 is evenly divisible by 2, 4, 5, 10, 20, 25, and 50.*

dol•phin /dŏl′
fĭn/ or /dôl′-/ *n.*
a sea mammal,
smaller than the
whale and having
a beaklike snout.
*Dolphins commu-
nicate with each
other by clicks
and whistles.*

dolphin

dou•ble-head•er /dŭb′ əl-hĕd′ ər/ *n.* two games played one after the other on the same day. *The Red Sox will play a double-header next weekend.*

down•stairs¹ /doun′ stârz′/ *adv.* to a lower floor. *I am going downstairs to finish the laundry.*

down•stairs² /doun′ stârz′/ *adj.* on the lower floor: *a downstairs bedroom.*

doz. dozen.

doz•en /dŭz′ ən/ *n.* (**doz•ens** or **doz•en** *pl.*) a set of twelve: *a dozen eggs.*

draft¹ /drăft/ *n.* **a.** a preliminary version; a rough copy. *Stacy asked her teacher to look over the first draft of her book report.* **b.** a movement of air. *A cold draft came from the open window.*

draft² /drăft/ *v.* to prepare the outline or design of. *The writer drafted the first chapters of his book.*

dra•ma /drä′ mə/ *n.* **a.** a story acted on a stage; a play. *Our class presented a drama about safety.* **b.** the writing, producing, or performing of plays. *She is planning a career in drama.*

dra•mat•ic /drə măt′ ĭk/ *adj.* **a.** having to do with plays or the theater. *An actor is a dramatic artist.* **b.** exciting and full of adventure. *The climbers made a dramatic attempt to reach the summit.*

draw /drô/ *v.* (**draws, drew, drawn, draw•ing**) to make a design or picture. *The artist drew a pencil sketch.*

draw•ing /drô′ ĭng/ *n.* a design, picture, etc. *Her drawing of a covered bridge won first prize in the art contest.*

drawn /drôn/ *v.* past participle of **draw.**

dur • ing /dŏŏr′ ĭng/ or /dyŏŏr′-/ *prep.*
a. throughout the entire time of. *The girls went to a camp during the summer.* **b.** at some time in; in the time of. *The phone rang during dinner.*

dust bowl /dŭst′ bōl′/ *n.* a dry, desertlike area with frequent dust storms. *A region may turn into a dust bowl when it does not have enough grass to keep the soil from blowing away.*

east • ern /ē′ stərn/ *adj.* of, in, or toward the east. *The eastern coast of the country was lined with mountains.*

edge /ĕj/ *n.* **a.** the side of a blade that cuts. *A knife edge must be sharp to cut well.* **b.** the outer part of anything; the line where anything ends. *The glass was resting on the edge of the table.*

ed • it /ĕd′ ĭt/ *v.* to check, correct, prepare, and arrange materials for publication. *My uncle edits children's books.*

ed • i • tor /ĕd′ ĭ tər/ *n.* **a.** a person who prepares writings for publication. *The editor marked her corrections in the margin.* **b.** a person in charge of the publication of a newspaper or magazine. *Sanjay is the editor of the school paper.*

eight • eenth¹ /ā′ tēnth′/ *n.* one of eighteen equal parts. *Two eighteenths make one ninth.*

eight • eenth² /ā′ tēnth′/ *adj.* next after the seventeenth: *the eighteenth person in line.*

eight • y /ā′ tē/ *n.* the next number after seventy-nine; eight times ten; 80. *Her grandmother will be eighty next month.*

e • lec • tric • i • ty /ĭ lĕk trĭs′ ə tē/ *n.* a kind of energy most often carried by wires, used to produce light and heat and to run motors. *Our house is heated by electricity.*

el • e • ment /ĕl′ ə mənt/ *n.* **a.** one of the more than one hundred substances in nature that make up all the material in the world. *Oxygen and iron are common elements.* **b.** a necessary, basic part. *Hard work is an element of success.*

em • blem /ĕm′ bləm/ *n.* an object or picture that stands for an idea; a symbol. *An oil lamp is an emblem of knowledge.*

em • ploy /ĕm ploi′/ *v.* to have in one's business as paid workers; to hire. *Factories employ hundreds of people.*

em • ploy • ment /ĕm ploi′ mənt/ *n.* **a.** one's work or occupation. *Mrs. O'Connor found employment as an accountant.* **b.** the hiring of people to do work. *The new computer firm provides employment for over seventy people.*

-en a suffix that means "to cause to be" or "to become," used to form verbs: *broaden.*

e • nam • el /ĭ năm′ əl/ *n.* the hard layer that protects the chewing surface of a tooth. *A dentist can fill a hole if it develops in the enamel.*

en • er • get • ic /ĕn′ ər jĕt′ ĭk/ *adj.* full of energy; active; vigorous. *We need energetic workers to help clean out the attic.*

en • er • gy /ĕn′ ər jē/ *n.* (**en•er•gies** *pl.*) the power, ability, or capacity to do work. *This swimming pool is heated by solar energy.*

e • nor • mous /ĭ nôr′ məs/ *adj.* very large. *The whale is an enormous sea animal.*

en • tire /ĕn tīr′/ *adj.* whole; complete. *We spent the entire day at the zoo.*

en • trance /ĕn′ trəns/ *n.* a doorway; a place for entering. *The statue stood by the front entrance to the building.*

en • ve • lope /ĕn′ və lōp′/ or /än′-/ *n.* a paper cover or holder used to hold papers and other materials. *Always put the correct address on the envelope.*

envelope

ep • i • sode /ĕp′ ĭ sōd′/ *n.* **a.** an event or happening in real life or in the course of a story. *Moving to a house in the country began an important episode in her life.* **b.** one of a series of events: *an episode of a TV show.*

e • quip /ĭ kwĭp′/ *v.* (**e•quips, e•quipped, e•quip•ping**) to supply; to furnish; to fit out with something needed. *Their house is equipped with air conditioning.*

-er a suffix that means "one who" or "one that does something": *buyer.*

es • say /ĕs' ā/ *n.* a short composition, often expressing a personal opinion on a single topic. *We each wrote an essay on world hunger.*

es • ti • mate /ĕs' tə māt'/ *v.* (**es•ti•mates, es•ti•mat•ed, es•ti•mat•ing**) to guess; to judge what the size, time, etc., will be. *We estimated that the book would contain six hundred pages.*

eve • ning /ēv' nĭng/ *n.* the beginning of the night; the time between sunset and bedtime. *In winter, evenings are longer because the sun sets earlier.*

e • vent /ĭ vĕnt'/ *n.* **a.** anything that happens. *To a child, a trip to the circus is a great event.* **b.** one of the contests in a sports meet. *The next event is the one-hundred-meter backstroke.*

e • vil¹ /ē' vəl/ *adj.* bad; wrong; harmful. *Deliberately hurting someone else is an evil thing to do.*

e • vil² /ē' vəl/ *n.* anything that causes pain and harm. *War is an evil.*

ex • act /ĭg zăkt'/ *adj.* correct; right; accurate in every detail. *When a bridge is built, every measurement must be exact.*

ex • cept /ĭk sĕpt'/ *prep.* but; not including. *The train runs every day except Sunday.*

ex • change¹ /ĭks chānj'/ *v.* (**ex•chang•es, ex•changed, ex•chang•ing**) to give something in return for another thing. *Juan exchanged his catcher's mitt for a fielder's glove.*

ex • change² /ĭks chānj'/ *n.* a giving and receiving. *The exchange of students between two countries can build goodwill.*

ex • cite /ĭk sīt'/ *v.* (**ex•cites, ex•cit•ed, ex•cit•ing**) to stir strong feelings in. *We were all excited to hear such good news.*

ex • er • cise¹ /ĕk' sər sīz'/ *v.* (**ex•er•cis•es, ex•er•cised, ex•er•cis•ing**) to develop or strengthen through regular practice or activity. *Solving puzzles is one way to exercise your mind.*

ex • er • cise² /ĕk' sər sīz'/ *n.* **a.** an activity that develops or strengthens the body or the mind. *He gets his exercise by walking.* **b.** a lesson provided to offer practice. *We do a math exercise every night.*

exercise

ex • ist /ĭg zĭst'/ *v.* **a.** to be; to be real. *Dinosaurs no longer exist.* **b.** to live; to be able to live; to go on living. *Most plants and animals cannot exist without air and water.*

ex • it /ĕg' zĭt/ or /ĕk' sĭt/ *n.* **a.** a way of going out of a place. *There was only one exit from the cave.* **b.** a going out of a place; a leaving. *The actress made a quick exit.*

ex • pand /ĭk spănd'/ *v.* **a.** to grow larger by spreading out or opening up. *The balloon expanded as it filled with air.* **b.** to express in fuller or more extended form. *You can expand the numeral 23 by writing it as 20 + 3.*

ex • pect /ĭk spĕkt'/ *v.* **a.** to look for something to happen; to look forward to. *We expected rain, but the sky was clear.* **b.** to require. *My parents expect me to study hard in school.*

ex • plain /ĭk splān'/ *v.* **a.** to make something clear; to tell what something means. *The teacher explained the difference between nouns and verbs.* **b.** to give a reason for; to tell the cause of. *Can you explain why you didn't do your homework?*

ex • tend /ĭk stĕnd'/ *v.* **a.** to lengthen. *We extended our vacation so we could visit another national park.* **b.** to stretch out. *The river extends for many miles.* **c.** to make larger; to increase. *You can extend your knowledge by reading books.* **d.** to offer. *He extended an invitation to the entire class.*

ex • ter • nal /ĭk stûr' nəl/ *adj.* outer; on the outside; exterior. *This old building is drab on the inside, but it has several interesting external features.*

Spelling Dictionary

face¹ /fās/ *n.* **a.** that part of the head on which the eyes, nose, and mouth are located. *I don't know him, but his face looks familiar.* **b.** a side or a surface of a solid geometric figure. *A cube has six faces.*

face² /fās/ *v.* (**fac•es, faced, fac•ing**) to be turned toward; to have the front toward. *The teacher faced the class and began to speak.*

fac•tor¹ /făk′ tər/ *n.* **a.** any of the things that cause a certain result. *Time is an important factor to consider in cooking.* **b.** any of the numbers that are multiplied to obtain a product. *3 and 7 are factors of 21.*

fac•tor² /făk′ tər/ *v.* to separate into factors. *If you factor 27, you get 9 and 3 or 3, 3, and 3.*

faith /fāth/ *n.* **a.** belief that does not require proof; trust; confidence. *The trapeze artist has complete faith in her partner.* **b.** devotion; loyalty. *The citizens pledged their faith to the new queen.*

false /fôls/ *adj.* **a.** not true. *It is false to say that 2 + 2 = 5.* **b.** not real or genuine. *The man wore a false beard.*

fa•mous /fā′ məs/ *adj.* widely known and talked about. *Colorado is famous for its mountains.*

far•ther /fär′ thər/ *adv.* at or to a greater distance. *We drove farther this summer than we did last year.*

fea•ture¹ /fē′ chər/ *n.* **a.** a part. *The interview was the best feature of the program.* **b.** something that attracts attention; an outstanding quality. *Her best feature is her ability to see mistakes.*

fea•ture² /fē′ chər/ *v.* (**fea•tures, fea•tured, fea•tur•ing**) to make prominent. *Most newspapers feature comic strips.*

fer•tile /fûr′ tl/ *adj.* **a.** producing many good crops. *The fertile soil of the Midwest gives us much corn.* **b.** able to bear seeds, fruit, or young. *A chick comes from a fertile egg.* **c.** having many ideas: *a fertile mind.*

fer•til•ize /fûr′ tl īz′/ *v.* (**fer•til•iz•es, fer•til•ized, fer•til•iz•ing**) **a.** to add something to soil to make it richer so it will produce more. *Lawns are fertilized with a combination of chemicals.* **b.** to cause a new animal or plant to develop. *Bees fertilize plants by carrying pollen from one flower to another.*

fes•ti•val /fĕs′ tə vəl/ *n.* a time of celebration and feasting to honor a special event. *Thanksgiving is a festival started by the early settlers in New England in 1621.*

fi•ber /fī′ bər/ *n.* **a.** a part that is like a thread. *The fibers of cotton are made into yarn.* **b.** the indigestible part of certain foods that is useful in regulating the digestive system. *A diet rich in fiber may help prevent cancer.*

fic•tion /fĭk′ shən/ *n.* writings about imaginary events and people. *Short stories and novels are types of fiction.*

fif•teenth¹ /fĭf′ tēnth′/ *n.* one of fifteen equal parts. *Each of the fifteen had one fifteenth of the cake.*

fif•teenth² /fĭf′ tēnth′/ *adj.* coming after fourteen others; the fifteenth in order. *I was the fifteenth person to arrive.*

fi•nal /fī′ nəl/ *adj.* **a.** last; closing; coming at the end. *Friday is the final day of the sale.* **b.** not to be changed. *The umpire's decision is always final.*

fire•place /fīr′ plās′/ *n.* an open place built of brick or stone for holding a fire. *A fireplace in a home is connected to a chimney so the smoke can escape.*

fireplace

flair /flâr/ *n.* **a.** a natural talent; a knack. *His use of color shows his flair for decorating.* **b.** a distinctive personal style. *She wore the unusual costume with a flair.*

▶ **Flair** sounds like **flare.**

flare¹ /flâr/ *v.* (**flares, flared, flar•ing**) to flame up suddenly and briefly. *A breath of wind made the candle flare.*

▶ **Flare** sounds like **flair.**

Spelling Dictionary

flare

282

flare[2] /flâr/ *n.* a sudden bright light, especially one used for signaling. *The army patrol sent up a flare to mark their location.*
▶ **Flare** sounds like **flair.**

flat•ten /flăt′ n/ *v.* to make or become flat. *Our cat flattens herself against the ground when she is stalking a bird.*

flaw /flô/ *n.* **a.** a defect; any crack, scratch, break, etc. *You can see the flaw in this glass.* **b.** any fault or mistake. *The flaw in his character is his thoughtlessness.* [Middle English *flaue,* splinter.]

flip /flĭp/ *v.* (**flips, flipped, flip•ping**) **a.** to put in motion with a snap of a finger and thumb; to toss: *flip a coin.* **b.** to turn through. *He flipped the pages of the book to find the picture he needed.* **c.** to turn over quickly. *You should flip the pancake only once.*

floor /flôr/ or /flōr/ *n.* **a.** the part of a room or hall on which we walk. *This room has a tile floor.* **b.** the bottom of something: *the floor of the ocean.* **c.** a story of a building. *Our apartment is on the sixth floor.*

Flor•i•da /flôr′ ĭ də/ *n.* a state in the southeastern United States. *Florida is a popular resort state.*

fluor•ide /floor′ rīd′/ or /flôr′-/ *n.* a chemical compound of fluorine with another element, often added to water to prevent tooth decay. *I use a toothpaste that contains fluoride.*

fog•gy /fô′ gē/ or /fŏg′ ē/ *adj.* (**fog•gi•er, fog•gi•est; fog•gi•ly,** *adv.*) **a.** having fog; misty enough to make seeing difficult. *No one wanted to drive on such a foggy night.* **b.** confused. *I have only a foggy memory of my vacation.*

folk song /fōk′ sông′/ or /-sŏng′/ *n.* a traditional song from a certain geographical region or ethnic group. *"Yankee Doodle" is a popular American folk song.*

fool•ish /foo′ lĭsh/ *adj.* senseless; silly; unwise. *Justin felt really foolish when he realized that his socks didn't match.*

foot /foot/ *n.* (**feet** *pl.*) **a.** that part of the body that is at the end of the leg and on which a person or animal stands and walks. *My feet were tired from so much walking.* **b.** a measure of length that equals twelve inches. *She is almost five feet tall.*

foot

Pronunciation Key

ă	pat	ŏ	pot	th	thin
ā	pay	ō	toe	*th*	this
âr	care	ô	paw, for	hw	which
ä	father	oi	noise	zh	vision
ĕ	pet	ou	out	ə	about,
ē	be	ŏŏ	took		item,
ĭ	pit	ōō	boot		pencil,
ī	pie	ŭ	cut		gallop,
îr	pier	ûr	urge		circus

force[1] /fôrs/ or /fōrs/ *n.* **a.** strength; power; energy. *The storm winds struck with great force.* **b.** any group of people who are trained to work together: *the police force.*

force[2] /fôrs/ or /fōrs/ *v.* (**forc•es, forced, forc•ing**) to make a person or thing do something. *No one can force you to do your homework; you should do it because it helps you learn.*

for•ev•er /fôr ĕv′ ər/ or /fər-/ *adv.* for all time; without ending. *Your allowance cannot be expected to last forever.*

for•get /fər gĕt′/ *v.* (**for•gets, for•got, for•got•ten** or **for•got, for•get•ting**) **a.** to have no memory of; to be unable to recall. *I will never forget my first sight of the Grand Canyon.* **b.** to neglect to do because of carelessness or lack of interest. *Did you forget to write Grandma a thank-you note for your birthday present?*

for•got•ten /fər gŏt′ n/ *v.* a past participle of **forget.**

for•mal /fôr′ məl/ *adj.* **a.** according to accepted customs, rules, or practices. *Slang expressions are out of place in formal writing.* **b.** done officially in an exact, definite manner. *The formal signing of the treaty came several weeks after the war ended.* **c.** elegant; fine: *a formal dinner.*

fort /fôrt/ or /fōrt/ *n.* a building or other place that is built for defense against an attack by enemies. *The soldiers entered the fort.*

for•tune /fôr′ chən/ *n.* **a.** a large amount of money, property, etc.; wealth. *Restoring this old hotel would cost a fortune.* **b.** luck. *She could scarcely believe her good fortune in finding the stolen jewelry.*

Spelling Dictionary

for•ty-four /fôr′ tē fôr′/ or /-fōr′/ *n.* the next number after forty-three; forty plus four; 44. *He found forty-four balls as he explored the golf course.*

for•ward /fôr′ wərd/ *adv.* toward the front. *The crowd pushed forward to see the pandas in the zoo.*

fos•sil /fŏs′ əl/ *n.* any traces or remains of animals or plants from an earlier age found in earth, ice, coal, or rock. *We saw the skeleton of the prehistoric creature in the fossil.*

fossil

frac•ture¹ /frăk′ chər/ *n.* a break or crack. *We could see a fracture in the exposed rock face.*

frac•ture² /frăk′ chər/ *v.* (**frac•tures, frac•tured, frac•tur•ing**) to break or crack. *Mr. MacDougal slipped on the icy sidewalk and fractured his arm.*

fran•tic /frăn′ tĭk/ *adj.* excited with fear or anxiety; agitated. *When I felt the dish slipping from my hand, I made a frantic attempt to catch it.*

free•dom /frē′ dəm/ *n.* the state of being free; liberty. *The Revolutionary War was fought to gain freedom for our country.*

freeze /frēz/ *v.* (**freez•es, froze, fro•zen, freez•ing**) **a.** to become ice; to turn to ice. *The lake froze during the night.* **b.** to chill something until it becomes cold and hard as ice. *We freeze the vegetables from our garden so they will keep through the winter.*

freight /frāt/ *n.* a load of goods carried from place to place by ship, truck, bus, train, or plane. *Most freight in the United States is carried by rail.*

fright•en /frīt′ n/ *v.* **a.** to make afraid; to scare. *The actors' costumes frightened the little girl.* **b.** to cause to move by making afraid. *The campfire frightened away the wolves.*

fron•tier /frŭn tîr′/ *n.* **a.** the farthest edge of the settled part of a country; the beginning of the unknown part. *The California gold rush brought new settlers to the western frontier.* **b.** boundary; border. *The United States and Canada have a peaceful frontier.* **c.** any new area or idea that is being explored: *the frontiers of space and medicine.*

frost•bite /frôst′ bīt′/ or /frŏst′-/ *n.* injury to the body's tissues caused by extreme cold. *If you dress warmly in winter, you won't get frostbite.*

froze /frōz/ *v.* past tense of **freeze**.

fro•zen¹ /frō′ zən/ *v.* past participle of **freeze**.

fro•zen² /frō′ zən/ *adj.* **a.** covered with ice. *Let's go ice skating on the frozen pond.* **b.** kept fresh by a process of freezing. *Frozen foods are used as often as canned foods these days.*

ft. foot.

full-time /fŏŏl′ tīm′/ *adj.* **a.** requiring all of one's time. *Taking care of young children can be a full-time occupation.* **b.** giving all of one's time to a certain job; working a full day. *Mr. Ellison is a full-time teacher.*

fur•ni•ture /fûr′ nĭ chər/ *n.* chairs, tables, beds, couches, etc., used in a home. *I help dust the furniture every week.*

fur•ther¹ /fûr′ thər/ *adj.* more; extra. *There has been no further news.*

fur•ther² /fûr′ thər/ *adv.* more; to a greater extent. *We will have to think further about going on the trip.*

fu•ry /fyŏŏr′ ē/ *n.* (**fu•ries** *pl.*) **a.** great anger. *Nathan flew into a fury when he couldn't find his homework.* **b.** violence; fierceness. *The old sea captain had been through the fury of many storms.*

fu•ture¹ /fyōō′ chər/ *n.* the time that is to come. *What are your plans for the future?*

fu•ture² /fyōō′ chər/ *adj.* in the time to come. *All future meetings will begin at three o'clock.*

gal. gallon.

gal•ler•y /găl′ ə rē/ *n.* (**gal•ler•ies** *pl.*) **a.** a long enclosed passageway, often with windows along one side; a hall. *We walked down the castle gallery and looked out at the lovely gardens.* **b.** a room or building where art objects are displayed. *The Art Institute of Chicago is a famous art gallery.*

gal•lon /găl′ ən/ *n.* a measurement of liquid. *Four quarts make a gallon.*

gar•den•er /gärd′ nər/ *n.* a person who takes care of a garden or does gardening. *Sharon worked as a gardener last summer.*

gas•o•line /găs′ ə lēn′/ or /găs′ ə lēn′/ *n.* liquid used as fuel for certain engines. *Gasoline is made from petroleum and burns fast.*

Gen. General.

gene /jēn/ *n.* a tiny part of a chromosome that helps pass down inherited traits from parents to offspring. *Your eye color, hair color, and blood type depend on the genes you received from your parents.*

gen•er•al[1] /jĕn′ ər əl/ *adj.* **a.** having to do with all or almost all. *The weather is a subject of general interest.* **b.** not given in detail; not definite; rough. *Everyone has a general idea of how an airplane stays in the air.*

General
George S. Patton

gen•er•al[2] /jĕn′ ər əl/ *n.* a top army officer, in command of many troops. *There are five ranks of general, who wear from one to five stars.*

gen•er•al•ize /jĕn′ ər ə līz′/ *v.* (gen•er•al•iz•es, gen•er•al•ized, gen•er•al•iz•ing) to talk or write in a general way without saying anything specific. *It is easy to generalize about the need for better education, but exactly what should be done?*

gen•er•ous /jĕn′ ər əs/ *adj.* willing to share; unselfish; giving happily. *The famous athlete was generous with her time in teaching girls how to play tennis.*

gen•ius /jēn′ yəs/ *n.* (gen•ius•es *pl.*) **a.** a person who has outstanding and remarkable ability in science, art, writing, music, etc. *The composer Mozart was a genius.* **b.** any special ability. *Charles has a genius for getting us to do what he wants.*

gen•tle•man /jĕn′ tl mən/ *n.* (gen•tle•men *pl.*) **a.** a man who is thoughtful, polite, educated, and honorable. *The word of a gentleman can be trusted.* **b.** a man of respected family or high social position. *Once only gentlemen were allowed to serve as attendants in a royal court.*

gen•tle•ness /jĕn′ tl nĭs/ *n.* **a.** mildness; softness. *The gentleness of the breeze was relaxing.* **b.** kindness; patience. *Her gentleness calmed the frightened animal.*

gleam[1] /glēm/ *n.* a beam of light. *Through the darkness we saw a small gleam from the cottage window.*

gleam[2] /glēm/ *v.* to shine. *The stars gleam.*

good-bye[1] or **good-by** /gŏŏd bī′/ *interj.* farewell. *Good-bye. See you later.*

good-bye[2] or **good-by** /gŏŏd bī′/ *n.* an expression of farewell. *We said our good-byes on the railway platform.*

gov•ern•ment /gŭv′ ərn mənt/ *n.* **a.** a system of ruling or managing. *Our American government is a democracy, which means that the power to make laws comes from the citizens.* **b.** the people in charge of such a system. *The government has approved the new dam.*

gov•er•nor /gŭv′ ər nər/ *n.* the person elected to be the head of a state of the United States. *In 1924 the people of Wyoming elected the first woman governor in the United States.*

gray[1] /grā/ *n.* a color obtained by blending black and white. *Gray is often used to paint ships.*

gray[2] /grā/ *adj.* **a.** having this color. *They live in a gray house.* **b.** dull; gloomy. *It is hard to be cheerful on a gray day like this.*

great /grāt/ *adj.* **a.** large in size or number; big: *a great redwood tree.* **b.** more than is ordinary or expected: *a great job.* **c.** important; skilled; famous: *a great leader.*

Spelling Dictionary

gro•cer•y /grō′ sə rē/ *n.* (**gro•cer•ies** *pl.*) a store that sells food and household supplies. *I went to the grocery for bread and milk.*

gro•cer•ies /grō′ sə rēz/ *n. pl.* anything sold by a grocer. *We carried two bags of groceries home from the store.*

growth /grōth/ *n.* **a.** the process of growing. *Social scientists are looking for ways to control population growth.* **b.** the development achieved by growing. *Some plants reach full growth in a single season.*

grudge¹ /grŭj/ *n.* a long-standing feeling of anger or dislike; resentment. *She held a grudge against him because of their old argument.*

grudge² /grŭj/ *v.* (**grudg•es, grudged, grudg•ing**) to be reluctant to allow; to resent; to envy. *He grudged them their success even though they deserved it.*

guard¹ /gärd/ *v.* to protect; to keep from harm; to defend. *There were soldiers on duty all night to guard the fort.*

guard² /gärd/ *n.* **a.** one who protects or watches over: *a security guard.* **b.** a protection; a watch; a defense: *a guard against infection.*

guide¹ /gīd/ *v.* (**guides, guid•ed, guid•ing**) to lead; to point out the way. *The museum director guided us through the exhibition.*

guide² /gīd/ *n.* one who leads or directs. *We hired a guide to take us down the river on our canoe trip.*

gui•tar /gĭ tär′/ *n.* a musical instrument having strings that are played with the fingers or with a pick. *The entertainer sat in a chair and played her guitar as she sang.* [Spanish *guitarra.*]

guitar

hab•it /hăb′ ĭt/ *n.* a custom; an action that has been done so often that one does it without thinking. *Brushing your teeth after every meal is a good habit to acquire.*

hai•ku /hī′ kōō/ *n.* a Japanese lyric poem of seventeen syllables, often on a subject in nature. *This haiku describes the beauty of a snowflake.*

hail¹ /hāl/ *v.* to greet; to welcome; to cheer. *Crowds hailed the king as he returned from the wars.*

hail² /hāl/ *n.* small pieces of ice that may fall during a rainstorm. *Hail makes a lot of noise on the top of a car.*

hail³ /hāl/ *v.* to pour down hail. *It hailed during the storm.*

ham•mock /hăm′ ək/ *n.* a kind of hanging bed or couch made of cloth, canvas, or cords. *We strung the hammock between two strong trees.* [Spanish *hamaca.*]

hand•some /hăn′ səm/ *adj.* very good-looking; pleasing in appearance. *What a handsome suit you're wearing today!*

har•bor /här′ bər/ *n.* a part of a sea, lake, or river that is sheltered; a port. *The ship sailed into the harbor.*

har•mon•y /här′ mə nē/ *n.* (**har•mo•nies** *pl.*) **a.** a getting on well together; accord. *The harmony among the workers has helped make the new store a big success.* **b.** a pleasing combination of musical sounds. *The choir sang in perfect harmony.*

har•vest¹ /här′ vĭst/ *n.* **a.** a crop. *This year's grain harvest will be larger than last year's.* **b.** the gathering in of a crop. *A farmer needs more workers during the harvest.*

har•vest² /här′ vĭst/ *v.* to gather in a crop. *Next week they will harvest the corn.*

hearth /härth/ *n.* **a.** the stone or brick floor of a fireplace. *I watched the coals glowing among the ashes on the hearth.* **b.** one's own fireside; home. *The poet wrote of his longing for his own hearth.*

he•red•i•ty /hə rĕd′ ĭ tē/ *n.* the passing down of physical and mental traits from parents to offspring. *Genetics is the study of heredity.*

he•ro /hîr′ ō/ *n.* (**he•roes** *pl.*) **a.** a person admired for courage, great deeds, or fine qualities. *George Washington is a national hero.* **b.** the most important male character in a story. *The plot usually permits the hero to triumph in the end.*

hex•a•gon /hĕk′ sə gŏn′/ *n.* a plane figure that has six sides and six angles. *All snowflakes have the shape of a hexagon.*

his•tor•ic /hǐ stôr′ ĭk/ *adj.* famous in history. *We visited historic monuments and buildings on our trip to England.*

his•to•ry /hǐs′ tə rē/ *n.* (**his•to•ries** *pl.*) **a.** the series of all past events, especially since the invention of writing. *Plato is one of the greatest philosophers in history.* **b.** the study of recorded facts of past events. *I am taking a course in the history of the United States.* **c.** an account or written record of past events: *a history of the Civil War.*

hol•low¹ /hŏl′ ō/ *adj.* **a.** empty; not solid. *The tree trunk is hollow.* **b.** not real; worthless; empty: *hollow promises.*

hol•low² /hŏl′ ō/ *n.* **a.** a hole; a hollow place. *Squirrels often use a hollow in a tree to store nuts.* **b.** a small valley. *Spring came early to the quiet hollow.*

hollow

home•less /hōm′ lǐs/ *adj.* without a home. *Our community center provides a shelter for homeless persons.*

home•mak•er /hōm′ mā′ kər/ *n.* a person with the responsibility of managing a household, including cooking, cleaning, and caring for children. *Being a homemaker is a demanding job.*

home run /hōm′ rŭn′/ *n.* a long baseball play that allows the batter to run to all the bases and score a point. *When the ball sailed over the fence, we knew it was a home run.*

home•stead /hōm′ stĕd/ *n.* a house with its land and outbuildings, especially on a farm. *The settlers chose a site by the river for their homestead.*

home•work /hōm′ wûrk/ *n.* work for school that is done at home. *Our class has ten arithmetic problems for homework.*

Pronunciation Key

ă	pat	ŏ	pot	th	**th**in
ā	pay	ō	toe	*th*	**th**is
âr	care	ô	paw, for	hw	**wh**ich
ä	father	oi	noise	zh	vi**si**on
ĕ	pet	ou	out	ə	**a**bout,
ē	be	ŏŏ	took		item,
ĭ	pit	ōō	boot		pencil,
ī	pie	ŭ	cut		gallop,
îr	pier	ûr	urge		circus

hom•o•graph /hŏm′ ə grăf/ or /hō′ mə-/ *n.* a word that has the same spelling as another word but a different meaning. *"Box" (to fight) and "box" (container) are homographs; so are "wind" (moving air) and "wind" (to turn).*

hom•o•nym /hŏm′ ə nǐm/ or /hō′ mə-/ *n.* a word that has the same pronunciation as another word but a different meaning. *"Box" (to fight) and "box" (container) are homonyms, as are "cent" and "sent," but "wind" (moving air) and "wind" (to turn) are not.*

hom•o•phone /hŏm′ ə fōn/ or /hō′ mə-/ *n.* a word that has the same pronunciation as another word but a different meaning and a different spelling. *"Cent" and "sent" are homophones.*

hor•i•zon•tal /hôr′ ĭ zŏn′ tl/ *adj.* going across, not up and down. *The lines of type on this page are horizontal.*

hour /our/ *n.* **a.** sixty minutes. *She said she had been waiting half an hour.* **b.** the time in which certain things are done. *The doctor's office hours are from ten to four.*

hr. hour.

hu•man•i•ty /hyōō măn′ ĭ tē/ *n.* **a.** people; the human race. *All humanity benefits from scientific research.* **b.** kindness; mercy. *The prisoners were treated with humanity.*

hu•man•i•ties, the /hyōō măn′ ĭ tēz/ *n. pl.* the study of languages, literature, and philosophy. *Studying the humanities helps widen our understanding.*

hum • ble /hŭm′ bəl/ *adj.* (**hum•bler, hum•blest; hum•bly,** *adv.*) **a.** modest; not proud. *She remained humble even after her huge success.* **b.** not important or grand. *That actor still lives in the humble house in which he grew up.*

hu • mid /hyoo̅′ mĭd/ *adj.* damp; moist. *Tropical climates are often humid.*

hu • mid • i • ty /hyoo̅′ mĭd′ ĭ tē/ *n.* dampness or moisture, especially of the air. *Coastal cities often have high humidity.*

hu • mor /hyoo̅′ mər/ *n.* **a.** something that makes a person laugh; a funny or amusing quality. *The essay used gentle humor to make its point.* **b.** a state of mind; a mood. *The cheerful story put me in a good humor.* **c.** ability to see the funny side of things. *She has a great sense of humor.*

hu • mor • ous /hyoo̅′ mər əs/ *adj.* funny; comical; amusing. *The audience laughed at the humorous movie.*

hun • dredth¹ /hŭn′ drĭdth/ *adj.* next after the ninety-ninth. *The college celebrated its hundredth anniversary.*

hun • dredth² /hŭn′ drĭdth/ *n.* one of one hundred equal parts; 1/100; 0.01. *A penny is one hundredth of a dollar.*

hur • ri • cane /hûr′ ĭ kān′/ *n.* a very strong storm, often causing great damage. *The hurricane's winds blew down trees and houses.*

hy • dro • gen /hī′ drə jən/ *n.* a very light, colorless gas that catches fire easily and burns quickly. *Hydrogen is the lightest chemical element.*

-ic a suffix, used with nouns, to form adjectives that mean: **a.** of: *allergic.* **b.** like: *heroic.* **c.** characterized by: *rhythmic.*

im- a prefix that means: **a.** not: *imprecise.* **b.** without; the opposite of: *immaturity.* **Im-** replaces **in-** before the letters **b, m,** and **p.**

im • age /ĭm′ ĭj/ *n.* **a.** a likeness or reflection. *You can see your image in a mirror.* **b.** a picture in the mind. *Tom is very different from the image I once had of him.*

i • ma • gine /ĭ măj′ ĭn/ *v.* (**i•ma•gines, i•ma•gined, i•ma•gin•ing**) **a.** to make up an idea or a picture in the mind. *I can imagine all the things I would do if I had the time.* **b.** to suppose. *I imagine they'll be there soon.*

im • pa • tient /ĭm pā′ shənt/ *adj.* not patient; restless. *We became impatient after the long delay.*

im • per • fect /ĭm pûr′ fĭkt/ *adj.* not perfect; having faults or defects. *The diamond was beautiful, but the single flaw made it imperfect.*

im • po • lite /ĭm pə līt′/ *adj.* not polite; showing bad manners. *It is impolite to interrupt when another person is speaking.*

im • por • tant /ĭm pôr′ tnt/ *adj.* **a.** meaning a great deal; serious. *Your birthday is important to you.* **b.** having power or authority. *These parking places are reserved for important officials.*

im • pos • si • ble /ĭm pôs′ ə bəl/ *adj.* (**im•pos•si•bly,** *adv.*) **a.** not possible; not able to happen. *It is impossible for us to live without breathing air, eating food, and drinking water.* **b.** difficult to get along with. *That impossible cat has clawed all the new furniture.*

in- a prefix that means: **a.** not: *indecisive.* **b.** without; the opposite of: *inefficiency.*

in. inch.

in • ac • tive /ĭn ăk′ tĭv/ *adj.* not active; idle; not moving around. *Hawaii has both active and inactive volcanoes.*

inch¹ /ĭnch/ *n.* (**inch•es** *pl.*) a measure of length. *Twelve inches are one foot.*

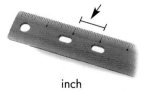

inch

inch² /ĭnch/ *v.* to move slowly; to go ahead little by little. *Sometimes heavy traffic causes automobiles to inch along.*

in • cis • or /ĭn sī′ zər/ *n.* a front tooth used for cutting. *Your first tooth was probably an incisor.*

in•clude /ĭn klōōd'/ v. (in•cludes, in•clud•ed, in•clud•ing) **a.** to contain; to cover. *The price of the radio includes the tax.* **b.** to put in as part of the total. *Don't forget to include the guests in the other room.*

in•com•plete /ĭn' kəm plēt'/ adj. not finished or complete; lacking something. *Your answer to the division problem was incomplete because you didn't give the remainder.*

in•cor•rect /ĭn' kə rĕkt'/ adj. **a.** not correct; wrong. *The answer is incorrect.* **b.** in poor taste; improper. *Slurping is usually considered incorrect.*

in•crease¹ /ĭn krēs'/ v. (in•creas•es, in•creased, in•creas•ing) to make or become greater. *The cost of living increases every year.*

in•crease² /ĭn krēs'/ n. an addition; growth. *There was an increase in the town's population.*

in•dent /ĭn dĕnt'/ v. to space or write farther in from the margin. *Writers often indent the first line of a paragraph.*

→ My dog Bill is lots of fun. He's always ready to play ball with me or to go for a walk.

indent

in•di•vid•u•al¹ /ĭn də vĭj' ōō əl/ n. one person; one thing; one animal. *Our constitution protects the rights of the individual.*

in•di•vid•u•al² /ĭn də vĭj' ōō əl/ adj. **a.** for one; separate. *Each person has an individual record in our files.* **b.** different from others; strongly unusual. *The musician has an individual style of playing.*

in•dus•try /ĭn' də strē/ n. (in•dus•tries pl.) **a.** the production of goods; business; manufacturing. *New technology has led to many improvements in industry.* **b.** hard work. *Jim's industry paid off when he made an A on the test.*

in•form /ĭn fôrm'/ v. to tell. *We informed her that she was on the wrong street.*

in•for•mal /ĭn fôr' məl/ adj. not formal; casual. *The party was informal, so we didn't have to dress up.*

in•ju•ry /ĭn' jə rē/ n. (in•ju•ries pl.) harm, damage, hurt. *The ship came through the terrible storm without injury.*

Pronunciation Key

ă	pat	ŏ	pot	th	thin
ā	pay	ō	toe	th	this
âr	care	ô	paw, for	hw	which
ä	father	oi	noise	zh	vision
ĕ	pet	ou	out	ə	about,
ē	be	ŏŏ	took		item,
ĭ	pit	ōō	boot		pencil,
ī	pie	ŭ	cut		gallop,
îr	pier	ûr	urge		circus

in•stall /ĭn stôl'/ v. **a.** to put something into a place where it can be used. *The new water heater was installed in the basement.* **b.** to put into office with ceremony. *The band played when the president of the college was installed.*

in•stinct /ĭn' stĭnkt'/ n. a natural tendency or ability. *Birds are not taught how to fly; they do it by instinct.*

in•struc•tor /ĭn strŭk' tər/ n. one who instructs; a teacher. *Our school has fine instructors.*

in•ter•est¹ /ĭn' trĭst/ or /-tər ĭst/ n. **a.** a feeling of wanting to know or take part in something. *Sandra has an interest in music.* **b.** the money paid for the use of another's money. *When you repay a loan, you pay the amount you borrowed plus interest.*

in•ter•est² /ĭn' trĭst/ or /-tər ĭst/ v. to get the attention of; to arouse curiosity in. *This book interests me.*

in•ter•est•ed /ĭn' trĭ stĭd/ or /-tər ĭ stĭd/ adj. showing interest. *The interested audience asked the speaker many questions.*

in•ter•est•ing /ĭn' trĭ stĭng/ or /tər ĭ stĭng/ adj. holding one's attention; arousing interest. *The story was so interesting that she read straight to the end without stopping.*

in•ter•nal /ĭn tûr' nəl/ adj. **a.** on the inside. *The heart is an internal organ.* **b.** within a country; domestic. *A civil war is an internal conflict.*

in•vent /ĭn vĕnt′/ *v.* **a.** to make something that has never been made before. *Thomas A. Edison invented the electric light and the phonograph.* **b.** to make up; to imagine. *A writer invents a story.*

in•ven•tor /ĭn vĕn′ tər/ *n.* one who invents. *Alexander Graham Bell was the inventor of the telephone.*

i•o•dine /ī′ ə dīn′/ or /-dĭn/ or /-dēn′/ *n.* a chemical element used in medicine, in photography, and in some industries. *Seafood can provide the iodine we need for good health.*

I•o•wa /ī′ ə wə/ *n.* a state in the north central United States. *Much corn is grown in Iowa.*

i•ris /ī′ rĭs/ *n.* (**i•ris•es** *pl.*) **a.** a plant with long pointed leaves and large brightly colored flowers. *Irises bloom in spring and summer.* **b.** the circle of color around the pupil of the eye. *Most people have blue, brown, or hazel irises.*

iris

-ish a suffix that means: **a.** having the qualities of: *childish.* **b.** rather; somewhat: *reddish.*

-ist a suffix that means "one who does" or "is connected with": *lobbyist, artist.*

it•self /ĭt sĕlf′/ *pron.* **a.** its own self. *The bird cleaned itself in the puddle.* **b.** a word used to make a statement stronger. *No wonder the house is expensive; the land itself cost thousands of dollars.*

-ity a suffix that means "the state or quality of being," used to form nouns: *reality.*

-ive a suffix used: **a.** to form adjectives that mean "tending toward or accomplishing": *descriptive.* **b.** to form nouns that mean "a person or thing that accomplishes an action": *detective.*

-ize a suffix that means "to cause to be" or "to become," used to form verbs: *specialize.*

jack•et /jăk′ ĭt/ *n.* **a.** a short coat that covers the upper part of the body. *When the weather became cooler, the children came into the house for their jackets.* **b.** any outer covering. *A book's jacket protects its cover.*

jazz /jăz/ *n.* a type of music or dance that features strong rhythm, unusual beats, and frequent improvisation. *We heard a band play jazz in New Orleans.*

jest•er /jĕs′ tər/ *n.* one who jests or tells jokes; especially, a person paid to entertain at a royal court in the Middle Ages. *The jester danced and sang for the king.*

jour•ney¹ /jûr′ nē/ *n.* a trip or voyage. *Our journey to England took only a few hours because we traveled by plane.*

jour•ney² /jûr′ nē/ *v.* to travel to a place. *My grandparents journeyed to the Philippines last year.*

joy•ous /joi′ əs/ *adj.* joyful; glad. *The air rang with joyous shouts from children playing.*

judg•ment /jŭj′ mənt/ *n.* **a.** a decision reached through careful thought. *The final judgment of the class was in favor of a picnic rather than a trip to the zoo.* **b.** opinion. *In my judgment such a plan will never succeed.* **c.** the ability to make wise decisions. *Consuela has excellent judgment concerning horses.*

ka•ra•te /kə rä′ tē/ *n.* a Japanese method of self-defense without weapons that features well-aimed blows with the hands and feet. *Loretta took a class in karate for exercise.* [Japanese *kara,* empty + *te,* hand.]

ker•nel /kûr′ nəl/ *n.* **a.** the soft, edible part inside the hard shell of a nut or fruit. *We shelled the pecans to eat the kernels.* **b.** a grain or a seed. *We eat kernels of wheat in cereals.*

▶ **Kernel** sounds like **colonel**.

key /kē/ *n.* **a.** a small metal device used to turn the bolt on a lock. *Don't forget your house key.* **b.** any of the parts that are pressed down to play a piano, operate a computer, etc. *Pianos have both black and white keys.* **c.** in music, a series of notes related to one tone. *The song is written in the key of C.*

kil•o•watt /kĭl′ ə wŏt′/ *n.* a unit of electric power equal to one thousand watts. *How many kilowatts does this generator produce?*

ki•mo•no /kə mō′ nə/ *n.* a loose outer garment bound with a sash in the middle. *Kimonos were first used in Japan.* [Japanese *ki*, to wear + *mono*, object.]

kitch•en /kĭch′ ən/ *n.* a room in which food is prepared and cooked. *When they walked into the kitchen, they could smell the bread baking.*

kitchen

knap•sack /năp′ săk/ *n.* a canvas or leather bag worn or carried on the back and used to hold food, clothing, equipment, etc. *The hikers carried knapsacks and sleeping bags.* [German *knappsack*.]

lan•guage /lăng′ gwĭj/ *n.* **a.** speech; words that are spoken or written. *Language is the main way human beings communicate.* **b.** the speech of a certain nation, tribe, or group of people. *The French language is spoken by the people of France.*

Pronunciation Key

ă	pat	ŏ	pot	th	**th**in
ā	pay	ō	toe	*th*	**th**is
âr	care	ô	paw, for	hw	**wh**ich
ä	father	oi	noise	zh	vi**s**ion
ĕ	pet	ou	**ou**t	ə	**a**bout,
ē	be	o͝o	t**oo**k		item,
ĭ	pit	o͞o	b**oo**t		penc**i**l,
ī	pie	ŭ	c**u**t		gall**o**p,
îr	p**ie**r	ûr	**ur**ge		circ**u**s

latch¹ /lăch/ *n.* (latch•es *pl.*) a lock or catch in which a movable piece fits into a notch or a slot. *The door wouldn't stay closed because the latch was broken.*

latch² /lăch/ *v.* (latch•es, latched, latch•ing) to close with a latch: *latch the door.*

launch /lônch/ or /länch/ *v.* (launch•es, launched, launch•ing) **a.** to send upward into space: *launch a spaceship.* **b.** to send into the water: *launch a ship.* **c.** to start; to begin. *Our school launched a cleaning and painting drive in the neighborhood.*

law•yer /lô′ yər/ *n.* a person who makes a living by practicing law; an attorney. *Ms. Castillo's lawyer helped her draw up the contract.*

lb. pound. [Latin *libra*.]

ledg•er /lĕj′ ər/ *n.* a book in which a business keeps records of all its sales and purchases. *The bookkeeper totaled a column of figures in the ledger.*

leg•is•late /lĕj′ ĭ slāt′/ *v.* (leg•is•lates, leg•is•lat•ed, leg•is•lat•ing) to pass laws. *Congress legislated a new tax bill.*

length•en /lĕngk′ thən/ or /lĕng′-/ *v.* to make or become longer. *This road has been lengthened since I last drove on it.*

lib•er•ty /lĭb′ ər tē/ *n.* (lib•er•ties *pl.*) **a.** freedom; independence. *The American Revolution won liberty for the former British colonies.* **b.** the right or opportunity to do something. *Our constitution protects our civil liberties.*

lift•off /lĭft′ ôf′/ or /-ŏf′/ *n.* the launching of a rocket. *If the weather is clear, the liftoff will occur on schedule.*

lig•nite /lĭg′ nīt′/ *n.* a low-quality brownish coal. *We saw workers mining lignite.*

lim•er•ick /lĭm′ ər ĭk/ *n.* a humorous verse of five lines with the rhyme scheme AABBA. *Edward Lear wrote many famous limericks.*

loaf /lōf/ *n.* (**loaves** *pl.*) the shape of bread baked as one piece. *Jay cut the first slice from the loaf.*

loaves /lōvz/ *n.* plural of **loaf.**

lo•cate /lō′ kāt/ or /lō kāt′/ *v.* (**lo•cates, lo•cat•ed, lo•cat•ing**) **a.** to find the position or place of. *Can you locate your town on the map?* **b.** to establish in a certain place. *The store is located in the shopping center.*

lodge /lŏj/ *n.* **a.** a building used as a temporary living place. *We stayed at a lodge on the lake.* **b.** the den of an otter or a beaver. *The beavers built a big lodge.*

loos•en /loo′ sən/ *v.* **a.** to make loose; to make less tight. *Loosen the collar around the dog's neck.* **b.** to become loose. *The knot in the rope loosened because it wasn't tied correctly.*

loss /lôs/ or /lŏs/ *n.* (**loss•es** *pl.*) **a.** ruin; destruction. *The forest fire caused the loss of many trees.* **b.** a failure to keep or to win. *The loss of the contract cost the company millions of dollars.* **c.** a losing. *Marci felt the loss of her old friends when she moved away.*

loy•al /loi′ əl/ *adj.* faithful. *Sam is a loyal friend.*

loy•al•ty /loi′ əl tē/ *n.* (**loy•al•ties** *pl.*) a sense of duty; being loyal. *No one could question our loyalty to our country.*

lug•gage /lŭg′ ĭj/ *n.* baggage; the suitcases, trunks, bags, or boxes that are taken on a trip. *We claimed our luggage at the station.*

lull•a•by /lŭl′ ə bī′/ *n.* (**lull•a•bies** *pl.*) a soft song to help lull a young child to sleep. *The baby fell asleep in the middle of the lullaby.*

lute /loot/ *n.* a stringed musical instrument with a flat head, long neck, and pear-shaped body. *Lutes were common in the fourteenth and fifteenth centuries.*

lute

lyr•ic[1] /lĭr′ ĭk/ *adj.* expressing feeling, as in music or poetry; lyrical: *a lyric poem.*

lyr•ic[2] /lĭr′ ĭk/ *n.* a short lyrical poem: *a lyric of love.*

lyr•ics /lĭr′ ĭks/ *n. pl.* the words of a song. *Do you know all the lyrics to our national anthem?*

M

mac•a•ro•ni /măk′ ə rō′ nē/ *n.* a type of noodle or pasta in the shape of hollow tubes. *We ate macaroni for supper.* [Italian *maccheroni.*]

mag•ic /măj′ ĭk/ *n.* **a.** in stories, the ability to do seemingly impossible things. *The prince was changed into a frog by magic.* **b.** anything that charms and delights; an enchanting quality. *Donna was fascinated by the magic of the coral reef.*

main i•de•a /mān′ ī dē′ ə/ *n.* the most important point; the central thought. *What is the main idea of this paragraph?*

Maine /mān/ *n.* a state in the northeastern United States. *Fishing is one of the major industries of Maine.*

ma•jor•i•ty /mə jôr′ ĭ tē/ *n.* **a.** a number that is more than half of a total; the larger part. *The majority of Americans can read and write.* **b.** the number of votes by which an election is won. *The vote was thirteen to nine, so they won the election by a majority of four votes.*

make-be•lieve[1] /māk′ bĭ lēv′/ *n.* a playful pretending of something that is not real. *Let's play make-believe; you be Batman and I'll be Robin.*

make be•lieve[2] /māk′ bĭ lēv′/ *v.* to pretend. *We made believe we were kangaroos.*

mam • mal /măm′ əl/ *n.* any
of a class of animals that are
warm-blooded, have a backbone, and whose females
have milk glands for feeding
their young. *Whales, human
beings, beavers, and bats are
mammals.*

mammal

man • do • lin /măn′ də lĭn′/ or
/măn′ də lĭn′/ *n.* a musical instrument
popular in the Middle Ages, similar to the
lute but having fewer pairs of strings. *The
singer carried his mandolin from castle to
castle.*

mar • gin /mär′ jĭn/ *n.* **a.** an edge; a border:
the eastern margin of the property. **b.** the
border around the writing or printing on a
page. *Please leave a margin of one inch on
all sides.*

mar • vel¹ /mär′ vəl/ *n.* a wonderful or marvelous thing. *Space capsules are marvels of
modern science.*

mar • vel² /mär′ vəl/ *v.* to be struck with
wonder; to be astonished. *We marveled at
the speed of the cheetahs.*

mar • vel • ous /mär′ və ləs/ *adj.* wonderful; astonishing. *The actors were marvelous
in their roles in the play.*

Mar • y • land /měr′ ə lənd/ *n.* a state in
the eastern United States. *Maryland and
Virginia border the District of Columbia.*

Mas • sa • chu • setts /măs′ ə cho͞o′ sĭts/
or /-zĭts/ *n.* a state in the northeastern
United States. *Massachusetts was one of the
original thirteen colonies that formed the
United States.*

ma • ture¹ /mə tyo͝or′/ or /-cho͝or′/ *adj.*
a. fully grown. *Adults are mature.* **b.** ripe.
Do not pick the fruit until it is mature.

ma • ture² /mə tyo͝or′/ or /-cho͝or′/ *v.*
(**ma•tures, ma•tured, ma•tur•ing**) to ripen;
to become fully grown. *The crops matured
earlier than we had expected.*

ma • yor /mā′ ər/ or /mâr/ *n.* a person who
is elected as the head of a city or town government. *The mayor gave a speech at the
opening of the new shopping center.*

meas • ure¹ /mězh′ ər/ *n.* a unit used in
finding the length, size, amount, etc., of
something. *Miles, pounds, and degrees are
common measures.*

meas • ure² /mězh′ ər/ *v.* (**meas•ures,
meas•ured, meas•ur•ing**) **a.** to find the
length, size, amount, etc., of something.
They measured the floor for the new rug.
b. to be of a certain size. *Mr. Elliott
measures over six feet in height.*

mem • brane /měm′ brān′/ *n.* a thin layer
of tissue that covers or lines a part of a
plant or an animal. *A clear membrane covers the pupil of the eye.*

mem • o • rize /měm′ ə rīz′/ *v.*
(**mem•o•riz•es, mem•o•rized,
mem•o•riz•ing**) to commit to memory; to
learn by heart. *We memorized a poem by
Emily Dickinson.*

mem • o • ry /měm′ ə rē/ *n.* (**mem•o•ries**
pl.) **a.** the power or the ability to remember
things. *She has a great memory for names.*
b. anything that is remembered. *Seeing our
old house again brought back happy
memories.*

-ment a suffix, used to form nouns, that
means: **a.** act or process of: *enjoyment.*
b. condition of: *astonishment.*

men • tion¹ /měn′ shən/ *v.* to talk about
briefly; to say something about. *She men-
tioned meeting the new teacher, but she
didn't tell me his name.*

men • tion² /měn′ shən/ *n.* a brief statement. *There wasn't even a mention of the
fire in the newspaper.*

mer • ry-go-round /měr′ ē gō round′/ *n.*
a round, rotating platform with seats and
animal figures on which people ride. *Sharla
rode a pink horse on the merry-go-round.*

mes • sage /měs′ ĭj/ *n.* any news, information, question, etc., sent from one person to another. *We left a message for him to meet us at the swimming pool.*

mid- a prefix that means "middle."

mid • af • ter • noon[1] /mĭd ăf′ tər nōōn′/ *n.* the middle of the afternoon. *Midafternoon is often the hottest part of the day.*

mid • af • ter • noon[2] /mĭd ăf′ tər nōōn′/ *adj.* in the middle of the afternoon: *a midafternoon swim.*

mid • air[1] /mĭd âr′/ *n.* the middle of the air. *A hummingbird can hover in midair.*

mid • air[2] /mĭd âr′/ *adj.* in the middle of the air: *a midair turn.*

mid • day[1] /mĭd′ dā′/ *n.* the middle of the day; noon. *The parade began at midday.*

mid • day[2] /mĭd′ dā′/ *adj.* in the middle of the day: *the midday meal.*

mid • land /mĭd′ lənd/ *n.* the middle or interior part of a country or a region. *We traveled to the midland of the desert.*

mid • night[1] /mĭd′ nīt′/ *n.* the middle of the night; twelve o'clock at night. *Midnight marks the end of the day.*

mid • night[2] /mĭd′ nīt′/ *adj.* in the middle of the night: *a midnight movie on TV.*

mid • term[1] /mĭd′ tûrm′/ *n.* the middle of the term. *The senator resigned in midterm for health reasons.*

mid • term[2] /mĭd′ tûrm′/ *adj.* in the middle of a term: *a midterm exam in school.*

Mid • west /mĭd wěst′/ *n.* a region of the north central United States. *Farmers in the Midwest grow much wheat and corn.*

mil • lion /mĭl′ yən/ *n.* a number equal to one thousand thousands; 1,000,000. *The numeral for one million has six zeros.*

mil • li • pede /mĭl′ ə pēd′/ *n.* a very small wormlike animal that has two pairs of legs for most segments of its body. *Millipedes live in damp, dark places and eat decaying plants.*

min • er • al /mĭn′ ər əl/ *n.* an inorganic substance; a substance that is neither animal nor vegetable, especially one that can be obtained from the earth by mining or drilling. *Copper and calcium are minerals.*

min • strel /mĭn′ strəl/ *n.* in the Middle Ages, a traveling entertainer who could sing and recite poems. *The minstrel tuned his lute before he began the ballad.*

mis • sion /mĭsh′ ən/ *n.* **a.** a group of people sent to carry on some particular business: *a mission to help foreign countries develop better methods of farming.* **b.** the business or job of such a group. *Their mission is to locate the missing files.* **c.** a person's calling. *Her mission in life was teaching.*

mix • ture /mĭks′ chər/ *n.* **a.** anything that is mixed or is being mixed. *The chemist was stirring a thick, blue-green mixture.* **b.** a combination of different things: *a mixture of forks and spoons.*

mo • bile /mō′ bəl/ *adj.* able to move or be moved; movable: *a mobile home.*

moc • ca • sin /mŏk′ ə sĭn/ *n.* a soft, flat leather shoe. *Some Native Americans made moccasins from the skins of deer.*

mo • dem /mō′ dəm′/ *n.* a device that can change data from one form to another. *A modem allows information to be sent from one computer to another over a telephone line.*

mod • ern • ize /mŏd′ ər nīz′/ *v.* (**mod•ern•iz•es, mod•ern•ized, mod•ern•iz•ing**) to make or become modern; to bring up to date. *We modernized our bathroom by adding a shower.*

mois • ture /mois′ chər/ *n.* the very small droplets of water that are in the air or that collect on a surface; wetness. *In the greenhouse, we could see the moisture that had collected on the leaves of the plants.*

mo • lar /mō′ lər/ *n.* a tooth in the back of a person's jaw that is used for grinding food. *The molars have double roots.*

molar

mol • e • cule /mŏl′ ĭ kyōōl′/ *n.* the smallest particle into which a thing can be divided and still remain that thing. *Molecules are made up of atoms.*

mon • i • tor[1] /mŏn′ ĭ tər/ *n.* a person assigned to supervise, keep order, or otherwise watch over. *Kate is the lunchroom monitor.*

mon•i•tor[2] /mŏn′ ĭ tər/ *v.* to keep track of; to watch over; to check up on. *The factory inspectors monitor the quality of their product.*

mon•soon /mŏn so͞on′/ *n.* **a.** a wind that causes wet and dry seasons by changing directions. *The monsoon blew from the southwest.* **b.** the rainy season caused by this wind. *The roads flooded during the monsoon.*

Mon•tan•a /mŏn′ tăn′ ə/ *n.* a state in the northwestern United States. *Glacier National Park is in Montana.* [Latin *montānus,* mountain.]

mo•tion[1] /mō′ shən/ *n.* **a.** the act of moving; movement. *The motion of the train made us sleepy.* **b.** a suggestion made at a meeting. *The motion was passed by the members.*

mo•tion[2] /mō shən/ *v.* to make a movement or a gesture. *The speaker motioned to us to sit down.*

mo•tor /mō′ tər/ *n.* an engine that turns power into motion. *The car would not move because the motor wouldn't start.*

mountain

moun•tain /moun′ tən/ *n.* any land that rises like a hill but is much higher than a hill. *We could see the snow on the mountains when we were still far away.*

mov•ie /mo͞o′ vē/ *n.* a series of pictures flashed on a screen so rapidly that what is shown appears to be moving. *Have you seen the movie* 101 Dalmatians?

mov•ies /mo͞o′ vēz/ *n. pl.* the showing of motion pictures at a theater. *We saw Greg at the movies.*

mul•ti•ple[1] /mŭl′ tə pəl/ *adj.* made up of many parts; being more than one. *His multiple interests include sports, music, and movies.*

mul•ti•ple[2] /mŭl′ tə pəl/ *n.* a number that is divisible by another number with no remainder. *4 and 6 are multiples of 2.*

mu•ni•ci•pal /myoͦo nĭs′ ə pəl/ *adj.* having to do with a city, town, or other local government. *Our town has a municipal bus service.*

mur•mur[1] /mûr′ mər/ *n.* a soft sound. *She spoke in a murmur.*

mur•mur[2] /mûr′ mər/ *v.* to make a soft noise. *Please do not murmur so softly.*

mu•se•um /myoͦo zē′ əm/ *n.* a building in which artistic, historical, or scientific objects are kept for display. *We saw an exhibition of famous paintings at the art museum.*

mu•si•cal[1] /myoͦo′ zĭ kəl/ *adj.* having to do with music: *musical instruments.*

mu•si•cal[2] /myoͦo′ zĭ kəl/ *n.* a musical comedy. Oliver! *is a musical based on a book by Charles Dickens.*

mys•te•ri•ous /mĭ stîr′ ē əs/ *adj.* full of mystery or the unknown; difficult to understand; puzzling. *Shooting stars were mysterious to people in ancient times.*

mys•ter•y /mĭs′ tə rē/ *n.* (**mys•ter•ies** *pl.*) **a.** something that is unknown or kept secret. *His reason for the trip was a mystery until he explained why he went.* **b.** a fictional work about a mysterious event; a suspense story. *Nancy Drew is a character in a series of mysteries.*

nar•row[1] /năr′ ō/ *adj.* **a.** not wide: *a narrow street.* **b.** close: *a narrow escape.*

nar•row[2] /năr′ ō/ *v.* to become less wide. *The river narrows as it reaches the city.*

na•ture /nā′ chər/ *n.* **a.** all things in the universe that are not made by human beings. *Plastics are not found in nature.* **b.** natural scenery. *The artist painted the beauties of nature.* **c.** the instincts that make a thing or person act in a certain way. *It is the nature of most birds to fly.*

nee•dle /nēd′ l/ *n.* **a.** a thin, pointed steel tool used in sewing. *Can you thread a needle?* **b.** a slender rod used in knitting. *We heard the needles clicking as you were knitting.* **c.** something thin and pointed like a needle. *A pine tree has needles.*

needle

neigh•bor /nā′ bər/ *n.* **a.** a person who lives nearby. *Our next-door neighbors have a gray cat.* **b.** a person or thing that is close to another. *Canada is a neighbor of the United States.*

-ness a suffix that means "state, quality, or degree of," used to form nouns: *loudness.*

Ne•vad•a /nə văd′ ə/ or /-vä′ də/ *n.* a state in the western United States. *Nevada's best-known cities are Reno and Las Vegas.*

New York /noo ′ yôrk′/ or /nyoo ′-/ *n.* a state in the eastern United States. *The state of New York has beautiful mountains and lakes.*

nine•teenth¹ /nīn tēnth′/ *n.* one of nineteen equal parts. *Two is one nineteenth of thirty-eight.*

nine•teenth² /nīn tēnth′/ *adj.* next after the eighteenth: *the nineteenth page.*

no. number. [Latin *numero.*]

non- a prefix that means "not": *nonprofit.*

non•fic•tion /nŏn fĭk′ shən/ *n.* writing that is based on fact, not made up; writing that is not fiction. *Histories and biographies are nonfiction.*

non•sense /nŏn′ sĕns′/ *n.* foolish actions or words; silly talk; anything that does not make sense. *Babies talk nonsense when they are learning to speak.*

non•stop¹ /nŏn′ stŏp′/ *adv.* without stopping. *We flew nonstop from Denver to Seattle.*

non•stop² /nŏn′ stŏp′/ *adj.* without stops; having no breaks: *a nonstop flight.*

non•vi•o•lent /nŏn vī′ ə lənt/ *adj.* not violent; opposed in principle to violence. *Diplomats use nonviolent methods to resolve conflicts.*

nor•mal¹ /nôr′ məl/ *adj.* natural; usual; average. *We had an inch less than the normal amount of rain this month.*

nor•mal² /nôr′ məl/ *n.* the usual condition. *Her temperature is two degrees above normal.*

North Da•ko•ta /nôrth′ də kō′tə/ *n.* a state in the north central United States. *North Dakota is a chief producer of wheat and rye.* [Sioux *dakota,* friend, ally.]

north•ern /nôr′ thərn/ *adj.* of, in, or toward the north. *Look in the northern sky for the Big Dipper.*

note•tak•ing /nōt′ tā′ kĭng/ *n.* the act of taking notes. *Careful notetaking can make writing reports easier.*

num•ber¹ /nŭm′ bər/ *n.* **a.** an amount; the total count: *a small number of people.* **b.** a word, figure, or numeral that shows how many. *"Thirty-two" and "176" are both numbers.*

num•ber² /nŭm′ bər/ *v.* to give a number to. *Always number the pages of your work.*

ob•tuse /ŏb toos′/ or /-tyoos′/ *adj.* containing more than 90 but fewer than 180 degrees. *A triangle can have only one obtuse angle.*

oc•ta•gon /ŏk′ tə gŏn/ *n.* a plane figure that has eight sides and eight angles. *A stop sign is an octagon.*

of•fice /ô′ fĭs/ or /ŏf′ ĭs/ *n.* **a.** a place or room where business is done or a service is supplied. *We waited in the doctor's office.* **b.** a position to which one is elected or appointed. *She holds the office of mayor.*

of•fi•cial¹ /ə fĭsh′ əl/ *n.* one who holds an office: *a public official.*

of•fi•cial² /ə fĭsh′ əl/ *adj.* **a.** having to do with a position of authority: *official duties.* **b.** coming from someone in authority: *an official announcement.*

O•hi•o /ō hī′ ō/ *n.* a state in the north central United States known for farm products and manufacturing. *Cincinnati is a city in Ohio.*

on•ion /ŭn′ yən/ *n.* a vegetable with a bulb that has a sharp smell and taste. *Onions can be eaten either raw or cooked.*

op•er•a /ŏp′ ə rə/ or /ŏp′ rə/ *n.* a play in which the actors sing instead of speak. *The soprano sang the leading role in the opera.* [Italian *opera,* from plural of Latin *opus,* work.]

op•er•ate /ŏp′ ə rāt/ *v.* (**op•er•ates, op•er•at•ed, op•er•at•ing**) **a.** to run or work. *Do you know how to operate a sewing machine?* **b.** to work on the body with instruments to restore it to health. *The doctor operated to remove the boy's tonsils.*

op•er•a•tor /ŏp′ ə rā′ tər/ *n.* one who runs or operates a machine, vehicle, business, etc.: *telephone operator.*

op•press /ə prĕs′/ *v.* to persecute; to govern cruelly or harshly. *Conquering soldiers often oppressed native peoples.*

-or a suffix, used with verbs to form nouns, that means: **a.** one who: *director.* **b.** thing that: *accelerator.*

or•ches•tra /ôr′ kĭ strə/ *n.* a group of players of various musical instruments. *Players in an orchestra must watch the conductor closely.*

or•gan•ize /ôr′ gə nīz′/ *v.* (**or•gan•iz•es, or•gan•ized, or•gan•iz•ing**) **a.** to work out the details for; to plan. *We helped organize the program for the school assembly.* **b.** to arrange; to put in order. *Organize your paper before you start to write it.*

or•na•ment /ôr′ nə mənt/ *n.* something pretty used for decoration. *A mirror can make an attractive wall ornament.*

ounce /ouns/ *n.* **a.** a unit of weight. *Sixteen ounces make one pound.* **b.** a measure of liquids. *An ounce is $\frac{1}{16}$ of a pint.*

-ous a suffix that means "having the qualities of" or "characterized by," used with nouns to form adjectives: *joyous.*

out•line¹ /out′ līn′/ *n.* a plan; a list of main subjects. *Martin made an outline of the points he wanted to cover.*

Pronunciation Key

ă	pat	ŏ	pot	th	**th**in
ā	pay	ō	toe	*th*	**th**is
âr	care	ô	paw, for	hw	**wh**ich
ä	father	oi	n**oi**se	zh	vi**s**ion
ĕ	pet	ou	**ou**t	ə	**a**bout,
ē	be	o͝o	t**oo**k		it**e**m,
ĭ	pit	o͞o	b**oo**t		penc**i**l,
ī	pie	ŭ	c**u**t		gall**o**p,
îr	pier	ûr	**ur**ge		circ**u**s

out•line² /out′ līn′/ *v.* (**out•lines, out•lined, out•lin•ing**) to make a plan of; to tell about the main ideas of something. *Outline your story before you write it.*

ov•en /ŭv′ ən/ *n.* the enclosed space of a stove used for baking, roasting, etc. *Keep the oven closed while the bread bakes.*

oven

ox•y•gen /ŏk′ sĭ jən/ *n.* a gaseous element that has no color, taste, or odor. *All animals need oxygen to live.*

oy•ster /oi′ stər/ *n.* a mollusk with a soft body surrounded by two rough shells, found in shallow parts of the ocean. *Some kinds of oysters are eaten and others form valuable pearls.*

oz. ounce [Italian *onza.*]

pack•age¹ /păk′ ĭj/ *n.* a bundle of things wrapped together. *Uncle Walter sent us a package of books.*

pack•age² /păk′ ĭj/ *v.* (**pack•ag•es, pack•aged, pack•ag•ing**) to wrap up; to place in a box. *The store will package all your purchases.*

pal•ace /păl′ ĭs/ *n.* the official residence of royalty. *The palace was protected by the royal guard.*

297

pan•el /păn′ əl/ *n.* **a.** a flat, rectangular section of a surface such as a wall. *The panels on the door are painted brown.* **b.** a group of persons sitting together to decide a question. *The panel met to discuss the state of the economy.*

par•cel /pär′ səl/ *n.* **a.** a package; a bundle of things wrapped together. *The shopper's arms were filled with parcels.* **b.** a piece; a section. *The farmer sold a parcel of land.*

par•don /pär dn/ *v.* to forgive or excuse. *Pardon me for disturbing you.*

part of speech /pärt′ əv spēch′/ *n.* one of the classifications of words according to how they function in sentences. *Common parts of speech include nouns, verbs, adjectives, and adverbs.*

pas•sen•ger /păs′ ən jər/ *n.* a person traveling in, but not operating, a vehicle. *Each passenger is allowed one piece of carry-on luggage.*

pas•ture /păs′ chər/ *n.* land covered with grass where cattle, sheep, etc., may graze. *Take the horses up to the pasture.* [Latin *pāscere*, to feed.]

pa•tient¹ /pā′ shənt/ *adj.* able to put up with pain, trouble, delay, etc., without complaint. *The passenger was patient despite the heavy traffic.*

pa•tient² /pā′ shənt/ *n.* a person under the care of a doctor. *The patients gave their nurse a birthday gift.*

pea•nut but•ter /pē′ nŭt bŭt′ ər/ *n.* a food made from roasted peanuts ground into a spreadable paste. *I like peanut butter on bananas.*

peat /pēt/ *n.* partly decayed plant matter found in bogs and used as fuel or fertilizer. *Peat is the first stage in the formation of coal.*

peer /pîr/ *v.* to look at with curiosity; to look long and hard. *The wide-eyed child peered at all the presents.*

▶ **Peer** sounds like **pier**.

pen•ta•gon /pĕn′ tə gŏn′/ *n.* a plane figure that has five sides and five angles. *You can draw a star inside a pentagon by connecting the corners.*

per•form /pər fôrm′/ *v.* **a.** to do; to carry out. *Elizabeth performs all her jobs well.* **b.** to entertain before an audience; to act out. *The actors performed a new play.*

per•fume /pûr′ fyo͞om′/ or /pər fyo͞om′/ *n.* **a.** a sweet smell. *The perfume of the flowers filled the air.* **b.** a sweet-smelling liquid used on the body and clothing. *My sister got a bottle of perfume for her birthday.*

pe•rim•e•ter /pə rĭm′ ĭ tər/ *n.* the distance around an area; the sum of the lengths of all sides of a figure. *The perimeter of a square with one-inch sides is four inches.*

phos•pho•rus /fŏs′ fər əs/ *n.* a nonmetallic element that burns easily and may glow in the dark. *Phosphorus is used to make matches.*

pi•an•o /pē ăn′ ō/ *n.* (**pi•an•os** *pl.*) a large musical instrument played by striking keys arranged in order of pitch from lowest to highest. *We played a duet on the piano.*

piano

pic•ture /pĭk′ chər/ *n.* **a.** a painting, drawing, or photograph. *The pictures in the magazine were beautiful.* **b.** a likeness; an image. *Larry is the picture of his father.* **c.** a description. *Her letter gave a good picture of army life.* [Latin *pingere*, to paint.]

pier /pîr/ *n.* a landing place for ships and boats. *Tie your rowboat to the pier.*

▶ **Pier** sounds like **peer**.

pierce /pîrs/ *v.* (**pierc•es, pierced, pierc•ing**) to make a hole in with a sharp, pointed instrument; to stab. *The balloon exploded when it was pierced with a pin.*

pint /pīnt/ *n.* a measure of volume equal to one-half of a quart or sixteen ounces. *We bought a pint of cream and a pint of strawberries.*

pi•o•neer /pī′ ə nîr′/ *n.* a person who goes first and opens the way for others. *The ancient Egyptians were pioneers in astronomy.*

pitch•er¹ /pĭch′ ər/ *n.* a player in a baseball game who throws the ball to a person at bat. *The pitcher threw a curve ball for a strike.*

pitch•er² /pĭch′ ər/ *n.* a jar with a large lip used for holding and pouring water, milk, oil, or other liquid. *Pitchers may have one or two handles.*

pkg. package.

place val•ue /plās′ văl′ yōō/ *n.* the value of the place a digit occupies in a numeral. *In the decimal system, the place value of each digit is ten times greater than that of the digit to its right.*

plaid¹ /plăd/ *n.* a pattern of checks or squares formed by stripes crossing at right angles. *Scottish clans have distinctive plaids, which they call tartans.* [Scottish Gaelic *plaide.*]

plaid² /plăd/ *adj.* having such a pattern: *a plaid scarf.*

plain¹ /plān/ *adj.* **a.** easy to see or understand; distinct; clear: *plain directions.* **b.** simple; not rich or fancy: *plain food.*

plain² /plān/ *n.* a large stretch of flat land. *The plains of the West are used for grazing cattle.*

plaque /plăk/ *n.* a thin film that forms on the surfaces of teeth. *Brushing and flossing daily will remove plaque and prevent cavities.*

plas•tic¹ /plăs′ tĭk/ *n.* any of a large number of synthetic chemical substances that can be molded into various forms by heat and pressure. *Vinyl and nylon are plastics.*

plas•tic² /plăs′ tĭk/ *adj.* made of plastic: *plastic dishes.*

pla•za /plä′ zə/ or /plăz′ ə/ *n.* a public square in a city or town. *The cathedral faces the plaza.* [Spanish, from Latin *platea*, broad street.]

pleas•ant /plĕz′ ənt/ *adj.* **a.** delightful; pleasing: *a pleasant vacation.* **b.** fair and warm: *a pleasant day.* **c.** agreeable; friendly: *pleasant teachers.*

pleas•ure /plĕzh′ ər/ *n.* **a.** joy; delight; satisfaction. *Her pleasure in meeting the famous guitarist showed on her face.* **b.** something that gives enjoyment or satisfaction. *Going to the zoo was a pleasure for the class.*

pledge¹ /plĕj/ *n.* a promise; an agreement. *We made a pledge to be home by ten o'clock.*

pledge² /plĕj/ *v.* (**pledg•es, pledged, pledg•ing**) to promise. *My father pledged to help with the fund drive.*

Pronunciation Key

ă	pat	ŏ	pot	th	thin
ā	pay	ō	toe	th	this
âr	care	ô	paw, for	hw	which
ä	father	oi	noise	zh	vision
ĕ	pet	ou	out	ə	about,
ē	be	ŏŏ	took		item,
ĭ	pit	ōō	boot		pencil,
ī	pie	ŭ	cut		gallop,
îr	pier	ûr	urge		circus

po•et•ry /pō′ ĭ trē/ *n.* poems; verse. *We studied the poetry of Shakespeare.*

poise /poiz/ *n.* the way the body is carried or held; grace; balance. *Ballet dancers move with superb poise.*

poi•son¹ /poi′ zən/ *n.* a substance that harms the body. *Some snakes give off a poison when they bite.*

poi•son² /poi′ zən/ *v.* to injure or kill by poison. *We poisoned the weeds in the yard.*

po•lice¹ /pə lēs′/ *n.* a group of persons who enforce law, deal with criminals, and keep peace. *Call the police in an emergency.*

po•lice² /pə lēs′/ *adj.* of or having to do with the police: *a police officer.*

po•lite /pə līt′/ *adj.* having good manners; courteous; thoughtful. *It is polite to shake hands when you meet someone.*

pol•ka /pōl′ kə/ *n.* a quick, lively dance for couples in 2/4 time. *Mr. and Mrs. Weiss were out of breath when they finished the polka.*

pop•u•late /pŏp′ yə lāt′/ *v.* (**pop•u•lates, pop•u•lat•ed, pop•u•lat•ing**) to live or reside in; to inhabit. *When the apartment building was finished, it was quickly populated by new residents.*

por•cu•pine /pôr′ kyə pīn′/ *n.* a small, slow-moving animal with stiff, sharp, needle-like hair on its back and tail. *Please don't pet the porcupine.*

porcupine

299

post- a prefix that means "after" or "later": *postwar.*

post•date /pōst dāt'/ *v.* (post•dates, post•dat•ed, post•dat•ing) to use a date on something that is later than the actual date. *I postdated the letter because I knew I wouldn't mail it until Monday.*

post•script /pōst' skrĭpt'/ or /pōs'-/ *n.* a note added to a letter after the writer's signature. *Rieko wrote in a postscript that she had found her socks after all.*

post•test /pōst' tĕst/ *n.* a test taken after information has been learned. *I did well on the posttest.*

post•war /pōst' wôr'/ *adj.* happening after a war: *the postwar boom in the economy.*

pound /pound/ *n.* a measure of weight equal to sixteen ounces. *Buy a pound of flour for me.*

prac•tice¹ /prăk' tĭs/ *n.* **a.** actual use. *The plan didn't work well in practice.* **b.** training by doing something over and over. *Playing the piano requires regular practice.*

prac•tice² /prăk' tĭs/ *v.* (prac•tic•es, prac•ticed, prac•tic•ing) **a.** to put into actual use. *He practices what he believes.* **b.** to do exercises in order to become skilled. *Let's practice our spelling.*

pre- a prefix that means: **a.** before: *preschool.* **b.** in advance: *prepaid.*

pre•cau•tion /prĭ kô' shən/ *n.* an action or care taken in advance, often for protection or safety. *We took the precaution of locking the car.*

pred•i•cate /prĕd' ĭ kĭt/ *n.* the part of a sentence that includes the verb and tells something about the subject. *In the sentence "The ball is red," "is red" is the predicate.*

pre•fix /prē' fĭks/ *n.* (pre•fix•es *pl.*) a group of letters added to the beginning of a word to change its meaning. *In the word "reheat," "re-" is a prefix that adds the meaning "again."*

pre•his•tor•ic /prē'hĭ stôr' ĭk/ or /-stŏr'-/ *adj.* having to do with the time before written history began. *Prehistoric paintings and tools have been found all over the world.*

pre•paid¹ /prē pād'/ *adj.* paid for in advance. *The package was prepaid.*

pre•paid² /prē pād'/ *v.* past tense and past participle of **prepay.**

pre•pare /prĭ pâr'/ *v.* (pre•pares, pre•pared, pre•par•ing) **a.** to make ready; to get ready. *The farmer prepares the soil for planting crops.* **b.** to make or to put together in a certain way. *The chef prepared her special salad.*

pre•pay /prē pā'/ *v.* (pre•pays, pre•paid, pre•pay•ing) to pay for in advance: *prepay the postage.*

prep•o•si•tion /prĕp'ə zĭsh' ən/ *n.* a word used in front of a noun, pronoun, or noun phrase to show its relation to something else in the sentence. *In the phrase "the chair in the hall," "in" is a preposition that shows the relation of "hall" to "chair."*

pre•re•cord /prē'rĭ kôrd'/ *v.* to record in advance for later use. *We are prerecording this program for airing over the holidays.*

prime /prīm/ *adj.* **a.** first in quality or importance: *the prime minister.* **b.** not able to be factored; having no factors except itself and 1. *19 and 23 are prime numbers.*

prin•ci•pal¹ /prĭn' sə pəl/ *adj.* most important; chief; main. *The principal product of Pittsburgh is steel.*

prin•ci•pal² /prĭn' sə pəl/ *n.* the head of a school. *The principal announced the winners of the spelling contest.*

▶ **Principal** sounds like **principle.**

prin•ci•ple /prĭn' sə pəl/ *n.* a basic fact; a rule upon which other rules are based: *the principles of science.*

▶ **Principle** sounds like **principal.**

prism /prĭz' əm/ *n.* a three-dimensional geometric shape that has two parallel, congruent polygons as bases. *A box is a rectangular prism.*

pri•vate /prī vĭt/ *adj.* belonging to a certain person or group of persons; not public. *Your letters are your private property.*

pro•claim /prō klām'/ or /prə-/ *v.* to announce publicly. *The president proclaimed a new federal holiday.*

pro•duce /prə dōōs'/ or /-dyōōs'/ *v.* (pro•duc•es, pro•duced, pro•duc•ing) **a.** to make or manufacture; to put out. *Boiling water produces steam.* **b.** to present to the public: *produce a play.*

pro•fes•sion /prə fĕsh′ ən/ *n.* a kind of work or occupation that requires special education. *To enter the medical profession, you must study for several years after college.*

pro•fes•sor /prə fĕs′ ər/ *n.* a college teacher of the highest rank. *After Mr. Patel received his Ph.D., he became an assistant professor at the university.*

pro•gram¹ /prō′ grăm′/ or /-grəm/ *n.* **a.** a list of events. *The musicians' names were printed on the program.* **b.** a performance; an entertainment: *a TV program.*

pro•gram² /prō′ grăm′/ or /-grəm/ *v.* (pro•grams, pro•grammed, pro•gram•ming) to write instructions for a computer. *Can you program the computer to solve this problem?*

prom•ise¹ /prŏm′ ĭs/ *n.* a statement that one will surely do something. *Jerry always keeps his promises.*

prom•ise² /prŏm′ ĭs/ *v.* (prom•is•es, prom•ised, prom•is•ing) to give one's word; to make a promise. *Margaret promised to be here at three o'clock.*

pro•nounce /prə nouns′/ *v.* (pro•nounc•es, pro•nounced, pro•nounc•ing) to make the sounds of; to speak. *If you pronounce words clearly, it will be easier for you to spell them.*

prose /prōz/ *n.* any spoken or written language that is not poetry; ordinary language. *Essays are written in prose.*

pro•tein /prō′ tēn′/ *n.* a substance containing nitrogen that is a necessary part of all living tissue and a requirement for a balanced diet. *Meats and beans are high in protein.*

proud /proud/ *adj.* feeling satisfaction and pleasure. *Brian felt proud when his science project won a blue ribbon.*

prove /prōōv/ *v.* (proves, proved, proved or prov•en, prov•ing) to show to be true. *The doctor's tests proved that Cindy was in good health.*

pt. pint.

pub•lic¹ /pŭb′ lĭk/ *n.* the people. *The library is used by the public.*

pub•lic² /pŭb′ lĭk/ *adj.* **a.** for the people; used by people. *Public parks are open to all.* **b.** of the people: *public opinion.*

Pronunciation Key

ă	pat	ŏ	pot	th	**th**in
ā	pay	ō	toe	*th*	**th**is
âr	care	ô	paw, for	hw	**wh**ich
ä	father	oi	noise	zh	vision
ĕ	pet	ou	out	ə	about,
ē	be	ŏŏ	took		item,
ĭ	pit	ōō	boot		pencil,
ī	pie	ŭ	cut		gallop,
îr	pier	ûr	urge		circus

pub•lish /pŭb′ lĭsh/ *v.* **a.** to prepare books, magazines, etc., for sale. *That company publishes a book we use in school.* **b.** to make known. *The newspaper published an account of the hearing.* [Latin *pŭblicāre,* to make public.]

pub•lish•er /pŭb′ lĭ shər/ *n.* a person or company whose business is to prepare, print, and sell books, magazines, newspapers, etc. *You will find the publisher's name on the second page in this book.*

punc•tu•ate /pŭngk′ chōō āt′/ *v.* (punc•tu•ates, punc•tu•at•ed, punc•tu•at•ing) to insert standard written marks such as periods or commas to make the meaning clear. *Did you punctuate this sentence correctly?*

pu•pil¹ /pyōō′ pəl/ *n.* a person being taught by a teacher; a student. *Sean is a pupil of hers.*

pu•pil² /pyōō′ pəl/ *n.* the dark opening in the center of the eye. *The pupil becomes smaller in bright light and larger in dim light.*

pur•pose /pûr′ pəs/ *n.* aim; plan; intention. *The purpose of the meeting was to plan our spring show.*

qt. quart.

quart /kwôrt/ *n.* **a.** a measure of liquid equal to two pints: *a quart of milk.* **b.** a measure of dry things equal to one eighth of a peck: *a quart of blueberries.*

quart

Spelling Dictionary

ra • di • ant /rā′ dē ənt/ *adj.* **a.** bright; shining. *Ann has a radiant smile.* **b.** sent out in waves. *The earth receives radiant heat from the sun.* [Latin *radiāre*, to emit beams.]

rat • i • fy /răt′ ə fī′/ *v.* (**ra•ti•fies, ra•ti•fied, ra•ti•fy•ing**) to make official or valid; to confirm; to approve. *The legislature ratified the treaty.*

ray /rā/ *n.* **a.** a thin beam of light: *the ray of the flashlight.* **b.** a part of a line that has one endpoint and extends infinitely far in the other direction. *Two rays with the same endpoint form an angle.*

re- a prefix that means: **a.** again: *regroup.* **b.** back: *rebound.*

re • al • ize /rē′ ə līz′/ *v.* (**re•al•iz•es, re•al•ized, re•al•iz•ing**) to understand; to know; to be aware. *Allen suddenly realized that he was late for school.*

re • ap • pear /rē′ ə pîr′/ *v.* to become visible again; to appear again. *The chipmunk vanished into a hole and then reappeared.*

re • call /rĭ kôl′/ *v.* **a.** to call back. *The soldiers were recalled to duty after a brief leave.* **b.** to remember. *Snapshots help us recall happy days.*

re • cent /rē′ sənt/ *adj.* done, made, or happening not long ago. *A recent news article told about the progress being made in building safer cars.*

re • charge /rē chärj′/ *v.* (**re•charg•es, re•charged, re•charg•ing**) to charge again; to restore to a former level of energy. *If you recharge the batteries, your radio will work again.*

re • cite /rĭ sīt′/ *v.* (**re•cites, re•cit•ed, re•cit•ing**) **a.** to say something learned or memorized out loud. *Dennis recited a poem.* **b.** to give a detailed account. *She recited the list of problems that need attention.*

re • claim /rĭ klām′/ or /rē-/ *v.* **a.** to restore to a usable condition. *We can reclaim land used for mining and set up a nature preserve.* **b.** to claim back; to ask for the return of. *They reclaimed their furniture from storage.*

re • cord • er /rĭ kôr′ dər/ *n.* **a.** a machine or device that records: *a tape recorder.* **b.** a wooden musical instrument that is held in a vertical position and blown into to produce a hollow, flutelike sound. *Recorders were popular during the Middle Ages.*

recorder

rec • tan • gu • lar /rĕk tăng′ gyə lər/ *adj.* having four sides and four right angles; shaped like a rectangle. *This page is rectangular.*

re • duce /rĭ dōōs′/ or /-dyōōs′/ *v.* (**re•duc•es, re•duced, re•duc•ing**) **a.** to make less. *Regular exercise helps reduce stress.* **b.** to change in form. *Reduce that fraction to its lowest terms.*

re • en • ter or **re-en • ter** /rē ĕn′ tər/ *v.* to go in again; to enter again. *When she reentered the room, we all clapped.*

re • flex /rē′ flĕks/ *n.* (**re•flex•es** *pl.*) an automatic action of the body in response to something. *Blinking and sneezing are reflexes.*

re • form[1] /rĭ fôrm′/ *v.* to make better by correcting or removing faults. *We discussed how to reform the old rules.*

re • form[2] /rĭ fôrm′/ *n.* an improvement; a correction of a wrong. *Reforms in the voting laws created a fairer system.*

re • fresh /rĭ frĕsh′/ *v.* to make fresh again; to revive; to renew. *The cool lemonade refreshed us after our hike.*

re • fund[1] /rĭ fŭnd′/ *v.* to give back something, especially money, that has been paid. *If you are not satisfied with your purchase, the store will refund your money.*

re • fund[2] /rē′ fŭnd/ *n.* a return or repayment of money. *When Molly's new radio wouldn't work, she asked for a refund.*

Spelling Dictionary

re • gard¹ /rĭ gärd'/ *v.* **a.** to look at closely; to examine. *He regarded me with interest.* **b.** to consider; to think of. *I regard her as a friend.*

re • gard² /rĭ gärd'/ *n.* respect; esteem. *The audience showed their regard for the soloist by applauding loudly.*

re • gion /rē' jən/ *n.* **a.** a large portion of the surface of the earth. *Cacti grow in desert regions.* **b.** any area or place. *We live in the northeast region of the state.*

re • hearse /rĭ hûrs'/ *v.* (**re•hears•es, re•hearsed, re•hears•ing**) to practice or prepare for a performance. *Our choir rehearsed for the spring concert.*

re • join /rē join'/ *v.* to join again. *When we came back, we rejoined the group in the living room.*

re • late /rĭ lāt'/ *v.* (**re•lates, re•lat•ed, re•lat•ing**) **a.** to tell about; to give an account of. *He related his experiences traveling in India.* **b.** to show a connection between. *Can you relate the science lesson to your experiment?*

rel • a • tive¹ /rĕl' ə tĭv/ *n.* a person connected to another by blood or marriage. *All my relatives attended the party.*

rel • a • tive² /rĕl' ə tĭv/ *adj.* comparative; compared with another. *We compared the relative sizes of moths and butterflies.*

re • mark¹ /rĭ märk'/ *v.* to say; to comment briefly. *Dad remarked that we had forgotten to brush our teeth.*

re • mark² /rĭ märk'/ *n.* a brief comment. *She made a flattering remark about my haircut.*

re • mem • ber /rĭ mĕm' bər/ *v.* **a.** to bring back to the mind; to recall. *I couldn't remember the answer.* **b.** to keep in mind. *Remember to turn off the light.*

re • move /rĭ mo͞ov'/ *v.* (**re•moves, re•moved, re•mov•ing**) to take away; to take off. *Remove everything from your desk before you leave.*

re • new /rĭ no͞o'/ or /-nyo͞o'/ *v.* **a.** to make new again; to make fresh again. *The bright paint renewed the dingy walls.* **b.** to restore; to fill again: *renew supplies.* **c.** to cause to continue for a new period of time: *renew a subscription.*

Pronunciation Key

ă	pat	ŏ	pot	th	**th**in
ā	pay	ō	toe	*th*	**th**is
âr	care	ô	paw, for	hw	**wh**ich
ä	father	oi	n**oi**se	zh	vi**s**ion
ĕ	pet	ou	**ou**t	ə	**a**bout,
ē	be	o͝o	t**oo**k		it**e**m,
ĭ	pit	o͞o	b**oo**t		penc**i**l,
ī	pie	ŭ	c**u**t		gall**o**p,
îr	p**ie**r	ûr	**ur**ge		circ**u**s

re • pair¹ /rĭ pâr'/ *v.* to bring back to good condition; to fix; to mend. *Do you know how to repair a flat tire?*

re • pair² /rĭ pâr'/ *n.* the act of repairing. *The repair of your car will be finished tomorrow.*

rep • re • sent /rĕp' rĭ zĕnt'/ *v.* **a.** to be a symbol of; to stand for. *The Statue of Liberty represents the freedom that can be found in the United States.* **b.** to speak or act for. *I will represent our class at the meeting.*

res • cue /rĕs' kyo͞o/ *v.* (**res•cues, res•cued, res•cu•ing**) to save from danger; to free from harm. *The volunteer rescued the bird from the oil spill.*

rescue

re • search¹ /rĭ sûrch'/ or /rē' sûrch'/ *n.* systematic investigation or careful study. *The scientist's research helped prove that her theory was accurate.*

re • search² /rĭ sûrch'/ or /rē' sûrch'/ *v.* to investigate; to study. *We researched the history of voting laws.*

re • side /rĭ zīd'/ *v.* (**re•sides, re•sid•ed, re•sid•ing**) to live; to make one's home at a place. *They reside in a nearby town.*

res • i • due /rĕz' ĭ do͞o'/ or /-dyo͞o'/ *n.* what is left after something else is removed or disappears, especially by a chemical process. *When the liquid evaporated, it left a gritty residue.*

re•tail[1] /rē′ tāl′/ *n.* the sale of goods directly to the consumer. *Storekeepers buy goods at wholesale and sell to their customers at retail.*

re•tail[2] /rē′ tāl′/ *adj.* having to do with selling in small amounts: *the retail price.*

ret•i•na /rĕt′ n ə/ *n.* a membrane at the back of the eye, made up of cells that respond to light. *The retina sends images from the lens to the brain.*

re•verse[1] /rĭ vûrs′/ *adj.* turned around in the opposite direction or position: *the reverse side of a coin.*

re•verse[2] /rĭ vûrs′/ *v.* (**re•vers•es, re•versed, re•vers•ing**) to change to the opposite direction or position. *Scott reversed the sign so we could see the back.*

re•vise /rĭ vīz′/ *v.* (**re•vis•es, re•vised, re•vis•ing**) **a.** to read over in order to improve; to edit. *My paragraph was much clearer after I revised it.* **b.** to alter or change: *revise an opinion.*

re•ward[1] /rĭ wôrd′/ *n.* something given in return for something done. *A medal is a reward for accomplishment.*

re•ward[2] /rĭ wôrd′/ *v.* to give a reward to or for. *Our efforts at cooking were rewarded with a delicious pie.*

rhyme[1] /rīm/ *n.* **a.** a word whose final syllable or sound is like that of another word. *"Block" is a rhyme for "clock."* **b.** a poem with lines that end with the same sound: *a nursery rhyme.*

rhyme[2] /rīm/ *v.* (**rhymes, rhymed, rhym•ing**) to be or to form a rhyme; to sound like another word. *"Feet" rhymes with "heat."*

ro•bot /rō′ bət/ or /-bŏt′/ *n.* a piece of machinery that does work like a human being. *Robots can do specific tasks, but they cannot think.* [Czech *robota,* drudgery.]

robot

ro•dent /rōd′ nt/ *n.* any one of a group of small mammals with large front teeth for gnawing. *Mice and squirrels are rodents.*

route /rōōt/ or /rout/ *n.* **a.** a road, path, etc. *We consulted the map to find the shortest route.* **b.** a regular course; a series of stops: *newspaper route.*

ru•ral /rŏŏr′ əl/ *adj.* having to do with the country; in the country. *Children who live in rural areas usually ride buses to school.*

sal•a•man•der /săl′ ə măn′ dər/ *n.* an amphibian that looks like a lizard but has no scales and is covered with moist skin. *Salamanders are related to frogs and live in dark, damp places.*

scald /skôld/ *v.* **a.** to burn with hot liquid. *Don't scald your tongue on the hot soup.* **b.** to heat to just under boiling: *scald the milk.* [Latin *excaldāre,* to wash in hot water, from *ex-,* from + *calidus,* warm.]

scan /skăn/ *v.* (**scans, scanned, scan•ning**) **a.** to look at carefully: *scan the fine print.* **b.** to look over or glance through quickly; to skim. *When you take a test, scan all the questions before you begin.*

scarce /skârs/ *adj.* hard to get; not abundant; rare. *Trees are scarce in the middle of a big city.*

scar•y /skâr′ ē/ *adj.* (**scar•i•er, scar•i•est**) causing one to feel scared; frightening. *Part of that movie was scary, but it had a happy ending.*

sci•en•tist /sī′ ən tĭst/ *n.* a person trained to be an expert in one or more fields of science. *Astronomers and geologists are scientists.*

scram•ble /skrăm′ bəl/ *v.* (**scram•bles, scram•bled, scram•bling**) **a.** to climb, crawl, or walk in a hurry. *The children scrambled up the side of the hill.* **b.** to mix in a messy way. *I scrambled my books and papers together and ran for the bus.*

scrap•book /skrăp′ bŏŏk′/ *n.* an album or book with blank pages for keeping pictures or clippings. *Our class made a scrapbook about our field trip.*

screen /skrēn/ *n.* **a.** wire woven together tightly, leaving tiny openings. *Screens keep out insects in summer.* **b.** a surface on which movies, slides, etc., are shown. *We put up the screen for the slide show.* **c.** the part of a TV set on which the picture appears: *a 25-inch screen.*

search[1] /sûrch/ *v.* to look for something. *All people search for happiness.*

search[2] /sûrch/ *n.* (**search•es** *pl.*) a hunt. *After a long search they found the cat under the sofa.*

sec•tion /sĕk′ shən/ *n.* **a.** a part; a division; a slice. *An orange is divided naturally into sections.* **b.** a region. *This hilly section of Missouri is beautiful.*

se•lect /sĭ lĕkt′/ *v.* to pick out; to choose. *Joanna selected the dress with the green ribbons.*

self•ish /sĕl′ fĭsh/ *adj.* thinking mostly of oneself; not caring much about others. *Refusing to share is selfish.*

semi- a prefix that means: **a.** half: *semicircle.* **b.** partly; somewhat: *semisweet.* **c.** twice during: *semiannual.*

sem•i•an•nu•al /sĕm′ē ăn′ yōō əl/ *adj.* happening twice a year. *The company holds semiannual sales meetings.*

sem•i•cir•cle /sĕm′ ĭ sûr′ kəl/ *n.* half of a circle. *The choir was in a semicircle on the stage.*

sem•i•co•lon /sĕm′ ī kō′ lən/ *n.* a punctuation mark (;) that stands for a break greater than a comma and less than a period. *A semicolon may be used to combine two related sentences.*

sem•i•fi•nal[1] /sĕm′ē fī′ nəl/ *adj.* coming just before the final, as in a competition: *the semifinal round.*

sem•i•fi•nal[2] /sĕm′ē fī′ nəl/ *n.* one of the two games, matches, or rounds that come just before the final. *If Mark wins the semifinal, he will advance to the final.*

sem•i•for•mal /sĕm′ē fôr′ məl/ *adj.* somewhat formal: *a semiformal dinner.*

sem•i•sweet /sĕm′ē swēt′/ *adj.* somewhat sweet: *semisweet chocolate.*

sen•a•tor /sĕn′ ə tər/ *n.* a member of a legislative group called a senate. *A senator in Congress is elected to serve six years.*

sense /sĕns/ *n.* **a.** a power of the body that makes a person aware of things. *Our five senses are sight, smell, taste, hearing, and touch.* **b.** a feeling: *a sense of satisfaction.*

sep•a•rate[1] /sĕp′ ə rāt′/ *v.* (**sep•a•rates, sep•a•rat•ed, sep•a•rat•ing**) to divide; to keep apart; to be between. *The fence separates the two yards.*

Pronunciation Key

ă	pat	ŏ	pot	th	thin
ā	pay	ō	toe	*th*	*th*is
âr	care	ô	paw, for	hw	which
ä	father	oi	noise	zh	vision
ĕ	pet	ou	out	ə	about,
ē	be	ŏŏ	took		item,
ĭ	pit	ōō	boot		pencil,
ī	pie	ŭ	cut		gallop,
îr	pier	ûr	urge		circus

sep•a•rate[2] /sĕp′ ər ĭt/ or /sĕp′ rĭt/ *adj.* not connected; set apart. *They work for the same factory but in separate buildings.*

ser•i•ous /sîr′ ē əs/ *adj.* **a.** thoughtful; solemn. *You look so serious; is something wrong?* **b.** in earnest; honest; not joking. *She is serious about becoming a dancer.*

serv•ice /sûr′ vĭs/ *n.* **a.** a help; an aid. *As a service to the passengers, the bus now stops at Oak Street.* **b.** work done for others. *He received an award for his service to the city.*

set•tler /sĕt′ lər/ *n.* one who settles in a new area. *The settlers worked together to clear the land.*

sev•en•teenth[1] /sĕv′ ən tēnth′/ *n.* one of seventeen equal parts: *a seventeenth of the casserole.*

sev•en•teenth[2] /sĕv′ ən tēnth′/ *adj.* coming next after the sixteenth: *the seventeenth book on the shelf.*

shad•ow /shăd′ ō/ *n.* a dark shape made on a surface by something that cuts off the light. *On a cloudy day you can't see your shadow.* [Old English *sceadu,* shade, shadow.]

shadow

shake /shāk/ *v.* (**shakes, shook, shak•en, shak•ing**) **a.** to move quickly up and down or from side to side. *The wind shook the windows.* **b.** to tremble. *Her hands were shaking from the cold.*

sham•poo[1] /shăm pōō′/ *n.* a liquid or cream used for washing the hair. *He uses an herbal shampoo.*

sham•poo² /shăm pōō′/ *v.* washing the hair with such a mixture. *She shampoos her hair often.* [Hindi *cãpō*, from *cãpna*, to wash.]

shawl /shôl/ *n.* a large piece of cloth worn over the shoulders or the head. *At the pueblo we saw a woman weaving a beautiful shawl.*

shawl

shel•ter¹ /shĕl′ tər/ *n.* something that covers, protects, or shields. *The old barn served as a shelter from the storm.*

shel•ter² /shĕl′ tər/ *v.* to protect; to give shelter to. *Our house shelters us from cold weather.*

shoul•der /shōl′ dər/ *n.* **a.** the part of the body between the neck and an arm. *The gym teacher said, "Shoulders straight!"* **b.** the edge of a road. *The truck driver pulled onto the shoulder.*

sick•ness /sĭk′ nĭs/ *n.* (**sick•ness•es** *pl.*) **a.** illness; poor health. *Good nutrition helps prevent sickness.* **b.** a certain disease. *Chicken pox is usually a mild sickness.*

sign¹ /sīn/ *n.* **a.** something that stands for something else; a symbol. *Shaking hands is a sign of friendship.* **b.** a board used for advertising or information: *a traffic sign.*

sign² /sīn/ *v.* to write one's name on. *Don't forget to sign your test paper.*

sil•ent /sī′ lənt/ *adj.* **a.** quiet; still; with no sound or noise. *The morning was silent until the birds began to sing.* **b.** not said out loud. *The "e" in "rake" is silent.*

sil•i•con /sĭl′ ĭ kən/ or /-kŏn′/ *n.* a common nonmetallic element found in rock, clay, and sand. *Silicon is used to make glass and computer chips.*

sim•pli•fy /sĭm′ plə fī′/ *v.* (**sim•pli•fies, sim•pli•fied, sim•pli•fy•ing**) **a.** to make something clearer or easier. *Mr. Golden simplified the story for the younger children.* **b.** to reduce to lowest terms. *You can simplify a fraction by taking out common factors.*

sin•cere /sĭn sîr′/ *adj.* honest; genuine; really meaning what one says. *Please accept our sincere thanks for the donation to the school.*

six•teenth¹ /sĭk stēnth′/ *n.* one of sixteen equal parts: *one sixteenth of a beat in music.*

six•teenth² /sĭk stēnth′/ *adj.* coming next after the fifteenth: *the sixteenth step on the stairs.*

skel•e•ton /skĕl′ ĭ tn/ *n.* the framework of a body, supporting or protecting the muscles and organs. *The shell of a snail is its skeleton.*

ski¹ /skē/ *n.* one of two long slender pieces of wood or metal that can be fastened to a shoe: *snow skis.*

ski² /skē/ *v.* to glide over snow or water on skis. *They skied swiftly down the hill.*

skim /skĭm/ *v.* (**skims, skimmed, skim•ming**) **a.** to remove from the top of a liquid: *to skim milk.* **b.** to read or glance over quickly. *I skimmed through a magazine article while I waited.*

slave /slāv/ *n.* a person who is the property of another person. *In ancient times, people captured in war often became slaves.*

slen•der /slĕn′ dər/ *adj.* **a.** thin; not big around. *This slender tree bends when the wind blows hard.* **b.** small; slight; not great or strong: *a slender chance.*

slim /slĭm/ *adj.* (**slim•mer, slim•mest**) **a.** thin; slender. *Jill chose a slim volume of poems at the library.* **b.** small; slight: *a slim hope.*

slo•gan /slō′ gən/ *n.* a word, phrase, or sentence used in advertising or business or by individuals to promote something. *The slogan for the toothpaste was "Gets teeth cleaner."*

slope¹ /slōp/ *n.* land that slants up and down. *We skied down a long slope.*

slope² /slōp/ *v.* (**slopes, sloped, slop•ing**) to slant. *The roof slopes to carry off rain.*

so•cial /sō′ shəl/ *adj.* **a.** having to do with human beings in a group. *The social problems of a city include heavy traffic and smog.* **b.** living in groups. *Bees are social insects.*

so•ci•e•ty /sə sī′ ĭ tē/ *n.* (**so•ci•e•ties** *pl.*) **a.** all people who are living and working together. *Laws are made for the good of society.* **b.** a club. *She joined a professional society.*

soft•ware /sôft′ wâr′/ or /sŏft′-/ *n.* any of the programs or languages through which instructions are given to a computer. *Most of the software for our computer is written in BASIC.*

sol•dier /sōl′ jər/ *n.* a person serving in an army. *Soldiers often receive both military and technical training.*

so•lu•tion /sə lōō′ shən/ *n.* **a.** the answer; the explanation. *The solution to the puzzle in the magazine is given on page 20.* **b.** a mixture formed by dissolving something. *You make a solution when you stir sugar into tea.*

solve /sŏlv/ or /sôlv/ *v.* (**solves, solved, solv•ing**) to find the answer to. *The police solved the crime.*

so•pra•no¹ /sə prăn′ ō/ *n.* the part in music sung by the highest singing voice. *Some boys can sing soprano.*

so•pra•no² /sə prăn′ ō/ *adj.* for a soprano: *the soprano part.*

sour¹ /sour/ *adj.* **a.** not sweet; acid. *A lemon has a sour taste.* **b.** spoiled. *This milk has gone sour.*

sour² /sour/ *v.* to become sour. *Milk sours if it is not kept cool.*

South Car•o•li•na /south′ kăr′ ə lī′ nə/ *n.* a state on the southeastern coast of the United States. *South Carolina raises much cotton and tobacco.* [Latin *Carolus*, Charles, after King Charles I of England.]

south•ern /sŭth′ ərn/ *adj.* of, in, or toward the south: *the southern side of the island.*

space•craft /spās′ krăft′/ *n.* a vehicle made for traveling to outer space. *Rockets are a type of spacecraft.*

speak /spēk/ *v.* (**speaks, spoke, spo•ken, speak•ing**) **a.** to talk; to say words. *Speak clearly so we can understand you.* **b.** to make known; to tell. *Always speak the truth.* **c.** to give a speech. *Charlene spoke first at the meeting.*

spe•cial /spĕsh′ əl/ *adj.* **a.** unusual; out of the ordinary. *The mayor declared a special holiday for the opening of the civic center.* **b.** great; particular: *a special friend.*

spe•cial•ize /spĕsh′ ə līz′/ *v.* (**spe•cial•iz•es, spe•cial•ized, spe•cial•iz•ing**) to emphasize or focus on a special area. *That reporter specializes in stories about Central America.*

spe•cial•ty /spĕsh′ əl tē/ *n.* (**spe•cial•ties** *pl.*) **a.** a special skill or occupation. *Sports photography is his specialty.* **b.** a special product or feature. *That store's specialty is toys.*

Pronunciation Key

ă	pat	ŏ	pot	th	**th**in
ā	pay	ō	toe	*th*	**th**is
âr	care	ô	paw, for	hw	**wh**ich
ä	father	oi	noise	zh	vi**s**ion
ĕ	pet	ou	out	ə	**a**bout,
ē	be	ŏŏ	took		it**e**m,
ĭ	pit	ōō	boot		penc**i**l,
ī	pie	ŭ	cut		gall**o**p,
îr	pier	ûr	**ur**ge		circ**u**s

spine /spīn/ *n.* **a.** the backbone of an animal or person. *The ribs are attached to the spine.* **b.** a stiff, sharp point. *A sea urchin has spines.*

splen•did /splĕn′ dĭd/ *adj.* **a.** bright; brilliant; magnificent. *What a splendid sunset!* **b.** good; excellent. *They have a splendid chance to win.*

spo•ken¹ /spō′ kən/ *v.* past participle of **speak.**

spo•ken² /spō′ kən/ *adj.* expressed orally. *The teacher gave us both spoken and written instructions.*

sq. square.

square¹ /skwâr/ *n.* a figure with four equal sides and four right angles. *A checkerboard is divided into squares.*

square

square² /skwâr/ *adj.* **a.** having the shape of a square: *a square box.* **b.** both long and wide; describing a measurement of area: *square inches.*

square³ /skwâr/ *v.* (**squares, squared, squar•ing**) to multiply by the same number. *If you square 4, you get 16.*

square dance /skwâr′ dăns′/ *n.* a dance for sets of four couples who stand in a square. *The caller for the square dance sang out, "Bow to your partner and do-si-do!"*

squir•rel /skwûr′ əl/ *n.* a small rodent with a long bushy tail. *Squirrels eat nuts and live in trees.*

staff /stăf/ *n.* **a.** a long cane or pole. *The shepherd carried a staff curved at one end.* **b.** a group of people working together under a leader or manager: *the teaching staff.*

stan • dard[1] /stăn′ dərd/ *n.* something that is used as a rule or model. *The government sets standards for foods and medicines.*

stan • dard[2] /stăn′ dərd/ *adj.* accepted; normal; conforming to a rule or model. *What is the standard size for typewriter paper?*

stat • ic[1] /stăt′ ĭk/ *n.* noise or interference on radio or television. *Sometimes static is caused by electricity.*

stat • ic[2] /stăt′ ĭk/ *adj.* having to do with charges of electricity produced by friction. *You can make static electricity by rubbing your feet on a rug.*

stat • ue /stăch′ ōō/ *n.* a figure of a person or animal shaped in stone, metal, or other material. *We saw the statue of Albert Einstein in Washington, D.C.*

steal /stēl/ *v.* (**steals, stole, sto•len, steal•ing**) to take dishonestly or without permission. *A burglar stole their television.*

stin • gy /stĭn′ jē/ *adj.* (**stin•gi•er, stin•gi•est; stin•gi•ly,** *adv.*) not generous; unwilling to spend or give. *Though he didn't have much money, he was never stingy.*

stock • ade /stŏ kād′/ *n.* an area enclosed by strong posts or timbers placed upright and close together in the ground; a fort. *The settlers' flag flew from a corner of the stockade.*

sto • len /stō′ lən/ *v.* past participle of **steal**.

stom • ach /stŭm′ ək/ *n.* the organ in the body into which food goes after it is swallowed. *The stomach helps digest the food.*

straight[1] /strāt/ *adj.* **a.** having no curves or bends. *Use a ruler to draw a straight line.* **b.** neat; in order. *A bank must keep its records straight.*

straight[2] /strāt/ *adv.* in a straight line; directly. *Go straight home after school.*

straight • en /strāt′ n/ *v.* **a.** to make or become straight. *After miles of curving, the road straightened.* **b.** to put in order. *Doug was supposed to straighten his room.*

strang • er /strān′ jər/ *n.* **a.** a person who is not known. *I know him, but she's a complete stranger.* **b.** someone from another place. *Many strangers came to town for the state fair.*

stu • di • o /stōō′ dē ō/ or /styōō-/ *n.* **a.** an artist's workshop. *We visited a sculptor's studio.* **b.** a place where radio or television programs or movies are made. *The actors arrive at the studio early in the morning.*

style /stīl/ *n.* **a.** a way of doing or making something. *Some authors have a simple style of writing.* **b.** fashion. *This year's style in dresses is different from last year's.*

styl • ish /stī′ lĭsh/ *adj.* in the current style; fashionable. *He wore a stylish new suit.*

sub • head /sŭb′ hĕd′/ *n.* a less important heading or title. *Rosa's outline had three subheads under each of the two main headings.*

sub • ject /sŭb′ jĭkt′/, *n.* **a.** the person or topic talked or written about. *Our subject for today is the invention of the steam engine.* **b.** in a sentence, the word or group of words about which something is said. *In the sentence "The boy throws the ball," the subject is "boy."*

suit[1] /sōōt/ *n.* a set of matching clothes. *Ms. Buckingham wore an elegant suit to the concert.*

suit

suit[2] /sōōt/ *v.* to please; to satisfy. *You can try very hard, but you can't suit everyone.*

suit • case /sōōt′ kās′/ *n.* a usually rectangular bag used to hold clothes when a person travels. *I had to sit on my suitcase to close it after it was packed.*

sum • ma • rize /sŭm′ ə rīz′/ *v.* (**sum•ma•riz•es, sum•ma•rized, sum•ma•riz•ing**) to give the main points of; to restate in fewer words. *Can you summarize Roger's speech?*

sun • ny /sŭn′ ē/ *adj.* (**sun•ni•er, sun•ni•est; sun•ni•ly,** *adv.*) bright with sunshine. *It's a shame to stay indoors on such a sunny day!*

sup • ply[1] /sə plī′/ *v.* (**sup•plies, sup•plied, sup•ply•ing**) to provide; to furnish; to give. *Who will supply the lemonade for the picnic?*

sup • ply[2] /sə plī′/ *n.* (**sup•plies** *pl.*) the amount or quantity needed or available. *When the snowfall started, the store got a supply of snow shovels.*

sup • pose /sə pōz′/ *v.* (sup•pos•es, sup•posed, sup•pos•ing) **a.** to guess; to think. *I suppose he's right.* **b.** to expect; to intend. *The kite wasn't supposed to rip.* **c.** to assume; to consider as a possibility. *Suppose she doesn't come—who will give the speech?*

sweat • shirt /swĕt′ shûrt′/ *n.* a heavy cotton pullover with long sleeves, often worn for exercise. *Grandpa wears a sweatshirt when he goes jogging.*

swift /swĭft/ *adj.* **a.** very fast: *a swift runner.* **b.** prompt: *a swift answer.*

swift • ness /swĭft′ nĭs/ *n.* speed; quickness. *The antelope's swiftness amazed us.*

syl • la • ble /sĭl′ ə bəl/ *n.* a word or a part of a word that is pronounced as a unit. *We divide words into syllables to know where to hyphenate them at the end of a line.*

syn • o • nym /sĭn′ ə nĭm′/ *n.* a word that has the same or almost the same general meaning as another word. *"Slim" and "slender" are synonyms.*

tar • di • ness /tär′ dē nĭs/ *n.* slowness; lateness. *Steve's forgetfulness contributes to his tardiness.*

tar • tar /tär′ tər/ *n.* a hard crust that forms on the teeth. *The dentist should remove the tartar from your teeth at least twice a year.*

tel • e • cast[1] /tĕl′ ə kăst/ *n.* a TV broadcast: *a sports telecast.*

tel • e • cast[2] /tĕl′ ə kăst/ *v.* (tel•e•casts, tel•e•cast or tel•e•cast•ed, tel•e•cast•ing) to broadcast by television. *The game will be telecast at eight o'clock.*

tenth[1] /tĕnth/ *adj.* next after the ninth; 10th: *the tenth person in line.*

tenth[2] /tĕnth/ *n.* one of ten equal parts. *A dime is a tenth of a dollar.*

term /tûrm/ *n.* **a.** a word or a group of words that has a special meaning. *Can you describe in scientific terms what causes rain?* **b.** a period of time. *The school term begins in September and ends in June.*

Pronunciation Key

ă	pat	ŏ	pot	th	**th**in
ā	pay	ō	toe	*th*	**th**is
âr	care	ô	paw, for	hw	**wh**ich
ä	father	oi	noise	zh	vi**s**ion
ĕ	pet	ou	out	ə	**a**bout,
ē	be	ŏŏ	took		item,
ĭ	pit	ōō	boot		pencil,
ī	pie	ŭ	cut		gall**o**p,
îr	pier	ûr	**ur**ge		circus

ter • mite /tûr′ mīt′/ *n.* a small insect that can eat and digest wood. *Termites can destroy wood products.*

Tex • as /tĕk′ səs/ *n.* a state in the south central United States. *Texas is the second largest state in the United States.*

the • a • ter /thē′ ə tər/ *n.* **a.** a place in which plays or movies are presented. *We sat in the front row at the theater.* **b.** drama; the art of writing or performing in plays. *Bob plans a career in theater.*

them • selves /thĕm sĕlvz′/ or /thəm-/ *pron.* **a.** their own selves. *They thought of the plan themselves.* **b.** their usual selves. *They were so tired after the circus that they weren't themselves.*

thor • ough /thûr′ ō/ *adj.* **a.** complete. *She did a thorough job.* **b.** careful and exact. *The police were thorough in examining the evidence.*

thou • sandth[1] /thou′ zəndth/ *n.* one of a thousand equal parts; 1/1,000; 0.001: *one thousandth of the population.*

thou • sandth[2] /thou′ zəndth/ *adj.* next after the 999th: *the thousandth ticket sold.*

throw[1] /thrō/ *v.* (throws, threw, thrown, throw•ing) **a.** to toss or cast through the air: *throw the ball.* **b.** to put into a particular state. *The power failure threw the office into confusion.*

throw

throw[2] /thrō/ *n.* an act of throwing; a toss. *The throw was caught for a touchdown.*

thrust¹ /thrŭst/ *v.* (thrusts, thrust, thrust•ing) to push or shove with force. *Jet engines thrust planes upward.*

thrust² /thrŭst/ *n.* a push. *A sudden thrust from behind knocked me off balance.*

thus /thŭs/ *adv.* therefore; as a result. *The car ran out of gas; thus we were unable to continue driving.*

tired /tīrd/ *adj.* weary; exhausted. *Even though we were tired, we kept on working.*

tone /tōn/ *n.* **a.** a sound, especially with reference to its quality. *The bell rang with a harsh tone.* **b.** a manner of speaking: *an angry tone.* **c.** a shade of color: *tones of green.*

tooth•brush /tōoth′ brŭsh′/ *n.* (tooth•brush•es *pl.*) a small, long-handled brush used to clean the teeth. *You should buy a new toothbrush often.*

top•ic /tŏp′ ĭk/ *n.* a subject of a conversation, piece of writing, etc. *The topic of her speech was how newspapers are written and printed.*

torch /tôrch/ *n.* **a.** a brightly burning stick of wood. *We carried a torch in the dark tunnel.* **b.** a small device that produces a very hot flame. *Welders use torches on metal.*

tour•ist /tōor′ ĭst/ *n.* a person traveling for pleasure. *The tourists all took pictures of the castle.*

tow•er¹ /tou′ ər/ *n.* a tall, narrow structure. *The bell tower stands next to the church.*

tow•er² /tou′ ər/ *v.* to rise high in the air. *The new building towered above the city.*

trea•ty /trē′ tē/ *n.* (trea•ties *pl.*) an agreement between nations. *The leaders signed a treaty to end the war.*

tri- a prefix that means "three."

tri•an•gle /trī′ ăng′ gəl/ *n.* a closed figure in which three straight lines form three angles. *There are 180 degrees in a triangle.*

tri•an•gu•lar /trī ăng′ gyə lər/ *adj.* having three angles; shaped like a triangle. *Yield signs are triangular.*

tri•cy•cle /trī′ sĭk′ əl/ or /-sĭ kəl/ *n.* a three-wheeled vehicle that is moved by pedals. *Small children ride tricycles.*

trim¹ /trĭm/ *v.* (trims, trimmed, trim•ming) to make neat by cutting some away. *I trimmed the grass along the sidewalk.*

trim² /trĭm/ *adj.* (trim•mer, trim•mest) neat and tidy. *Trim hedges grew in the garden.*

tri•sect /trī′ sĕkt′/ or /trī sĕkt′/ *v.* to divide into three equal parts: *trisect an angle.*

trom•bone /trŏm bōn′/ or /trəm-/ *n.* a large brass instrument, usually with a long sliding section used to vary the pitch. *A band with seventy-six trombones would make loud music.*

tru•ly /trōo′ lē/ *adv.* **a.** really; truthfully. *Do you think he told us what he truly thought?* **b.** in fact; indeed. *The music sounded truly glorious.*

trum•pet /trŭm′ pĭt/ *n.* a brass instrument with a mouthpiece, valves for changing pitch, and a wide bell at one end. *Liz blew a rousing call on her trumpet.*

trumpet

tu•ba /tōo′ bə/ or /tyōo′-/ *n.* a large brass instrument with a low pitch. *The big-belled tuba that is played in marching bands is called a sousaphone.*

tun•dra /tŭn′ drə/ *n.* a large treeless area in the arctic regions. *Because its ground remains frozen all year beneath the surface, the tundra can support only mosses and shrubs.*

turn•ta•ble /tûrn′ tā′ bəl/ *n.* a round, rotating platform on which phonograph records are played. *Does your turntable spin at various speeds?*

twen•ty-sev•en /twĕn′ tē sĕv′ ən/ *n.* the next number after twenty-six; twenty plus seven; 27. *His football career ended when he was twenty-seven.*

twi•light /twī′ līt′/ *n.* the very dim light in the sky just before sunrise or just after sunset. *The street lights are turned on at twilight.*

type¹ /tīp/ *n.* a particular kind; a sort; a class. *What type of book do you like best?*

type² /tīp/ *v.* (types, typed, typ•ing) to write with a typewriter. *Linda typed her report.*

type•writ•er /tīp′ rī′ tər/ *n.* a hand-operated machine for putting letters and figures on paper. *How many characters are on the keyboard of your typewriter?*

typ • ist /tī′ pĭst/ *n.* a person who uses a typewriter. *A good typist must also be a careful proofreader.*

um • brel • la /ŭm brĕl′ ə/ *n.* a light metal frame covered with waterproof material, used as a protection against sun or rain. *I got wet because I forgot my umbrella.*

umbrella

un- a prefix that means: **a.** not: *unhappy.* **b.** the opposite of: *undress.*

un • but • ton /ŭn bŭt′ n/ *v.* to unfasten the buttons of. *Unbutton your shirt before you pull it off.*

un • der • line /ŭn′ dər līn′/ *v.* (un•der•lines, un•der•lined, un•der•lin•ing) to draw a line under. *Underline the part of the sentence that contains an error.*

un • e • qual /ŭn ē′ kwəl/ *adj.* **a.** not the same; not equal: *unequal amounts.* **b.** poorly matched; unfair. *The race between the tortoise and the hare was an unequal contest.*

u • nit /yōō′ nĭt/ *n.* **a.** a single thing or a group of things thought of as one. *These shelves join to form a portable unit.* **b.** a standard measure. *Meters are units of distance.*

un • known /ŭn nōn′/ *adj.* not known; strange; unfamiliar. *A stranger is an unknown person.*

un • sure /ŭn shŏŏr′/ *adj.* not certain or sure. *He was unsure of his ability to win.*

up-to-date /ŭp′ tə dāt′/ *adj.* including any recent changes; current; modern. *This edition of the dictionary is the most up-to-date version.*

Pronunciation Key

ă	pat	ŏ	pot	th	**th**in
ā	pay	ō	toe	*th*	**th**is
âr	care	ô	paw, for	hw	**wh**ich
ä	father	oi	noise	zh	vi**s**ion
ĕ	pet	ou	**ou**t	ə	**a**bout,
ē	be	ŏŏ	took		it**e**m,
ĭ	pit	ōō	boot		penc**i**l,
ī	pie	ŭ	cut		gall**o**p,
îr	pier	ûr	urge		circ**u**s

va • cant /vā′ kənt/ *adj.* **a.** empty; not occupied. *I found a vacant chair and sat down.* **b.** not aware; not thinking; not recognizing or understanding: *a vacant look.* [Latin *vacare,* to be empty.]

vain /vān/ *adj.* **a.** too proud of oneself. *After Elaine won the prize she became vain about her accomplishment.* **b.** not successful; useless. *I soon gave up my vain efforts to attract his attention.*

▶ Vain sounds like **vane** and **vein**.

val • ley /vǎl′ ē/ *n.* an area of low land between hills or mountains. *A clear river flowed through the valley.*

val • ue¹ /vǎl′ yōō/ *n.* **a.** worth; importance. *No one doubts the value of a good education.* **b.** a moral principle or standard. *Your values determine your character.*

val • ue² /vǎl′ yōō/ *v.* (val•ues, val•ued, val•u•ing) to think of as having great worth. *He values the time that he spends with his children.*

vane /vān/ *n.* a device to show which way the wind is blowing. *The weather vane turns as the wind changes direction.*

▶ Vane sounds like **vain** and **vein**.

van • i • ty /vǎn′ ĭ tē/ *n.* **a.** an excessive pride in one's abilities or appearance; vainness. *Patrick's vanity makes him worry about what others will think.* **b.** uselessness; worthlessness. *We realized the vanity of our efforts to kill every weed in the yard.*

var•y /vâr′ ē/ *v.* (var•ies, var•ied, var•y•ing) **a.** to change. *The temperature varies with the seasons.* **b.** to cause to change or be different. *People can vary their appearance by wearing different clothes.*

vein /vān/ *n.* one of the many branching tubes through which blood is carried to the heart from all parts of the body. *Can you see the veins in your arms?*

▶ **Vein** sounds like **vain** and **vane.**

verse /vûrs/ *n.* **a.** poetry; the opposite of prose. *Shakespeare's plays are mostly in verse.* **b.** a poem. *A limerick is a funny verse.* **c.** a group of lines in a poem or song; a stanza. *Do you know the second verse of "Jingle Bells"?*

ver•te•bra /vûr′ tə brə/ *n.* (ver•te•brae or ver•te•bras *pl.*) a bone in the backbone. *The thick cord of nerves that runs down the back is protected by the vertebrae.*

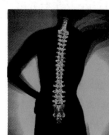

vertebrae

ver•te•brae /vûr′ tə brē/ *n.* a plural of **vertebra.**

ver•te•brate /vûr′ tə brĭt/ or /-brāt/ *n.* an animal that has a backbone. *Fish, mammals, reptiles, and amphibians are all vertebrates.*

ver•tex /vûr′ tĕks′/ *n.* (ver•ti•ces or ver•tex•es *pl.*) the point at which two or more lines or edges of a geometric figure intersect; a corner. *An angle has one vertex.*

ver•ti•ces /vûr′ tĭ sēz′/ *n.* a plural of **vertex.**

ver•ti•cal /vûr′ tĭ kəl/ *adj.* straight up and down. *Draw a vertical line down the middle of your paper to divide it into columns.*

ve•to[1] /vē′ tō/ *n.* (ve•toes *pl.*) the power or right to stop an action from being put into effect. *By not signing the new bill passed by Congress, the President used the veto.*

ve•to[2] /vē′ tō/ *v.* (ve•toes, ve•toed, ve•to•ing) to refuse to consent or agree to. *Mom vetoed our plan to stay up all night.*

view•point /vyoo′ point′/ *n.* a point of view; an opinion; a way of thinking. *From a bird's viewpoint, worms are delicious.*

vig•or•ous /vĭg′ ər əs/ *adj.* full of vigor; energetic. *We made a vigorous attempt to rake all the leaves in an hour.*

vi•ta•min /vī′ tə mĭn/ *n.* an organic substance found in foods and necessary for growth and good health. *Lack of certain vitamins may cause disease.* [Latin *vita*, life + English *-amine*, amine, a chemical.]

volt /vōlt/ *n.* a unit used to measure electrical force or potential. *Batteries are often sized in volts.*

voy•age /voi′ ĭj/ *n.* a journey by water or through air or space. *Christopher Columbus made a famous voyage to America.*

waf•fle /wŏf′ əl/ *n.* a kind of pancake cooked between two metal plates with rough surfaces. *The surface of a waffle is marked by a pattern of small squares.* [Dutch *wafel.*]

waltz[1] /wôlts/ *n.* a smooth, graceful dance in three-quarter time. *The first dance of the ball was a waltz.*

waltz[2] /wôlts/ *v.* to dance a waltz. *The couples waltzed around the room.*

warmth /wôrmth/ *n.* **a.** the state of being warm. *The warmth of the sun felt good.* **b.** friendly or affectionate feeling. *We appreciated the warmth of their welcome.*

Wash•ing•ton /wŏsh′ ĭng tən/ or /wôsh′-/ *n.* **a.** a state in the northwestern United States. *Washington is known for its delicious apples.* **b.** the capital of the United States; Washington, D.C. *The White House is in Washington.*

wa•ter•proof /wô′ tər proof′/ *adj.* unaffected by water. *The raincoat is made from waterproof material.*

watt /wŏt/ *n.* a unit of electrical power. *This lamp needs a bulb that has 75 watts.*

wea•ry /wîr′ ē/ *adj.* (wea•ri•er, wea•ri•est; wea•ri•ly, *adv.*) tired; exhausted. *The weary travelers went to sleep at once.*

wea•sel /wē′ zəl/ *n.* a small, wild animal with a long body and short legs. *Weasels eat mice and birds.*

weight /wāt/ *n.* **a.** a measure of the heaviness of an object. *The assistant recorded my dog's weight.* **b.** the measured heaviness of a specific object. *Muffin's weight is twenty-eight pounds.*

west•ern /wĕs′ tərn/ *adj.* of, in, or toward the west. *We found the berries in the western half of the valley.*

west•ward /wĕst′ wərd/ *adv.* toward the west; in a westerly direction. *The wagon train rumbled slowly westward.*

whole /hōl/ *adj.* (**whol•ly,** *adv.*) **a.** in one piece. *Don't slice the apples; just leave them whole.* **b.** complete; entire. *There are twenty-four volumes in the whole set of books.*

wise /wīz/ *adj.* (**wis•er, wis•est; wise•ly,** *adv.*) **a.** showing good sense or judgment. *He made a wise decision.* **b.** having much knowledge or information. *England's Queen Elizabeth I was recognized as an unusually wise woman for her time.*

wolf /wŏŏlf/ *n.* (**wolves** *pl.*) a wild animal of the dog family, slightly larger than a German shepherd. *Arctic wolves eat mice and travel in packs.*

wolves /wŏŏlvz/ *n.* plural of **wolf.**

wood•wind /wŏŏd′ wĭnd′/ *n.* a musical wind instrument such as a flute or clarinet. *Once all woodwinds were made of wood.*

world /wûrld/ *n.* **a.** the earth. *There are many different languages spoken in the world.* **b.** all of the people on the earth. *The world rejoiced when the vaccine for polio was discovered.*

worst[1] /wûrst/ *adj.* most evil, bad, or unpleasant. *This is the worst book I ever read.*

worst[2] /wûrst/ *n.* that which is worst. *The worst of the winter is yet to come.*

worth[1] /wûrth/ *n.* **a.** merit; value. *This book has little real worth, but it's fun to read.* **b.** the quantity of something that can be bought for a certain amount. *Grandma bought ten dollars' worth of gasoline.*

worth[2] /wûrth/ *adj.* **a.** worthy of. *If a thing is worth doing, it's worth doing well.* **b.** having the value of. *That book is worth twenty dollars.*

Pronunciation Key

ă	pat	ŏ	pot	th	**thin**
ā	pay	ō	toe	*th*	**this**
âr	care	ô	paw, for	hw	**which**
ä	father	oi	noise	zh	vision
ĕ	pet	ou	**out**	ə	about,
ē	be	ŏŏ	took		item,
ĭ	pit	ōō	boot		pencil,
ī	pie	ŭ	cut		gallop,
îr	pier	ûr	**ur**ge		circus

writ•er /rī′ tər/ *n.* **a.** a person who writes. *She is the best writer in our class.* **b.** a person whose profession is writing. *The author of this book has been a writer for twenty years.*

wt. weight.

yard[1] /yärd/ *n.* a measure of length equal to three feet or thirty-six inches. *He bought a yard of cloth.*

yard[2] /yärd/ *n.* the open ground around a house, school, or any building. *Let's go play in the yard.*

yard

yd. yard.

year /yîr/ *n.* a period of 365 days or 12 months. *From one birthday to another is a year.*

yo•del /yōd′ l/ *v.* to sing so that the voice wavers between a normal and a high sound. *My friend Hans from Switzerland can yodel.* [German *jodeln.*]

yo•gurt /yō′ gərt/ *n.* a creamy, slightly tart food made from milk that may be flavored with fruit. *Yogurt is both nutritious and delicious.* [Turkish *yoğurt.*]

youth /yōōth/ *n.* **a.** a young person, especially a young man. *Who is the tall youth with the red hair?* **b.** the quality or the time period of being young. *Youth is followed by adulthood.*

yr. year.

Spelling Dictionary

ze • ro /zîr′ ō/ or /zē′ rō/ *n.* **a.** the figure 0. *In the number 1,000 there are three zeros.* **b.** nothing. *Two minus two equals zero.*

zero

USING THE Thesaurus

The **Writing Thesaurus** provides synonyms—words that mean the same or nearly the same—and antonyms—words that mean the opposite—for your spelling words. Use this sample to identify the various parts of each thesaurus entry.

- **Entry words** are listed in alphabetical order and are printed in boldface type.

- The abbreviation for the **part of speech** of each entry word follows the boldface entry word.

- The **definition** of the entry word matches the definition of the word in your **Spelling Dictionary**. A **sample sentence** shows the correct use of the word in context.

- Each **synonym** for the entry word is listed under the entry word. Again, a sample sentence shows the correct use of the synonym in context.

- Where appropriate, **antonyms** for the entry word are listed at the end of the entry.

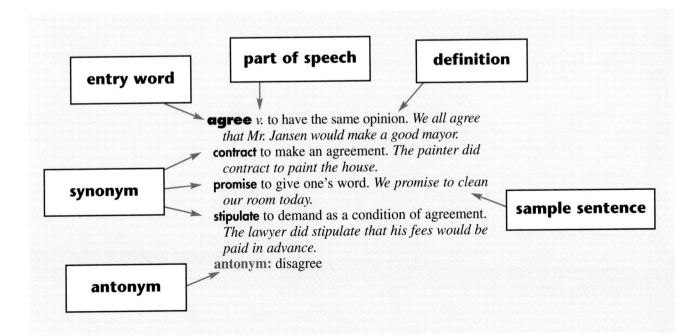

entry word   part of speech   definition

agree *v.* to have the same opinion. *We all agree that Mr. Jansen would make a good mayor.*
contract to make an agreement. *The painter did contract to paint the house.*
synonym
promise to give one's word. *We promise to clean our room today.*
stipulate to demand as a condition of agreement. *The lawyer did stipulate that his fees would be paid in advance.*
sample sentence
antonym: disagree
antonym

allow *v.* to let; permit. *Our parents allow us to watch TV if we have finished our homework.*

admit to let in. *At Gate 7 they will admit fans with season passes.*

consent to give permission. *The ranger did consent to our plan to build a campfire.*

stand for to put up with. *The leader would not stand for carelessness.*

antonyms: to refuse, deny

amusement *n.* entertainment; sport; pastime. *Chess is her favorite amusement.*

enjoyment fun; entertainment. *The film was produced for our enjoyment.*

pleasure a good feeling. *Reading brings pleasure to many people.*

recreation relaxation. *Swimming is Heather's favorite form of recreation.*

ancient *adj.* belonging to times long ago. *There are many ancient temples in Greece, Italy, and Egypt.*

antique of a previous time. *Their house is furnished with antique furniture.*

olden from long ago. *The workers found several pieces of pottery from olden days.*

primitive before modern technology. *Their homes were solid but primitive.*

antonyms: modern, recent

apology *n.* words saying one is sorry; asking pardon. *Please accept my apology for coming so late; I was delayed by heavy traffic.*

acknowledgment statement of responsibility. *The printer made an acknowledgment of his mistake.*

confession admission of error. *In her confession, she explained how she cracked the safe.*

regret repentance. *The woman expressed her regret about the accident.*

repentance feeling of regret. *She showed repentance for her rudeness.*

antonym: denial

argue *v.* 1. to disagree; dispute; quarrel. *Tanya will often argue with Michael.* 2. to give reasons for or against. *The lawyer did argue her case effectively.*

contend to struggle with. *The ranchers had to contend with the angry farmers.*

debate to disagree formally. *Members of the school board did debate the building of a new science lab.*

antonym: to agree

average *adj.* 1. determined by averaging. *The average score on the test was 75.* 2. common; ordinary; usual. *Today was an average day, neither great nor awful.*

fair neither very good nor very poor. *My grades were just fair.*

mean a middle point or score. *The class's mean grade was 88.*

normal ordinary. *The dog's behavior was normal while it was in the vet's office.*

passable just satisfactory. *His performance at the chess match was barely passable.*

typical as expected. *My sister acts like a typical teenager.*

antonyms: extraordinary, uncommon

avoid *v.* to stay away from; to keep from meeting. *I tried to avoid him when he had measles.*

dodge to get out of the way of. *I always try to dodge the snowballs.*

duck to move out of the way of. *Jim called to me to duck his wild pitch.*

escape to avoid danger. *We barely did escape the storm's damage.*

shirk to avoid; put off. *A responsible person won't shirk a duty.*

shun to ignore; to stay away from. *We won't shun a friend who is having trouble.*

steer clear of to keep away from. *Let's try to steer clear of that question.*

antonyms: to accept, welcome, meet, face, seek

awful *adj.* very bad; very ugly; unpleasant. *That was an awful movie.*

disagreeable not pleasant. *The weather was very disagreeable during most of our vacation last summer.*

fearful causing awe or fear. *The enormous bear was a fearful sight.*

miserable causing discomfort. *Harry's cold made him feel miserable.*

objectionable causing offense. *Her serious audience found the speech objectionable.*

offensive hurtful. *That was an offensive thing to say.*

terrible dreadful. *The way they sang that song was really terrible.*

unpleasant not pleasing. *The rainy day was an unpleasant one for a picnic.*

antonyms: nice, pleasant, agreeable, charming, likable, good, lovely, delightful

beautiful *adj.* having beauty; pleasing to the eye, ear, or mind; lovely. *That is a beautiful painting.*

attractive arousing interest. *Jean has an attractive smile.*

good-looking pleasing in appearance. *Jack's new suit is really good-looking.*

handsome good-looking. *That's a handsome jacket Steven is wearing.*

antonyms: ugly, unattractive

beauty *n.* the quality that makes a person or thing pleasing to the senses. *The beauty of the music made us forget everything else.*

attractiveness quality that draws one to something. *The wooden frame adds to the picture's attractiveness.*

charm personal quality that attracts. *His charm made many friends for him.*

grace smooth, beautiful movement. *The grace of the dancers captivated the audience.*

belief *n.* the acceptance of something as true or real. *His belief in life on other planets was questioned.*

confidence trust. *Have confidence in yourself!*

faith confidence; trust. *Joey has faith in his father.*

antonyms: disbelief, distrust, suspicion, uncertainty

beret *n.* a round, soft, flat cap of wool or felt. *She wore her beret at a jaunty angle.*

hat head covering. *A wool hat gives good protection on a cold day.*

tam Scottish cap. *The knit tam kept her ears warm on the coldest days.*

bother *v.* 1. to give trouble to. *Don't bother me while I'm writing.* 2. to take the time and trouble. *Don't bother to wash the dishes now.*

annoy to disturb; trouble. *That dog's bark really does annoy me.*

disturb to keep from concentrating. *Will my typing disturb you?*

irritate to annoy. *The sound of his lawn mower can irritate me.*

pester to bother repeatedly. *Try not to pester your brother when he's doing his homework.*

trouble to annoy. *Don't let me trouble you.*

upset to cause distress. *Did that remark upset you?*

broad *adj.* 1. wide; large from side to side. *The West contains broad stretches of prairies and forests.* 2. plain; easy to understand. *Alf dropped a broad hint that he wanted a puppy for his birthday.* 3. of wide range; not small. *My father has a broad view of life.*

extensive huge. *We couldn't believe that anyone would have such an extensive library in a private home.*

general broad. *The president made a very general statement about education.*

large enormous. *"We have a large selection of coats," the clerk told the customer.*

roomy having plenty of space. *Six of the cousins could sit together on the roomy couch.*

spacious roomy. *The living room was spacious and had a fireplace at one end.*

sweeping inclusive. *Her promise of help was so sweeping that it covered everything we wanted.*

vague not clear. *Terry had only a vague idea of the rules.*

wide broad; large. *Their yard is so wide that we can play football in it.*

antonyms: narrow, slim, small, detailed, clear

building *n.* a structure such as a house, school, or factory. *Our new building is larger than the old one.*

construction anything made of parts. *After hours of work, the construction of wooden blocks came tumbling down.*

structure something put together. *This strange-looking structure is our new library.*

bunch *n.* a group of things of the same kind, growing together or put together. *We took a bunch of flowers to Edward when he was in the hospital.*

band group of people. *Have you read about Robin Hood and his band of merry men?*

batch set; group of items. *Take this batch of rolls and put them on the table.*

clump bunch. *The weeds grew in a clump in the broken sidewalk.*

cluster things sharing a small space. *The school buildings are arranged in a cluster.*

collection set put together. *Have you seen her collection of dolls?*

company organized group of people. *The company of scouts marched by.*

crew group assembled for work. *The crew of workers cleaned up the picnic area.*

crowd unorganized group. *A small crowd gathered outside the theater.*

heap group of things piled on one another. *His clothes lay in a heap on the floor.*

herd group of animals. *The herd of cows grazed calmly.*

knot things tightly packed. *A knot of travelers blocked the aisle in the bus.*

lot set of things. *We found a huge box of baseball cards at a yard sale and bought the whole lot.*

number uncounted set. *We found a number of valuable books at the flea market.*

pack number of animals or items. *A pack of wild dogs lives in the woods.*

party group of people. *The waitress tried to seat the party of eight at one table.*

troop group of persons. *The small troop of soldiers moved quickly.*

caution *n.* 1. care. *Cross streets with caution.* 2. a warning. *Did you read the caution on the label?*

attention watchfulness. *Don't let your attention wander while you take this test.*

care caution. *Did you take care to turn off the iron?*

watchfulness caution. *The fox's watchfulness saved its kits from the flood.*

antonyms: neglect, carelessness

character *n.* 1. a person in a play or book. *The character of Pinocchio appeals to children.* 2. a way of behaving, thinking, and feeling. *Her character changed when she became a success.* 3. a letter; a sign. *Chinese and Japanese writing and printing have characters different from ours.*

characteristic trait; mark of personality. *List a characteristic of the hero in the legend of King Arthur.*

cipher letter; sign. *The famous artist often used a special cipher in her designs.*

figure sign; letter. *Each figure on the sign was carefully made.*

logo letter or design relating to a group. *The business used its logo for many years.*

nature way of behaving. *A wild animal won't change its nature.*

personality nature. *Jane had a very friendly personality.*

role an assigned part. *Josie played the leading role in the school play.*

trait mark of personality. *What trait do you value most in a friend?*

citizen *n.* a member of a nation who has rights, such as voting, and who also has the duty of being loyal to the nation. *Any person born in this country is a citizen of the United States.*

inhabitant resident. *We are all inhabitants of the planet Earth.*

native one born in a place. *Jeanne's grandfather is a native of France.*

resident one who lives in a place. *I'm glad to be a resident of the United States.*

subject one who is under another's rule. *The hero of the story was a loyal subject of the queen.*

voter one who casts a ballot. *Don't you agree that every citizen should be a voter?*

antonyms: foreigner, alien, outsider, visitor

common *adj.* 1. frequent; usual. *A temperature of ninety degrees is common in the summer.* 2. belonging to more than one person or company. *The city parks are common property.*

familiar well-known. *Snow is a familiar sight in the mountains.*

general occurring everywhere. *General confusion followed the explosion.*

ordinary usual; expected. *The undercover detective wore ordinary clothes.*

popular appealing to many. *Popular music played over the loudspeaker.*

public open to all. *Our park system is for public use.*

regular daily; frequent. *She visits us at regular intervals.*

social including all. *The Labor Day parade is a special social event.*

widespread general; occurring everywhere. *After the peace treaty, there was widespread celebration.*

antonyms: unusual, strange, private, personal, scarce, rare

correct *adj.* having no mistakes; right. *Gary was sure he had the correct answer to the problem.*

accurate carefully done. *The figures in the report are accurate.*

all right acceptable. *She said that the way I shoveled the driveway was all right.*

errorless without mistakes. *An almanac is supposed to be errorless.*

exact correct in detail. *The carpenter's measurements had to be exact.*

OK all right. *"That's OK for now," the boss shouted.*

true accurate; correct. *Did Mark Twain tell a true story of life on a riverboat?*

antonyms: untrue, false, wrong, faulty, incorrect

couch *n.* a piece of furniture that can seat several people; a sofa. *My friends and I sit on the couch to watch TV.*

divan a low couch without a raised back or arms. *We spread red pillows on the divan.*

sofa couch with back or arms. *Our old sofa is in the basement now.*

coworker *n.* a fellow worker. *One coworker took Juanita out to lunch on her birthday.*

associate a friend or coworker. *The businesswoman's associate enjoys working with her.*

companion one who accompanies another. *In what story is a rooster the companion of a dog and a donkey?*

partner one who shares a task. *My partner did most of the research, and I wrote the report.*

create *v.* 1. to make a thing that has not been made before; form. *The artist wanted to create a painting.* 2. to cause; produce. *It takes only one loud person to create a disturbance.*

build to put together. *Let's build a doghouse for Bowser.*

cause to bring about. *They can cause a lot of trouble through their carelessness.*

design to plan something new. *The architect will design a new library for our school.*

discover to find the unknown. *Archaeologists want to discover how people lived in ancient times.*

dream up to think of a new idea. *How do cartoonists dream up such great drawings?*

invent to create an object or system. *Do you think someone might invent wings for people so each of us can fly?*

make to construct. *Peter dreamed that someday he would make a home for his friends.*

mold to form. *The leader wanted to mold each scout to be resourceful.*

produce to bring forth. *He worked all afternoon to produce a single poem.*

shape to form. *She can shape the driftwood into a sculpture by careful carving.*

credit *n.* 1. recognition; favorable regard. *He deserves credit for his work.* 2. a system of buying goods by charging the amount and paying the bill, with interest, later. *Using credit is convenient but expensive.*

approval sign of support. *The principal gave approval for our work on Cleanup Day.*

honor show of approval. *Let us pay honor to those who work for our safety.*

praise approval. *She was generous with praise for each student.*

regard recognition. *Their work deserves our regard.*

damage *v.* to break, injure, or harm something. *The accident did damage their car.*

deface to spoil the appearance of. *Those posters would deface the walls.*

harm to cause injury. *When you build, don't harm the environment.*

hurt to cause pain. *I hurt my ankle on the long hike.*

injure to cause damage. *Fortunately, the fall did not injure the little girl.*

ruin to spoil. *The chemicals will ruin the ancient stone buildings.*

spoil to ruin. *Be careful or you will spoil the newly painted desk.*

wreck to destroy. *The terrible storms did wreck the old fishing boat.*

decide *v.* to reach a decision; to make up one's mind. *I did finally decide to tell them.*

arrange to bring about. *I will arrange to take the test one day early.*

referee to judge. *She is going to referee the debate.*

resolve to find a solution. *I count on my parents to help me to resolve problems that are too big for me.*

rule to make a decision. *The judge will rule on the case.*

settle to bring to an end. *My friend can settle almost any argument.*

umpire to judge; referee. *He will umpire the school intramural games.*

declare *v.* 1. to announce publicly and formally; to make known to others. *Only Congress can declare war.* 2. to say positively and surely; to state openly. *Mark decided to declare that he would never again be late for school.*

announce to make a statement. *Lois heard the reporter announce the success of the space mission.*

express to state an idea. *Writing is a great way to express your ideas and to share your feelings.*

proclaim to declare formally. *We expect the mayor to proclaim a day of celebration for the city's ninety-fifth birthday.*

profess to state a belief. *The senator continued to profess his belief in his party.*

state to say; to declare. *The coach is always ready to state his opinion.*

decrease *v.* to become less; to diminish. *The noise will decrease sharply when the window is closed.*

drop to become less. *The number of fans seems to drop each year.*

fall off to lessen. *Attendance began to fall off after a week.*

lessen to become less; to make less. *We tried to lessen the noise by turning the volume down.*

reduce to make smaller. *Can you reduce the danger by driving more slowly?*

shorten to make shorter. *I ruined the jeans when I tried to shorten the legs.*

shrink to become smaller in size. *Those jeans might shrink if you wash them in hot water.*

wane to become smaller. *The moon will wane until next Sunday.*

weaken to make less strong. *Adding water will weaken the orange juice.*

antonyms: to increase, grow, rise, soar, strengthen, expand

delight *n.* enjoyment; pleasure; joy; something delightful. *Her sense of humor is a delight.*

gladness happiness. *The song about joy and gladness made me feel happy.*

happiness pleasurable feeling. *I've found happiness with my friends.*

joy intense pleasure. *Grandpa's visit brought us all so much joy!*

pleasure enjoyment. *Being outdoors gives me a lot of pleasure.*

antonyms: disgust, displeasure, dissatisfaction, distaste, bore

deny *v.* 1. to state that something is untrue or incorrect. *The prisoner did deny that she had robbed the store.* 2. to refuse to give or allow. *The court continued to deny his request for a new trial.*

contradict to declare untrue. *Please be courteous if you contradict a statement.*

disown to deny connection with. *Will you disown your brother because of what he did?*

dispute to disagree. *Teresa hates to dispute about anything.*

forbid to refuse approval. *Their parents did forbid them to swim there.*

protest to object. *The fans started to protest the referee's call.*

refuse to not allow or give. *I'm going to refuse to help them.*

turn down to refuse. *Why did you turn down his request?*

veto to vote against. *The President will veto that bill.*

withhold to hold back. *Just withhold your support and see what they do.*

antonyms: to affirm, believe, allow, let, permit, give, offer, provide

destroy *v.* to put an end to; to ruin; to tear down; to wreck completely. *The fire did destroy the beautiful cathedral.*

cancel to bring to an end. *We might have to cancel our vacation plans.*

consume to eat; to use up. *We watched the fire consume the pile of leaves.*

end to finish. *This snow does end the nice, warm autumn.*

erase to rub out. *Please erase your answer neatly.*

exterminate to destroy completely. *The company promises to exterminate the termites.*

remove to take away. *Can you remove the remains of the bonfire?*

ruin to spoil. *The storm might ruin the corn.*

undo to reverse. *She tried to undo the harm done by her lie.*

wipe out to destroy. *Hail can wipe out the young crops.*

antonyms: to create, make, erect, raise

diary *n.* a written record of the things that the writer has done or thought day by day. *Ricardo kept a travel diary of his trip to New York.*

appointment book a list of daily events or business. *James wrote each day's activities in his appointment book.*

journal a daily record. *Martha found the journal that her mother kept during her trip to America.*

director *n.* a person who directs or manages the work done by other people. *He became the director of sales.*

boss a person who directs; one who gives orders. *The detective story is about two office workers and their missing boss.*

chief director; head. *The police chief retired this week.*

commander a leader, usually of a military group. *The President is the Commander-in-Chief of all the United States armed forces.*

head the person in charge. *Nora Charles is the head of the science department.*

leader a person whom others follow. *The leader of the band became famous.*

manager a person who directs a group. *The team's manager was known for making funny remarks during press interviews.*

organizer a person who plans activities. *Suki's grandfather was an organizer for labor unions.*

supervisor one who directs others in their work. *Mr. Washington is the supervisor for all the local sales representatives.*

dislike *v.* to have a feeling against; to object to. *At first I wanted to dislike him, but now we are friends.*

despise to dislike and look down upon. *Sports fans despise cheating.*

detest to hate. *Andrew did detest the way the forest was being destroyed.*

disapprove to deny support. *The coach said that she does disapprove of my diet.*

hate to dislike strongly. *"I hate seeing the river polluted," Maggie cried.*

resent to feel displeased. *Greg said that he does resent being taken off the team.*

scorn to look down on. *Mark seemed to scorn the opinion of his neighbor.*

shun to avoid. *A good rule is to shun dishonesty.*

antonyms: to like, enjoy, admire

dramatic *adj.* 1. having to do with plays or the theater. *An actor is a dramatic artist.* 2. exciting and full of adventure. *The climbers made a dramatic attempt to reach the summit.*

make-believe imaginative; not real. *Little children love make-believe games.*

remarkable worth noticing. *I think circus performers are remarkable people.*

sensational dramatic. *The high-wire acts are sensational.*

spectacular impressive and striking. *The parade was really spectacular.*

stagy artificial; not realistic. *The costumes were too stagy to suit me.*

striking noticeable. *The dance numbers were really striking.*

theatrical overly dramatic or emotional. *Georgia's reaction to the news seemed rather theatrical.*

thrilling exciting. *Do you think circuses are thrilling?*

vivid bright; noticeable. *The scenery for the show was vivid and will long be remembered.*

antonyms: flat, common, everyday, dull

energetic *adj.* full of energy; active; vigorous. *We needed energetic workers to help clean out the attic.*

active lively. *Koalas are active at night.*

brisk quick. *Make your daily walk brisk and energetic.*

forceful strong. *His speech to the band members was forceful.*

lively active; energetic. *The lively music was great for dancing.*

tireless endlessly energetic. *Walter is a tireless supporter of our senator.*

vigorous full of energy. *We gave the classroom walls a vigorous scrubbing.*

antonyms: lazy, slothful, inactive

entire *adj.* whole; complete. *We spent the entire day at the zoo.*

complete finished. *The complete set of Stevenson's books is on the top shelf.*

full having no empty space. *The children ate a full bowl of popcorn.*

perfect with nothing missing; faultless. *Everything about the dance performance was perfect.*

single one; whole. *The mobile was formed from a single strand of wire.*

total complete. *The total cost was almost three hundred dollars.*

unbroken not in parts. *The dish he dropped was unbroken.*

undivided in one part; complete. *The play had our undivided attention.*

whole having all parts. *For a change, we finished the whole crossword puzzle.*

antonyms: partial, incomplete, divided

event *n.* 1. anything that happens. *To a child, a trip to the circus is a great event.* 2. one of the contests in a sports meet. *The next event is the one-hundred-meter backstroke.*

activity sports event. *In the triathlon, Mark's favorite activity is the bike race.*

adventure exciting event. *Kevin says that finding snakes for the zoo is quite an adventure.*

experience an event. *He thought that wading through a swamp was an interesting experience.*

happening something that occurs. *Our winter festival was a successful happening.*

milestone important event in a series. *Being chosen quarterback was a milestone in Shawn's career.*

explain *v.* to make something clear; to tell what something means. *The teacher will explain the difference between nouns and verbs.*

clarify to make clear. *Annie tries to clarify her thoughts by writing in her journal.*

demonstrate to teach by showing. *Please demonstrate the last step in dividing fractions.*

instruct to teach. *Uncle Jake will instruct his nieces and nephews in the skill of square dancing.*

spell out to explain step-by-step. *Last year, Ms. Arthur had to spell out how to use the Dewey Decimal System.*

teach to instruct. *To teach well takes knowledge and orderly thinking.*

extend *v.* 1. to lengthen. *We want to extend our vacation so that we can visit another national park.* 2. to stretch out. *The river does extend for many miles.* 3. to make larger; to increase. *You can extend your knowledge by reading books.* 4. to offer. *He did extend an invitation to the entire class.*

broaden to make more inclusive. *Seeing both sides of a situation will broaden your understanding of it.*

continue to make longer; extend. *The family wanted to continue the drive along the waterfront.*

draw out to extend in time. *The opposing team tried to draw out the final minutes of the basketball game.*

enlarge to make greater. *Carl says that reading the encyclopedia will enlarge his collection of trivia.*

expand to make broader. *It's true that reading will expand your mind and your imagination.*

give to present. *"We give this medal only to heroes," the governor said.*

lengthen to make longer. *Do you think it would be good to lengthen the school year?*

offer to hold out. *The store will offer a discount on every purchase this week.*

present to extend. *"We present you with this medal," said the mayor.*

straighten to uncurl. *When Beth does straighten her hair, it looks longer.*

stretch to pull; to make longer. *When I tried to stretch the rubber band, it snapped.*

uncurl to straighten. *The caterpillar will uncurl when I put it back on the ground.*

unroll to open to full length. *"Unroll the scroll and read it to us," they said.*

widen to make broader. *They will widen this road to reduce the traffic problem.*

antonyms: to shorten, contract, curl, roll, fold, cut short, narrow, limit, reduce

external *adj.* outer; on the outside; exterior. *This old building is drab on the inside, but it has several interesting external features.*

outer covering. *Wear warm outer clothing for cold-weather hikes.*

outside outdoors. *Although it was cold outside, it was warm in the house.*

antonyms: interior, internal, inner

false *adj.* 1. not true. *It is false to say that 2 + 2 = 5.* 2. not real or genuine. *The man wore a false beard.*

artificial not real. *The flowers looked real, but were artificial.*

dishonest deliberately untrue. *The answers they gave the travelers were dishonest.*

fake artificial. *The coat was warm and was made of soft, fake fur.*

lying deliberately false. *Lying words can cause real harm.*

make-believe not real; imaginary. *"Don't be afraid," we told the little boy. "Bambi is just make-believe."*

misleading leading to a wrong conclusion. *Some clues in the mystery story were very misleading.*

untrue not correct. *It is untrue to say that Texas is the smallest state.*

wrong not right or correct. *Kim's answer to the history question was wrong.*

antonyms: true, loyal, faithful, honest, genuine, real, correct

famous *adj.* widely known and talked about. *Colorado is famous for its mountains.*

noted famous; honored. *Jesse's grandmother is a noted author.*

publicized made known. *They asked the scientists about the widely publicized discovery.*

well-known noted. *"Cinderella" is a well-known story.*

antonyms: unknown, hidden

feature *n.* 1. a part. *The interview was the best feature of the program.* 2. something that attracts attention; outstanding quality. *Her best feature is her ability to see mistakes.*

characteristic quality. *Honesty is a characteristic most people admire.*

highlight noticeable feature. *A highlight of the parade was the huge, striped balloon.*

final *adj.* 1. last; closing; coming at the end. *Friday is the final day of the sale.* 2. not to be changed. *The umpire's decision is always final.*

closing ending; last. *The audience sang the national anthem at the festival's closing ceremonies.*

concluding ending. *The concluding song on Lucy's recital was a well-known lullaby.*

finishing ending. *For the finishing touch, she drew a silver stripe along the side.*

last at the end. *Our float was the last one in the parade.*

latest most recent. *You are reading the paper's latest edition.*

antonyms: first, original, beginning, opening, earliest, introductory

foolish *adj.* senseless; silly; unwise. *Justin felt really foolish when he realized that his socks didn't match.*

absurd not reasonable. *My question didn't seem absurd at the time.*

empty-headed foolish. *It's not a compliment to be called empty-headed.*

improper not appropriate. *Joy's behavior was improper for a formal dinner.*

senseless without reason. *Destroying the picture was senseless.*

silly foolish. *The baby acted silly when she saw everybody was watching her.*

stupid not intelligent. *The puppy isn't stupid; it just isn't trained yet.*

thoughtless unthinking. *Sometimes Judy's words are thoughtless and harmful.*

unwise not sensible. *We felt that their decision was unwise.*

antonyms: wise, sensible, reasonable, intelligent

freedom *n.* the state of being free; liberty. *The Revolutionary War was fought to gain freedom for our country.*

discharge release from a duty or job. *The soldier asked for a discharge.*

elbowroom adequate space. *At the ranch, we have lots of elbowroom.*

independence freedom from control by others. *Do you think complete independence is possible?*

liberty independence. *People all over the world want liberty.*

release getting free. *The prisoners' release was celebrated by their families.*

right freedom. *In America, we have the right to share our ideas.*

scope space to move or think freely. *The children were given the scope they needed to become confident in themselves.*

self-rule independence from other governments. *The nation wants self-rule.*

antonyms: burden, pressure, confinement

frighten *v.* 1. to make afraid; to scare. *The actor's costume will frighten the little girl.* 2. to cause to move by making afraid. *They used the campfire to frighten away the wolves.*

alarm to frighten. *A strange noise alarmed the campers.*

awe to cause fear and respect. *A violent storm will awe those who experience it.*

dismay to cause concern. *Her failure to get better should dismay her doctors.*

horrify to frighten and dismay. *That mask is sure to horrify the people who see you.*

scare to alarm. *The costume will scare the little children.*

shock to surprise and frighten. *The dog's snarl seemed to shock its owner.*

startle to surprise and scare. *The doorbell managed to startle the man from his sleep.*

terrify to frighten badly. *The monster movie might terrify the young child.*

unnerve to upset seriously. *The earthquake did unnerve all of us.*

antonyms: reassure, encourage

generous *adj.* willing to share; unselfish; giving happily. *The famous athlete was generous with her time in teaching girls how to play tennis.*

abundant plentiful. *The harvest of corn was abundant this year.*

bountiful generous. *At Thanksgiving, we think of the bountiful land.*

openhanded generous. *Our neighbor is always openhanded when she bakes bread and rolls.*

overflowing more than is needed. *The overflowing cornucopia is a harvest symbol.*

unselfish willing to share. *Our neighbors are unselfish.*

antonyms: stingy, mean, scarce, small-minded, petty

good-bye or **good-by** *n.* an expression of farewell. *We said good-bye on the railway platform.*

adieu French word for good-bye. *We sadly bade them adieu on the dock.*

departure going from a place. *The plane's departure was delayed by snow.*

dismissal sending away. *Our dismissal from school was early today because of parent-teacher meetings.*

farewell parting; parting words. *They made their farewell brief.*

leave-taking parting. *The workers' leave-taking was cheerful.*

parting leave-taking. *Our parting was easier because we knew we would see them soon.*

send-off a formal leave-taking; celebration of a leave-taking. *Our block had a big send-off party when one family moved away.*

antonym: arrival

government *n.* 1. a system of ruling or managing. *Our American government is a democracy, which means that the power to make laws comes from the citizens.* 2. the people in charge of such a system. *The government has approved the new dam.*

command rule. *The army has a strict system of command.*

congress body that governs. *Members of the Congress are elected by the people.*

control power; influence. *Who has control of decisions like that?*

management method of rule. *The mayor heads our city's management.*

rule government. *How long did their rule of that region last?*

rulers persons who govern. *Who are the present rulers of the Middle East?*

antonyms: chaos, lawlessness

habit *n.* a custom; an action that has been done so often that one does it without thinking. *Brushing your teeth after every meal is a good habit to acquire.*

custom practice; habit. *It is Jake's custom to do his homework before he reads or plays.*

practice habit; routine. *Marcia's practice of reading every morning has helped her in school.*

routine regular practice. *Maggie follows the same routine every school day.*

harvest *n.* 1. a crop. *This year's grain harvest will be larger than last year's.* 2. the gathering in of a crop. *A farmer needs more workers during the harvest.*

product something that is made. *The dairy sold milk products of all kinds.*

profit gain. *The result of their work was a good profit.*

reward that which is gained. *The farm family reaped the reward for the hard work of the past year.*

yield the amount produced. *The farmer was pleased with the year's yield.*

hero *n.* 1. a person admired for courage or great deeds. *George Washington is a national hero.* 2. the most important character in a story. *The plot usually permits the hero to triumph.*

adventurer person who seeks danger and excitement. *People who like action may look up to an adventurer.*

champion person who stands up for others. *The ancient folktale is about a champion who saved the people in times of trouble.*

star person who stands out; entertainer. *Fans admire the star of that TV series.*

winner person who triumphs. *Marie Curie was the winner of a Nobel prize in chemistry.*

humanity *n.* 1. people; the human race. *All humanity benefits from scientific research.* 2. kindness; mercy. *The prisoners were treated with humanity.*

charity concern for others. *Helping a friend is an act of charity.*

consideration concern for others. *Think of others and act with consideration.*

humankind all people. *Traveling adds to our knowledge of humankind.*

human race humankind. *Members of the human race are alike in important ways.*

kindness treating others well. *Most people value kindness.*

world all people; humankind. *They announced their findings to the world.*

humble *adj.* 1. modest; not proud. *She remained humble even after her huge success.* 2. not important or grand. *That actor still lives in the humble house in which he grew up.*

insignificant unimportant. *The humble artist said his work was insignificant when compared with that of artists in the past.*

lowly plain or common. *People thought of Harriet Tubman as a lowly woman until they learned about her heroic acts.*

meek quiet; making no protest. *I like my meek friend because she is so calm.*

respectful thinking well of others. *It's important to be respectful of other people's rights and ideas.*

shy timid; lacking self-confidence. *When Ted was little, he was very shy.*

simple plain; not showy. *The great writer's home is simple and looks like all of the other houses on the street.*

antonyms: arrogant, proud, haughty, boastful, important, significant

humid *adj.* damp; moist. *Tropical climates are often humid.*

damp containing water. *The damp clothes dried slowly because the air was humid.*

misty humid; foggy. *We could not see far in the misty air.*

moist slightly wet. *The tabletop was moist after I wiped it off.*

muggy hot and damp. *Even pets suffered during the muggy summer afternoons.*

steamy hot and moist. *The swamp is always steamy this time of year.*

watery full of water. *The watery soup did not look very tasty.*

wet watery. *I hung the wet towel on the clothesline.*

antonyms: dry, arid, parched

humor *n.* 1. something that makes a person laugh; a funny or amusing quality. *The essay used gentle humor to make its point.* 2. a state of mind; mood. *The cheerful story put me in a good humor.*

comedy humorous language or situations. *My favorite TV show is a comedy.*

disposition attitude; feeling. *The sunny day improved my disposition.*

frame of mind attitude; disposition. *Seeing my friend always puts me in a good frame of mind.*

temper disposition. *A good joke will improve his temper.*

wit humor; cleverness. *Daniel M. Pinkwater is a writer who uses wit on every page.*

humorous *adj.* funny; comical; amusing. *The audience laughed at the humorous movie.*

amusing entertaining; comical. *The cartoon is just barely amusing.*

comical funny; amusing. *The cartoon was so comical that everybody had to laugh.*

funny humorous; laughable. *Did you ever notice that people don't all find the same things to be funny?*

laughable inspiring laughter. *Mark didn't think that the situation was laughable.*

witty clever; intelligently humorous. *Clive is so witty that we want him to do a stand-up comic routine for the talent show.*

antonyms: serious, grave, stern, sad

imagine *v.* 1. to make up an idea or picture in the mind. *I can imagine all the things I would do if I had the time.* 2. to suppose. *I imagine they'll be there soon.*

create to make something original. *Alexander Calder created a new art form called a "mobile."*

fancy to imagine something never experienced. *Just fancy living without any machines!*

invent to make something new. *The Wright brothers invented a machine that would fly.*

picture to see in one's mind. *Can you picture my sister on a motorcycle?*

suppose to think. *Do you suppose the picnic will be fun?*

think of to imagine; to consider. *How did you ever think of zebra-striped walls?*

visualize to picture. *Try to visualize the way your room will look before we move all the furniture.*

impatient *adj.* not patient; restless. *We became impatient after the long delay.*

abrupt short in speech; impatient. *The clerk became abrupt when she realized that we weren't going to buy anything.*

eager impatient to do something pleasant. *We were all eager to start on the trip to Florida.*

fidgety restless. *Did you ever try to entertain a fidgety three-year-old?*

fussy irritable; nervous. *Eddie told his brother to stop being so fussy about his clothes.*

hasty in a hurry. *Slow down and don't be so hasty.*

irritable cross. *Having to wait makes me feel irritable.*

nervous anxious; concerned. *Waiting for the doctor made Rosie nervous.*

reckless careless. *Martin is often reckless with his spending money.*

restless jumpy; impatient. *The rainy day made us all restless.*

antonyms: patient, restful, quiet, calm, cool, easygoing

imperfect *adj.* not perfect; having faults or defects. *The diamond was beautiful, but the single flaw made it imperfect.*

crude natural; rough. *My uncle is drilling for crude oil on his property.*

defective having a fault. *Because the computer hookup was defective, a fuse blew.*

faulty defective. *Faulty wiring is very dangerous.*

flawed having a spot or blemish. *The surface of the beautiful table was flawed.*

incomplete missing a part. *The drawing was interesting but still incomplete.*

inferior of lower quality. *The desktop cracked because it was made of inferior wood.*

limited having limits; imperfect. *The self-emptying pencil sharpener Will invented is limited in its usefulness.*

marred spotted or spoiled. *The new mirror was marred by a long, thin scratch.*

unfinished incomplete. *Jed had shoveled snow for an hour, but the job was still unfinished.*

unsound not free from defects. *Katie's plans were unsound, so her great invention wouldn't work.*

antonyms: perfect, flawless, thorough

impolite *adj.* not polite; showing bad manners. *It is impolite to interrupt when another person is speaking.*

discourteous not courteous. *Loud talking in public places is discourteous.*

rude deliberately discourteous. *While he was upset, his behavior seemed rude.*

ungracious not mannerly or polite. *Never be ungracious to a guest.*

unmannerly lacking in manners; not showing courtesy. *When they were together, they were often loud and unmannerly.*

antonyms: polite, courteous, mannerly

important *adj.* 1. meaning a great deal; serious. *Your birthday is important to you.* 2. having power or authority. *Those parking places are reserved for important officials.*

critical capable of making a difference. *The decision you make now may be critical to your future.*

influential powerful. *The most influential woman in town owns the newspaper.*

major of first importance. *Clem's decision to go to the academy was a major move.*

meaningful having importance. *She and I had a very meaningful conversation.*

notable well-known; important. *The mayor and other notable officials were present.*

powerful holding authority. *Who is the most powerful elected official in our country?*

serious important; weighty. *Ms. Adamson's discussion with Tina was serious.*

weighty of great seriousness. *Mary Lynn had weighty plans for her future.*

antonyms: unimportant, slight, minor, weak

impossible *adj.* 1. not possible; not able to happen. *It is impossible for us to live without breathing air, eating food, and drinking water.* 2. difficult to get along with. *That impossible cat has clawed all the new furniture.*

unimaginable not able to be imagined. *I find it unimaginable that Sandy would have said that.*

unreal lacking reality. *The danger of an earthquake or a hurricane will seem unreal to those who have never experienced them.*

unreasonable not logical. *It is unreasonable to expect everybody to help.*

unthinkable not capable of being thought of. *A trip to the moon was once unthinkable.*

antonyms: reasonable, likely

inactive *adj.* not active; idle; not moving around. *Hawaii has both active and inactive volcanoes.*

idle not active; accomplishing little. *To be idle during vacation is pleasant.*

immobile unable to move. *The bike was so badly rusted that its wheels were immobile.*

motionless not moving. *The tiger lay motionless as she watched the grazing deer.*

antonyms: energetic, active, busy

include *v.* 1. to contain; to cover. *The price of the radio includes the tax.* 2. to put in as part of the total. *Don't forget to include the guests in the other room.*

admit to allow in. *Will the library club admit students in the lower grades, too?*

contain to hold; surround. *Sam said that no box in the world could contain his collection of treasures.*

cover to include. *The newspaper article did not cover everything that happened at the school board meeting.*

have to include. *Does that game have all the pieces we need?*

hold to contain. *The box Dad made will hold all of the chess pieces and the board.*

involve to bring into a situation. *My brother doesn't want us to involve him in our plans for the ball game.*

take in to admit. *The club hasn't room to take in everyone in school.*

antonyms: to exclude, eliminate, omit

incomplete *adj.* not finished or complete; lacking something. *Your answer to the division problem was incomplete because you didn't give the remainder.*

defective missing a part; incomplete. *I think that radio is defective.*

half-finished partly finished. *Dad complained when Jack left the mowing half-finished.*

imperfect missing a quality or part. *This opal costs less because it is imperfect.*

partial incomplete. *That is only a partial answer to your question.*

undone not completed. *Al always leaves some homework undone.*

unfinished incomplete; not yet done. *Every sewing project Janet ever began was left unfinished.*

antonyms: whole, complete, finished

incorrect *adj.* 1. not correct; wrong. *This answer is incorrect.* 2. in poor taste; improper. *Slurping is considered incorrect.*

false untrue. *It is false to say that terriers make better pets than spaniels.*

faulty not correct; not thought through. *The workers couldn't complete the swimming pool because the plans were faulty.*

improper not correct. *It would be improper to talk to our guest without an introduction.*

inaccurate not exact; not correct. *Jerry's estimate for the damage was inaccurate.*

inappropriate not suitable for a situation. *The music was inappropriate for a serious gathering.*

inexact containing error. *The door didn't fit because the measurements she took were inexact.*

unfit unsuitable. *Your gym shoes are unfit for a formal dance.*

unsuitable not right for a situation. *Most people would agree that jeans are unsuitable for a wedding.*

untrue incorrect. *The statement is completely untrue.*

wrong incorrect. *I think your answer to the math problem is wrong.*

antonyms: accurate, exact, faultless, right, true, proper

increase *v.* to make or become greater. *The cost of living continues to increase every year.*

add to make larger by adding a part. *We decided to add two rooms to our house rather than move into a bigger one.*

develop to grow. *Our neighborhood will develop when the new workers move to this area.*

enlarge to make larger. *The photographer promised to enlarge our favorite snapshot.*

expand to stretch. *The balloon began to expand.*

extend to lengthen. *Grandma can extend her dining room table by adding sections.*

grow to become larger. *That tree can grow about one inch a year.*

inflate to make grow by filling with gas. *The huge balloons inflate very slowly.*

magnify to cause to appear larger. *The lens will magnify fine print.*

multiply to increase. *Sometimes, problems seem to multiply more quickly than solutions.*

prolong to make longer in time. *We couldn't prolong our winter vacation.*

raise to increase pay. *The company will raise everyone's salary.*

swell to puff up. *When Joey fell, his wrist began to swell.*

antonyms: lessen, decrease, shrink, reduce

inform *v.* to tell. *We had to inform her that she was on the wrong street.*

advise to inform; to suggest. *Would you advise her to study harder?*

educate to enlighten. *The students agreed to educate each other on local problems.*

enlighten to give information that will improve knowledge. *Gwen doesn't know what a pueblo is, so we will enlighten her.*

explain to provide information. *Gus's parents are going to explain speed skating and bike racing.*

instruct to teach. *My mother will instruct students who want to learn how to play hockey.*

notify to inform of a situation. *Please notify us if another meeting is to be held.*

teach to educate. *David's father will teach us how to ski.*

tell to inform. *Can Thomas tell us more about the carnival?*

informal *adj.* not formal; casual. *The party was informal, so we didn't have to dress up.*

casual not serious; informal; without plan. *Lunch at our house is usually very casual.*

easy relaxed; not formal. *Life around our house is pretty easy in the summertime.*

familiar well-known; casual. *I relax more easily in familiar surroundings.*

free casual; informal. *The big end-of-year dance was free and easy.*

relaxed without rules; informal. *The beach picnic had a relaxed atmosphere.*

simple plain; casual. *She wore a simple dress to the party.*

unofficial not part of an office or position. *The mayor's visit to our house was unofficial.*

antonyms: formal, official, stiff

install *v.* 1. to put something into a place where it can be used. *They will install the new water heater in the basement.* 2. to put into office with ceremony. *There was a special ceremony to install the new president of the college.*

admit to allow into; to install as part. *The Honors Club will admit twelve new members.*

establish to set up. *We might establish the deck as the place for our family breakfast.*

invest to admit with ceremony. *The society will invest the new members by giving them medals.*

locate to set in a planned place. *Where will they locate their new store?*

place to put in position. *Please place the tray on the table.*

position to put in place. *We tried to position the TV set so everyone in the crowded room could watch the game.*

seat to establish in office. *A special ceremony was held to seat the city council members.*

set up to establish officially. *The position of class president has been set up for the first time in our class.*

instructor *n.* one who instructs; teacher. *Our school has a good art instructor.*

adviser one who offers suggestions. *Anyone planning a career needs an adviser.*

educator a person who teaches or studies teaching methods. *Do you want to be an educator when you are older?*

guide a person who leads through an unknown area. *The ranger was our guide through the mountain pass.*

teacher a person who instructs. *The students at Borough School named Ms. Cantor teacher of the year.*

trainer one who teaches a skill. *Beth does well with her new trainer in gymnastics.*

interest *n.* 1. a feeling of wanting to know or take part in something. *Sandra has an interest in music.* 2. the money paid for the use of another's money. *When you repay a loan, you pay the amount you borrowed plus interest.*

attention notice; interest. *The cheerful shouting caught our attention.*

attraction a pull; an interest. *History has a strong attraction for Holly.*

care concern; interest. *Show your care for the environment by not littering.*

concern interest; worry. *People in our town feel concern about the pollution of the river.*

curiosity desire to know; desire to experience. *Curiosity led Alice to meet the Mad Hatter and the March Hare.*

notice attention. *Will that poster attract their notice?*

profit gain; interest. *The bank made a profit on the loan to the city.*

antonyms: boredom, coolness, disregard

internal *adj.* 1. on the inside. *The heart is an internal organ.* 2. within a country; domestic. *A civil war is an internal conflict.*

buried hidden. *Katie's real feelings often stay buried.*

domestic national. *What are our biggest domestic problems?*

hidden personal; private; internal. *Until you know her, Della's real personality is hidden.*

inner internal; inside. *The library's inner walls have been replastered and repainted.*

inside inner. *The safest place in a wind storm is near an inside wall of your house.*

secret internal; private. *Mandy had a secret desire to be a singer.*

antonyms: exterior, outer, outside, exposed

invent *v.* 1. to make something that has never been made before. *Thomas wants to invent a new type of electric light.* 2. to make up, to imagine. *A writer can invent a story.*

create to make something new. *Maggie and Mark will create a new toy for their brother.*

falsify to deliberately change facts. *The spy in the story had to falsify a passport.*

fashion to put together. *Together they want to fashion an unusual routine for the marching band.*

fib to tell a trivial lie. *I know the minute my little sister tries to fib.*

lie to make up a false statement. *Do you ever lie about your age?*

originate to begin. *Where did the planting of potatoes originate?*

inventor *n.* one who invents. *Alexander Graham Bell was the inventor of the telephone.*

creator a person who makes something; an artist. *Michelangelo was the creator of the sculpture called "David."*

designer one who plans. *Frank Lloyd Wright was an architect and a designer of homes.*

originator a person who begins something. *Benjamin Franklin was the originator of bifocal lens.*

pioneer an originator; one who is first in a field. *Amelia Earhart was a pioneer in aviation.*

jacket *n.* 1. a short coat that covers the upper part of the body. *When the weather became cooler, Jimmy came into the house for his jacket.* 2. any outer covering. *A book's jacket protects the cover.*

case a cover. *The CD case had the artist's name on it.*

coat an outdoor garment. *Jackie's bright green coat caught everyone's attention.*

envelope a covering. *I put all of my letters in a large envelope.*

folder something that surrounds; a jacket. *Collect all of your papers and put them in a folder.*

wrapper a jacket; a cover. *The wrapper kept the snow from ruining Joe's book.*

joyous *adj.* joyful; glad. *The air rang with joyous shouts from children playing.*

cheerful happy. *The movie is mostly cheerful, but sometimes a little sad.*

happy joyful; content. *When Joe is sad, he finds that a good story will make him happy again.*

merry cheerful; joyful. *The merry, oddly dressed clown entertained the children.*

antonyms: depressing, grim, sad

judgment *n.* 1. a decision reached through careful thought. *The final judgment of the class was in favor of a picnic rather than a trip to the zoo.* 2. opinion. *In my judgment, such a plan will never succeed.* 3. the ability to make wise decisions. *Consuela shows good judgment about horses.*

award a judgment or decision. *What award did the court give them?*

conclusion a decision made after considering facts. *Her conclusion was that recycling is necessary.*

decision a conclusion; judgment. *The referee made an unpopular decision.*

decree a formal ruling. *In the fable, the cruel king's decree forbade all singing.*

finding formal ruling. *The lawyer said the court's finding was a reasonable one.*

intelligence cleverness; good judgment. *The coach says that good runners must have intelligence as well as speed.*

notion an idea; a personal judgment. *How did you arrive at that notion?*

order a ruling or decree. *He sent an order to the army.*

ruling a formal decision. *The court's ruling ended the confusion.*

sentence a legal ruling. *The judge gave a hard sentence to the careless driver.*

thought an opinion. *Tell us your thoughts after hearing our arguments.*

understanding wisdom; good judgment. *These ancient people had an understanding of how to keep the earth safe.*

verdict a legal conclusion. *The jury finally announced its verdict.*

wisdom good personal judgment. *Mr. Chee says his ancestors showed great wisdom in their care of the land.*

antonym: foolishness

kernel *n.* a grain or seed. *We eat the kernels of wheat in cereal.*

grain a small piece; kernel. *I watched as the squirrel ate every grain of corn.*

seed kernel from which grain or grass will grow. *The wheat seed is very tiny.*

kimono *n.* a loose outer garment bound with a sash in the middle. *The kimono was first used in Japan.*

costume native clothing. *The sari is still the costume of many women from India.*

dressing gown robe; kimono. *David sent his mother a beautiful silk dressing gown when he visited Japan.*

knapsack *n.* a canvas or leather bag worn or carried on the back, and used to hold food, clothing, equipment, etc. *The hiker carried a knapsack and a sleeping bag.*

backpack knapsack; bag. *Jody's backpack held at least ten pounds of food and water.*

kit equipment for a soldier; equipment for a particular activity. *The hikers carried a first-aid kit at all times.*

language *n.* 1. speech; words that are spoken or written. *Language is the main way human beings communicate.* 2. the speech of a certain nation, tribe, or group of people. *The French language is spoken by the people of France.*

communication language; sharing meaning. *Using words correctly is important for good communication.*

dialect language of a region or people. *A story that uses dialect makes the setting and characters seem real.*

jargon language of a group or of experts. *I don't understand computer jargon.*

speech voice; language. *The visiting poet talked about the importance of rhythm in speech.*

latch *n.* a lock or a catch in which a movable piece fits into a notch or slot. *The door wouldn't stay closed because the latch was broken.*

bolt wooden or metal sliding bar on a door or window. *The bolt was made of wood.*

catch fastener; latch. *The metal catch broke off during the struggle.*

fastener device used for holding something in place. *Use the fastener to keep the curtains out of the way.*

launch *v.* 1. to send upward into space. *As we watched, the satellite was launched.* 2. to send into the water. *At the dock, workers prepared to launch the newest ship.* 3. to start; to begin. *Our school will launch a cleaning and painting drive in the neighborhood.*

begin to start. *Soon we will begin volleyball practice.*

eject to push out. *Student pilots learn to eject from their planes.*

institute to begin; to start. *The city will institute a plan for a new library.*

propel to push. *Escaping air will propel the balloon upward.*

push to launch; to propel. *We had to push the car to the gas station.*

set afloat to push into water. *The children used a long stick to set afloat the boats they had made.*

liberty *n.* 1. freedom; independence. *The American Revolution won liberty for the former British colonies.* 2. the right or opportunity to do something. *Our Constitution protects our liberty.*

freedom liberty; independence. *Every day the newspaper carries a story of people who work for freedom.*

independence freedom from rule. *The nation claimed its independence from Great Britain.*

permission freedom to act. *Our parents gave us permission to stay here all day.*

antonyms: denial, veto, ban

lodge *n.* 1. a building used as a temporary living place. *We stayed at a lodge on the lake.* 2. the den of an otter or beaver. *The beavers built a big lodge.*

cabin a small wooden shelter. *Early American settlers often built log cabins.*

cottage a simple house; a country home. *The Joneses have a cottage near Lake George.*

gatehouse a house at the entrance to an estate. *The owners rent the gatehouse to my friend's family.*

hut a temporary shelter; a small cabin. *The girls built a hut at the edge of the woods and used it as their clubhouse.*

loosen *v.* 1. to make loose; make less tight. *Loosen the collar around the dog's neck.* 2. to become loose. *The knot in the rope started to loosen because it was badly tied.*

decrease to lessen. *Gradually, the number of rules decreased, and Jackson was free to plan his own long summer days.*

deliver to free. *The army scouts were able to deliver their comrades from those who had captured them.*

ease to loosen to a degree. *Max's piano teacher promised to ease the practice rules after the recital.*

let up to ease. *The puppies let up on their demands for our time.*

reduce to lessen. *Kate reduced the pressure she had been putting on herself to succeed as a gymnast.*

relax to reduce an obligation. *During vacation, Gigi's parents relax her bedtime rules.*

release to let go. *The ski should release your foot if you fall.*

set free to let go. *The children wanted to set free the penned-in herd of deer.*

unbind to undo; release. *My hands are so cold I can't unbind these bales of hay.*

unbridle to loosen bindings. *Riders learn to unsaddle and unbridle their own horses.*

unchain to set free. *They won't unchain the elephant when there are visitors in the circus tent.*

unclasp to unhook. *Please unclasp the binder so I can add some pages.*

undo to unfasten. *Undo your scarf if you are too hot in here.*

unfasten to undo. *Can you unfasten the snaps on the baby's snowsuit, please?*

untie to undo a binding. *Untie your shoe and you will feel more comfortable.*

unyoke to release from a bond. *Anyone who wanted to unyoke the team of oxen had to be strong.*

weaken to grow less strong. *The bond between Joanne and her friend began to weaken.*

antonyms: to tie, bind, clasp, fasten, yoke, imprison, bridle, capture, stiffen, tighten, strengthen

loss *n.* 1. ruin; destruction. *The forest fire caused the loss of many trees.* 2. a failure to keep or to win. *The loss of the contract cost the company millions of dollars.* 3. a losing. *Marcia felt the loss of her old friends when she moved away.*

damage harm; ruin. *Covering books helps to prevent damage.*

defeat a failure to win. *The team's defeat was a surprise to the fans.*

forfeiture loss. *The breakdown of the bus caused our forfeiture of the game.*

harm hurt; destruction. *Pesticides cause harm to wild birds.*

ruin loss; destruction. *The film showed us the ruin of cities during the war.*

antonyms: excess, plus, surplus, profit, gain, return, improvement

loyal *adj.* faithful. *Sam is a loyal friend.*

devoted loyal; faithful. *Jack is devoted to his grandfather and helps him in many ways.*

faithful dependable; loyal. *That dog is so faithful that it follows Addie everywhere.*

reliable dependable; loyal. *Janet is a reliable friend.*

antonyms: faithless, disloyal, traitorous

loyalty *n.* a sense of duty; being loyal. *No one could question our loyalty to our country.*

allegiance loyalty. *We pledge allegiance to the flag and to the country for which it stands.*

devotion love and loyalty. *He showed devotion to his ideals.*

faithfulness allegiance. *History shows many examples of men and women who proved their faithfulness to their countries.*

obedience loyal following of orders. *The commander praised the sailor's obedience.*

antonyms: treachery, faithlessness, disloyalty

luggage *n.* baggage; the suitcases, trunks, bags, or boxes that are taken on a trip. *We claimed our luggage at the station.*

baggage luggage; portable equipment. *Our family always takes along more baggage than is needed.*

bags suitcases; luggage. *The tour guide limited us to four bags apiece.*

equipment gear. *A painter's equipment is lightweight and portable.*

gear luggage; equipment. *The photographer carried her gear everywhere.*

pack a soft bag, usually carried on the shoulder or back. *Tom traveled all summer with just a small pack.*

paraphernalia assortment of materials; gear. *Juan carried all kinds of drawing paraphernalia on our class trip.*

suitcases bags. *Hard-sided suitcases are heavier but safer.*

magic *n.* 1. in stories, the ability to do seemingly impossible things. *The prince was changed into a frog by magic.* 2. anything that charms and delights; an enchanting quality. *Donna was fascinated by the magic of the coral reef.*

appeal interest; glamour. *We felt the castle's appeal because we knew what had happened within those walls.*

enchantment wonder. *Many folktales are stories of enchantment.*

fascination wonder. *The beauty of the old buildings held a fascination for us.*

glamour enchantment; wonder. *Our visit to the ancient castle was full of glamour.*

spell enchantment. *A spell had been cast upon the little green troll.*

wonder-working act of enchanting; casting spells. *In the cartoon, the wizard's wonder-working was always for the good of the people.*

majority *n.* 1. a number that is more than half of a total; the larger part. *The majority of Americans can read and write.* 2. the number of votes by which an election is won. *The vote was thirteen to nine, so they won the election by a majority of four votes.*

bulk large part. *The bulk of the food was eaten before the party began.*

lion's share largest part. *The Great Dane got the lion's share of the dog food.*

antonyms: minority, few, little

margin *n.* an edge; border. *We left a wide margin on our printed report.*

border edge; margin. *The scarf of white silk had a picture of a Chinese home and garden and was edged with a red border.*

edge boundary. *The farmer built a stone wall at the edge of the field.*

rim edge where depth changes. *At the rim of the canyon, we stopped the horses and looked down at the river.*

midday *n.* the middle of the day; noon. *The parade began at midday.*

noon midday. *The cafeteria begins to serve lunch exactly at noon.*

twelve o'clock noon; midday. *The sun is highest in the sky at twelve o'clock standard time.*

midterm *adj.* in the middle of a term. *Jim failed the midterm exam, but did well on the final exam.*

midquarter halfway through a quarter. *If your school year is divided into quarters, you probably have a midquarter exam.*

midsemester halfway through a semester. *The midsemester vacation was a welcome break.*

midyear halfway through the year. *The Fourth of July is a great midyear celebration for Americans.*

modernize *v.* to make or become modern; bring up to date. *To modernize our bathroom we converted the tub into a shower.*

renew to make new. *The faculty decided to renew some class procedures.*

renovate to make like new. *The owners have promised to renovate those old buildings.*

streamline to make modern and efficient. *The fire department will streamline its emergency procedures.*

update to make modern. *The city announced that it would update its phone system.*

antonyms: to age, date, outdate, antique

motor *n.* an engine that turns power into motion. *The car would not move because the motor wouldn't start.*

dynamo a small generator. *At the flea market we found an old dynamo.*

engine a motor. *The car's old engine needed to be overhauled.*

generator a machine that converts mechanical energy into electricity. *The hospital can use a backup generator if the electricity in the city fails.*

narrow *adj.* 1. not wide. *The house is on a narrow street.* 2. close. *The careless riders had a narrow escape.*
  close by a small amount; narrow. *We had a close call while driving on the freeway yesterday.*
  slender thin; narrow. *The baby's cap was tied with a slender strip of ribbon.*
  thin slender; narrow. *The wire on which the mobile hung was so thin it was almost invisible.*
  antonyms: wide, fat, thick, broad

nonsense *n.* foolish actions or words; silly talk; anything that does not make sense. *Babies talk nonsense when they are learning to speak.*
  foolishness silly talk or behavior. *We all laughed at their foolishness.*
  poppycock an old-fashioned word for nonsense. *"Balderdash and poppycock!" the officer cried impatiently.*
  rubbish nonsense; something with no merit. *The magazine was really just rubbish, and Pat found it boring.*
  silliness nonsense. *The silliness of the cartoons helped me to relax.*
  trivia unimportant facts. *The book reported a lot of trivia, but didn't contain much helpful information.*
  antonyms: sense, logic, basics

nonstop *adv.* without stopping. *We flew nonstop from Denver to Seattle.*
  ceaselessly without ceasing. *The puppy whined ceaselessly when we left him alone in the basement.*

office *n.* 1. a place or room where business is done or a service is supplied. *We waited in the doctor's office.* 2. a position to which one is elected or appointed. *She holds the office of mayor.*
  position office; role; job. *The position of scout leader is challenging.*
  post position; official work. *The ambassador's family joined him at his new post in Europe.*
  role a position; office. *The governor seems comfortable in his new role.*
  room place for business. *When they began their business, they rented a small room in the building across the street.*
  suite a set of rooms. *The magazine editors work in the suite on the second floor.*

operate *v.* to run or work. *Do you know how to operate a sewing machine?*
  go to run; to work. *The engine is made to go on very little energy.*
  run to operate; to make go. *Brian likes to run the electric train he received for his birthday.*
  work to run; to operate. *After practice, most people learn how to work the controls on a microwave oven.*
  antonyms: to fail, stop, break down

operator *n.* one who runs or operates a machine, vehicle, business, etc. *The telephone operator helped us find the correct number.*
  conductor operator. *The conductor on the trolley car was very good-natured.*
  mechanic one who operates or repairs machines. *The factory needs good mechanics.*
  pilot operator. *The riverboat pilot finished a long period of training.*
  technician trained operator. *The huge water-processing plant employs that technician.*
  worker operator. *Some fancy, older hotels have a worker running each elevator.*

organize *v.* to arrange; to put in order. *Organize your ideas before you start to write your paper.*
  catalogue to organize by type. *There are several ways to catalogue library books.*
  classify to put in a particular order. *Classify your notes according to topic.*
  group to put in like sets. *The dancing teacher wants to group the children according to height.*
  order to arrange. *Please order the books alphabetically on each shelf.*

sort to decide on an order. *Would you sort these papers according to their subjects, please?*
  antonyms: to scramble, jumble, confuse, mix up, disorganize, disarrange

ornament *n.* something pretty used for decoration. *A mirror can make an attractive wall ornament.*
  accessory something that is decorative or extra. *Clement added a gold chain as an accessory to the black shirt he wore for the party at school.*
  adornment decoration. *Ms. Carter wears simple clothes with little adornment.*
  decoration ornament; trimming. *The city put up beautiful decorations for its hundredth anniversary celebration.*
  trimming decoration; adornment. *We will use ribbons as the trimming on the package.*

outline *n.* a plan; a list of main subjects. *Martin made an outline of the points he wanted to cover.*
  diagram a plan; an outline. *Can you make a diagram so that I can understand your idea?*
  plan an outline. *A good plan will make the job easier.*
  sketch a plan. *Make a quick sketch of main ideas before you begin to write.*
  summary statement of main ideas. *Be sure the summary is complete.*

parcel *n.* 1. a package; a bundle of things wrapped together. *The shopper's arms were filled with parcels.* 2. a piece; a section. *The farmer sold a parcel of land.*
  box a container with a flat base. *We tried to find a box large enough for the bicycle.*
  bundle package; load. *The teddy bear and the stuffed monkey made a bundle too awkward to carry easily.*
  carton box; container. *The neighborhood children played in the cardboard carton from our refrigerator.*
  package bundle; parcel. *We received a package of cheese from our friends in Italy.*

packet a small package. *The earrings came in a small packet.*
  portion part; piece. *Grandfather sold a portion of the orchard to a neighbor.*

patient *adj.* able to put up with pain, trouble, delay, etc., without complaint. *The driver was patient despite the heavy traffic.*
  persistent keeping at a task or problem. *Eve was persistent until she finally learned to play the computer game.*
  resigned patient; able to put up with. *The driver was resigned to frequent traffic delays.*
  sympathetic understanding; able to feel as others feel. *Families are usually sympathetic to each other's problems.*

picture *n.* 1. a painting, drawing, or photograph. *The picture in the magazine was beautiful.* 2. a likeness; image. *Larry is the picture of his father.* 3. a description. *Her letter gave a good picture of army life.*
  description picture made in words. *I love novels that use a lot of description.*
  drawing picture made with lines, not colored in. *One student in our class made a very lifelike drawing of horses.*
  illustration picture; drawing. *Jamie drew a realistic illustration of our class trip to the circus.*
  image likeness. *Steven is the image of his grandfather at Steven's age.*
  likeness picture similar to its live object. *That is a perfect likeness of my parents when they were younger.*
  painting picture; work of art. *Amy spent all of her time studying one painting.*
  photograph a picture taken with a camera. *Elise showed us a photograph she took on her vacation in Hawaii.*
  portrait likeness of a person. *Sally had an artist paint her portrait.*
  portrayal description. *C. S. Lewis's portrayal of the land beyond the wardrobe is my favorite fictional description.*
  sketch picture showing only the main lines of an object. *The artist at the mall made a quick sketch of me.*

pioneer *n.* a person who goes first and opens the way for others. *The ancient Egyptians were pioneers in astronomy.*

developer one who develops. *Henry and Camille Dreyfuss were among the first developers of manufactured fibers that would replace natural fibers.*

forerunner person who goes first. *A forerunner in aviation was Harriet Quimby, who received a pilot's license in 1911.*

originator a person who begins something. *Elisha Otis was the originator of the passenger elevator.*

antonyms: follower, imitator, copier

plaza *n.* a public square in a city or town. *The cathedral faces the plaza.*

courtyard an enclosed area next to a building. *The office building where Mr. Scott works has a beautiful courtyard with a fountain.*

mall collection of shops, often under one roof. *Three new stores have just opened in the mall.*

marketplace place where products are sold. *The farmers brought fruit and vegetables to sell in the marketplace.*

piazza public square. *Restaurants in the piazza have outdoor tables.*

shopping center mall. *We like to meet at the shopping center downtown.*

square central public area. *In our town, the square is flooded for ice skating every winter.*

pleasant *adj.* 1. delightful; pleasing. *We had a pleasant vacation.* 2. fair and warm. *The weather was pleasant.* 3. agreeable; friendly. *The natives were pleasant to the tourists.*

agreeable pleasant; cheerful; obliging. *Mom asked us to be agreeable to our visiting aunt because she didn't feel well.*

cheerful pleasant; agreeable. *We think it's nice to have such a cheerful traffic officer near our school crossing.*

comfortable giving comfort; giving pleasure. *Our house is a comfortable place to be.*

enjoyable pleasurable. *Just about everyone said that the music was enjoyable.*

pleasing giving pleasure. *Ben was surprised to find that pomegranates have a pleasing taste.*

pleasurable giving pleasure. *Swimming in the cool water was pleasurable on hot summer days.*

refreshing making fresh; giving pleasure. *Orange juice is a refreshing drink.*

satisfying supplying enjoyment. *Our family Thanksgiving was a satisfying experience.*

antonyms: unpleasant, distressing, annoying

pledge *n.* a promise; an agreement. *We made a pledge to be home by ten o'clock.*

guarantee a promise to keep an agreement. *The teacher said he could not guarantee that the field trip was still possible.*

promise pledge. *"Give me your promise that you'll come to my party," Jan said to Mike.*

word pledge; promise. *Your friends know you will keep your word.*

polite *adj.* having good manners; courteous; thoughtful. *It is polite to shake hands when you meet someone.*

civilized polished; gracious. *Manners are a sign of civilized behavior.*

considerate thoughtful; well-mannered. *Politeness is a sign of a considerate person.*

courteous polite. *People who serve the public should be courteous at all times.*

gracious courteous; welcoming. *Lori's Aunt Maisie is the most gracious hostess I've ever met.*

nice pleasant. *Well-mannered people are nice to be around.*

polished well-mannered; knowing what is correct. *The butlers in English TV shows usually have very polished manners.*

well-mannered courteous. *Everybody was impressed by the well-mannered little boy.*

antonyms: rude, discourteous, impolite, impudent, crude, insolent

postscript *n.* a note added to a letter after the writer's signature. *Rieko wrote in a postscript that she had found her socks after all.*

addition something added. *Suki found a good addition to fill out her report.*

afterthought postscript; addition. *Jim's invitation to the party gave the location at the end, as if it were an afterthought.*

supplement addition. *The newsletter sent out by the school included a dress code as a supplement to the list of rules.*

practice *v.* 1. to put into actual use. *He does practice what he believes.* 2. to do exercises in order to become skilled. *Let's practice our spelling.*

do to practice. *Do the examples before going on to the next page.*

drill to practice; to train. *Drill regularly to learn the dance.*

employ to use. *Let the science students employ the ideas they have developed.*

engage in to practice; to follow. *My cousin will engage in a live demonstration of lion training.*

exercise to do; to practice. *The hall guards in our school are quick to exercise their authority.*

follow to practice. *A good athlete must follow a regular program of exercise.*

perfect to make right; to rehearse. *After a week, Judy should perfect her playing of the folk song.*

polish to perfect. *Let's polish our performance and be ready to win our blue ribbon at the talent show.*

rehearse to practice, usually an art. *The actors rehearse every afternoon.*

sharpen to make correct; to perfect. *Sharpen those math skills!*

train to practice. *Triathletes train daily during the season.*

work out to drill intensely. *Does the football squad work out daily?*

precaution *n.* action or care taken in advance, often for protection or safety. *We took the precaution of locking the car.*

foresight seeing needs ahead of time. *Their foresight made the day pleasant.*

preparation getting ready. *The police department helped with preparation for the governor's visit.*

prevention planning to stop something. *Eating well helps in the prevention of illness.*

prudence foresight; planning. *Saving money shows prudence.*

safeguard prevention. *They took extra water on the run as a safeguard.*

principal *adj.* most important; chief; main. *The principal product of Pittsburgh was steel from the many huge mills.*

central main; most important. *The central idea of the novel is that people can overcome their fears.*

chief central; main. *The chief reason we called was to invite you to dinner.*

foremost primary; main. *The town's foremost industry is textiles.*

leading major; principal. *The leading department store is closed for inventory.*

main most important. *Two of Iowa's main farm products are corn and pork.*

major most important. *Kit went to work for a major newspaper.*

prime most important. *The prime suspect was easy to spot in that show.*

antonyms: minor, secondary, lesser

principle *n.* a basic fact; a rule upon which other rules are based. *Learning from experimentation is a basic principle of science.*

doctrine beliefs; teachings. *What doctrine do you live by?*

law rule; principle. *Gravity is a natural law.*

rule law; basis. *It's a rule of nature that most plants need light.*

truth principle; basic fact. *What truth does this fable try to convey?*

private *adj.* belonging to a certain person or group of persons; not public. *Your letters are your private property.*

confidential secret; private. *Most secrets should be kept confidential.*

hidden not seen; not public. *The house has a small, hidden garden in the back.*

nonpublic private. *The telephones inside that office building are all nonpublic.*

secret personal; hidden. *The spy kept a secret diary.*

unofficial not official. *The mayor travels on official business, but some of his traveling is also unofficial.*

unpublished not public; unrevealed. *The famous poet's letters to his friends are unpublished.*

unrevealed not made known. *The whole story is still unrevealed.*

antonyms: available, general, public, official

purpose *n.* aim; plan; intention. *The purpose of the meeting was to plan our spring show.*

aim plan; purpose. *The girls' aim was to collect a hundred toys for children who had none of their own.*

design plan; aim. *Their design was to complete the work early.*

desire wish; plan. *The parents' club expressed its desire to build a bigger library for the school.*

plan aim; purpose. *Wally's plan was to surprise the coach.*

scheme complicated, secret plan. *Tom Sawyer's scheme to watch his own funeral was a success.*

wish desire. *The boys cleaned the playground out of a wish to be helpful.*

radiant *adj.* bright; shining. *Ann has a radiant smile.*

bright brilliant; shining. *The bright day made us all feel better.*

brilliant radiant; bright. *Sunlight shining through the prism made a brilliant rainbow on the classroom wall.*

glowing radiant. *Glowing brightly, Jupiter appeared low in the eastern sky.*

shining bright; giving light. *The shining yard light outside the window lit up the room and made it hard for Jan to sleep.*

realize *v.* to understand; to know; to be aware. *Allen was startled to realize that he was late for school.*

know to understand; to have knowledge. *The neighbors wanted to know why Pat played basketball all day.*

understand to comprehend; to know. *Reading about the Revolutionary War helped Betsy understand the history of her country.*

reappear *v.* to become visible again; to appear again. *The chipmunk seemed to vanish into a hole and then to reappear again.*

recur to come up again; to be repeated. *Once Janie had learned the new word, it seemed to recur in every TV show she watched.*

recent *adj.* done, made, or happening not long ago. *A recent news article told about progress being made in building safer cars.*

contemporary new; current. *Wicker furniture is a contemporary style.*

fresh recently made; recently discovered. *The hunters followed the fresh tracks through the canyon.*

late recent. *Dad listens to the radio for the late news stories.*

modern up-to-date; of recent make. *Joy wants a kitchen with modern appliances.*

new modern; recent. *Information in the newspaper should be new every day.*

novel unknown; original and fresh. *Katie's ideas for having fun are usually novel.*

up-to-date contemporary; current. *Jason reads a lot of up-to-date scientific journals.*

antonyms: old, ancient, early, old-time

reclaim *v.* 1. to restore to a usable condition. *We can reclaim used cans and newspapers by recycling them.* 2. to claim back; to ask for the return of. *I will reclaim my furniture from storage.*

recover to get back; to make available. *The company wants to recover the business it lost during the strike last year.*

recycle to make reusable. *The city plans to recycle plastic bottles and have them formed into boards for playground benches.*

restore to make like new; to make usable. *Donna worked hard to restore the old furniture.*

antonyms: to discard, waste, abandon, neglect, lose, reject

region *n.* 1. a large portion of the surface of Earth. *Cactuses grow in that desert region.* 2. any area or place. *We live in the northeast region of the state.*

area place; region. *I come from a heavily populated area of the country.*

barrio Spanish-speaking part of a city. *The houses in the barrio were made of stucco and painted in pale colors.*

district part of an area regarded as a unit. *The beautiful old city has an area called the Garden District.*

place area; region. *What places in this country have you visited?*

section measured part of a space. *Each family had its own section of the garden area in which to grow vegetables or flowers.*

space region; area. *We planted flowers in the large, empty space near the parking lot.*

spot small area. *On this spot by the river, Josh saw a crane for the first time.*

territory area claimed by a group, person, or animal. *The red-winged blackbird's soft whirring sound warns other birds to stay away from its territory.*

tract stretch of land. *The tract by the river will become a park.*

zone area with a special purpose. *Most cities set aside a residential zone where only houses can be built.*

rehearse *v.* to practice or prepare for a performance. *Our choir will rehearse for the spring concert.*

itemize to list. *Itemize everything that you want me to get at the store.*

practice to repeat to make correct. *Jason is good at drawing because he has practiced for years.*

recount to tell. *The old sailor began to recount the story of his first voyage.*

repeat to do again. *Please repeat that story about the weasel.*

relative *n.* a person connected to another by blood or marriage. *My favorite relative is Uncle Ed.*

kin relatives. *Mother said we could never count all of our kin.*

relation a person in one's family. *"He is no relation of mine!" Marge exclaimed.*

repair *v.* to bring back to good condition; to fix; to mend. *Do you know how to repair a flat tire?*

fix to repair. *Jonas can fix any toy you bring him.*

freshen to renew. *A coat of paint will freshen the room's appearance.*

mend to make whole. *Grandmother tells me she used to mend holes in my dad's socks.*

overhaul to examine and repair. *Last month Zach needed to overhaul the engine in his truck.*

patch up to make small repairs. *Maybe Billy should patch up the holes in the fence.*

restore to make like new. *When she got her first apartment, Gina learned to restore wooden furniture.*

separate *v.* to divide; keep apart; be between. *The fence will separate the two yards.*

break to separate into many pieces. *Don't drop the vase or the handles will break off.*

come apart to separate. *The old bike began to come apart as Hugo rode down the street.*

come between to divide; to separate. *He decided not to let a move to a distant neighborhood come between Joe and his friends.*

cut to sever with a sharp instrument. *In kindergarten, children are taught to cut straight.*

detach to take off; separate. *You can detach the training wheels and use the bicycle without them.*

divide to separate into parts; come between. *The Mississippi River divides Iowa from Wisconsin.*

part to put space between. *Many novels tell about someone's efforts to part a boy or girl and a pet.*

sever to cut apart. *It was hard to sever the drumstick from the thigh with a dull knife.*

split to divide wood on the grain. *Abe Lincoln is sometimes called "the rail-splitter" because he split wood for fence rails.*

tear to separate; rip. *The tailor could tear the material smoothly.*

antonyms: to unite, connect, join, mix, put together

serious *adj.* 1. thoughtful; solemn. *You look so serious; is something wrong?* 2. in earnest; honest; not joking. *She is serious about becoming a dancer.*

earnest showing serious feeling. *The little girl was earnest about helping her grandfather shovel the sidewalk.*

solemn very serious. *The funeral is a solemn ceremony for the family.*

thoughtful serious; earnest. *Wally was thoughtful as he worked at the computer.*

antonyms: lighthearted, humorous

shelter *v.* to protect; give shelter to. *Our house will shelter us from the cold weather.*

care for to protect. *Barb tries to care for birds in the winter by providing them with food and water.*

cover to give protection; to shelter. *Cover the sleeping bags so they don't get wet.*

harbor to give protection. *The old house was built to harbor many generations of Wallaces.*

house to give shelter. *The city wants to house anyone who has no shelter from the cold.*

lodge to give shelter to. *The rangers said they would lodge any campers whose tents had been destroyed.*

look after to care for; safeguard. *Rick is going to look after Eric's dog during Eric's vacation.*

preserve to save; keep. *The photographer is trying to preserve all of the old photographs of the city.*

protect to shield. *Police officers promise to protect citizens.*

provide for to care for; look after. *The Red Cross can provide for thousands of people in emergencies.*

safeguard to protect by prevention. *Drink bottled water to safeguard against illness.*

shield to cover; protect; give shelter. *Tents did shield the campers from the storm.*

take in to shelter; provide housing. *The motel owners offered to take in flood victims.*

slim *adj.* 1. thin; slender. *Jill chose a slim volume of poems at the library.* 2. small; slight. *There was a slim hope that he would win.*

narrow not wide. *The river is narrow at its source.*

skinny very thin. *The skinny cat slid past me as I tried to push it outside.*

slender fine; thin. *A slender path wound through the field.*

small very little. *There was a small chance that Lou would win the tournament.*

thin slim; slender. *The little girl was thin enough to slip between the fence rails.*

antonyms: stout, thick, broad, wide, abundant, large

summarize *v.* to give the main points of; to restate in fewer words. *Can you summarize Roger's speech?*

condense to summarize. *The newspaper will condense the mayor's talk.*

outline to list main ideas. *A good listener can easily outline a report.*

review to summarize. *The TV reporter didn't review the movie soon enough for me to know that it was a waste of time.*

sum up to summarize; give main ideas. *Try to sum up the short story without telling the details.*

antonyms: to enlarge on, expand

supply *v.* to provide; furnish; give. *Who will supply the lemonade for the neighborhood block party?*

equip to supply materials. *It is expensive to equip oneself for horseback riding.*

furnish to supply; provide. *The girls agreed to furnish decorations for the party.*

give to provide. *Andy's mother decided to give him a new winter jacket.*

provide to furnish; supply. *The class had to decide how to provide food for the field trip.*

stock to store supplies. *The men agreed to stock the cabin where they stayed when they went fishing.*

swiftness *n.* speed; quickness. *The antelope's swiftness amazed us.*

haste speed; hurry. *Students entered the gym in haste.*

speed quickness; fast movement. *The cheetah's speed reaches seventy miles an hour!*

suddenness quickness. *The owl swooped down with such suddenness that the rabbit didn't know it was there.*

antonym: slowness

thorough *adj.* 1. complete. *She did a thorough job.* 2. careful and exact. *The police were thorough in examining the evidence.*

all-inclusive including all; thorough. *The sports almanac that Manny brought to school is all-inclusive.*

exhaustive including all details. *Janie gave an exhaustive account of her vacation.*

sweeping generalizing. *Her statements were too sweeping to be taken seriously.*

throw *v.* 1. to toss or cast through the air. *I'll throw the ball to you.* 2. to put into a particular state. *A power failure can throw the office into confusion.*

cast to throw; to bring about. *The news of the coming storm cast us into panic.*

fling to throw hurriedly. *The boys stopped to fling their coats on before leaving.*

hurl to throw violently. *The athlete tried to hurl the discus with all his strength.*

pitch to throw in a controlled way. *Ted can pitch the ball across the plate.*

toss to throw gently. *Patiently, Pat continued to toss the ball over and over again to his little cousin.*

tone *n.* 1. a sound, especially with reference to its quality. *The bell rang with a harsh tone.* 2. a manner of speaking. *She used an angry tone.*

mood feeling; tone. *The first song set a cheerful mood for the concert.*

note a musical tone. *The pianist gave the singers their starting note.*

sound noise. *The sound of the school bell startled everyone.*

style tone; mood. *How would you describe that author's style?*

tourist *n.* a person traveling for pleasure. *The tourist took pictures of the famous German castle.*

globe-trotter person who travels constantly. *Janet's Uncle Arthur is a globe-trotter.*

journeyer person who is on a trip; a person who takes trips. *The short story was about a journeyer through space and time.*

pilgrim person who travels for religious reasons or to a holy place. *The American Pilgrims were searching for religious freedom.*

sightseer person who travels to see famous places. *Traveling with a sightseer can be very tiring.*

traveler person who travels. *The traveler rode the bus from coast to coast.*

voyager person who travels by ship or in space. *Thor Heyerdahl is a famous voyager in modern times.*

wanderer person or thing moving without a settled route or pattern. *A comet is a wanderer around the solar system.*

truly *adv.* 1. really; truthfully. *Do you think he told us what he truly thought?* 2. in fact; indeed. *The music sounded truly glorious.*

actually in fact; truly. *The top speed of a greyhound may actually be close to 70 miles an hour.*

as a matter of fact honestly; truly. *The fans, as a matter of fact, want a victory.*

honestly truly; in fact. *The team is honestly trying to play better than they did last season.*

indeed truly; actually. *Deer are indeed beautiful animals.*

in fact actually. *In fact, no one knows the size of the universe.*

really actually; truly. *Josie told the class that she really wanted to be president of student council next year.*

type *n.* a particular kind; sort; class. *What type of book do you like best?*

kind a type; a category. *Catherine and Jane couldn't decide which kind of books they liked best at the public library.*

sort a type; kind. *The new mall has shops of every sort, including places to buy food.*

unit *n.* a standard measure. *Meters are a unit of distance.*

measure unit; standard. *Which measure is longer, an inch or a centimeter?*

quantity amount; unit. *The travelers bought a small quantity of milk.*

unknown *adj.* not known; strange; not familiar. *A stranger is an unknown person.*

hidden not known; not recognized. *Paul's talent for mimicry was hidden for a long time.*

mysterious unknown; not understood. *The source of the noise remained mysterious.*

unrecognized strange; not known. *The famous author was unrecognized when she visited our city.*

up-to-date *adj.* including any recent changes; current; modern. *This edition of the dictionary is the most up-to-date version.*

current up-to-date; recent. *The weekly school newspaper always tries to have information on current events.*

latest most recent. *My sister's latest interest is painting.*

recent modern; new. *I'm looking for a recent copy of that magazine.*

antonyms: old, former, out-of-date

vain *adj.* 1. too proud of oneself. *After Elaine won the prize, she became vain of her accomplishment.* 2. not successful; useless. *I soon gave up my vain efforts to attract his attention.*

boastful bragging. *The boastful athlete angered his teammates.*

conceited vain; proud. *Conceited people are usually not very patient with others.*

useless of no value. *Because they lost the match, the members of the tennis team felt that their practice had been useless.*

valley *n.* an area of low land between hills or mountains. *A clear river flowed through the valley.*

glen a narrow valley. *The houses and yards in the glen were nearly always dark.*

hollow space surrounded by hills. *The little town in the hollow was old and beautiful.*

ravine a deep cleft between mountains. *Fog rolled down into the ravine and hid the houses from sight.*

antonyms: hill, highland, upland, rise

value *n.* worth; importance. *No one doubts the value of a good education.*

advantage benefit. *Doing homework carefully has many advantages.*

merit value; worth. *The idea is unusual, but it has merit and will be considered.*

worth value; merit. *Wilma Rudolph knew the worth of ambition and hard workouts.*

vary *v.* to cause to change or be different. *People can vary their appearance by wearing different clothes.*

alter to change. *Please alter the jacket to make it fit properly.*

mix to combine parts. *We asked the band to mix modern music with old favorites.*

modify to make a small change. *Zeke modified his appearance by curling his hair.*

reshape to vary the shape. *The cleaners said they could reshape Grandpa's old felt hat when they cleaned it.*

voyage *n.* a journey by water or through air or space. *Christopher Columbus made a famous voyage to America.*

cruise a voyage for pleasure. *The family took a cruise to Alaska.*

sail a trip on a sailing ship or boat. *Every Sunday afternoon, people take a sail on the lake.*

warmth *n.* 1. the state of being warm. *The warmth of the sun felt good.* 2. friendly or affectionate feeling. *We appreciated the warmth of their welcome.*

affection warmth of feeling. *Members of Roger's family clearly felt a strong affection for one another.*

heat warmth; high temperature. *The heat in the house felt good after we walked home in the cold.*

worth *n.* merit; value. *This book has little real worth, but it's fun to read.*

cost price. *What is the cost of that portable cassette player?*

merit worth; value. *Peggy saw the merit of daily practice on the piano.*

price cost. *Do they ever lower the price of cars?*

value worth; merit. *The value of a thing cannot always be measured in dollars.*